AFTER THE WASHINGTON CONSENSUS

Restarting Growth and Reform in Latin America

AFTER THE WASHINGTON CONSENSUS

Restarting Growth and Reform in Latin America

edited by
Pedro-Pablo Kuczynski
and John Williamson

Institute for International Economics
Washington, DC
March 2003

John Williamson, senior fellow at the Institute for International Economics since 1981, was project director for the UN High-Level Panel on Financing for Development (the Zedillo Report) in 2001; on leave as chief economist for South Asia at the World Bank during 1996-99; economics professor at Pontificia Universidade Católica do Rio de Janeiro (1978-81), University of Warwick (1970-77), Massachusetts Institute of Technology (1967, 1980), University of York (1963-68), and Princeton University (1962-63); adviser to the International Monetary Fund (1972-74); and economic consultant to the UK Treasury (1968-70). He is author, coauthor, editor, or coeditor of numerous studies on international monetary and developing-world debt issues, including *Dollar Overvaluation and the World Economy* (2003), *Delivering on Debt Relief: From IMF Gold to a New Aid Architecture* (2002), and *Exchange Rate Regimes for Emerging Markets: Reviving the Intermediate Option* (2000).

Pedro-Pablo Kuczynski was minister of economy and finance of Peru in 2001-02 and minister of energy and mines in 1980-82. He has been president and chief executive officer of the Latin America Enterprise Fund LP since its inception in 1994. From 1992 to 1994, he was vice chairman of CAP SA, a steel and forest products company in Chile. From 1982 to 1992, he was chairman of First Boston International and managing director of First Boston Corporation. He was also a partner at Kuhn, Loeb & Company International (1973-75), deputy director of the Peruvian Central Bank (1967-69), and president and chief executive officer of Halco Mining (1977-80). He began his career at the World Bank in 1961 and held senior positions there and at the International Finance Corporation. He is the author of several books on the economics of Latin America.

INSTITUTE FOR INTERNATIONAL ECONOMICS
1750 Massachusetts Avenue, NW
Washington, DC 20036-1903
(202) 328-9000 FAX: (202) 659-3225
www.iie.com

C. Fred Bergsten, *Director*
Valerie Norville, *Director of Publications and Web Development*
Brett Kitchen, *Director of Marketing and Foreign Rights*

Typesetting by BMWW
Printing by Automated Graphic Systems, Inc.
Cover Photo: Pete Turner/Getty Images

Printed in the United States of America
05 04 03 5 4 3 2 1

Library of Congress Cataloging-in-Publication Data

After the Washington consensus : restarting growth and reform in Latin America / John Williamson, Pedro-Pablo Kuczynski, co-editors
p. cm.
Includes bibliographical references and index.
ISBN 0-88132-347-0

1. Latin America—Economic policy. 2. Latin America—Economic conditions—1982- I. Williamson, John, 1937- II. Kuczynski Godard, Pedro-Pablo, 1938-

HC125 .A3187 2003
330.98—dc21 2003040745

Contents

Preface

Latin America has been a focus of research at the Institute for International Economics throughout the life of the Institute. Our numerous studies of the debt crisis of the 1980s of course centered on that region. Examples included John Williamson's analysis of the *Prospects for Adjustment in Argentina, Brazil, and Mexico: Responding to the Debt Crisis* (1983) and of *Inflation and Indexation: Argentina, Brazil, and Israel* (1985), and William R. Cline's highly influential *International Debt and the Stability of the World Economy* (1983) and *International Debt: Systemic Risk and Policy Response* (1984).

In the mid-1980s, we began to look "beyond the debt crisis" in an effort to chart a path for restoring sustained prosperity in the region. As a central part of that effort we assembled a team of leading Latin American economists (Gerardo Bueno from Mexico, Pedro-Pablo Kuczynski from Peru, and Mario Henrique Simonsen from Brazil) to work with our own Senior Fellow Bela Balassa to produce *Toward Renewed Economic Growth in Latin America,* which proposed a plan to that end. We assessed the changing mood of the region in a conference held in 1989, proceedings of which were published in *The Progress of Policy Reform in Latin America* in 1990, in which editor John Williamson coined the phrase the "Washington Consensus."

This new study takes a fresh look at developments over the ensuing decade in an effort to understand why the results of reform, while clearly positive in many respects, are still so disappointing. It assesses the successes and failures (and omissions) of the policy reforms to date and develops a policy agenda attuned to the present situation. We deliberately entitle it *After the Washington Consensus* to emphasize our belief that it is high time the world moved on from tendentious ideological debates in which the Washington Consensus is caricatured as a neoliberal manifesto to a serious discussion of the new wave of reform the region needs to restart growth and make it more equitable than it has been in the past.

This volume was produced largely by economists from Latin America itself, each addressing his or her issue-area of particular expertise. Twelve of the fifteen authors are Latin American, including two former finance ministers (Pedro-Pablo Kuczynski of Peru and Ricardo Lopéz Murphy of Argentina). The idea for the project was in fact initiated by a Latin American, Dr. Kuczynski (before he reentered the government of his country for a period in 2002, which delayed the completion of the volume), who had coauthored our earlier study in 1986 and rightly believed that the time had come for a comprehensive reassessment of the situation and what needed to be done to improve it.

The Institute for International Economics is a private nonprofit institution for the study and discussion of international economic policy. Its purpose is to analyze important issues in that area and to develop and communicate practical new approaches for dealing with them. The Institute is completely nonpartisan.

The Institute is funded largely by philanthropic foundations. Major institutional grants are now being received from the William M. Keck, Jr. Foundation and the Starr Foundation. A number of other foundations and private corporations contribute to the highly diversified financial resources of the Institute. About 31 percent of the Institute's resources in our latest fiscal year were provided by contributors outside the United States, including about 18 percent from Japan. The Charles Stewart Mott Foundation provided generous support for this study.

The Board of Directors bears overall responsibility for the Institute and gives general guidance and approval to its research program, including the identification of topics that are likely to become important over the medium run (one to three years), and which should be addressed by the Institute. The Director, working closely with the staff and outside Advisory Committee, is responsible for the development of particular projects and makes the final decision to publish an individual study.

The Institute hopes that its studies and other activities will contribute to building a stronger foundation for international economic policy around the world. We invite readers of these publications to let us know how they think we can best accomplish this objective.

C. Fred Bergsten
Director
March 2003

Acknowledgments

This study originated during a conference at Princeton University in the fall of 1999, when Pedro-Pablo Kuczynski expressed his dissatisfaction about economic stagnation in Latin America to John Williamson and suggested that the time was ripe for a new assessment of the issues similar to that in which he had previously participated (see Balassa et al., 1986). Fred Bergsten agreed, and the Institute for International Economics went about assembling a team of authors familiar with what we regarded as the main economic issues facing the region. The study has taken longer than we initially planned due to other commitments such as Kuczynski's appointment as minister of finance in Peru in 2001-02 and Williamson's appointment as project director for the Zedillo Report in 2001.

The group held three meetings, two in Washington (in 2000 and 2002) and one in Montevideo (in 2001). All of the 15 members who have written for the study attended at least one of these meetings and a number attended all three. The meetings involved intense debate and much cross-fertilization among the authors, so there are many intellectual debts owed by some members of the team to others. They are here acknowledged collectively rather than individually at the start of each chapter.

A number of other knowledgeable economists attended one or other of these meetings, in many cases to act as discussants of drafts of the papers. We hereby acknowledge with gratitude valuable inputs made by C. Fred Bergsten, Jorge Buendía, William R. Cline, Jonathan Eaton, Kimberly Ann Elliot, Richard Feinberg, Carol Graham, Gary Hufbauer, Miguel Kiguel, José Luis Machinea, Antonio Ortiz Mena, Guillermo Perry, Jeffrey Puryear, Pedro Ravela, Paulo Renato Souza, Sebastián Saiegh, Vito Tanzi, Mariano Tommasi, Edwin M. Truman, and Roberto Zahler.

We are also pleased to acknowledge the valuable suggestions of three referees who did not insist on anonymity: William R. Cline, Ricardo Ffrench-Davis, and Nora Lustig.

Overview

An Agenda for Restarting Growth and Reform

JOHN WILLIAMSON

These may not be the worst of times, but few view them as among the best of times in Latin America. The region has lived through another decade of slow growth. Crises seem to have become ever more frequent, with the consequences of the Argentine crisis particularly painful. Poverty fell in the first half of the 1990s but has been increasing again since 1997. Growth in employment in the formal sector has been agonizingly slow. Investment remains substantially lower than it was in the 1970s. The world economy is in recession, the prices of many primary products were recently at record low levels, and emerging markets are out of fashion with investors. In many countries, there is disillusionment with political leaders, though in most cases—according to Latinobarómetro—not with democracy.

Of course, the pessimism can be overdone. Growth did revive in Latin America in the first half of the 1990s, until the crises started exploding. Inflation, the great enemy of the poor, has been conquered. Growth follows

John Williamson has been a senior fellow at the Institute for International Economics since 1981.

recessions: Primary product prices, like stock markets, do not go down forever. The statistics tell us that social progress—as measured specifically by longevity, literacy, and infant mortality—continued even through the decade of the debt crisis and the 1990s (see table 0.1).

But when all is said and done, Latin Americans are entitled to feel disappointed that the past decade did not live up to the hopes that were kindled at the start of the 1990s, when it was widely expected that reforms would get the region back on a growth path that would allow living standards to start catching up with those in industrial countries. The first two years of the new century saw no net increase in output at all—by far the worst performance since 1982-83, at the start of the debt crisis. Latin Americans want to know what went wrong, and they want a new agenda that promises to correct the weaknesses of the past. The chapters in this volume were primarily seeking answers to the second of those questions, but it is useful to start by confronting the first.

The authors who have contributed to this volume are 15 economists from, or associated with, Latin America. Twelve of the 15 are actually Latin Americans, 2 of whom are former finance ministers (Pedro-Pablo Kuczynski of Peru and Ricardo López Murphy of Argentina). All 15 have contributed to the development of the set of ideas that are explored in the volume and that are summarized here, and all of them sympathize with the general thrust of the argument, but they have not individually endorsed everything in this overview.

What Went Wrong?

The authors of this volume do not take the view that the liberalizing reforms of the past decade and a half, or globalization, can be held responsible for the region's renewed travails in recent years. To consider why not, it is natural to focus attention on Argentina, the country that is now embroiled in the deepest crisis that has been experienced in the region at least since the 1980s, and that not long ago was widely regarded as the poster child for the Washington Consensus.

Argentina did indeed undertake many excellent reforms, particularly in the first half of the 1990s. It improved its fiscal performance, and the central government even had a small budget surplus in 1993. It liberalized trade. It welcomed foreign direct investment. It reformed its pension system. It privatized most state companies—though some of them perhaps too quickly, before an effective regulatory mechanism had been put in place, and in some cases with questionable propriety. It liberalized and strengthened its financial system. It legislated a world-class bankruptcy law. Most of the public-sector debt was long term, and contingent credit lines were arranged with commercial banks. And all these good policies were indeed rewarded: hyperinflation was replaced by price stability, and

Table 0.1 Basic social statistics for selected Latin American countries and other developing regions, 1960-2000

	Literacy rate (percent)				Life expectancy (years)					Infant mortality (per 1,000 live births)				
Country or region	**1970**	**1980**	**1990**	**2000**	**1960**	**1970**	**1980**	**1990**	**2000**	**1960**	**1970**	**1980**	**1990**	**2000**
Argentina	93	94	96	97	65	67	70	72	74	60	52	35	25	17
Brazil	68	76	81	85	55	59	63	66	68	114	95	71	48	32
Chile	88	82	94	96	57	62	69	74	76	113	77	32	16	10
Colombia	78	84	89	92	57	61	66	68	72	97	70	41	30	20
Mexico	75	82	78	91	57	62	67	71	73	93	73	51	36	29
Peru	72	80	86	90	48	54	60	66	69	141	108	81	54	32
Venezuela	76	84	89	93	60	65	68	71	73	79	53	36	25	19
Latin America and Caribbean	74	80	85	88	56	61	65	68	70	105	84	61	41	29
East Asia and Pacific	55	68	79	86	39	59	64	67	69	131	79	57	44	36
Europe and Central Asia	94	95	96	97	—	—	68	69	69	—	—	41	28	20
Middle East and North Africa	30	42	54	65	47	52	58	64	68	165	134	98	56	43
South Asia	32	39	47	55	44	49	54	59	62	163	139	119	87	73
Sub-Saharan Africa	28	38	50	62	40	44	48	50	47	164	138	116	103	91
Developing countries	53	62	69	75	44	55	60	63	64	143	108	88	67	59

— = not available

Source: World Bank, *World Development Indicators.*

real per capita GDP rose by a cumulative 46 percent between 1990 and 1998, which was by far the country's best performance since at least the 1920s. Assertions that the 1990s were a decade of decline for Argentina are simply wrong.

Nevertheless, the euphoria of the early 1990s was carried altogether too far. The currency board that was adopted in 1991 to help the country exit hyperinflation was very successful in that aim, but it was an extremely rigid system that risked making the peso an overvalued currency. That risk materialized big time through a conjunction of unfortunate developments:

- The use of a fixed exchange rate to terminate an ongoing inflation normally results in the price level overshooting equilibrium, to leave an overvalued currency in its wake, and that happened in Argentina.
- The Brazilian real was drastically devalued in 1999, and this mattered a lot, given that by then Brazil was by far Argentina's most important trading partner.
- The US dollar (to which the Argentine peso was pegged) levitated against virtually all other currencies, especially the euro, from the late 1990s to early 2002.
- Argentina's large current account deficits throughout the 1990s meant that it would have needed a progressively more competitive real exchange rate to generate the foreign exchange with which to service its increasing foreign debt.

Although Argentina did succeed in making modest gains in its competitiveness vis-à-vis the United States in the last years of the currency board, by dint of a painful process of internal price deflation, this did not suffice to prevent a progressive increase in the overvaluation of the peso (Perry and Serven 2002). Perhaps a more flexible labor market could have made those competitiveness gains somewhat greater, but it was an essentially hopeless task; the overvaluation was simply too great to be corrected that way.

Another big policy error was, as so often in Argentina's past, fiscal laxity. Although there was a radical improvement in the fiscal position in the early years of the decade, this was allowed to erode after 1993. The ratio of public debt to GDP rose from 29 percent in 1993 to 41 percent in 1998, and then to 55 percent in 2001. This eliminated the scope for the government to run a fiscal expansion to help stabilize the economy when it fell on hard times at the beginning of the present decade. The exchange rate straitjacket plus the inadequate fiscal effort in the good times doomed the Argentine experiment (Mussa 2002). The political implosion was the straw that broke the camel's back, but it is difficult to see how it could have been avoided given the economic dead end.

Argentina was unique in adopting a currency board,[1] yet most other countries also had a disappointing decade of slow growth, low investment, very modest increases in employment in the formal sector, and little progress in poverty reduction. That was true of most countries, but not all. In particular, Chile had the fourth fastest growing economy in the world during the 1990s. Hence a diagnosis of why things went wrong in Latin America in the 1990s needs to be evaluated in relation to Chile as well, to make sure that we have an explanation that can account for Chilean success as well as the general disappointment.

Surely the factor that has been most damaging to economic growth is the series of crises that emerging markets have suffered, starting with that in Mexico at the end of 1994 and continuing through East Asia, Russia, Brazil, Argentina, and then Brazil again (to mention only the major victims). Too many countries encouraged money to flood in and overvalue the currency when the capital markets were throwing money at the region,[2] or used a fixed or crawling exchange rate as a nominal anchor, or pursued a procyclical fiscal policy. They thereby made themselves vulnerable to "sudden stops" in capital inflows, and they left themselves no scope to relax fiscal policy in difficult times.

The policy agenda of a decade ago certainly did not warn countries against such foolish acts, and indeed in certain cases countries may even have been encouraged to do some of those things. Note that Chile used the *encaje* to try and prevent the Chilean peso from becoming overvalued when foreign investors were flooding it with money; it avoided using the exchange rate as a nominal anchor but reduced inflation gradually through a policy of inflation targeting; and it pursued a distinctly anticyclical fiscal policy (Ffrench-Davis 2000). These policy choices explain why Chile, unlike almost all its neighbors, managed to avoid a macroeconomic crisis in the 1990s.

A second reason that outcomes did not match the hopes of a decade ago is that reforms were incomplete. For one thing, some of the "first-generation reforms" were neglected (perhaps most conspicuously regarding the labor market, which has remained strongly dualistic everywhere, resulting in an ever-growing informal sector) or incomplete (e.g., with regard to fiscal reform, where the massive budget deficits were eliminated but opportunity was not taken in the good times to run budget surpluses that

1. Admittedly, two other, much smaller, countries have gone even further in tying themselves irrevocably to the dollar in recent years; both Ecuador and El Salvador have actually adopted the dollar. El Salvador seems a rather natural candidate for dollarization (it is a small country whose trade is overwhelmingly with the United States or other countries with currencies closely linked to the dollar). Ecuador is a medium-sized economy with moderate ties to the United States, so it offers an interesting experiment.

2. Ironically, this was a particular danger to countries whose economic officials were regarded as a "dream team" by the international capital markets.

would allow deficit spending in bad times). Note that Chile is the country that pushed first-generation reforms the furthest (and that had started them first), although it has to be conceded that even Chile has not done anything to liberalize its labor market. And, as already noted, it sought to make fiscal policy anticyclical and pursue structural fiscal balance.

In addition, there is a whole generation of so-called second-generation reforms, involving the strengthening of institutions, that is necessary to allow full advantage to be taken of the first-generation reforms unless institutions are already strong. Once again, Chile shows up relatively well. It has long boasted a qualified, legitimate, and uncorrupt civil service. It is also among the countries that have implemented the most ambitious agenda of institutional reforms, with the grant of independence to a central bank with a technically competent staff, significant and fiscally responsible decentralization, major modernization of the machinery to collect income tax, an ambitious judicial reform in process, and significant improvements in education (chapter 8), including full-day schooling at the secondary level. (But it lags in the medical field, as is noted in chapter 10.) Most countries of the region started from a lower institutional base and achieved far less in the way of institutional reform.

A third reason for the region's disappointing performance is that the main objective informing policy was excessively narrow. That is, policy remained focused on accelerating growth, not on growth plus equity. There remained relatively little concern for income distribution or the social agenda, despite the fact that the region's income is more concentrated than anywhere else in the world except a few African countries. It may make sense to focus policy overwhelmingly on growth in places where income is less unequally distributed and virtually everyone is poor, like South Asia. But that is not true of Latin America, where the elite is so rich relative to the masses that it is inconceivable that the living standards of the average person will ever catch up with those in industrial countries just through growth without a narrowing of the gap between rich and poor. A minor redistribution of income from the rich to the poor would have the same impact in reducing poverty as many years of growth with a constant income distribution, let alone of growth accompanied by further widening of the income gap.

Moreover, the denial of opportunities to the poor results in a waste of human talent that helps explain the dismal growth performance of the region. Of course, there are enormously destructive (populist) ways of trying to narrow the income gap or advancing the social agenda, and many of these have periodically been unleashed on Latin America in the past. But the mere fact that it is possible to pursue an objective destructively does not imply that one should not seek constructive ways to achieve it. In this dimension, it has to be said that Chile does not distinguish itself from the rest of Latin America. Poverty has indeed fallen in Chile during the past decade, but overwhelmingly because of growth, not because income distribution has become much less unequal nor because of any great improvement in social policies.

New Agenda I: Crisis Proofing

Our proposed reform agenda stems directly from the preceding diagnosis of what went wrong in the 1990s. To begin with, given that we now know that crises can blow up so easily and have such devastating consequences, it needs to be an objective of the highest priority to reduce the vulnerability of the region's countries to crises. It is true that Latin America has been chronically crisis prone practically since it achieved independence, but change is essential if the region is to have any chance of maturing into a group of stable, high-income countries.

Not only is this reduced vulnerability to crises the key to the ability to maintain a respectable average growth rate over time, but there are good reasons to believe that, because rich people are better able to protect themselves against crises (mainly by holding dollars abroad), the volatility of the region helps explain why income remains so concentrated. Some of the actions that are needed to curb volatility, like moving from an export profile dependent on a few primary commodities to a diversified industrial base, are inherently long term. But the core ones (developed in chapters 4, 5, and 6) could be implemented in the space of less than a business cycle:

- Achieve budget surpluses in times of prosperity so as to reduce debt to prudent levels and provide scope for stabilizing deficits to emerge by operation of the automatic stabilizers in bad times.[3]
- Make sure that subnational governments are subject to hard budget constraints, and define their entitlement to transfers from the central government as a proportion of *national public expenditure* rather than *tax revenue*, so that they cannot undermine an anticyclical policy directed by the central government.
- Accumulate reserves and build a stabilization fund when exports (particularly those of cyclically unstable primary commodities) are strong.
- Adopt a sufficiently flexible exchange rate regime to allow external competitiveness to be improved through currency depreciation when there is a sudden stop to capital inflows or other balance of payments difficulties emerge, but do what is possible (e.g., by using measures

3. The need to maintain consistency between fiscal and exchange rate policy is likely to curb the scope for expansionary fiscal measures during a recession in a country that maintains a less flexible exchange rate regime.

like an *encaje*) to avoid this leading to overvaluation if capital inflows threaten to become excessive.[4]

- Except in small countries that have close relations with the United States in both trade and financial flows, where full dollarization makes sense, aim to minimize the use of the dollar as a currency in which residents hold savings and in which loans are contracted. Unless and until this aspiration is achieved, make banks insure risks that they incur in lending in dollars to the nontradable sector.
- Complement a flexible exchange rate with monetary policy focused on targeting a low rate of inflation.
- Strengthen prudential supervision of the banking system and enforce capital adequacy ratios to minimize the danger of banking collapses.
- Increase domestic savings so that investment can rise without undue dependence on capital imports.[5] This will involve a further strengthening of structural fiscal positions, and it can also be promoted by completing the process of pension reform that has already been started in many countries.

One interesting idea discussed in chapter 4 is for some regional body to develop standards analogous to the European Union's Maastricht criteria for fiscal discipline. We would hope that these would be more sophisticated than Maastricht's limits of a 3 percent of GDP cap on the noncyclically adjusted budget deficit and a 60 percent cap on the ratio of public debt to GDP, and would instead aim to build pressure for a consistent anticyclical policy.

For example, the growth of government expenditures might be capped at the estimated trend rate of growth of the economy, whereas tax revenue could be required to grow at least in line with nominal GDP. A government that wished to enlarge government expenditures, or cut taxes, by more than this allowed would be expected to demonstrate to its peers in the regional monitoring organization that its plans did not prejudice the maintenance of fiscal discipline. It is to be hoped that its peers would not tolerate any chicanery of "supply-side economics" that might be presented to them to rationalize fiscal lapses. If there is a convincing need for higher public expenditures, they need to be financed soundly, if necessary by raising taxes.

4. A good review of the possibilities in this direction is provided by Ocampo (forthcoming).

5. Although it is not discussed much in the book, my own view is that one of the benefits of cutting dependence on foreign savings is that it would increase the latitude to use capital controls strategically where they can reduce the amplitude of boom-bust cycles. It would still be important to avoid the main danger of resorting to capital controls, which is the tendency to overrate the impact they can have.

We do not offer a candidate for the regional body that should be given this monitoring responsibility, because none of those presently available appears to fit the bill. Mercosur started to seek macroeconomic policy coordination before the recent crises blew up, though without any clear concept of the strategic role that such coordination should seek to achieve. But the problems with using Mercosur for this purpose are (1) that it is currently in disarray and, more seriously, (2) that it covers only a part of the region.

The International Monetary Fund has much expertise in this area, but it has not in the past distinguished itself by a concern for cyclical stabilization, and it is not controlled from within the region. The Inter-American Development Bank, the Organization of American States, and the United Nations Economic Commission for Latin America and the Caribbean all cover the right geographical area, but none has in the past developed the appropriate sort of expertise. Perhaps it would make a useful function for a Free Trade Area of the Americas (FTAA) to perform, although the North American Free Trade Agreement (NAFTA) eschews dealing with this topic and so hardly constitutes an encouraging precedent. The United States actually used its bilateral free trade agreement with Chile to bully it into curtailing use of the *encaje* for anticyclical purposes.

Then there is of course a further institutional question beyond identifying the body to monitor the rules: to specify a penalty for breaking the rules and an enforcement mechanism to secure payment of the penalty when it is due. We note these issues but pass them by. Our contribution is limited to identifying a need, rather than suggesting an institutional way to satisfy that need.

New Agenda II: Completing First-Generation Reforms

But crisis proofing the regional economy is not enough to ensure future growth. The region also needs a faster underlying rate of growth. Although much was done in the past decade and a half to implement what are now referred to as first-generation reforms, and the evidence says that these did indeed serve to accelerate rather than retard the growth rate (Fernandez-Arias and Montiel 1997; Lora and Panizza 2002; Stallings and Peres 2000), the process is still incomplete in several dimensions. Perhaps the most egregious omission has been to fail to make the labor market more flexible.

The reason for this is not difficult to comprehend, insofar as those who think they are beneficiaries of the status quo—those who have unionized formal-sector jobs—constitute an interest group that is sufficiently powerful politically to deter potential reformers, and sufficiently underprivileged economically to evoke public sympathy. Nevertheless, as chapter 9 illuminates, the rigidity in the labor market constitutes a major obstacle to an expansion of employment in the formal economy. This does not just impede faster growth, but does so primarily at the cost of some of the poorest members of society—those who are denied the opportunity to move out of the informal economy.

Is there therefore a dilemma in choosing between the interests of organized labor in maintaining the rigidities of the labor market and the interests of those in the informal sector? A crude program focused on nothing but rolling back the benefits that labor has won over the years, from severance payments to the social wage to restrictions on hours worked to prohibitions on what children (for example) are allowed to do, would indeed pose such a dilemma. But, as a perusal of chapter 9 will make clear, it is possible to envisage ways of restoring flexibility that would not prejudice the interests of organized labor (as has been achieved during the past 20 years in the Netherlands).

For example, severance payments can be replaced by a system of individual accounts, as in Colombia. The social wage can be modified to forms that give the individual worker a direct stake in the payments made on his or her behalf (e.g., by adopting defined-contribution rather than defined-benefit pension schemes, which also benefits workers by allowing much greater portability of pensions). Existing workers can be grandfathered (if they so desire, and by no means all of them would) in arrangements allowing for more flexible working hours.

Not all regulations—certainly not those limiting child labor—deserve to be scrapped. And improvements in labor market information, skill certification, and occupational training systems could improve the functioning of the labor market so as to raise productivity and reduce the waste that results from mismatches between demand and supply. It is in fact possible to design a program that would liberalize the labor market and that enlightened trade unionists would recognize as consistent with their interests.

A number of other first-generation reforms are also incomplete. In trade policy, substantial progress has been made in liberalizing imports, but apart from Mexico (with NAFTA), more recently Central America, and in the future Chile, there has been essentially no progress in improving access to the markets of developed countries (chapter 7). Latin America certainly needs an FTAA, and a successful Doha Round of negotiations in the World Trade Organization, to open up export opportunities in industrial countries, as well as to provide stability in the regulations that govern intraregional trade.

Similarly, though a lot of privatization has happened, there remain sectors—most notably in banking, with the continued existence of many state-owned banks—where the process is seriously incomplete. Latinobarómetro has discovered that privatization is by far the most unpopular of the first-generation reforms with the Latin American public, but—as is discussed in chapter 2—the evidence simply does not support the view that privatization has not benefited the general public. It must be admitted that privatizations have sometimes been carried out badly. The remedy, however, is not to stop the process of privatization but rather to make sure that it is done carefully, and with newly privatized firms either exposed to competition or subject to proper regulation.

Finally, in the financial sector, there remain countries where the process of liberalization has not been supplemented by the necessary strengthening of prudential supervision.

New Agenda III: Second-Generation Reforms

But it would be wrong to give the impression that the only task at this juncture in history is to complete first-generation reforms. The major thrust of development economics in the 1990s was recognition of the crucial role of institutions in permitting an economy to function effectively. The importance of institutional reforms in complementing first-generation reforms in Latin America was first emphasized by Naím (1994), who dubbed these "second-generation reforms."[6] A recent paper by Levine and Easterly (2002) concludes that the state of institutional development furnishes the *only* variable that reliably predicts how developed a country is.

An important role for the state of institutions is perfectly consistent with mainstream economics, which posits a crucial role for the state in creating and maintaining the institutional infrastructure of a market economy, in providing public goods, in internalizing externalities, and, depending on political views, in correcting income distribution. (Note that none of these roles serve to rationalize a government responsibility for running steel mills, electricity generators, or banks.)

Second-generation reforms have sometimes been pictured as politically boring esoterica like creating budget offices or securities and exchange commissions. Chapter 10 argues that in fact they are liable to involve political confrontation with some of society's most potent and heavily entrenched interest groups, such as the judiciary and public school teachers. This is surely right. The judiciary in Latin America is notorious for ignoring economic considerations, for example, by overriding creditor rights to the point where creditors are reluctant to lend. Or worse still, they are so corrupt that judges have to be paid to permit money to be recovered. Also, as noted in chapter 8, many teachers' unions have been captured by small

6. It can be argued that this is a misnomer, inasmuch as decently functioning institutions may be a precondition for certain liberalizing reforms, which implies that the second generation ought to precede the first!

groups with political agendas unrelated to the teaching profession. The answer, it is argued, is not to initiate a campaign to "break the unions," but rather to seek to professionalize teaching so that teachers will want their unions to become positive partners for reform. A third politically powerful group whose attitudes and working practices often need to be transformed is the civil service.

One institutional reform that would seem a mistake is introduction of an industrial policy, that is, a program that requires some government agency to "pick winners" (to help companies that are judged likely to be able to contribute something special to the national economy). There is little reason to think that industrial policies were the key ingredient of success in East Asia (see Noland and Pack 2003); though it is true that several of those economies had some form or other of industrial policy at some stage of their development, it is also true that one of the most successful, Hong Kong, never did.

It is difficult to explain the success of a group of countries by something that one of them conspicuously lacked. One needs to look instead at the common features of those countries, such as their high saving rates, outward orientation, macroeconomic stability, work ethic, and strong educational systems. This is not to say that an industrial policy would necessarily be a disaster, because in a country with strong private firms one can expect these to ignore misguided government pressures (e.g., the attempt of the Japanese Ministry of International Trade and Industry to rationalize the Japanese car industry by telling Honda not to make cars). But we believe that government has more useful things to do than issue advice that can only be defended by arguing that firms are free to ignore it.

Specifically, though government should stay out of making business decisions—and leave those to the people who stand to gain if the decisions are good and lose if they are not—it has an important role in creating a business-friendly environment. This is partly the old-fashioned business of providing decent infrastructure, a stable and predictable macroeconomic, legal, and political environment, and a strong human resource base. But it also includes the modern task of building a national innovation system to promote the diffusion of technological information and fund precompetitive research, as well as providing tax incentives for research and development and encouraging venture capital, and may extend to encouraging the growth of industrial clusters.

Latin America has lagged badly in developing high-technology industries, as shown in the region's poor placement in the proportion of technically sophisticated exports as well as its low ranking in the Competitiveness Indices of the World Economic Forum. Although there is still ample scope for productivity to increase in the region by copying best practices developed in the rest of the world, it may need an act of Schumpeterian innovation—and therefore the sort of technologically supportive infrastructure that constitutes a national innovation system—to bring global best practices to Latin America.[7]

In addition to reforming the judiciary, teachers, and the civil service (especially budget offices, securities and exchange commissions, and central banks, which deserve autonomy even if not complete independence from the political process) and building up national innovation systems, second-generation reforms need to address two major economic areas. One involves modernizing the institutional infrastructure of a market economy. Unlike the economies in transition, which had the challenging task of creating such an infrastructure from scratch, Latin America already had the essential features of a market economy in place when the present wave of reform started in the late 1980s. Nonetheless, there are deficiencies in property rights (particularly the lack of property rights in the informal sector, to which Hernando de Soto has repeatedly drawn attention) and, in many countries, bankruptcy laws.[8]

The other major need for institutional reform is in the financial sector. What is needed here, in addition to strengthening prudential supervision, is a whole series of apparently minor changes such as improving transparency, upgrading accountancy, strengthening the rights of minority shareholders, facilitating the recovery of assets pledged as collateral, and developing credit registries (see chapter 5). There are also some useful ideas as to how to build financial systems based on the local currency rather than the dollar at the end of chapter 6, including requiring banks that accept dollar deposits and then relend in dollars to the nontradable sector to insure the additional risk this entails. Although such reforms may appear minor, in fact they are of fundamental importance—but quite difficult to implement.

Doubtless none of these economic institutions begin to compare in importance to the political institutions that can allow a Hugo Chávez to capture control of the state and ravage an economy, as is happening in Venezuela as this goes to press. Patricio Navia and Andrés Velasco make some suggestions in chapter 10 about the political reforms that might increase the likelihood of the political process generating the sort of progressive but responsible reforms that we advocate in this volume. They argue for the need to have a balance of power between president and legislature, rather than for gutting the legislature, with the legislators con-

7. See ECLAC (1995, part 2) for a review of the policies that would assist enterprises to catch up with global best practices.

8. Argentina had a world-class bankruptcy law until January 2002, when the Congress replaced it with a law that made debt collection virtually impossible under the misapprehension that this would limit the damage of the crisis. Of course, it would have ensured the collapse of any still-solvent banks in Argentina, which is why the IMF insisted on its amendment.

sisting of career professionals responsible to their constituents rather than either the executive or party bosses.

Navia and Velasco also tend to favor first-past-the-post electoral systems, but their thoughts on how to design proportional systems are perhaps even more interesting: keep electoral districts relatively small (about five members) and use open rather than closed lists, so as to maximize the power of voters. Hold elections for different positions simultaneously rather than subjecting countries to almost permanent electioneering. Because the other contributors to this volume have credentials as economists rather than political scientists, we cannot vouch for this reform agenda, but our impression is that it constitutes a thoughtful attempt to tackle what is without question a critical problem.

New Agenda IV: Income Distribution and the Social Sector

There are two ways through which the poor can become less poor. One is by an increase in the size of the economic pie from which everyone in society draws their income. The other is by redistribution of a given-sized pie, so that rich people get a smaller proportion and the poor get a bigger proportion. In most cases, the most effective way to give the poor a bigger proportion will be to equalize opportunities by paying more attention to the social agenda.

The evidence shows more or less clearly that growth benefits the poor, even if nothing is consciously done to make it "pro-poor" growth. Benefits do trickle down. One influential analysis concluded that the poor typically benefit more or less in proportion to what they already have (Dollar and Kraay 2000), although others have concluded that the elasticity of low incomes with respect to aggregate growth is significantly less than one (Foster and Székely 2001). But even if the poor do benefit in as great a proportion as others, they will not gain very much from economic growth if they do not have very much to start with, as is the case almost everywhere in Latin America.

Because most people believe that improving the lot of the poor matters more than securing an equal income gain for rich people, there is an abstract case for supplementing the gains from growth with a measure of income redistribution. And because a country where the poor receive a very small proportion of income needs to reallocate a relatively small part of the income of rich people to make a big dent in poverty, that case applies in spades to Latin America. If one learns that poverty increased in Mexico in the 1990s even though average per capita income increased (Székely 2001b), one may feel that the case for action to improve the distribution of income is rather compelling.

Figure 0.1 Okun's big trade-off

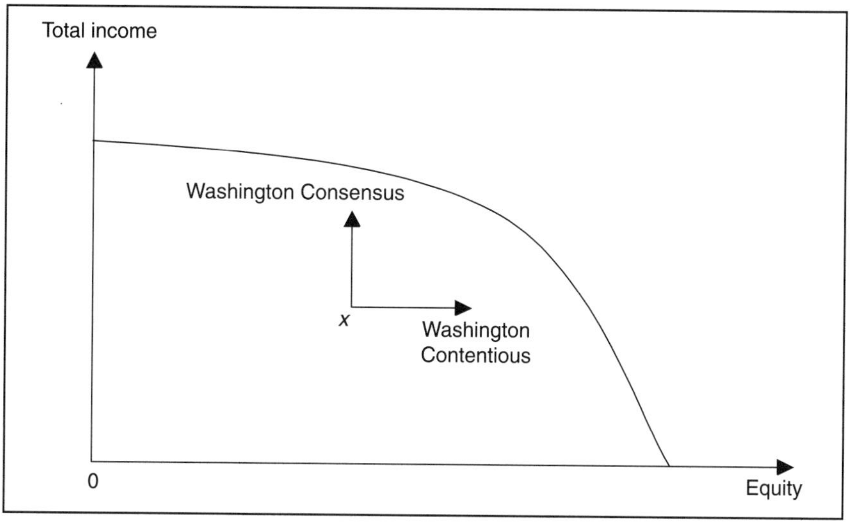

Source: Okun (1975).

Figure 0.1 shows what Okun (1975) called "the big trade-off"—between the level of income and its equitable distribution. If society were efficiently organized, then we would be on the frontier, and any gain in equity would have to be paid for by a reduction in the level of income. If, for example, we tried to redistribute income from the rich to the poor through higher taxes and increased welfare benefits, then there would be a cost in the disincentive effects of high marginal tax rates reducing effort and therefore income. In practice, most societies are usually operating somewhere like point *x* in figure 0.1 within the efficient frontier so that there are opportunities for win-win solutions, and obviously one wants to identify and exploit these wherever one can. The Washington Consensus reforms that were in vogue a decade ago were focused on increasing growth without harming equity. Birdsall and de la Torre (2001) offered a list of 10 Washington Contentious reforms (along the general lines of the discussion in chapter 3) that they argued would push countries to the right in figure 0.1, improving equity without reducing growth.

Their 10 reforms constitute a sensible list, even if one can debate whether they all quite fit the rubric of improving equity without diminishing growth.[9] For example, their first two proposals concern the devel-

9. The 10 reforms are rule-based fiscal discipline; smoothing booms and busts; social safety nets that trigger automatically; schools also for poor people; taxing rich people and spending more on the rest; giving small business a chance; protecting workers' rights; dealing openly with discrimination; repairing land markets; and consumer-driven public services.

opment of fiscal rules that would secure an anticyclical fiscal policy, such as were discussed above under the heading of crisis proofing; one could argue these are at least as important for increasing the average rate of growth as for improving income distribution. But the more fundamental point is that there is no intellectual justification for arguing that *only* win-win solutions deserve to be considered. One always needs to be aware of the potential cost in efficiency (or growth) of actions to improve income distribution. But in a highly unequal region such as Latin America, opportunities for making large distributive gains for modest efficiency costs deserve to be seized.

Progressive taxes are the classic instrument for redistributing income. One of the more questionable aspects of the reforms of the past decade in Latin America has been the form that tax reform has tended to take, with a shift in the burden of taxation from income taxes (which are typically at least mildly progressive) to consumption taxes (which are usually at least mildly regressive). Although the tax reforms that have occurred have been useful in developing a broader tax base, it is time to consider reversing the process of shifting from direct to indirect taxation, including recently the growth of taxes on check payments. In particular, one needs an effort to increase direct tax collections. For incentive reasons, one wants to avoid increasing the marginal tax rate on earned income, which suggests that attempts to collect more from direct taxes should be focused on the following three elements:

- the development of property taxation as a major revenue source (it is the most natural revenue source for the subnational government units that are being spawned by the process of decentralization that has rightly become so popular);
- the elimination of tax loopholes, which not only can increase revenue but can also simplify tax obligations and thus aid enforcement; and
- better tax collection, particularly of the income earned on flight capital parked abroad, which will require the signing of tax information-sharing arrangements with at least the principal havens for capital flight.

Any increase in tax revenue then needs to be devoted to spending on basic social services, including a social safety net as well as education and health, so that the net effect will significantly reduce inequality, particularly by expanding opportunities for the poor. But it may be a mistake to limit the benefits exclusively to the poor, because at least in some circumstances it is only a middle-class stake in public spending that gives the extra spending a chance of being politically sustainable. At the same time, it must always be remembered that spreading expenditures more broadly to include nonpoor people inevitably reduces the antipoverty impact of a given level of expenditures.

Even with the best will in the world, however, what is achievable through the tax system is limited, in part by the fact that one of the things that money is good at buying is advice on how to minimize a tax bill. Really significant improvements in distribution will come only by remedying the fundamental weakness that causes poverty, which is that too many people lack the assets that would enable them to work their way out of poverty.

The basic principle of a market economy is that people exchange like value for like value. Hence, to earn a decent living the poor must have the opportunity to offer something that others want and will pay to buy; those who have nothing worthwhile to offer because they have no assets are unable to earn a decent living. The solution is not to abolish the market economy, which was tried in the communist countries for 70 years and proved a disastrous dead end, but instead to give the poor access to assets that will enable them to make and sell things that others will pay to buy. This means

- ***Education.*** There is no hope unless the poor get more human capital than they have had in the past. Latin America has made some progress in improving education in the past decade (see chapter 8), but it is still lagging on a world scale.
- Titling programs to provide property rights to the informal sector and allow Hernando de Soto's (2000) "mystery of capital" to be unlocked.
- ***Land reform.*** The Brazilian program of recent years to help peasants buy land from *latifundia* landlords provides a model. Landlords do not feel their vital interests to be threatened and therefore they do not resort to extreme measures to thwart the program. Property rights are respected. The peasants get opportunities but not handouts, which seems to be what they want.
- ***Microcredit.*** Organizations to supply microcredit are spreading, but they still serve only about 2 million of Latin America's 200 million poor people. The biggest obstacle to an expanded program consists of the very high real interest rates that have been common in the region. These high interest rates mean either that microcredit programs have a substantial fiscal cost and create an incentive to divert funds to the less poor (if interest rates are subsidized), or (otherwise) that they do not convey much benefit to the borrowers. We expect our macroeconomic program to reduce market interest rates and thus facilitate the spread of microcredit.

Mechanisms like these are becoming more and more realistic because of the strengthening of civil society, which is one of the most positive trends in the region. They will nonetheless take time to produce a social revolution, for the very basic reason that they rely on the creation of new assets, and it takes time to produce new assets. But unlike populist programs, they do have the potential to produce a real social revolution if they are pursued steadfastly. And they could do so without jeopardizing the interests of rich people, thus holding out the hope that these traditionally fragmented societies might finally begin to develop real social cohesion.

Criticisms

It is not difficult to anticipate some of the criticisms that will be directed at this agenda. It is all about reforms that need to be made in Latin America, whereas many of the region's problems are due to, or at least intensified by, policies that are made outside the region. True enough, but we have written an agenda directed at the leaders of the region, not at their peers in the rest of the world. Apart from a few brief paragraphs in chapter 11, we are silent on the illegal drug problem and environmental issues. True again; we plead the benefits of a division of labor, and we do not question the importance of these issues.

Another possible criticism is that the agenda we have sketched out is a medium-term one that omits any discussion of how Argentina and Brazil can escape from the crises of 2002. That again is a valid criticism, to which we again plead division of labor. In addition, we would say that the region will never escape from the treadmill of repeated crises unless policymakers begin to pay more attention to long-term issues rather than being constantly mesmerized by the latest crisis. We look primarily to fiscal reform to enable countries to gradually work down the level of public debt and thus escape the vulnerability to panics by foreign creditors that now hangs over the region.

A more pertinent criticism is that the policy agenda laid out above does not offer an alternative model of development; it is very much in line with the sort of national economic policies that developing countries subscribed to when they endorsed the Monterrey Consensus. That is a perfectly legitimate criticism from anyone who believes they do have such an alternative, but the view of the authors of this book is that past alternatives failed and that the antiglobalization movement of today has so far not provided a coherent alternative at all. The way forward is to complete, correct, and complement the reforms of a decade ago,[10] not to reverse them.

Others may criticize our agenda as unrealistically broad. No country can be expected to implement everything suggested here all at once, and we fail to give much guidance on sequencing. Those criticisms also have

10. This is to "reform the reforms," in the felicitous phrase of Ffrench-Davis (2000), which was subsequently adopted by the Inter-American Development Bank in the program for its 2002 annual meeting.

substance. Of course, it will be necessary to sequence the reforms, and it would be foolish to try and do everything at once. But does anyone really believe that there exists some unique sequence that should be prescribed for all 32 countries of the region? Surely how quickly reforms are implemented and which are tackled first has to depend on the situation in each country and the political priorities of its leaders, and to suggest otherwise would be an attempt to subvert the democratic process.

The key question is whether the agenda we have laid out will reignite growth in Latin America. Those who look to tax cuts to puff up demand or work magic with incentives, or who look to new inflows of foreign capital to avoid the need for hard choices, will doubtless be skeptical. But our view is that what the region needs is not so much an immediate boom, nice as that would be, as the sustainable and sustained growth that comes from making it worthwhile for the private sector, from multinationals to microentrepreneurs, to invest and sell.

Our agenda is directed at creating the conditions from which such growth can emerge. Perhaps the biggest risk of all is that the region's leaders will lack the patience that is needed for such an approach to succeed.

1

Setting the Stage

PEDRO-PABLO KUCZYNSKI

Latin America—excepting Argentina, whose golden age was in the decades before 1914—grew as never before or since in the years between 1940 and 1980. The commodity price booms ignited by World War II finally laid to rest the Great Depression. When the war ended, rapid worldwide growth and the active developmentalist policies adopted throughout the region, which included first-stage import substitution, maintained rates of growth that averaged 5.2 percent a year between 1945 and 1981 (Thorp 1998, 318). Social indicators also improved rapidly (table 1.1).

Yet even during this time, there was a lot to be concerned about. The income gains that were being achieved were concentrated on those who were already best off, so that the pattern of highly unequal distribution bequeathed by the region's colonial history continued. And the income gains, though impressive by historical standards, did not match those being realized elsewhere in the world at the same time. While GDP per capita increased by between 60 percent in Venezuela and almost 240 percent in Brazil from 1950 to 1980, comparable increases were much larger elsewhere, especially in Southern Europe and East Asia (table 1.2). Moreover, in the last decade of this golden age, there were more and more reasons to doubt the sustainability of the growth model, as budget deficits

Pedro-Pablo Kuczynski has been president and chief executive officer of the Latin America Enterprise Fund LP since its inception in 1994. He was the minister of economy and finance of Peru from July 2001 to July 2002 and minister of energy and mines (1980-82).

Table 1.1 Social indicators for selected Latin American countries and East Asia, 1960-98

Country	Approximate year	Life expectancy at birth (years)	Infant mortality to age 5 years (per 1,000 live births)	Adult literacy (percent)	Access to safe water (percent)
Argentina	1960	65.2	72	91.0	51
	1980	69.6	38	94.4	58
	1998	73.3	22	96.6	65
Brazil	1960	54.9	177	61.0	32
	1980	62.7	80	74.5	56
	1998	67.1	40	84.5	72
Mexico	1960	57.3	134	65.0	38
	1980	66.8	74	82.2	50
	1998	72.1	35	90.8	83
Latin America	1960	56.5	154.1	74.0	35
	1980	64.7	78.5	79.9	53
	1998	69.7	37.7	87.8	76
East Asia	1960	39.2	198.2	—	—
	1980	60.0	81.7	68.8	—
	1998	68.9	42.6	84.5	84

— = not available

Sources: World Bank, *World Development Indicators*; Edwards (1993a); Morawetz (1977).

grew, inflation accelerated, foreign borrowing exploded, and in consequence debts accumulated faster than the ability to service them.

The growing macroeconomic imbalances made the region progressively more vulnerable, and so it proved unable to withstand the strains induced by the anti-inflationary tightening of monetary policy in the United States in the early 1980s. Interest rates soared; the dollar, in terms of which most foreign debts were denominated, appreciated; the price of commodity exports collapsed; and the markets for noncommodity exports shrank. In August 1982, Mexico ran out of reserves and was unable to borrow more, and so it was forced to declare a moratorium on debt service. Within weeks, the whole region was immersed in what became known as the debt crisis.

Growth ground to a halt in the following months and years. But because population continued to grow, the result was an erosion of living standards and a reversal of the downward trend in poverty of the preceding decades. The region entered what was before long labeled the "lost decade."

Toward New Policies to Promote Growth

It was in the midst of this lost decade, in the darkest days of the debt crisis, that the Institute for International Economics sponsored a study titled

Table 1.2 GDP per capita for selected Latin American countries and countries in other regions, 1950-2000
(US dollars at 1995 prices)

Region and country	1950	1966	1980	1998	2000	Ratio of 2000 to 1950
Latin America						
Argentina	5,314	6,678	9,084	11,230	10,981	2.1
Brazil	1,803	2,788	6,092	6,193	6,094	3.4
Chile	4,009	5,617	6,715	8,214	8,217	2.0
Colombia	2,687	3,383	5,328	5,615	5,226	1.9
Mexico	2,987	4,898	7,210	7,202	7,625	2.6
Venezuela	6,021	9,588	9,370	5,430	4,911	0.8
Southern Europe						
Greece	2,562	5,730	11,171	13,035	13,829	5.4
Portugal	2,075	4,349	8,753	13,743	14,679	7.1
Spain	3,292	7,728	12,071	15,156	16,408	5.0
Turkey	1,984	3,573	5,857	6,004	5,728	2.9
East Asia						
China	—	—	780	2,903	3,286	—
South Korea	1,274	2,259	5,682	12,600	12,795	10.0
Singapore	1,699	3,697	11,177	22,633	23,026	13.6
Taiwan	1,438	2,845	7,140	15,425	16,500	11.5

— = not available

Sources: For 1950 (at 1995 prices and exchange rates), Balassa et al. (1986, table 1.2); for 1950, 1966, 1980, and 1998 (at 1995 prices and purchasing power parity), World Bank, *World Development Indicators 2000;* US Central Intelligence Agency, *World Factbook 2000.*

Toward Renewed Economic Growth in Latin America. The authors were Bela Balassa, then a visiting fellow at the Institute, and three Latin American economists: Gerardo Bueno of Mexico, Pedro-Pablo Kuczynski of Peru, and Mario Henrique Simonsen of Brazil.

This study laid out a policy agenda that was starkly at variance with conventional thought in Latin America at that time. It argued that the still-prevalent policy of import substitution, which may have been constructive during its first easy phase, had long since outlived its usefulness and become a drag on industrial development, for it had largely precluded a boom in manufactured exports such as that experienced in the more dynamic developing regions. The study viewed the large fiscal deficits that were almost ubiquitous at the time as a demand on the savings needed to finance growth rather than as a Keynesian stimulus to output. And it criticized the overwhelming economic role of the state (including the prevalence of state-owned enterprises) as undermining the ability of the private sector to generate growth.

The sort of policy reversal called for by the study had in fact been pioneered by Chile in the 1970s. This did not immediately strike other countries as an example that they might want to emulate—partly because of the dictatorial political regime that was responsible, and partly because the initial fits and starts did not suggest this to be an attractive economic model. But from the mid-1980s onward, Chile developed a sustained economic boom. Economists such as Balassa had for years been arguing that Latin America was making a mistake in not emulating the policies of openness and macroeconomic discipline that had served East Asia well and led to an economic miracle there; the presence of a local model powerfully reinforced this message. And so, in the second half of the 1980s, policy started to shift in a similar direction in other countries of the region.

The Birth of the Washington Consensus

This change surely encouraged the incoming US administration of George H.W. Bush to propose the Brady Plan for resolving the debt crisis soon after it took office in 1989. The extent to which Latin American policy reforms were being implemented was, however, not widely understood in the United States when the Brady Plan was being discussed in Congress. In an attempt to remedy this, the Institute for International Economics convened a conference in November 1989 under the title "Latin American Adjustment: How Much Has Happened?" And with the aim of providing some coherence to the papers that were commissioned to examine the extent to which individual countries had already embraced reform, the conference's organizer, John Williamson, laid out in a background paper what he understood to be the main reforms that were widely agreed in Washington to be needed to restore Latin American economic growth.[1]

This was the origin of what Williamson termed the Washington Consensus. The term has been used and misused in all sorts of ways in the subsequent years, to mean laissez-faire and minimalist government and disdain for all values but the growth of GDP, but its original meaning was vastly less ideological. It was intended to identify those policies that mainstream Washington institutions like the US Treasury, the International Monetary Fund, the World Bank, and the Inter-American Development Bank agreed to be key to the restoration of growth in Latin America.

Some of these policies, like privatization, had indeed been pioneered by such market-oriented regimes as Margaret Thatcher's government in Britain but had subsequently won wide endorsement. Others, like free trade and fiscal discipline, had been advocated for decades for industrial

1. Williamson (1990); this book contains country papers by Juan Cariaga, Patricio Meller, Pedro-Pablo Kuczynski, Juan Carlos de Pablo, Eliana Cardoso and Daniel Dantas, Javier Beristain and Ignacio Trigueros, Rudolf Hommes, Ricardo Hausmann, DeLisle Worrell, Sylvia Saborio, and Enrique Iglesias.

countries by the Organization for Economic Cooperation and Development, but general recognition of their appropriateness in developing countries was more recent. The agenda of the conference omitted ideologies like supply-side economics and monetarism that were widely questioned just as much as it excluded the socialist dream that was collapsing in Eastern Europe at the very time that the conference was held. It was largely the agenda sketched out in *Toward Renewed Economic Growth in Latin America*: a mainstream agenda that recognized the importance of both the market and the state.

The hope of a better future for Latin America in the 1990s rested on a combination of liberalizing and stabilizing policy reforms, the Brady Plan for debt relief, and democratization. Mexico had already joined the GATT in 1986, and substantial other reform efforts were reported in a number of countries in the Institute's November 1989 conference, but the year 1989 was nonetheless something of a watershed. The plebiscite in favor of the return of civilian elected government in Chile marked the effective end of military rule in most of the region. Privatization started in a big way with the sale of the controlling interest of the state in Teléfonos de Mexico to a private consortium, and Mexico secured the first Brady debt reconstruction in September of that same year. Argentina began to put its fiscal house in order during a period of unprecedented hyperinflation, and it also sold off control of its state-owned telephone company. And Venezuela attempted a radical adjustment program.

By the early 1990s, a majority of the countries in the region, including several of the smaller economies in Central America and the Caribbean, were engaged in opening up their foreign trade, cutting budget deficits, and selling off state assets, including many utilities. The combination of domestic privatization and declines in US interest rates from 1990-91 and on unleashed a flood of foreign portfolio investment onto the larger Latin American stock markets, which appreciated by 25 percent annually from 1989 to 1994. Economic growth began to pick up, and for the region as a whole it averaged 4.2 percent annually in the period 1990-95, compared with barely 1 percent in 1982-89. Per capita incomes started to increase after a decade of decline, although unemployment remained high and real wages recovered only slowly.

Two important positive events occurred in the region in 1994. In Brazil, the trade liberalization and privatization (initially of the steel and petrochemical industries) of the early 1990s were finally complemented by an effective stabilization plan, the Plano Real. This brought the largest economy of the region into line with the policies of the other major countries. And Mexico completed its entry into the North American Free Trade Agreement (NAFTA) after lengthy negotiations with Canada and the United States, setting the stage for the fourfold expansion of its export earnings in the following 6 years.

Crisis Returns

However, that same year witnessed the return of crisis to the region. Shortly after a new administration had been inaugurated in Mexico in December 1994, the unsustainable current account deficit of the years 1992-94 created a crisis of confidence that ultimately led to a large and disorderly devaluation. To avoid a debt default, an international mega-rescue package that in principle totaled almost $50 billion had to be organized, and this led to much controversy in the US Congress because it followed so shortly the accession of Mexico to NAFTA.

The large devaluation (eventually threefold in terms of pesos per dollar) was beneficial to Mexican exports, but it sparked renewed protectionist sentiment in some sectors in the United States. The devaluation caused devastation to the Mexican banking and capital markets: interest rates had to stay at high levels for balance of payments reasons, choking off investment and growth; massive domestic defaults, especially of mortgages and consumer credit debt, wiped out the capital of most banks; that, combined with a "moral hazard" culture that encouraged default even by those who could pay, eventually led the Mexican government to put in close to $100 billion to rescue the banking system, six times what it had collected when the banks were reprivatized in 1991-92; the emerging domestic bond and equity markets, which had made a promising recovery in 1990-94, went into dormancy. The "tequila crisis" reverberated throughout the region, especially in Argentina, although in the end no other country was engulfed.

Just over 3 years after the start of the Mexican devaluation, Brazil faced a similar problem with some similar causes, reinforced by the world financial crisis that had started in Thailand in July 1997, and exposed the fragility of the East Asian economic miracle, then surfaced in Russia, and devastated the Long-Term Capital Management hedge fund based in the United States. At $42 billion, the international rescue package for Brazil was almost as big as that of Mexico. Fortunately, it proved more effective in limiting the damage than most of the preceding rescues had been: the devaluation was smaller, the banking system was stronger, and the determined actions of the central bank limited inflation; so after a few months of uncertainty, Brazil returned to weak growth. Nevertheless, Brazil has had to maintain high domestic real interest rates to limit the devaluation of the real (60 percent, in reais per dollar, in 1999) and hold inflation within single digits.

The traumatic financial events in the two largest economies of the region, which together account for 60 percent of regional GNP, undoubtedly affected all of Latin America. For the second half of the 1990s, regional growth barely reached 2.5 percent annually, well below the performance of the United States (3.9 percent annually in the same period). To be sure, the East Asian economic crisis, particularly its negative impact on commodity prices and on the availability of private international debt finance, contributed to the poor result, especially in Argentina, Chile, and the Andean countries. The Russian crisis of 1998 reinforced the virtual shutdown of the flow of finance from the international bond market and from banks to emerging markets that had begun a year earlier.

The outcome of these internal as well as external events is that the 1990s were another disappointing decade for Latin American economies. Of the several possible causes of this disappointment—such as an apparently secular commodity downturn, the high dependence on volatile foreign financing, and the persistence of weakness in public finances—one in particular stands out: the proclivity of key countries in the region to be unable to manage their macroeconomic policies—the combination of fiscal, monetary, and exchange policies—in a sustainable manner that avoids periodic crises. This has been the case for Mexico, then Brazil, and now Argentina.

There are several reasons for this inability. One is the desire of policymakers to reconcile what are in practice irreconcilable objectives: exchange rate stability to achieve low inflation on one hand, and balance of payments viability in a world of volatile capital flows on the other. A second is political myopia, which has again and again led policymakers to spend during good times without thought for the future. That is one reflection of a more general problem, the weakness of key institutions, so that decisions that are considered essential and normal in more advanced economies in practice become highly politicized in a Latin American setting.

There is of course nothing of particular statistical significance about a decade or about a collection of fairly diverse countries that stretch over 10,000 kilometers. Nonetheless, international investors and financial markets tend to look at the geographic region as a whole, and the slow economic growth in almost all these countries during a long period of about 20 years hardly inspires them to regard this as a dynamic region in which they must have a presence.

Social Progress—Nevertheless

Despite Latin America's disappointing economic growth, it has made much progress during the past two decades in improving standards of longevity, nutrition, public health, and literacy, keeping its averages above those of East Asia. Yet it has shown no sign of progress in remedying its long-standing and endemic maldistribution of wealth; indeed, the region may have retrogressed in what were already among the most highly skewed distributions in the world. And its progress in longevity and health poses an additional challenge to countries that have slow economic growth. As I have written elsewhere:

> In the case of a number of South American nations there is a danger that they will grow old before they grow up: rapidly improving health care and declining birth rates will eventually lead to an aging population (as in Argentina and Uruguay) before these countries have had an opportunity to reach reasonably modern living standards. Once the population stabilizes, only a near-miraculous productivity gain can propel a country to modernity. In other words, there is the risk of growing old before growing up. Of all the elements necessary in order to avoid this economic *progería* (premature aging), what countries in the region perhaps need most is a tradition of solid, competent and honest institutions. (Kuczynski 2002)

The unsteady and in the end disappointing growth of the past 50 years, and in particular the past 15—since *Toward Renewed Economic Growth* was written—poses some key questions. Can most Latin American countries do better? What policies would allow the region's countries to realize their potential? As a significant part of the region's population starts aging, are the next few years its last chance for a real period of sustained economic growth?

The 1940-80 period was one of special blessings for Latin American economies: a commodity boom in the wake of three wars, after the drought of the Great Depression; abundant international credit, first from international agencies that had few other outlets, and then in the 1970s from international banks that needed to place newfound profits from energy exporters; and goodwill from the United States, which was worried about the spread of communism, especially after the accession of Fidel Castro in 1959. Yet, despite these favorable circumstances, annual growth averaged barely above 5 percent, with much of that concentrated initially in Mexico and then in Brazil. Admittedly, rapid population growth held back saving and thus made investment highly dependent on capital imports.

Growth Prospects

Making a careful judgment on the region's growth prospects therefore requires looking at its past experience. Unless Latin Americans, and especially their governments, are able to significantly raise their rate of saving, it is unlikely that growth on a sustained basis will top 5 percent annually. Even to achieve such a target, the macroeconomic mix of policies has to be scrupulously maintained, avoiding major imbalances that can lead to setbacks such as the Mexican devaluation and financial crisis of the mid-1990s, the Brazilian devaluation of early 1999, and the Argentine and Brazilian crises of 2002. Without these events, growth for the region would have been in the range of 4.5 to 5 percent, close to the target. Thus, the maintenance of a coherent and realistic set of macroeconomic policies is essential to achieve even minimum growth.

As economies grow, they increase their domestic savings, and this in turn reinforces growth. The fact that few Latin American countries have gross domestic savings as a percentage of GDP above the high teens (the main exceptions being Chile, Ecuador, Mexico, and Panama; see table 1.3) is due in part to the high proportion of poor people. In Peru, for example, as of 2001 the proportion of people living in poverty (defined as living on $2.00 a day or less) was 54 percent; of those, one-quarter live in extreme poverty (defined as less than $0.75 a day). Although most other countries have less extreme situations, with those living in poverty accounting for one-quarter to half of the population, the extent of poverty makes it impossible to create a mass market for industry and services, and impedes the creation of the savings necessary to finance rapid growth.

The task of reaching higher levels of savings is a complex one. But the experience of other countries—including Chile in Latin America—suggests several avenues. First, there must be income growth; high growth rates are the easiest way to generate savings. Second, governments must lead the way and provide the example by being savers themselves, particularly in their social security systems—a rare occurrence in Latin America. Public pension systems are a major fiscal drag in a number of countries and need to be reformed.

Governments must also have enough revenue to finance substantial productive investment expenditure, especially on education and basic infrastructure, so as to provide opportunities to the large masses in the middle and at the lower end of the economic spectrum. If governments spend most of their limited resources on paying wages and servicing their external debt—the situation of a number of the region's governments—they make little or no contribution to savings. A determined effort has to be made in education, raising both quantity (coverage and the years of schooling) and quality. In East Asia, economic growth, savings, and education have gone hand in hand. There is no reason why the same combination—hard as it may be to implement—cannot work in Latin America.

New ways also have to be found to mobilize private savings through independent pension systems, following the example of Chile. This is being done in a number of countries, although many improvements still need to be made. Private pension systems are the most hopeful innovation for the development of local capital markets in the region.

Will Latin American countries be able to reach high growth rates, in the 7 percent range, on a sustained basis? History suggests not, at least not without more profound policy changes than currently seem on the horizon. Matching the growth performance of the 1945-81 era (5.2 percent) will already be a stretch and would be a major achievement, especially in light of recent experience (no net growth in 2001-02, as this is being written). Aspirations beyond that are wonderful. But for now, a steady, moderate rate of growth could set the stage for better performance in the future.

Table 1.3 Gross domestic savings for selected Latin American and Caribbean countries, 1990-2000
(percent of GDP)

Country	1990	1991	1992	1993	1994	1995	1996	1997	1998	1999	2000
Argentina	19.7	16.2	15.2	16.7	16.9	17.6	17.5	17.2	17.4	17.2	15.3
Brazil	21.4	20.5	21.4	22.3	22.5	20.5	18.6	18.6	18.6	19.3	20.1
Chile	28.4	27.0	25.2	24.1	25.4	27.6	24.7	24.5	22.4	23.0	24.5
Colombia	24.3	23.4	18.7	19.0	19.8	19.6	16.5	15.0	13.5	11.3	13.3
Costa Rica	20.6	15.7	16.6	15.8	15.7	17.1	14.1	15.4	17.6	23.8	18.9
Ecuador	22.9	23.8	25.0	21.7	22.0	19.7	24.4	21.2	18.0	24.2	28.4
El Salvador	1.2	2.1	2.2	3.8	4.6	4.2	2.3	4.2	4.5	4.2	1.8
Mexico	22.0	20.4	18.3	17.1	16.9	22.5	25.2	25.8	22.2	21.9	21.5
Panama	21.4	18.7	22.7	24.5	28.0	28.2	28.7	27.1	23.0	24.0	24.1
Peru	18.4	15.0	14.4	15.5	18.9	19.4	18.4	20.2	18.9	19.7	18.2
Uruguay	17.6	18.0	16.2	15.2	15.3	15.3	15.1	15.1	14.9	13.6	12.5

Source: World Bank, *World Development Indicators.*

The Purpose of This Book

The purpose of this study is to develop a policy agenda for reviving economic momentum in Latin America. A resumption of growth is undoubtedly a key aspect of this objective, but we believe that the region needs more than faster growth if the bulk of its population is one day to reach the sort of living standards typical of industrial countries, while achieving a decent social system and preserving the physical environment in the process. Clearly, achieving industrial country living standards for the bulk of the population requires that the rate of economic growth be a lot higher than it has been for the past 20 years; by itself, redistribution of income could not begin to do the job. At the same time, aggregate economic growth alone will not remedy the highly skewed distribution of income and wealth that gives Latin America much more poverty than any industrial country would have at those levels of average income. Hence, our focus is on both accelerating growth and improving income distribution. We believe that both are possible and both are necessary.[2]

The region's poor growth performance during the past 20 years—certainly a long enough period to detect a trend—has bred a skeptical attitude among some policymakers about the importance of economic dynamism and growth; mediocre expansion rates of 3 to 4 percent a year are often received with comfort and complacency. It is crucial, if Latin America is to have a chance at overcoming unemployment and poverty, to set aside this attitude of resignation and refocus policy thinking on the urgency of rekindling economic growth on a long-term, sustainable basis.

The same can be said emphatically about issues of economic equity. The challenge now is not only to rekindle a bare minimum of 5 percent growth over a long period, a base target that can hopefully be exceeded, but to do so in a far more egalitarian and equitable manner than in the past. Unless the region's great masses, who constitute the overwhelming majority of its 500 million inhabitants, have a meaningful stake in its development, development itself will not be achievable.

The study has a further nine topical chapters, plus a concluding summary chapter and an appendix. The nine chapters cover the broad subjects that we believe are essential for the main purpose of the book. The first deals with reforming the state. The second focuses on poverty, equity, and social policy. The next six are devoted to specific policy areas: fiscal and budgetary policy, the financial system, exchange rates and monetary policy, trade policy, education and training, and labor markets. Chapter 10 deals with the political-economy problems of reform, specifically with so-called second-generation reforms.

2. Is there a conflict between them? We think not, which is a condemnation of the existing state of policy in the region. Efficient policies would have put countries on the frontier, where any improvement in one would come at the expense of the other. That is not where we see the region as being.

Clearly, this is not an all-encompassing compendium of the subjects that affect development. But the contents of the book reflect our judgment of the topics that are of key importance in achieving rapid and equitable growth. Two of the most important issues that we omit and that are likely to be of great importance in determining the quality of life in Latin America are the drug trade and environmental issues. We touch briefly on these in the final chapter, where we also summarize the policy agenda that emerges from the nine chapters on specific topics. An appendix deals with the relationship between the reform agenda we develop in this book and the Washington Consensus.

2

Reforming the State

PEDRO-PABLO KUCZYNSKI

Even though Latin American governments and their activities represent a far smaller percentage of GNP than those in more advanced economies, governments have a large role in the economy. In the past, government decisions have had a significant and sometimes deleterious effect on economic activity, creating instability and unpredictability, especially in the period before and during the external debt crisis of the early and mid-1980s. Subsequently, many governments embarked on economic reform programs. Today, after several years of very slow growth and in some cases, notably Argentina, outright economic depression, there is widespread frustration with the role of governments as reformers.

Nonetheless, since *Toward Renewed Economic Growth in Latin America* was published by Balassa et al. in 1986, there have been three significant improvements and changes in the role of the state in the economies of Latin America. First and most important, the destabilizing element of public finances has been reined in; the very large public-sector deficits and their impact in stimulating domestic inflation have been brought under reasonable control (see chapter 4), although significant fiscal weaknesses remain in most countries. Second, as part of fiscal stabilization, but also to increase economic efficiency, the role of the government as provider of commercial goods and services has been drastically reduced through privatization. Third, most governments have made some effort to cut back their overregulation of economic activity, both domestically and in external trade and payments, although their efforts and results have been uneven.

Have these efforts been sufficient to create a more just society and to stimulate growth? The performance of the 1990s suggests not. In all three areas, with a wide variety of ranges among countries but with clear underlying trends, a retrospective review suggests an "incomplete" grade.

Making the State More Effective

After 20 years of limited or nonexistent economic growth in the majority of Latin American economies, a major political debate is beginning in the region on the role of the state. In rather oversimplified terms, there are two basic questions: Should the state shrink to do fewer things but do them more effectively? Or should it have a larger role, taking up the slack left by low levels of private (and public) investment during the recent recession?

Certainly, the record of the past 20 years or so suggests four basic conclusions. First, fiscal resources are severely limited in most countries, and governments have little room to maneuver, at least in the short run (see chapter 4). Second, despite some progress, especially in Brazil, Latin American countries are far behind in the crucial area of educational achievement, particularly in providing education and training to those from low-income groups (chapter 8). Third, despite the progress in a number of countries in getting the state out of commercial activities, a number of the remaining but basic governmental functions are either not provided or are provided deficiently, especially public security and a functioning and honest judicial system. Fourth, government attempts to reduce poverty have in general been ineffective, while the maldistribution of income and wealth, one of the most skewed in the world (with a few exceptions, e.g., Costa Rica and Uruguay), continues much as in the past and, if anything, has probably deteriorated somewhat during the past two decades (see chapter 3).

An essential ingredient for any of these reforms is efficient, open, and competent public administration. Without it, market reforms cannot work properly. Most Latin American countries, both large and small, still have a long way to go in creating modern institutions of public administration. Civil service entry in most cases is not yet organized on a competitive basis. Because political interference in administrative decisions is the norm rather than the exception, young talent is discouraged from entering public administration, with the exception of a few semi-independent agencies such as central banks and in some cases finance ministries and the diplomatic service. Crucial sectors—such as the administration of education, health care, and public infrastructure—suffer from political interference, lack of a career path for civil servants, and pay that is substantially lower than in comparable private-sector positions. The result is sometimes a confrontational attitude toward the private sector—and sometimes corruption and ineptitude.

Although European countries today are backtracking from the elitist and competitive civil services that flourished (especially in France and the United Kingdom) in the postwar period, a dose of both elements might be productive today in Latin America, introducing more order and competence in public administration. By creating a kind of elite "officer corps" in the civil service, Latin American countries would not only raise the professional level of the civil service—as Spain has done in the past 50 years—but by raising the social and economic status of senior civil servants, governments would also in time sharply curtail the temptations for corruption.

Another essential element is to define more clearly than in the past the scope and range of government regulation of the economy. This goes from tariffs and trade to the exchange system and labor markets. Substantial progress has been made in virtually all countries in deregulating prices; not coincidentally, inflation has fallen sharply in most countries. However, most countries lag in having a transparent and effective system of bankruptcy proceedings, thereby introducing unnecessary rigidities into the economic system, especially during times of recession, as now.

A crucial area of economic regulation is that of public utilities. With the privatization of basic utilities, particularly telephones and electricity, regulatory reform has assumed increasing importance. Although most countries have created ostensibly independent regulatory agencies, many are still having growing pains in setting up a regulatory process that is fair, predictable, and transparent. Tariff changes are sometimes sudden and politically motivated, as happened with Chilean telephone tariffs in 1997; the public is given little information on the reasoning behind regulatory decisions and therefore has no stake in the system. Moreover, regulators sometimes have hidden motives, such as trying to assuage authorities by appearing to be tough; at other times, they are too close to the companies they are supposed to regulate.

Some of these problems also occur in more advanced economies and are complex to tackle. Besides better professional preparation and the time it takes to develop objective regulatory systems, perhaps the most important missing ingredient that needs to be developed is public education on regulatory issues.

Deregulation, or rather sensible regulation, is but one element necessary for economic growth. Nonetheless, it is an important element for investors, both domestic and international. The periods of intense progress in deregulation, such as in 1991-93 in Argentina and Peru, were accompanied by a substantial inflow of direct and portfolio investment from abroad—including the reflow of flight capital—as well as the start of industrial restructuring and of domestic investment. It is not a coincidence that deregulation, capital inflows, and privatization all went together, each one influencing the other, making the other possible, and reinforcing one another.

Privatization

Privatization came about in most Latin American countries in the 1990s from a mixture of two main motives. The overriding one was the financial crisis in the public sector (e.g., Salinas 2000, chap. 14), where the losses of state-owned enterprises and the subsidies they received from the central government accounted for as much as half of the public-sector deficits of the largest countries and for most of the deterioration of public finances from the mid-1970s to the early and mid-1980s (Larraín and Selowsky 1991, chapter 8). The other motive was the appalling decline of public services in the 1980s, especially in electric power and telephones, after most of the utilities had been taken over by governments in the 1960s and 1970s.

The combination of financial crises and high inflation (hyperinflation in Argentina and Peru) and the utter failure of essential public services in a number of countries provided a propitious setting for governments to push privatization through reluctant legislatures. A third motive, particularly important in Chile, the precursor and pioneer in privatization, was the strong ideological conviction among the economic advisers to the government that privatization was essential to raise the low level of efficiency of the economy.

There is no doubt, more than 10 years after the start of privatization in 1990 in Mexico and Argentina (emulating the earlier example of Chile, and followed later by Peru, Brazil, and most of the countries of the region), that the provision of basic public services—particularly electricity and telephones—has vastly improved in comparison with the erratic and expensive delivery of the 1970s and 1980s. The power interruptions (*apagones*) so typical of the late 1980s in Argentina, Colombia, and Peru, among other countries, probably lopped 1 percent off their GDP annually in those years (OLADE 1993). The very large improvements in the efficiency of privatized electric distribution systems in the 1990s—eliminating clandestine connections, reducing distribution losses by replacing obsolete networks, and stimulating competition among generators—not only eliminated the huge costs to industry arising from power outages but also made possible a reduction in prices for users, as is noted below.

The record in other activities is less clear-cut. In telephone systems, the lengthy monopoly positions granted the carriers in Argentina, Mexico, Peru, and Venezuela at the time of privatization—to improve the price for the selling governments and to give time to the buyers to make the large investments required as a condition for privatization—enabled the privatized monopolies to maintain high prices, especially for long-distance service, and to exclude potential competitors until the monopolies expired in the late 1990s. Nonetheless, because of investment and performance commitments made at the time of privatization, service improved dramatically over the pitifully low standards of the 1970s and 1980s.

Privatization in other sectors was stimulated by the selling governments' absorbing a major part of existing debt. In steel, the strategy by and large was successful, especially in Argentina and Brazil. In airlines, however, in line with the difficulties of commercial aviation worldwide, privatization simply shifted the burden of maintaining national carriers of dubious potential from the public sector to the commercial banks, some of which were at that point still state owned. The privatized Mexican airlines in effect went bankrupt—along with a smaller private-sector competitor; the Peruvian and Venezuelan carriers also went bankrupt and were closed in the late 1990s, while Aerolíneas Argentinas, privatized in 1990, struggles on to avoid formal bankruptcy. Seen from another perspective, the gradual disappearance of these airlines was hastened by privatization, a positive and in the end unavoidable development in an industry with worldwide overcapacity.[1]

The major contribution of privatization in its various forms (outright sales, concession agreements, and management agreements) has been in public utilities, where the two or three decades in the 1960s, 1970s, and 1980s of state ownership in Latin America resulted in erratic prices, underinvestment, wastage, and large-scale foreign borrowing, and in various countries (though not all) in poor coverage. Privatization corrected these flaws, substantially increasing coverage. The areas that needed this increased coverage were the poor ones, where governments had already in the 1970s and 1980s made a significant effort. As a result of the investment programs mandated under privatization, privatized electricity companies were able in the 1990s to extend coverage to virtually 100 percent in their concession areas. Blackouts were eliminated, and shut-offs for maintenance were sharply curtailed (table 2.1).

It is true that to prepare electric utilities for privatization, electricity tariffs had to be sharply raised; the state-owned companies were not viable without these increases. But simply raising tariffs without changing ownership and management would not have been enough; many old habits died hard, particularly that of stealing electricity, not only a very dangerous activity but also one that raised costs for those who did pay. Before privatization, most state-owned companies had nontechnical losses (i.e., stealing) of about 12 to 15 percent. This percentage has today been reduced in most cases to 1 to 3 percent, with corresponding benefits in coverage and cost to the customer.

Much has been made by some politicians of supposedly high electricity tariffs. First, in reality, because of the mandatory productivity improvements included in tariff formulas in most countries, tariffs have gone down in dollar terms. In Chile, they have fallen by about 15 percent since privatization, and by much more in Argentina (table 2.1). Second, a

1. Ramamurti (1996); see chapters 6, 7, 8, and 9. Also see Grosse (1996) on Aerolíneas Argentinas (in the Ramamurti volume).

Table 2.1 Coverage, average tariff, and efficiency of privatized electric systems in selected Latin American countries (at the time of privatization compared with the latest year, 2001 or 2002)

	Coverage (percent)		**Average tariff** (cents per kilowatt-hour)		**Losses from distribution system** (percent)		**Hours of interruption per month**	
Country	**At privatization**	**Latest year**	**At privatization**	**Latest year**	**At privatization**	**Latest year**	**At privatization**	**Latest year**
Chile	90	98	10.0	8.6	14	5	—	—
Peru (Lima area)	75	100	9.2	9.0	20	9	72	1
Peru (national)	48	75	—	—	21	9	—	—
Argentina	94	95	3.8	2.9	22	10	17	5
Brazil	90	94	7.7	9.0	9	8	26	15

— = not available

Sources: Utility companies and regulatory bodies, plus ECLAS, CCPE (Brazil), U. Católica (Chile).

Table 2.2 Basic statistics of privatized telephone systems in selected Latin American countries (at the time of privatization compared with the latest year, 2001 or 2002)

Country	Statistic	At privatization	Latest year	**Percent coverage in latest year** (total number of phones ÷ population)
Argentina	Fixed lines (thousands)	1,700	8,400	41
	Mobile phones (thousands)	12	7,200	
	Average tariff (cents per minute for local call)	3.1	0.9	
Brazil[a]	Fixed lines (thousands)	22,000	48,000	48
	Mobile phones (thousands)	7,000	29,000	
	Average tariff (cents per minute for local call)	0.8	0.3	
Chile	Fixed lines (thousands)	600	3,500	59
	Mobile phones (thousands)	—	5,500	
	Average tariff (cents per minute for local call)	3.2	1.8	

— = not available

a. Privatization occurred in 1998.

Sources: Telephone companies and regulatory bodies for the respective countries.

number of governments have introduced cross-subsidies for really poor consumers, namely, those using in the range of 100 to 200 kilowatt-hours a month. Where this has been done, complaints about the cost of electricity have all but disappeared.

The story of telephone systems has been more complicated, but in the end a wide swath of the population has benefited from the spread of cellular or mobile telephones, an area of intense competition (table 2.2). To maximize fiscal revenue at the time of privatization, governments that privatized telephone monopolies (Mexico, Argentina, Peru, and Venezuela—in that order—and earlier Chile) offered a guaranteed fixed telephone monopoly for a period of years, usually 5 to 7, which was extended in some cases (Argentina and Mexico).

The acquiring companies, having seen 20 years of nationalizations and defaults, were also hesitant to participate without a guarantee period. Much of this was inevitable, given the difficulties of attracting investment at the time, but a fair criticism can certainly be made about the time it took to bring long-distance rates down from the extremely high levels prevailing in most countries other than Chile—which already had among the lowest and most competitive long-distance rates in the world, as befits an export-oriented economy. It is in mobile telephones that the fastest gains in coverage in urban areas were achieved, once they were opened to competition; intense price competition and special economy rates have extended mobile telephone use to people with modest incomes.

A review of the status of privatization in Latin American economies suggests that very significant progress has been made in a number of countries, but that progress has been uneven, both by sector and by country. Some countries have not embraced privatization because of strong historical resistance by an aging population (this has been the case in Uruguay) or because of political instability (e.g., Ecuador). Others, such as Colombia, have not been able to get very far because of investor resistance; the state-owned parts of the Venezuelan aluminum industry are another example.

The privatization pioneer, Chile, basically stopped significant privatizations after 1989, with the exception of the main rail line; water systems and the copper-mining industry remain partially in state hands. Large state-owned commercial banks continue to exist in a number of countries, such as Banco do Brasil, Banco de la Nación and Banco de la Provincia de Buenos Aires in Argentina, and Banco del Estado in Chile. After much discussion, the state of São Paulo sold off its state bank, Banespa, to BSCH of Spain in an international bid in 2000. The energy area in Mexico remains largely untouched, except for a few private electricity-generating plants—whether state-owned or privately owned, a generating plant will have similar performance, so that the efficiency benefits of competitive private management are smaller for generation than for distribution.

Did privatization contribute to economic growth? In a general way, there is no doubt that privatization was one of the key elements that helped to jump-start economic revival in the countries that were the most aggressive privatizers (Chile, Argentina, and Peru). But in other countries that did less in privatization (Brazil, Mexico, and Venezuela), the effects were also less clear-cut. More systematic surveys (e.g., by Lora and Panizza 2002) that group the effects of all the various reforms together show major gains in productivity and income in Argentina and Peru in the 1990s, as well as in a number of smaller countries (and of course in Chile in the 1980s). As for the distributional effects, on which there has been much political commentary but little analysis, it is clear that the privatizations in Latin America, which focused principally on carefully structured sales of utilities, avoided the excesses and concentration of wealth that came with the sales and privatizations of state-owned industrial and energy firms in Russia and Eastern Europe (Birdsall and Nellis 2002).

The unpopularity of privatization in recent years in most Latin American countries has come from a variety of sources. First, some presidents turned publicly against privatization when they saw that they had run out of big-ticket items to sell off (e.g., Alberto Fujimori in Peru and Carlos Menem in Argentina, both of whom were trying to get elected to unconstitutional third terms) and therefore that there was limited political mileage in pursuing privatization. Second, the memories of the very poor utility services of 10 years ago are fading in a number of countries. Third and most important, very little effort was made to create a wide shareholding for privatized companies. The exceptions were some of the telephone companies and the energy company YPF in Argentina, but in the end it was sold in its entirety to Repsol of Spain.

Privatization is a work in progress in Latin America. Because of worldwide overinvestment in telephone and electricity systems, major players in the United States and Europe—pressed by their regulators—are trying to exit from areas that are not central to their main business. That means selling Latin American assets, where growth peaked in the late 1990s and the Argentine crisis and the 2002 presidential election in Brazil have cast a pall in boardrooms. Many assets will be sold at knockdown prices in the next year or two. What that will do to concession agreements and to service is still very much an open question.

The Rule of Law—Personal Security

If there is one area where the government has a clear role it is that of controlling crime and providing physical security for its citizens. Yet, in the words of a recent report by the Inter-American Development Bank, "Crime and violence have become staple features in most Latin American countries. Despite the persistent lack of reliable data, what statistics are available indicate that the region has one of the highest crime rates in the world" (IDB 2000b, 71).

The economic cost of crime in Latin America is not quantified, but there is no doubt that it is very substantial. A country such as Colombia, admittedly at the top end of the insecurity spectrum, annually spends 6 percent of GDP on private security and criminal justice—not counting the direct costs of crimes committed, from assaults, in property damage (e.g., pipelines cut and oil spills), in ransom paid, in investment forgone, in emigration to cities and abroad, in large-scale psychological damage, and so on.

Crime and insecurity show no sign of abating. Estimated statistics show a dramatic increase in the 1980s in homicide rates, which have in most cases stayed at high levels since then, with variations by countries. There were reductions in Peru, for example, and increases in Argentina, Mexico, and Venezuela (table 2.3).

Other than unemployment, crime consistently ranks at the top of citizen concerns in most Latin American countries. No government can afford to be complacent about this problem. The difficulty with crime control in Latin America, as elsewhere, is what approach to take. As in the United States, the public and the police favor punishment—sentencing offenders and building more jails—whereas social scientists usually emphasize prevention—such as supervision of troublesome adolescents and incentives for children to complete school. In the United States in the early

Table 2.3 Homicide rates for selected Latin American and Caribbean countries, 1980-2000 (homicides per 100,000 inhabitants)

Country	Circa 1980	Circa 1990	Circa 2000	2000/1980
Argentina	3.9	4.8	8.2	2.1
Brazil	11.5	19.7	17.4	1.5
Chile	2.6	3.0	1.7	0.7
Colombia	20.5	89.5	65.0	3.2
Mexico	18.2	17.8	26.0	1.4
Peru	2.4	11.5	4.9	2.0
Trinidad and Tobago	2.1	12.6	—	—
United States	10.7	10.1	5.5	0.5
Venezuela	11.7	15.2	25.9	2.2

— = not available

Source: World Bank data, as shown in Instituto Apoyo, *Seguridad Ciudadana* (2001), based on local police and Ministry of Interior reports.

1990s, 94 percent of law enforcement budgets was aimed at crime control and punishment, and little at prevention; according to the Inter-American Development Bank (IDB 2000b, 74), this proportion is likely to be even more skewed in Latin America.

In this regard, much can be learned from Japan, a country with one of the lowest crime rates. There is a police presence at the local level, physically visible every few blocks in a Koban, a sort of miniprecinct where the public is invited in and can give the police good information on their particular area, thus building up the trust of citizens in the police. Although the setting is different, elements of this system—a combination of local pressure with "big brother" watchfulness—might work in some Latin American countries.

In much of Latin America, on the contrary, the police inspire little trust. In Argentina in the 1996-98 period, even before the recent crime wave that accompanied the recession, almost 80 percent of urban residents did not trust the police.[2] A similar percentage prevails in Peru (Ortíz de Zevallos and Pollarolo 2000, 198), and high levels of distrust occur in such other countries as Brazil, Mexico, and Venezuela. Insecurity is the major factor behind the recent part-time emigration of businesspeople from Colombia, Mexico, and Venezuela, among other countries, to places such as Miami. Needless to say, this is accompanied by a movement of savings abroad—in short, by capital flight.

Seventy-five percent of Latin Americans consider that there is no equality before the law. They believe that the police and the courts protect the powerful rather than the broad mass of the population. Even in a socially more developed country such as Uruguay, the percentage is still relatively

2. As stated in IDB (2000b, 76).

high at 49 percent. The first thing that is therefore required in the fight against insecurity and crime is to restore trust in the police and the judicial system. This will require training, time, and especially funds. Moreover, crime prevention is a broad subject that encompasses a large variety of subjects, ranging from aid to abandoned children—a major tragedy in large urban areas—to public works programs and supervision for students seeking to complete secondary school. (The last, incidentally, is a salient weakness of Latin American public education systems and is the main reason that Latin Americans average only 5 years of schooling compared with 7.5 years for Southeast Asians.)

An approach to security that emphasizes crime prevention involves more public spending. The difficulty is that legislatures and the voting public do not directly connect the additional savings to society from crime prevention, which takes time to show results, to the additional public expenditures, which are immediate. In any case, it is clear that public expenditures on police and related matters would have to rise above their present very low level of 1 to 2 percent of GDP in most countries—not counting additional expenditures on related priority social services, particularly education.

The Rule of Law—the Judiciary and Civil Society

Any effort to improve public security needs to include judicial reform. Many good recommendations have been made on the subject, and over the years a number of countries have made efforts to streamline judicial procedures, raise administrative efficiency, and make the judiciary independent and honest. But these efforts still have a very long way to go. The average Latin American judiciary is still very far from being independent from the government in power or from previous governments that appointed the judges; procedures focus on formality rather than substance (partly a result of the intellectual inheritance of Roman Law plus the Napoleonic Code, in contrast to the Anglo-Saxon tradition of common law), thus bypassing norms usually taken for granted in countries practicing common law, such as the presumption of innocence until proven guilty.

Judicial efficiency is still a distant objective, with huge backlogs of both civil and criminal cases. Inefficiency and bureaucratic slowness create large costs for society, in effect making recourse to justice an experience only the wealthy and influential can afford. If corruption is added to inefficiency, a state of affairs in a number of countries—notably Peru in the late 1990s—then the judiciary ceases to fulfill its role as a central pillar of civil society.

Among the recommendations frequently made to improve the judiciary is that of raising the salaries of judges. Comparisons are often made between the compensation of judges and those of the top lawyers that litigate before them; as in industrial countries, however, there is a large difference between the earnings of top lawyers and those of the vast majority of lawyers, most of whom are solo practitioners and are often only partially employed. Although it is important to improve the level and the predictability of judges' real earnings, it is just as important to establish a career path for them, with recognized standards of selection and promotion. Only in this way will the judicial profession over time gain the respect of society at large and have a better chance of avoiding corruption. Taking again the example of Peru, almost half of the 800 judges there are on temporary contract, with no clear career prospects; this failing is fertile ground for corruption (Instituto Apoyo 2000).

One area that holds promise for unclogging judicial systems and bringing them closer to the people is that of the justice of the peace (*juez de paz*), who sits at the local level. He or she can resolve the type of local disputes that tend to occur in rural areas—such as disagreements over water rights, cattle rustling, rights-of-way, and property boundaries—without clogging up the judicial system, which is usually represented by a court in a distant city. Some sort of central quality control is needed for such a system to work, so as to avoid the petty favoritism that tends to occur in small localities all over the world.

In a number of Latin American countries, the judiciary operates under very difficult circumstances. In Colombia today and in a number of Central American countries in the past, for example, judges have been threatened and even killed by both guerrillas and paramilitaries in civil wars. Gigantic cases of corruption—in Argentina, Brazil, and Peru, for example—have put enormous political pressure on judges to reach quick verdicts when the judicial system has very limited budgets to marshal and analyze evidence.

Another obstacle is the nature of legislation, which is often vague and leaves too much room for discretion; in the words of a well-known Mexican political and economic analyst: "Curiously, the Mexican legal system is analogous to that of the former communist regimes. Laws and regulations are written in discretionary terms. . . . This makes government action unpredictable, not only because ambiguous law is easy to manipulate."[3] The results of this ambiguity have also been evident elsewhere, perhaps most conspicuously in Argentina, where judicial decisions that are out of touch with economic reality have periodically upset macroeconomic policies.

The needed improvement in the judiciary is thus not a task that can be tackled in a vacuum, independent of other aspects of social and economic development. To ease the transition to a more open civil society, the essential ingredient of an independent judiciary must be accompanied by a

3. Luis Rubio, "A Rule of Law Emerges in Mexico, Slowly," *Wall Street Journal*, April 27, 2001.

free press and an active participation of nongovernmental organizations that can publicize the concerns of particular groups of citizens and over time can lead to informed debate about the issues facing government. This evolution will lead to a better informed, more independent judiciary; conversely, a more independent judiciary will lead to a better informed, more open government and society. The development of an effective judiciary is thus an interdependent part of social and economic development.

Decentralization

A key issue in the management of Latin American economies is decentralization. One of the legacies of the external debt crisis in Latin America during the 1980s, as well as of the return to democratically elected governments at about the same time, has been a desire to decentralize government from the center down to the local level.

This pressure for change comes after almost 500 years of unusually strict although often ineffective centralization. In the words of a leading student of the subject: "Spain's [and also, but to a lesser extent, Portugal's] legacy to Latin America was a tradition of extreme centralization in government decision making and an elitist social structure that impeded the implementation of central government policies. Local government was grossly neglected during the post-independence period" (Nickson 1995). This tendency continued right up through the 1970s and early 1980s, partly reinforced by international aid agencies, including the US Agency for International Development, that liked the simplicity of dealing with one decision maker per country—in sharp contrast to the federal principles of the US government (Nickson 1995, 16). An exception to this centralization has been the Inter-American Development Bank, which has traditionally supported local and municipal investments.

The centralizing trend was an accident of history. Spain had had a long tradition of autonomously run city-states, going back to Roman times. By the end of the 15th century, just before the conquest, the desire of the Crown to assert national control ran straight into local autonomy. The Comunero rebellion of 1521 and the confrontation between the Crown and the Santa Hermandad (Holy Brotherhood) of cities sealed the fate of local autonomy. In the colonies, conquistadors (known as *adelantados*, those who go ahead) were given special powers over the town councils (*cabildos*), and under Philip II municipal positions were sold to raise royal revenues. In Brazil, town councillors were restricted in the 17th century to *homens bons*, landed gentry untainted by commerce or labor.

In general, a long tradition was established of weak local government, with the bulk of local revenue channeled upward to the capital and from there to the Crown (Nickson 1995, 7-25). These arrangements, which have continued with some changes until today, have sparked periodic local rebellions and unrest, especially in such far-flung and diverse countries as Argentina, Brazil, Colombia, Mexico, and Peru, where impoverished local populations feel they are getting a bad bargain from a distant capital.

Today, decentralization is widely seen as a test of democracy, a necessary reversal of past authoritarian trends. However, the long tradition of centralization and authoritarianism dies hard, and change is not easy. Despite this difficulty, there is no doubt that the benefits of properly managed decentralization can be considerable for economic development: the ability to relate investments to local needs, a sense of local involvement that breeds greater interest in how public money is spent—especially if it is seen as coming from local taxation—and better knowledge of local conditions, which is especially important in the agricultural areas where low-income people usually are concentrated.

At the same time, the fiscal perils of excessively rapid decentralization, without formal arrangements for control of local expenditures and of revenue sharing, are well known and have been the subject of much comment and discussion (Fukasaku and Hausmann 1998; Giugale and Webb 2000). Rapid decentralization of revenues without proper control of expenditures was undoubtedly one of the major causes of Argentina's and Brazil's fiscal problems in the 1980s (see chapter 4).

Several issues need to be faced to achieve efficiently functioning decentralization. These include training of local officials; a clear framework that delineates responsibilities among the central government, states (or provinces), and municipalities; financially viable municipal units (many are too small to operate efficiently), or schemes to share revenues and functions among municipalities; and, given the large income disparities between large cities and rural areas, functioning schemes that equalize or reduce these disparities through transfers.

In the United States, state and local governments collect and keep sales taxes and property taxes as well as income taxes (in most states); these revenues are roughly equivalent to 10 percent of GDP (compared with 22 percent for federal revenues). In Latin American countries, by contrast, the autonomous sources of revenue for local governments are few and far between—other than transfers from the central government. The main sources of local revenue are fees and some payroll taxes; urban property taxation is relatively underdeveloped, and taxation of land is virtually nonexistent. In Mexico, for example, property taxes on average are only 13 percent of municipal revenues (Giugale and Webb 2000, 17), although the proportion is higher in some of the large cities. Whatever the composition of local revenues, without a strong local revenue base, decentralization cannot be a functioning reality.

The organization of the relationship between the center and the states and municipalities in Latin America spans a wide variety of systems. At one end is Brazil's federal system, in which states raise their own revenue (as well as receiving substantial federal transfers) and control their own expenditures—although the federal government intervenes, sometimes decisively (Giugale and Webb 2000, 3). From there on, a combination of federal and central systems prevail. Some countries have a large number of municipalities and others not many—for instance, Peru has roughly 1,900 (with only 14,000 inhabitants per municipality), whereas Uruguay has only 19 (each with an average population of almost 170,000 in 1994). Peru tried in the 1980s to bring cohesion to the dispersion and small size of local government by creating a few large regions, but these had difficulty in getting established because voters, especially outside the capital city of Lima, felt too remote from them.

Decentralization is an ongoing process that is not subject to relatively simple prescriptions. It is a more complex subject than others, such as fiscal balance, privatization, or opening up trade, where one-size-fits-all appears more or less to have worked in most countries in the region.

Nevertheless, even though different systems are likely to work in different countries, the devolution of more responsibility and economic power to provinces and localities is important so as to give voters and local governments a sense of participating in the development of their country. The problem is how federal governments can cap state and provincial deficits, so as to avoid the pressure for the center to periodically assume decentralized debts, thus undermining national fiscal stringency. Brazil, with its "internal IMF programs" and Law of Fiscal Responsibility, provides an encouraging model. If decentralization can be combined with fiscal responsibility in the coming decades—reversing the practice of several centuries—a stronger base will have been laid for development and democracy.

A Final Comment

For Latin American governments, the next several years will be a period of special challenge. After a period of restructuring the state—especially shedding commercial functions and deregulating the economy—the lack of growth in the recent past is leading to calls to augment government's role in the economy. If this larger role means more and better investments in high-priority areas—such as education, preventive health care, and rural infrastructure—then the call for change will have been worthwhile. But if it leads to the type of unfinanced fiscal expansions that took place in the 1970s, then it will be a setback for the region.

3

Bootstraps, not Band-Aids: Poverty, Equity, and Social Policy

NANCY BIRDSALL AND MIGUEL SZÉKELY

After a decade of economic reform that dramatically altered the structure of economies in Latin America, making them more open and more competitive, and a decade of substantial increases in public spending on education, health, and other social programs in virtually all countries, poverty and high inequality remain deeply entrenched. By the 1990s, most countries of the region had adopted in some form the recipe that seemed to produce dramatic rates of growth in East Asia: a combination of open markets and substantial commitment of public resources to investment in human capital.[1]

Yet the proportion of poor people, in most countries 40 percent or higher, failed to decline much if at all—the only exceptions were Chile,

Nancy Birdsall is president of the Center for Global Development in Washington, DC. Miguel Székely is the undersecretary for planning at Mexico's Ministry for Social Development.

1. Of course not everything was the same. But in the 1990s, the differences (see the essays in Birdsall and Jasperson 1997) in macroeconomic and in social policy were subtle, and probably no greater between, say, Peru and Malaysia than between South Korea and Malaysia. In particular, spending on social programs as a percentage of GDP was as great in Latin America in the 1990s as it had been and is in the tigers of East Asia. The differences may well have been in pre-1990s policies and economic characteristics, in particular the unhappy history of inflation in much of Latin America; the longer period of import-substitution policy, with its protection of local industry; and Latin America's greater inequality, with its political as well as economic implications.

with a reduction from an estimated 32 to 16 percent between 1990 and 1998, and Uruguay, from 23 to 13 percent. Not surprisingly, the proportion of poor people actually increased in countries that had low rates of growth, such as Venezuela. But the proportion also increased in countries such as Mexico and Peru where there was growth, at about 2 percent per capita annually. In no country was there any obvious improvement in what are generally very high rates of income inequality.[2]

What is wrong, and what can be done to alter this bleak picture? Obviously, higher rates of growth would help. But they continue to elude most countries, even Chile in the past few years. Moreover, it may be that the problems of poverty and inequality help explain the persistently low rates of growth, rather than only or primarily slow growth explaining persistent poverty.

In this chapter, we ask the question whether a fundamentally different approach to what we call "social policy" in Latin America could make a difference—both in increasing growth and in directly reducing poverty. We define social policy broadly to include economywide (macroeconomic and employment and other structural) policies that affect poverty and social justice in foreseeable ways, as well as social investment programs, such as health, education, and social protection programs, including cash and other transfers targeted to poor people and others vulnerable to economic and other shocks.

We begin with a brief review of what is known about the links among poverty, inequality, and growth in the region and elsewhere. We emphasize the relevance of empirical work, showing that income poverty, combined with inequality in access to credit and to such assets as land and education, contributes to low growth and directly to the low income growth of poor people. Then we focus on the effects of the market reforms of the past 10 to 15 years on poverty and inequality in the region, on the basis of empirical studies using household data. We emphasize our finding that the reforms have not contributed to reducing poverty and inequality.[3] Though reforms have not particularly worsened the situation of poor people, they have not addressed the underlying structural causes of high poverty: the lack of access of the poor to credit and to productivity-enhancing assets.

We then go on to briefly describe four stages of social policy in the region during the past four decades. Finally, we propose a more explicitly "bootstraps"-style social policy, focused on enhancing productivity via better distribution of assets. We set out how this broader social policy could ad-

2. The data on poverty and inequality to which we refer are set out in Behrman, Birdsall, and Székely (2001b). The data are from household surveys in the late 1980s and 1990s.

3. In Behrman, Birdsall, and Székely (2001a), we show that reforms as a group, especially financial-sector liberalization and the opening of the capital market, have tended to increase wage inequality (between those with higher or secondary education compared with primary education).

dress the underlying causes and not just the symptoms of the region's unhappy combination of high poverty and inequality with low growth.

Poverty, Inequality, and Growth in Latin America

Latin America suffers from a vicious circle in which low growth contributes to the persistence of poverty, particularly given high inequality, and high poverty and inequality contribute to low growth.[4] Consider first the former part of the statement: that low growth contributes to poverty, especially combined with initially high income inequality. Across all developing countries during the past several decades, GDP growth per capita has been necessary for reducing the number of poor people.[5] The most obvious example is China, where growth has been high and the number of poor people has been reduced dramatically.

Economic growth reduces poverty mainly through its effect on employment. Low GDP growth in Latin America has meant limited creation of new jobs in the modern sector—in contrast to East Asia in the 1960s through the 1980s, where employment increased rapidly and, as the labor market tightened, so did wages. In Latin America, the limited growth of the 1990s was not employment intensive, exacerbating the problem.[6] Of course, low growth implied fewer public resources in an absolute sense for the kind of public spending—on basic education and health—most likely to reach poor people and reduce inequality in the long run.

Compounding the problem, low growth in Latin America has been combined with unstable growth. Rich people seem better able to protect their incomes during downturns, at least in relative terms; this may be more the case where the initial distribution of income (and as we shall suggest, of assets and thus of economic as well as political power) favors the rich. The 1980s recession in Latin America led to more than proportionate increases in poverty.[7] Downturns in the 1980s and 1990s also probably exacerbated inequality, because some poor people had to sell their land or other assets and withdraw their children from school—undermining their future income-earning ability (Lustig 1995 and World Bank 2001, chap. 9).

In addition, high inequality meant that whatever the rate of growth, the growth effect on poverty was less than it might have been with a more

4. This section is based on Birdsall and de la Torre (2001).

5. Dollar and Kraay (2000) show that on average across countries the income of poor people (defined as the bottom fifth of the population) rises about one for one with growth in per capita GDP. This has not been necessarily true of course in every country. Foster and Székely (2001) criticize their approach and discuss some of the limitations of their interpretations.

6. Stallings and Peres (2000) provide evidence on this point.

7. Morley (1994) provides extensive evidence on this point.

Table 3.1 Change in the poverty rate and decomposition of the change into growth and redistribution effects, selected Latin American countries, various years (percent)

Country	Period	Poverty line	Initial poverty rate	Final poverty rate	Total change	Percent of total change due to: Growth	Redistribution	Residual
Brazil	1985-95	Extreme	10.0	11.1	10.2	–40	145	–5
		Moderate	30.4	28.0	–7.9	–40	–70	10
Bolivia	1990-95	Moderate	52.4	47.1	–10.1	–147	44	3
Chile	1987-96	Moderate	45.1	23.2	–48.6	–85	–7	–8
Colombia	1991-95	Moderate	58.5	58.5	–0.1	–103	6	–3
Costa Rica	1986-95	Moderate	29.4	25.6	–12.9	–117	17	0
Peru	1985-96	Moderate	43.1	50.5	17.2	99	–27	28

Source: Attanasio and Székely (2001).

equal distribution of income to start with, and a better distribution of the gains from growth. Even in countries that benefited from higher rates of growth, growth alone failed to translate into proportionate reductions in poverty. Consider the following two examples from Attanasio and Székely (2001). Between 1996 and 1998, GDP per capita increased in Mexico by 9.7 percent in real terms, a spectacular gain compared with the previous 16 years. However, poverty hardly declined. In fact, the incomes of the poorest 30 percent of the population contracted during this period. The huge increase in mean income was due entirely to income gains among the richest 30 percent—particularly the richest 10 percent—of the population (Székely 2001b).

The second example is Chile. Between 1992 and 1996, Chilean GDP per capita expanded by more than 30 percent in real terms, and moderate poverty (head count ratio) declined by 20 percent. But income inequality increased (the Gini index rose 7 percentage points). Had income distribution remained as it had been in 1992, the proportion of poor people would actually have declined much more—by 50 percent.[8]

Table 3.1 presents the result from a decomposition of the change in poverty in various countries into three components for selected years (based on household survey data) in the late 1980s and 1990s. The three

8. This result is obtained by using household surveys of the government of Chile for 1992, and multiplying all incomes by 1.3 to simulate the growth rate registered between 1992 and 1996. The poverty rate computed after this adjustment can be interpreted as the poverty that would have been observed had the distribution remained unchanged between the 2 years. Obviously, this is only a simulation for illustrative purposes, because there is no guarantee that growth would have been the same under a static distribution. The levels and the change in poverty head count differ from that in table 3.1 because of differences in the dates and in the definition of poverty in the CASEN data from the standardized (across countries) definition applied to all surveys covered in table 3.1.

components are a growth effect, a redistribution effect, and a residual.[9] During these years for the most part, distribution undermined and in some cases reversed the small positive effect of growth. In Bolivia, Colombia, and Costa Rica, the reductions in poverty registered in each period were due exclusively to growth. Income distribution deteriorated in these countries, and without growth, poverty would have increased. In Chile, inequality had a slight poverty-reducing effect; most of the poverty reduction was attributable to growth. Peru is the only country where an improvement in income distribution played a potentially important role in poverty reduction, although there it was outweighed by the negative growth effect.

Growth in Latin America in the 1990s made little difference for poverty reduction, for two reasons. First, growth was modest to start with in most countries of the region. Second, growth provided less than proportionate gains for poor people, certainly failing to offset their disproportionate losses in the 1980s, and in some cases increasing those losses.

Let us turn to the latter part of the statement about the vicious circle made above: that high poverty and inequality contribute to low growth. This is pertinent to social policy because it suggests there is no necessary trade-off between "economic" policies—for example, to maintain macroeconomic stability and enhance growth—and "social" policies to reduce poverty and inequality.

Theory suggests that poverty accompanied by an unequal distribution of such assets as land and human capital can inhibit growth by magnifying the adverse effects of imperfect markets and weak government institutions on savings and investment.[10] The obvious examples include the inability of landless poor people, without collateral, to borrow against the future human capital of their children so as to keep the children in school; and the inability of even small business owners with movable collateral to borrow where the legal and regulatory framework does not guarantee that creditors can seize that collateral. Moreover, if relatively poor people were able to invest, they would be likely to achieve higher returns than

9. To perform the decomposition, the researchers (Attanasio and Székely 2001) used the methodology developed by Datt and Ravallion (1992). The decomposition simulates the change in poverty that would have been observed if average income had changed as it actually did but the distribution had remained constant (the growth effect). The redistribution component is obtained by simulating the change in poverty that would have occurred if average income had remained constant but the distribution had shifted as it actually did.

10. Aghion, Caroli, and Garcia-Penalosa (1999) summarize the economic literature. Particularly relevant to our discussion of social policy is Benabou (1996). Birdsall, Ross, and Sabot (1995), in their analysis of inequality and growth in East Asia, emphasize that region's experience seems to belie the assumption, e.g., of Kaldor, that high savings are related to high income inequality.

those with greater wealth, because the latter move farther down their list of potentially good investments; the outcome for the economy as a whole is lower average returns on investment.[11]

Empirical evidence from cross-country studies supports the general proposition for developing countries that those with higher levels of income inequality have experienced lower levels of growth. Best known but problematic are the early studies of Persson and Tabellini (1994) and Alesina and Rodrik (1994). These relied on cross-sectional estimates without controlling for fixed country effects; they were therefore showing that unequal countries tended to grow more slowly, but not necessarily that inequality and not other characteristics associated with inequality was a cause of low growth.

More recent studies—including those on industrial as well as developing countries and those controlling for country effects—tend to come to the opposite conclusion (Forbes 2000). But Barro (2000) shows that the distinction between industrial and developing countries is important. In developing but not industrial countries, inequality does seem to reduce growth. Inequality of income, not surprisingly, matters where capital and other markets do not work well and also probably where government does not work well. Market and policy failures combine with high inequality to undermine growth.

A second series of cross-country studies clarifies that the fundamental problem is not inequality of income itself, but the underlying inequality of such assets as land and human capital (Birdsall and Londoño 1997; Deininger and Olinto 2000). Figure 3.1 illustrates Latin America's high inequality of land and human capital relative to other regions. Once the inequality of the latter two "assets" is taken into account, the "Latin America" effect (of lower growth than elsewhere) disappears (Birdsall and Londoño 1997); moreover, across countries, the effect of inequality of land and education is twice as great in reducing the income growth of the poorest 20 percent of households as in reducing average growth. De Janvry and Sadoulet (2000) present compelling evidence that in Latin America, where land inequality is high, growth in agricultural production and productivity has *worsened* rural income inequality because it has failed to raise employment and income levels of landless poor people.

Country studies provide evidence of what can be a vicious circle in which low income constrains the ability to acquire assets. In Brazil and Honduras, children in low-income households acquire relatively little edu-

11. Aghion, Caroli, and Garcia-Penalosa (1999) model this point. See also Birdsall, Pinckney, and Sabot (1999), who develop a household model in which income and work effort are endogenous to investment opportunities for liquidity-constrained households; one outcome is high returns on own investment, e.g., among small farmers in East Asia.

Figure 3.1 Asset inequality in various regions, about 1990

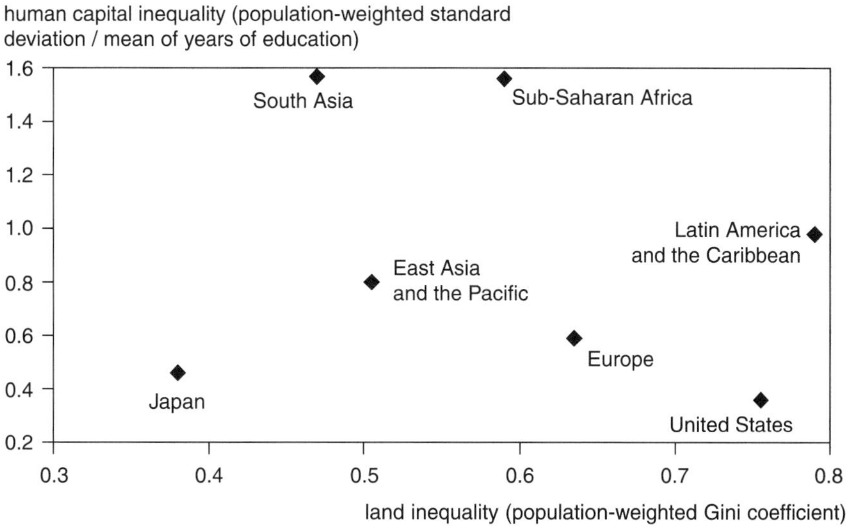

Note: Human capital inequality was calculated using data reported in Barro and Lee (2000a, b).
Source: Birdsall and Londoño (1997).

cation.[12] The point is obvious but important in magnitude. For example, if Brazil had had Malaysia's distribution of income in the 1980s (when the per capita income of the two countries was similar), and given empirical estimates of the income effect on children's enrollment in school, Brazil would have had an estimated doubling of secondary school enrollment (from 20 to 40 percent).[13] In Brazil, because poor people have few assets, they are not able to insure against income risk, compounding the effect of low income on the further acquisition of assets (Attanasio and Székely 2001). Uncertainty combined with the absence of adequate insurance mechanisms becomes a restriction on acquiring assets. Even when uncertainty induces precautionary savings, the savings go to relatively unproductive assets, such as cash holdings, instead of to human and physical capital.

Country studies also indicate the benefits to poor people of a combination of assets. For example, better access to credit or owning land is much more effective where the poor have more education, and vice versa. These studies also show systematic differences in returns on assets between rich and poor people, possibly reflecting differences in quality but also a

12. Country studies reported in Attanasio and Székely (2001) include assessments, using probit or logit regressions, of the association between ownership or access to human, physical, and social capital and the probability of a household being below the poverty line. In all six countries where the assessments were done, there was a strong inverse relation between years of schooling and the probability of being poor.

13. Birdsall, Ross, and Sabot (1995) provide this estimate and the calculations that underlie it.

greater likelihood that the poor suffer ethnic or racial discrimination—for example, in the form of a lower return on their human capital or greater difficulty in obtaining access to jobs or credit to put their human capital to work. In Chile, the difference between the average years of schooling of children at the top and bottom of the income distribution is not that large at young ages, but children from poor families attend schools with the lowest scores in terms of student achievement, whereas those from rich families mostly attend the best-scoring schools. In Costa Rica, the differential return on assets is an important determinant of poverty. If poor people were to receive the same return that the rich receive on the same asset, poverty would decline rapidly. Understanding the causes of differential returns—whether the systematically lower quality of education received by the poor or discrimination in the labor market—would provide insight into critical policy tools.

The fundamental problem boils down to the reality that inequality in Latin America is a good proxy for the poor having limited access to economic and social assets and thus limited economic opportunities, and limited economic returns on the assets they do have. Finally, given that the region's unusually high inequality compared with countries elsewhere is largely due to the extremely high concentration of income in the top decile,[14] the problem of limited assets at the bottom is probably compounded by the politics of power at the top, but we do not have analytic models to test this latter proposition.

The Effects of Market Reforms on Poverty and Inequality

A series of market reforms began in the 1980s in some Latin American countries and then spread to others, deepening everywhere in the 1990s. Estimates suggest (e.g., IDB 1997, 50-53 and appendix 1) that the reforms had a strong positive effect on growth, on the order of an annual increase of 1.9 percentage points for the period 1986-95. However, more recent analyses covering the period through 2002 would be less positive, given that growth rates have declined in the past few years.

The effects of the reforms on poverty and inequality have been less clear. Here we describe what we believe are the best recent estimates of these effects, based on analyses reported in detail in Behrman, Birdsall and Székely (2001a and 2001b). These estimates are based on household data for more than two decades from 17 countries of the region, covering more than 90 percent of the region's population; and on country- and year-specific measures of the intensity of five different types of economic

14. See IDB (1999) for a detailed assessment of this point. Karl (2001) elaborates on the corrosive interaction of economic and political privilege in the region.

reform. In these two papers, Behrman and we use reform indices developed in a series of papers by Lora (1997 and 2001) and Morley, Machado, and Pettinato (1999). These indices summarize data on trade reform, financial liberalization, tax reform, domestic liberalization of external capital transactions, and privatization for the period 1970-99, and they are comparable across time and countries.

Because it is not easy to compile an indicator to represent the extent of a government's economic liberalization, the literature has traditionally relied on various "proxies."[15] This approach is problematic because the proxies often present outcomes that have little to do with the actual decisions of governments and instead reflect reaction to markets, international prices, or the domestic private sector. In contrast, the Lora and Morley variables are based on direct indicators of governmental policies, and more accurately represent policy "effort."

The trade reform index reflects the average level of tariffs and the dispersion of those tariffs. The index for liberalization of the external capital account averages four components: sectoral controls of foreign investment, limits on profits and interest repatriation, controls on external credits by national borrowers, and capital outflows. The index for domestic financial reform takes into account borrowing and lending rates at banks and the reserves to deposit ratio. The tax reform index takes into account four factors: the maximum marginal tax rate on corporate incomes, the maximum marginal tax rate on personal incomes, the value-added tax rate (higher rates reduce the index), and the efficiency of the value-added tax.[16] The privatization index is calculated as 1 minus the ratio of value added in state-owned enterprises to nonagricultural GDP. The index of labor-market reform reflects legislative mandates affecting the ease of hiring and layoffs (the latter in terms of employer's cost) and of overtime pay.

All the indices are normalized between 0 and 1, where in each case 0 refers to the minimum value of the index across all Latin American countries in the relevant time period, and 1 is the maximum registered in the whole sample.[17] Figure 3.2 shows the average value of the indices for the region and displays the well-known intensification of liberalization at the end of the 1980s, especially after 1987.[18]

15. Two examples of common proxies used in the literature are exports plus imports over GDP, used as an indicator of trade liberalization, and M2 over GDP, used as an indicator of financial market reform.

16. Efficiency of the value-added tax is defined as the revenue collected under the tax as a percentage of GDP, given the tax rate.

17. Thus, the indices are comparable across countries in the region, which is critical for making comparisons among countries, including in our econometric estimates.

18. Liberalization of the external capital account is not included in figure 3.2. The figure shows the indices as updated by Lora (2001), who did not cover this reform. In figure 3.3, Behrman, Birdsall, and Székely (2001a) show this index as one where the reform has been greatest relative to the other reforms.

Figure 3.2 Evolution of reforms in Latin America, 1985–99
(regional average structural reform indices)

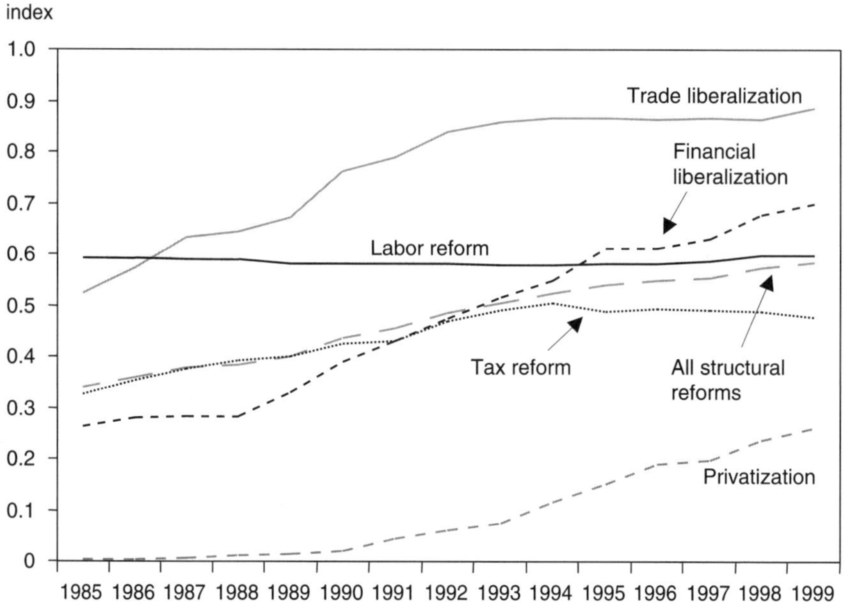

Note: Reform indices range from 0 to 1; 1 indicates a greater depth of reform. The regional average does not include the Dominican Republic, Honduras, or Nicaragua.

Source: Lora (2001).

With these indices in hand, it is possible to assess the effects of reform on the relative gains or losses in income of different groups during the periods covered by the various country surveys. Behrman, Birdsall, and Székely (2001b) do such estimates, grouping individuals (at the beginning and end of each period) as poor (*P*), rich (*R*), or in the middle (*M*). They assess the effects of the reforms on inequality by looking at the relative changes in the average income of the top decile (*R*) compared with the bottom three deciles (*P*).[19] Table 3.2 shows the correlation (0.925) between the resulting inequality variable (in logs) and the Gini coefficient. Similarly, they assess the effects of reforms on poverty by looking at relative changes in the average income of all those with per capita income below $2 a day (in 1985 purchasing power parity dollars) compared with all those above that threshold who are not rich (*M*).[20] Table 3.2 shows the cor-

19. See the appendix to this chapter. They proceed in this manner, i.e., comparing relative gains and losses across income groups, to minimize econometric problems. They adapt the approach from Behrman, Birdsall, and Székely (2001a).

20. This is not a measure of change in absolute poverty; it measures the change in the average income of poor people compared with others. Using a variable that measures change in the income difference has econometric advantages, which are explained in the appendix.

Table 3.2 Correlation between inequality and poverty indicators

Variable	Gini index	Poverty head count	Poverty gap[a]	Poverty intensity[a]
	Poverty and inequality indicator			
Variables correlated with inequality				
Log *R* – log *P* (poorest 10 percent)	0.726	0.569	0.633	0.673
Log *R* – log *P* (poorest 30 percent)	0.925	0.645	0.682	0.700
Variables correlated with poverty				
Log *R* – log *P*	0.576	–0.094	–0.004	0.046
Log *M* – log *P*	–0.219	–0.815	–0.785	–0.754

a. On these alternative measures of poverty, see Foster, Greer, and Thorbecke (1984).

Source: Behrman, Birdsall, and Székely (2001b).

relation (–0.815) between the resulting poverty variable (in logs) and more standard measures of poverty.

Table 3.3 presents their results for inequality.[21] Financial-sector liberalization has had a significant positive impact on inequality (table 3.3); trade liberalization has not affected inequality. (The coefficient of trade liberalization is negative, reducing income inequality, but insignificant.) There is no evidence to support the widespread belief that trade openness is the principal reason why the distribution of income has worsened in Latin America.[22] The other reforms (combined here to simplify presentation)[23] do not appear to have had any impact on inequality. Volatility and inflation, not surprisingly, show a significant positive effect (worsening inequality). An improvement in the terms of trade and an increase in the real exchange rate (a real appreciation of the local currency) seem to make the distribution of income more equal, though the coefficient of the former variable is not significant in the first-column estimation of table 3.3 (which is our preferred estimation).

21. The estimations refer to ordinary-least-squares first-differences regressions, in which the standard errors are robust and they are corrected to eliminate biases introduced by correlation between observations of the dependent variable. The technique used is the Huber correction. The reform variables are lagged 4 years to take into account that the reforms have a lagged effect on income distribution. This lag structure is tested, explored, and justified in Behrman, Birdsall, and Székely (2001a) for wage differentials. Lagging the reform variables increases the number of observations in the regression and allows for the incorporation of changes in poverty and inequality until 1999. The lag increases observations because the reform variables are available until 1995 and the household data analyzed for the dependent variables cover the period up until 2000.

22. This result is consistent with that of other studies, in particular, Behrman, Birdsall, and Székely (2001a) and Spilimbergo, Londoño, and Székely (1999), who obtain a similar result using panel data for countries from various regions of the world.

23. The "other reform" variable here refers to an index (the simple average) of privatization, the external capital account, and tax reform. Labor-market reform is not used here; it had not changed much in any country in the period covered.

Table 3.3 Effects of reforms and macroeconomic changes on wage inequality

	Variable		
	Preferred estimation	Other estimations	
Independent variable	Log *R* – log *P* (*P* = poorest 30 percent)	Log *R* – log *P* (*P* = poorest 10 percent)	Gini index
Trade liberalization	–0.39	–0.60	–0.43
	–1.32	*–0.91*	*–2.40*
Financial liberalization	0.16	0.18	0.06
	2.33	*1.60*	*2.91*
Other reforms	–0.09	–0.12	0.40
	–0.41	*–0.41*	*2.06*
Macroeconomic volatility	0.13	0.14	0.04
	2.65	*1.66*	*3.47*
Inflation	0.09	0.12	0.02
	2.43	*1.52*	*3.24*
Terms of trade	–0.35	–0.31	–0.14
	–1.47	*–0.86*	*–2.38*
Real exchange rate	–0.30	–0.40	–0.10
(local currency to dollar)	–6.17	–4.27	–7.58
Constant	2.16	2.57	1.34
	6.95	*4.25*	*15.01*
Number of observations	75	75	75
$F(7,46)$	15.22	8.53	20.31
Probability > F	0.000	0.000	0.000
R^2	0.297	0.141	0.485

Note: *t* statistics are in italics.

Source: Behrman, Birdsall, and Székely (2001b).

The last two columns of table 3.3 show results using the Gini coefficient as the dependent variable, and using solely the bottom decile for *P* (instead of the bottom three deciles). Using the Gini does not allow us to control the many missing variables at the country level that are controlled for in the first column. In this estimation, trade openness actually has a significant negative effect, reducing inequality, and financial liberalization and the other reforms have a significant positive effect. However, we cannot be sure if these results are genuine or simply represent problems of omitted variables.

Table 3.4 presents the results for the relationship between liberalizing reforms and our proxy for poverty, the income of absolutely poor people relative to others. Again, the results indicate that trade openness has no effect on poverty. (The coefficient is negative but insignificant.) Financial liberalization, conversely, has a significant positive effect on our measure of poverty. Again, not surprisingly, inflation and volatility in per capita GDP have significant positive effects on poverty. Poor people have less capability to weather shocks. The terms of trade do not have any effect on poverty, and appreciation in the real exchange rate appears to reduce poverty.

Table 3.4 Liberalization, macroeconomic context, and poverty

Independent variable	Dependent variable: Preferred estimation: Log M – log P (P = \$2 a day)	Other estimations: Log R – log P (P = \$2 a day)	Poor people ratio	Poverty gap[a]	Poverty density[a]
Trade liberalization	–0.03	–0.12	–0.38	–0.43	–0.60
	–1.21	*–1.68*	*–1.18*	*–1.53*	*–1.66*
Financial liberalization	0.27	0.21	0.26	0.26	0.34
	2.54	*2.02*	*1.25*	*1.70*	*1.75*
Other reforms	–0.03	–0.04	0.46	0.33	0.38
	–1.64	*–0.73*	*1.21*	*1.03*	*0.92*
Macroeconomic volatility	0.18	0.23	0.26	0.42	0.51
	2.10	*1.79*	*3.62*	*5.42*	*4.83*
Inflation	0.21	1.16	0.05	0.08	0.09
	2.99	*3.88*	*0.91*	*1.83*	*1.71*
Terms of trade	–0.22	–0.38	–0.60	–0.83	–1.05
	–0.10	*–0.19*	*–1.98*	*–2.22*	*–2.32*
Real exchange rate	–0.37	–0.35	–0.20	–0.25	–0.32
(local currency to dollar)	*–2.23*	*–4.38*	*–2.13*	*–3.53*	*–3.57*
Constant	1.09	1.25	1.39	1.83	2.17
	29.90	*12.77*	*3.06*	*3.45*	*3.30*
Number of observations	75	75	75	75	75
$F(7,46)$	4.82	7.65	10.51	13.01	11.49
Probability > F	0.000	0.000	0.000	0.000	0.000
R^2	0.321	0.395	0.363	0.459	0.437

a. On these alternative measures of poverty, see Foster, Greer, and Thorbecke (1984).

Note: *t* statistics are in italics.

Source: Behrman, Birdsall, and Székely (2001b).

As in table 3.3, we present in table 3.4 the results for other dependent variables. But because these three regressions suffer from omitted variable biases, we do not use them in our conclusions.[24]

In summary, our preferred estimates (the first columns of tables 3.3 and 3.4) suggest that except for financial-sector reform, the economic reforms of the past two decades have not contributed to increased poverty and inequality. On the other hand, it is also the case that the reforms have not contributed to *reducing* poverty and inequality. It should not be particularly surprising that increasing reliance on market mechanisms has not in itself created income opportunities for poor people. The constraint may be poor people's limited assets, including human capital, a constraint that market reforms alone cannot change. Financial-sector liberalization in particular appears to have made poor people worse off, at least relative to the rich and the middle groups. This is also not surprising; without collateral,

24. There are three differences with the first regression in the table. First, the effect of financial liberalization with regard to these three variables is not significant from a statistical standpoint. Second, inflation seems to increase poverty, but it is also insignificant. Third, improved terms of trade do seem to significantly reduce poverty.

poor people are less able to exploit liberalized financial markets. (Indeed, the end of repressed interest rates alone may make credit more costly in the short run. In addition, new higher-yield financial instruments will mostly help those with special and diverse investment needs.[25])

That market reforms in themselves do not help poor people is consistent with our observation that assets matter. Without assets, the poor are not in a position to exploit the potential benefits of less distorted markets. The economic reforms apparently failed to address the underlying structural problems that continue to inhibit growth in the productivity and incomes of poor people.

Poverty and the Evolution of Social Policy in Latin America

Social policy in the region today is a healthy combination of reasonable spending on basic investments in health and education; an emphasis on reaching poor people, which though far from perfectly implemented is a substantial improvement over earlier periods; and an impressive array of administrative reforms, including decentralization to more accountable local governments and such institutional innovations as cash subsidies to poor households that keep their children in school.[26]

Today's social policy evolved over what might be considered four phases or periods. The first covers the period between World War II and the late 1970s, the "golden years" of Latin America in terms of economic growth. The industrial sector in most countries was growing vigorously, fueled by the import-substitution development strategy that prevailed in those decades. The urban middle-income group also was expanding.[27]

During this period, social policy was seen as a fundamental part of the overall development strategy. Social policy consisted mainly of the widespread provision of subsidies for goods and services, from which the expanding urban middle-income groups benefited most. Some of the subsidies—such as those to fuel consumption—were justified as supporting higher real industrial-sector wages. Rural areas played the role of providing primary goods and natural resources for industrial production at low prices, as well as low-cost goods for urban consumers. This implied in many cases subsidizing rural production—and in a few cases, land redistribution—to minimize idle resources and the underutilization of land.

25. Székely (1998) analyzes the effect of financial liberalization in increasing inequality in Mexico in the early 1990s. He shows that owners of physical capital were better able to exploit the availability of new higher-yield financial instruments that could be adapted to specific investment needs.

26. This section is based largely on Székely (2001a).

27. See, e.g., Székely (1998) for a description of the case of Mexico.

For the most part, however, the needs of structurally poor people were neglected, though of course many households that began the period as poor benefited from the overall growth in incomes. Indeed, there were healthy declines in poverty and inequality during the period.[28] But the industrial growth strategy and the subsidies relied heavily on public borrowing and were ultimately unsustainable. They ended in the early 1980s with the debt crisis.[29]

In the second period, under the new macroeconomic constraints of the early 1980s, social policy in effect went underground. With escalating inflation rates, devaluation, and GDP declines, the policy priority was to stabilize the economy at all costs. Widespread subsidies and social transfers were seen as an obstacle to growth, rather than a powerful engine of development as in the past. Fiscal pressures and the burden of debt combined with low growth to severely restrict new investments in health and education. Spending did not decline much as a proportion of the budget in most countries, because the political pressure to sustain civil service jobs and limit wage declines, which take up the bulk of social spending, was considerable. However, spending on new investments collapsed, and annual spending in absolute terms per child and per health client declined because overall government spending was declining.

Moreover, uncertainties and the lack of any new investment contributed to overall deterioration in the institutions—health and school systems—as teachers and health workers coped with limited access to complementary inputs—books, medicines, and so on; and as the systems no doubt lost some of their better personnel and suffered from constantly changing leadership. The remnants of the old policy provided limited but insecure job guarantees for that portion of the middle-income group that was lucky enough to hold a civil service or state enterprise job, and few if any services to rural and urban poor people. By the end of the 1980s, there was increasing evidence of growing inequality and, most worrying, of substantial increases in poverty.[30]

The third period began in the middle to late 1980s with the acknowledgment that structural adjustment programs and economic reform were not addressing the needs of the large number of poor people—about 40 percent of the region's population. Social policy became focused on protecting poor people in the unfavorable macroeconomic environment, and in the face of increasingly global competition. It was recognized that the

28. See Londoño and Székely (2000) for evidence on poverty and inequality trends for Latin America during the 1970s.

29. The public subsidies, including to industry through import protection, relied heavily on foreign and domestic public borrowing, not domestic public savings, and could not be sustained once access to borrowing and the cost of borrowing rose.

30. See Morley (1995) and, for the effect of adjustment programs on social problems, see Cornia, Jolly, and Stewart (1987).

poor generally have fewer means of protecting their incomes from unexpected shocks and from the erosion of liquid assets that high inflation brings. They were also seen as the most disadvantaged in their chances of engaging in high-productivity sectors with the best chances of surviving external competition.

The policy solution was the introduction of compensatory policies through the implementation of safety net programs, including social emergency and social investment funds (which became favored programs for support by the multilateral development banks). In the face of continuing fiscal pressures, the approach became one of targeting resources to poor people, that is, allocating limited budget resources to obtain the most poverty reduction possible per peso spent. Poverty maps and poverty profiles were developed to identify the population with the highest poverty rates. Resulting programs were designed as small, specific, and tightly focused.[31] Social policy and overall development and growth strategies of countries became totally disconnected. As in the second period, emphasis remained on the fiscal trade-off between macroeconomic policies and social programs, with social programs seen as a potential threat to public deficits and to macroeconomic stability.

By the mid-1990s, with the recovery of positive economic growth in most countries of the region, a fourth phase of social policy had emerged. Though growth in the region was still modest, with the exception of Chile, it was sufficient to encourage governments and the policy community to implement real increases in public spending on broad social programs—in a manner seen as fiscally responsible. Public spending on education and health increased in most countries of the region by at least 20 percent between 1990 and 1996 (Birdsall and Londoño 1997).

The opening of Latin America's economies to world markets, which had begun in the mid-1980s in most countries, created more interest in ensuring that economies could compete effectively in the global economy, and thus in ensuring that a larger proportion of the workforce could be more productive. Having an army of unskilled workers with low wages was no longer seen as a basis for global competitiveness. Emphasis on meeting the needs of poor people continued, but with much more attention to increasing their productive capacity, consistent with the view that competitiveness in open economies required much greater investment in human capital.

In many countries, the increases in spending on health and education favored primary and secondary education relative to university spending (e.g., in Brazil and Mexico; this change and other reforms began in the

31. The actual performance of the social funds in reaching the poor was not always good (Lustig 2000b). Poor performance reflected the political difficulty of avoiding use of new funds for patronage, and the technical difficulty of balancing between, on the one hand, the administrative (and political) costs of finding poor people and avoiding leakage of benefits to nonpoor people and, on the other hand, undercoverage of poor people.

1980s in Chile and was reinforced in the 1990s).[32] New programs such as Progresa (recently renamed Oportunidad) in Mexico, Bolsa Escola in Brasília, and Chile Joven in Chile,[33] though targeted to poor households, were designed not only as safety nets protecting consumption capacity but also as investments in the human capital of the poor. Increases in social spending were accompanied in some countries by major new efforts to deal with reforms of the structure of health and education systems, particularly through an emphasis on decentralization and on greater parent and community control of schools (e.g., in Bolivia, in El Salvador, and in Minas Gerais, Brazil).

This fourth (and for all practical purposes still current) generation of social policy is thus essentially focused on programs to address the needs and increase the human capital of people who are currently poor. That makes good sense in a region where at least 30 percent of the population is poor, and where reducing poverty and encouraging future growth rely heavily on harnessing the potential for increasing poor people's productive engagement in the economy. Moreover, with its emphasis on building the human capital of the poor, this approach to social policy is more visibly a part of an overall development strategy.

But there are drawbacks to this approach. First, it is highly vulnerable politically; social programs must compete fiercely for public resources and so far have not been institutionalized in any country. Social programs are seen primarily as long-term investments in uncertain future growth, given the demands of the global market. But as growth falters and the sense of unreasonable vulnerability to external markets increases, this approach to social policy, sound as it is, is at risk of unwinding—threatened

32. These efforts probably led to reduced gaps in the 1990s between schooling of children from rich vs. poor households, based on a lower gap in most countries for 15-year-olds than for 21-year-olds—though the evidence is not yet clear or convincing, because there is a natural tendency for the gaps to increase with age (data from Filmer and Pritchett 1999). But the gaps in many countries remained dramatically high—consistent with other evidence that for the most part, differences in education of parents by income group in Latin America are replicated in differences in the education of children in the next generation (Behrman, Birdsall, and Székely 2000b; Birdsall 1999).

33. Progresa is the Spanish acronym for the Programa de Educación, Salud y Alimentación (Education, Health and Nutrition Program). The program provides cash transfers and a nutritional supplement to families in extreme poverty in rural areas. Cash transfers are conditioned on children's school attendance rates of at least 85 percent, and regular attendance to health clinics for checkups and follow-ups. The cash transfer is given to the mother, who also has to attend a series of talks and courses on health practices. Bolsa Escola is a similar program that provides scholarships for disadvantaged children. Part of the cash transfer is held in a special account, which the beneficiary can access after completing a schooling cycle. Chile Joven is also a program of cash transfers, but in this case they are provided to young adults for incentive training. A detailed description and evaluation of Progresa can be found at www.ifpri.org/country/mexico.htm. A description of Bolsa Escola can be found at www.mec.gov.br/home/bolsaesc/default.shtm. See De Janvry and Sadoulet (2000) for a discussion of Progresa's targeting.

by another necessary round of fiscal austerity, or by a return to populist-style broad and fiscally irresponsible programs and subsidies.

Fundamentally, this approach to social policy does not effectively address the underlying causes of continued high levels of poverty and stubborn inequality. For instance, increased spending on education has raised schooling levels among poor children, but (as we will refer to below) has not appreciably raised their expected future income, because low growth and high real interest rates continue to limit job creation; because the average return from primary and secondary education has remained low; and because in some countries continuing ethnic, racial, and gender discrimination and its historical effects have kept wage returns low for many unskilled poor households. Nor will social investments raise incomes if poor people cannot accumulate physical and financial capital, or if recurrent economic downturns force periodic "de-cumulating" of their limited assets. Social policy alone, as currently conceived, cannot change the economic environment or the underlying elements in the structure of the economy that are contributing to poverty and slowing overall growth.

Social and Development Policy: One and the Same

Latin America's high inequality of assets poses a deep structural barrier to raising the productivity and incomes of poor people. In the discussion above, we emphasized both the failure of the economywide, efficiency-enhancing economic reforms to reduce poverty and the still-limited extent to which social policy affects the larger economic environment in which the poor work, save, and invest. In this section, we conclude by outlining briefly the key ingredients of a social policy that would address explicitly the need to ensure that poor people acquire the assets and have real access to the economic opportunities that would allow them to raise their *own* productivity and pull themselves up by their own bootstraps.

This approach implies policies that support the poor in a way that enables them to contribute to growth and to be themselves engines of growth and development. This can only be done if social policy is at the heart of the development strategy of a country, rather than an opponent constantly competing for public resources that may undermine macroeconomic stability. The solution is not compensatory or Band-Aid measures, but policies that promote efficiency in the economic system and that improve the productivity of poor people.[34]

We see this approach as consisting of three parts: mainstreaming of the equity objective into traditional macroeconomic and economywide poli-

34. Birdsall (2002) proposes an open-economy social contract for Latin America that would emphasize fiscal soundness and labor market reform as the foundation for a social contract.

cies so as to protect poor people's assets; policies and programs to increase their assets; and policies to increase the return on their assets. We outline these only briefly here, referring the reader to other studies for detail.

Mainstreaming Poverty Reduction into Economywide Policy

The cost of economic instability has been high for poor people in Latin America (IDB 1997 and Lustig 2000a)—largely because the busts that follow booms reduce returns on their principal asset, labor, and often force them to withdraw children from school and sell land or small businesses. A central objective of fiscal and monetary policy should be to reduce instability (recall the effects of volatility on poverty shown in table 3.4)—including via lower inflation and, to protect exchange rates and minimize capital flight, through fiscal discipline rather than recourse to high interest rates.

As outlined in Birdsall and de la Torre (2001), and in chapter 4 of this volume, this approach implies both fiscal regimes that are more rules-based and also more emphasis in monetary policy on tough, prudential norms for the banking system. It also implies fiscal policies that are disciplined enough in good times to finance countercyclical social insurance—including unemployment insurance and public works employment programs—in bad times.

Changing the Distribution of Assets

Social policy is already well understood to include strengthening the ability of poor people to acquire human capital by increasing public spending on health and education programs. We have already referred to the importance of programs, such as Progresa in Mexico, that enhance household demand for schooling through cash transfers to mothers (in this case) tied to children's school attendance.[35] But social policy should also embrace more explicit efforts to ensure poor people's access to land and financial markets. Market-friendly land reform programs in Brazil and Colombia provide models for what can be done, but they remain small and underfunded. In other countries, even less is being done. As was

35. For an analysis of this and other cash-for-education programs, see Morley and Coady (2003). A new proposal in Mexico would build on Progresa's (now named Oportunidad) emphasis on using cash transfers to help poor people accumulate an asset (human capital). It would make deposits to individual accounts of students from qualified households who stay in secondary and higher education, which could be accessed in the future. They could have earlier access to the funds under certain schemes that ensure that the funds are used to scale up their own assets or acquire new ones. This is based on information from the Secretaría de Desarrollo Social (Sedesol), Government of Mexico.

noted above, the liberalization of the financial sector has not helped poor people; those with other assets, including information, education, and land or physical capital to provide collateral, have been much better able to exploit the liberalized financial markets.

To increase access to credit for poor people requires a long list of arcane, technical fixes in the system. It does not require subsidized loans by state-owned banks. In the past, that approach has mostly generated perverse incentives for rent seeking, waste, and at times, corruption. Promoting institutions that make microloans is one step—but to date these institutions account for not even 1 percent of the credits provided by commercial banks. Legal changes that make movable assets collateralizable and that allow leasing and factoring, the creation of credit bureaus, fiscal incentives that encourage group lending, and more timely bankruptcy procedures all would contribute to increasing the supply of conventional bank credits for poor people. Emphasis on competition in the banking sector and, as noted above, on macroeconomic policy to minimize recourse to high real interest rates should also be seen as fundamental to sensible social policy.

Raising the Return on Poor People's Assets

Poor people's principal asset is their own labor. A striking difference between poor and rich households in Latin America is the lower labor force participation (in the wage sector) of the former, less educated group. One reason for this outcome is that traditional mechanisms for protecting labor in Latin America were designed by males, for males. The objective was to generate formal employment with benefits, and with guarantees for stable jobs. But the resulting rules end up discouraging the hiring of females, on the one hand by imposing higher costs for them on employers (due to maternity leave and allowances) and on the other by restricting their employment to full time and limiting flexibility in hours. These efforts at protection result in much lower labor participation rates for poor, uneducated females.

Again, many incremental (and fiscally cheap) policy changes would help: subsidized child care services (through public subsidies or tax incentives provided to employers); socializing of maternity benefits; labor legislation that allows more flexibility in contracting conditions; and a labor framework that encourages collective bargaining while enforcing the accountability of labor union leaders to their members and reduces the politicization of unions.

But apart from the differences in labor force participation between rich and poor individuals, poor people also face the strong disadvantage of receiving lower remuneration to the precarious human capital that they own. Part of the reason may be ethnic and racial discrimination, which

Figure 3.3 Change in the marginal return to education in Latin America in the 1990s (average and by education level)

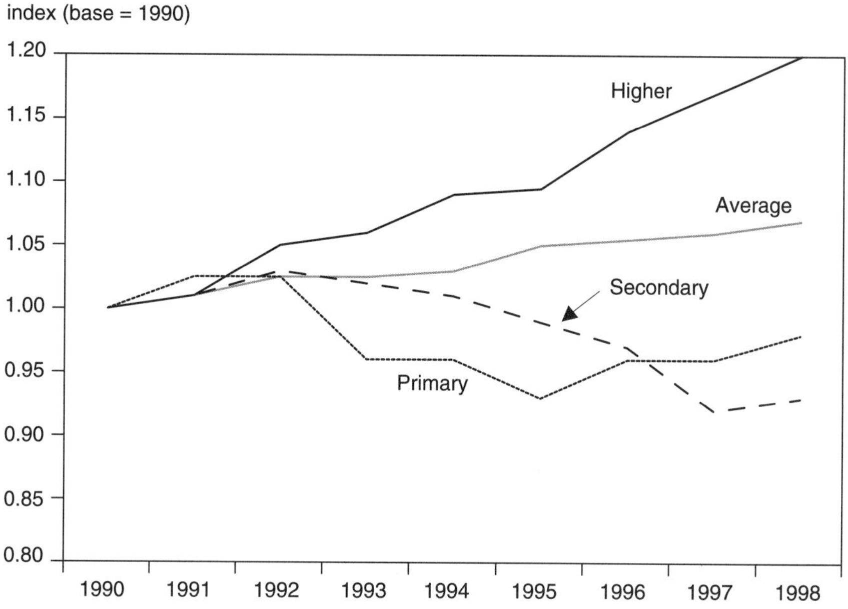

Source: Behrman, Birdsall, and Székely (2001a).

translates into lower wages for nonwhites with the same skills and experience as whites.[36] Part of the reason is that the economic benefits of less than university education stagnated in the 1990s. In Latin America, the wage returns on higher education have been high and rising compared with returns on primary and secondary schooling (figure 3.3); the result has been a notable increase in the wages of those with any postsecondary education compared with those with primary and secondary education at most (figure 3.4).

In an era of globalization, it is difficult to think of policies that promote higher wages and employment for poor people without referring to trade policy. Our analysis above showed that trade liberalization has not hurt the poor and may have helped them. More steps could be taken. According to the Inter-American Development Bank (IDB 1999), what would make sense are flat and moderate tariff structures that protect all sectors alike and do not privilege imports of capital-intensive activities that normally complement skilled labor. Tariff structures that favor intermediate inputs or factors of production that complement relatively unskilled labor

36. Birdsall and de la Torre (2001) discuss the problems of gender and racial discrimination. For evidence of wage differences associated with differences in skin color, see Saavedra (2003).

Figure 3.4 Differential returns to education in Latin America during the 1990s

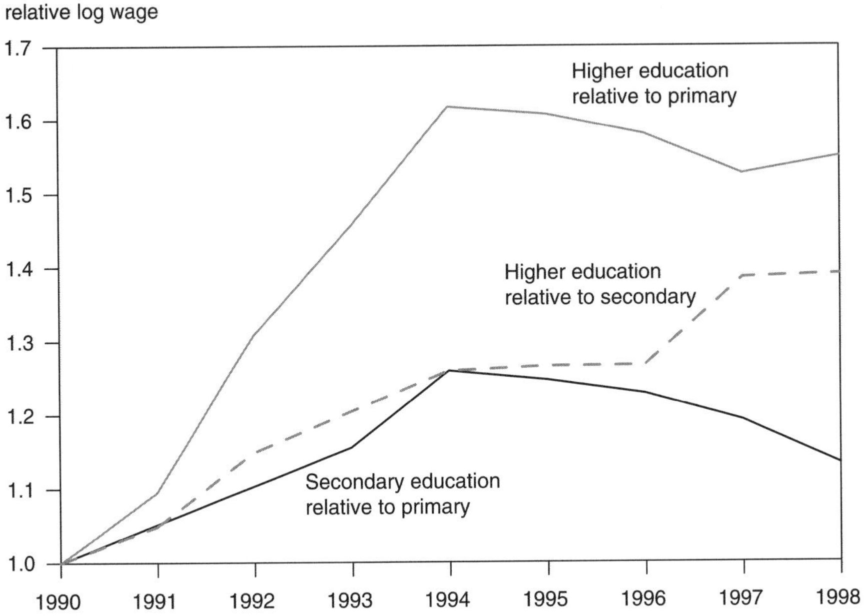

Source: Behrman, Birdsall, and Székely (2001a).

(by Latin America standards) would increase the demand for poor people's labor.

A Final Comment

Our review of the outlines of a broader approach to social policy illustrates a simple point: When we focus on assets and opportunities for poor people, we end up talking about the economic system as a whole. Much of what we propose is rarely conceived of as part of social policy. But in Latin America, and in many other parts of the developing world, it is becoming more and more obvious that social policy needs to be thought of and implemented in a new way. A singular focus on achieving growth via market reforms has not hurt poor people, but neither has it helped them. At the same time, a focus solely on the traditional "Band-Aids" of narrowly defined social programs is not the answer either. It will increase welfare levels temporarily but will not bring the sustained increases in poor people's productivity that would raise their incomes and make them an engine of overall growth.

What is needed is what might be called a bootstraps approach, one that focuses on increasing poor people's assets and their opportunities for high returns on those assets, putting their economic future into their own hands.

Appendix 3.1
Assessing the Effects of Reform on Poverty and Inequality

To assess the effects of reform on poverty and inequality, the most rigorous way to proceed would be to use a complete model of the determinants of poverty and inequality, from which the econometric equation for estimation could be identified. But it is, of course, impossible to include all variables that affect poverty and inequality, so we instead use a specification that minimizes the effects of omitted variables.[37] We use a specification similar to that in Behrman, Birdsall, and Székely (2001a), in which we extend the traditional Mincer-type semi-log wage regression to include the differential effects of liberalization and other macroeconomic variables, depending on an individual's position in the distribution of income:[38]

$$\ln y = (\alpha_p + \beta_p L + \gamma_p E)P + (\alpha_m + \beta_m L + \gamma_m E)M + (\alpha_r + \beta_r L + \gamma_r E)R + (\alpha_T + \beta_T L + \gamma_T E) + \delta I + \gamma C + \epsilon \qquad (1)$$

where P, M, and R are dichotomous variables that indicate if an individual is poor (P) (bottom of the income distribution), in the middle of the distribution (M), or can be classified as rich (R) (top of the distribution). Our empirical definition of the groups P, M, and R is based on income (see below). Because income is a reflection of the assets that generate income, their rate of utilization and the price paid for them, membership in these three groups can be thought of as a function of assets. For example, belonging to group P indicates low levels of human and physical capital and/or that the price assigned in the market to these assets is relatively low.

The variable y represents an individual's income. The vector L is a combination of variables that represent the policies of economic liberalization

37. The work of Li, Squire, and Zhu (1998) is one of the recent attempts to design a model to guide empirical analyses, but even this type of work suffers from not being able to put forward a complete model of income distribution.

38. This equation is not exactly the same as that in Behrman, Birdsall, and Székely (2001a). The difference is that Behrman et al. concentrate on differences among groups based on their level of schooling, whereas here the focus is on detecting differences having to do with distribution of income. Also, for Behrman et al., the critical variables were only L and y, not E.

(the reform indices), whereas E represents a group of macroeconomic variables that affect each income group differently. I is the vector of individual characteristics (e.g., age, sex); C is a vector of variables that change over time in each country (e.g., capital per worker or technology), and ϵ is stochastic shock. All of these variables could have subscripts for time and country, and the individual variables could also have subscripts for individuals, but these are suppressed to lessen clutter.

In relation (1), the effect of liberalization policies and of macroeconomic variables for individuals below the poverty line is $(\alpha_p + \beta_p L + \gamma_p E)$. The impact for the middle class is $(\alpha_m + \beta_m L + \gamma_m E)$, whereas for rich people it is $(\alpha_r + \beta_r L + \gamma_r E)$. Therefore, as well as taking into account the effect on the entire population $(\alpha_T + \beta_T L + \gamma_T E)$, the specification identifies the differential effect of liberalization and macroeconomic variables on individuals depending on their position in the distribution of income and also controlling for personal and country-specific characteristics. The idea is to obtain estimates for the coefficients β_p, β_m, and β_r, and for γ_p, γ_m, and γ_r.[39]

As explained in Behrman, Birdsall, and Székely (2001a), there are a number of problems in obtaining good estimates of the coefficient vectors of interest—β_p, β_m, β_r, γ_p, γ_m, and γ_r—from direct estimates of relation (1). The first is the number of parameters. The second is that the (possibly large number of) economywide variables is likely to be fairly highly correlated, leading to further imprecision and possible problems in sorting out the effects of particular variables. The third is omitted-variable bias. If the unobserved variables are correlated with the interaction between the reform indices and income, the result is unobserved variable bias.

The solution proposed in Behrman, Birdsall, and Székely (2001a) is an estimation strategy that consists of obtaining estimates of the relative impact of the economic reform variables on gains or losses in income. To accomplish this, the information in relation (1) is aggregated by groups, and the difference between groups is estimated in the following manner:

$$\ln y_M - \ln y_P = (\alpha_m - \alpha_p) + (\beta_m - \beta_p)L + (\gamma_m - \gamma_p)E + (\epsilon_m - \epsilon_p) \qquad (2a)$$

$$\ln y_R - \ln y_M = (\alpha_r - \alpha_m) + (\beta_r - \beta_m)L + (\gamma_r - \gamma_m)E + (\epsilon_r - \epsilon_m) \qquad (2b)$$

$$\ln y_R - \ln y_P = (\alpha_r - \alpha_p) + (\beta_r - \beta_p)L + (\gamma_r - \gamma_p)E + (\epsilon_r - \epsilon_p) \qquad (2c)$$

where $\ln y_I$ (for $I = P, M, R$) is the average for each of the three groups. Only two of these relations are independent, as can be seen by subtracting (2b) from (2c) to obtain (2a).

Estimation of relations (2a), (2b), and (2c) yields both direct estimates of the parameters of principal interest and direct statistical tests of the sta-

39. Estimates of the impact of personal characteristics and of fixed country-specific variables are of less interest to this investigation.

tistical significance of these differences. These estimates have a number of advantages over efforts to estimate relation (1). First, the number of the parameters is much lower, and there are no restrictions on the degrees of freedom of the coefficients. Second, there are many fewer variables for estimating relations (2a), (2b), and (2c) than relation (1), so the problems of colinearity are reduced. Third, this specification controls for all unobserved country characteristics whether fixed over time or time varying, so there are no problems with omitted variable bias.[40]

40. Furthermore, whether relation (2) is estimated in first-differential or fixed effects, it resolves another problem that has not yet been mentioned. If one of the motives for a country to initiate or intensify structural reforms is precisely the level of inequality or poverty that exists at time 0, then there will be a problem of endogeneity. Nonetheless, as is shown in table 3.1, income inequality did not change dramatically from one year to the next in any country. One could argue that the elevated level of inequality in Latin America is a phenomenon that has characterized the region for many years, and that it could be seen as a historical characteristic of these countries. If high inequality is in some sense a characteristic fixed across time, the first-differential estimation of the relation eliminates the problem.

4

A Fiscal Policy Agenda

DANIEL ARTANA, RICARDO LÓPEZ MURPHY,
AND FERNANDO NAVAJAS

Almost everywhere in Latin America, fiscal deficits were one of the critical problems that led to the debt crisis and rapid inflation during the 1980s. As table 4.1 shows, the situation improved very significantly during the 1990s, although there has again been a marked deterioration in recent years, presumably at least partly because of recession. In itself, fiscal deterioration during a recession should not be considered undesirable, for it is exactly what should happen if countries have good automatic stabilizers. But the size of recent deficits does raise the issue of whether countries have yet strengthened their underlying positions enough to be able to afford an anticyclical policy.

Making fiscal policy anticyclical is one of the critical dimensions of the design of fiscal policy and fiscal institutions in Latin America that we take up in this chapter. The policy objectives are to improve macroeconomic stability, allocative efficiency, and income distribution, and to

Daniel Artana is a chief economist at Fundación de Investigaciones Económicas Latinoamericanas (FIEL) in Buenos Aires and professor of economics at the National University of La Plata and the Universities of San Andrés and Torcuata di Tella. He was formerly secretary of the Argentine Treasury. Ricardo López Murphy is currently a candidate for president of the Argentine Republic. He has formerly been a minister of economy and minister of defense of Argentina, and also a chief economist at FIEL. Fernando Navajas is a chief economist at FIEL and professor of economics at the National University of La Plata and the University of San Andrés. He was formerly chief of the Cabinet of Advisers to the Ministry of Economy in Argentina.

Table 4.1 Central government balances in selected Latin American countries, 1980s-2001 (percent of GDP)

Country	1980s	1990s	1991-94	1994-98	1999	2000	2001
Argentina	–3.7	–1.1	–0.5	–1.2	–2.9	–2.4	–3.2
Brazil	–8.7	–5.8	–4.9	–7.1	–5.8	–3.3	–3.5
Chile	0.3	1.4	1.9	1.7	–1.4	0.1	–0.3
Colombia	–1.7	–2.7	–1.4	–3.2	–5.9	–6.9	–5.9
Ecuador	–1.5	0.5	1.6	– 0.4	–0.7	0.7	0.1
Mexico	–8.5	0.0	1.9	–0.7	–1.6	–1.3	–0.7
Peru	–4.3	–1.5	–1.7	0.9	–2.2	–2.0	–2.3
Venezuela	–1.0	–1.5	–2.3	–1.8	–2.4	–2.1	–2.6

Note: This table shows data only for central governments. A better estimate of the underlying public-sector deficit would take into account the deficit of all public agencies (including the central bank) and subnational governments. It is not possible to obtain a long series for all the countries included in the table. But there are figures available for the 1990s that show that when all public agencies are included, the 1990s deficit doubles in the case of Argentina (mostly because of the deficit of the provincial governments); it increases by about 1 percent of GDP in Peru and Venezuela; and it is reduced to 1.6 percent of GDP in Colombia because subnational governments and the pension system run surpluses.

Source: IMF data.

reduce poverty. The topics discussed here are restricted to those we have studied during the past decade, both in academic discussions and policy involvement.

These themes are particularly relevant to Latin American countries, given the interaction between their fragile economic and financial institutions and the macroeconomic shocks they faced during the 1990s, which hit while they were undergoing structural reforms to lower inflation, free trade, and broaden the use of market mechanisms. We hope it is clear from the analysis that our recommendations seek to avoid getting countries into a situation like the one Argentina suffered in 2001-02. The idea is to prevent a debt crisis through prudent fiscal policies before it becomes too late and countries must then deal with the severe policy dilemma of not having access to financing in voluntary credit markets while being forced to reduce their fiscal deficit in the midst of a recession.

Although good fiscal policy and national fiscal institutions cannot substitute for an adequate global financial architecture, they still are much needed—whether they strategically complement global reform or serve to make the best of a difficult situation in the absence of reform. Our agenda emphasizes rules that favor growth by taking advantage of opportunities in a competitive world, which is the key starting point for improving welfare. This emphasis leads to reforms that avoid both an inefficient use of productive resources and also an increase in the cost of capital stemming from lax fiscal rules and deteriorating fiscal savings. This last aspect is fundamental, because much of Latin America's macroeconomic vulnerability has been caused by an excessive use of foreign savings, resulting in part from lax fiscal institutions.[1]

One theme we will stress again and again is how the proposed agenda complements other macroeconomic policies. For example, a hard monetary regime can coexist successfully with neither an inconsistent fiscal policy nor public behavior that involves high risks resulting from non-transparent or unstable rules of the game. Even if a superficial reading of indicators does not reveal an imminent crisis, the constant danger is that the system will unravel, as indeed happened in Argentina with such tragic consequences for growth and social cohesion in 2001.

This chapter covers seven topics.

- The well-known problem of procyclical fiscal policy in emerging-market economies.
- The problem of hidden liabilities in the form of implicit or unregistered debts.
- The issue of tax expenditures (i.e., tax exemptions or differential tax rates designed to aid particular sectors), which aggravate intertemporal fiscal balance and distort resource allocation.
- Fiscal decentralization, taking into account both microeconomic incentives and macroeconomic coordination.
- The issue of designing, reforming, and administering a tax system.
- Budget mechanisms and the system of incentives and monitoring of public spending in such critical areas as social policy.
- Proposals for explicit institutional rules, such as laws enforcing fiscal responsibility and international agreements, to strengthen the effectiveness and credibility of public policies.

---

1. E.g., Dayal-Gulati and Thimann (1997) compared savings behavior in Southeast Asia and Latin America for the period 1975-95. They found that the mean of national savings to GDP was 28 percent in Southeast Asia and only 19.5 percent in Latin America, and the mean of the central government balance was virtually zero in Southeast Asia compared with a deficit of 2.4 percent of GDP for Latin America. Moreover, while in Southeast Asia fiscal deficits turned into surpluses after 1987, they never were eliminated in Latin America. In their empirical results, these researchers found that the higher national savings rate observed in Southeast Asia can be attributed to higher public savings rates over the period of the study. (In this study, Southeast Asia comprised Indonesia, Malaysia, Philippines, Singapore, and Thailand, while Latin American data were for Argentina, Brazil, Chile, Colombia, Mexico, Paraguay, Peru, Uruguay, and Venezuela.)

Reversing Procyclical Fiscal Policy

In Latin American countries, an expansion of economic activity and the resulting increase in fiscal revenues is typically not accompanied—as in industrial countries—by a significant reduction in fiscal deficits.[2] This is true despite the fact that in developing countries the aggregate tax base fluctuates more than output, which rises and falls as the economy is exposed to shocks. In Latin America, the standard deviation of GDP from its trend is more than twice that of industrial countries, and the relative figure is even wider for private consumption. The problem is that there is a strong positive correlation between government expenditure and GDP, as strong as that between tax revenues and GDP. Talvi and Vegh (2000) find these correlations to be similar, about 0.53 for developing economies in the past 25 years or so, while the equivalent numbers are much smaller (0.17 and 0.38, respectively) for industrial countries, and even lower—in fact, close to zero in the case of public expenditures—for Group of Seven economies. Among developing economies, including those of Latin America, the differences are minor and not significant.

Some observers have tried to make the case that this behavior is caused by developing economies' vulnerability to capital flows. However, the fact that there have been several episodes of deficits during booms, and even when there are very favorable and clearly unsustainable terms of trade, unambiguously indicates that the problem lies primarily with fiscal institutions. Of course, capital flow reversals and terms of trade shocks can have an acute impact on public finances that cannot be neutralized overnight. However, this calls for developing hard rules of conduct to protect national economies as well as possible, and not for resorting to a "market failure" excuse that neglects domestic institutional buildup and tries to shift responsibility abroad.[3]

2. See, e.g., López Murphy (1988, 1994) for Argentina and Gavin et al. (1996) for Latin America. With a broader sample, Talvi and Vegh (2000) find evidence that procyclical fiscal policy (understood as expenditures (taxes) rising (decreasing) in booms and the opposite in recessions) is a pervasive fact in developing economies and to some extent in industrial countries other than the Group of Seven.

3. What we are going to suggest is the creation of sound fiscal institutions that will mitigate "market failure." Other alternatives appear to be less efficient. E.g., restrictions on short-term capital inflows cannot solve the problem of abnormally high dollar receipts caused by transitory improvements in the terms of trade, even if such restrictions could not be circumvented by the private sector. The experience of Argentina and Chile during the 1990s is interesting. Both countries had some regulations on capital inflows (although Argentina opted for imposing regulations that increased the liquidity of the banking sector to very high levels and allowed the banks to invest these requirements abroad), but fiscal behavior was completely different. Although Chile ran surpluses during many years of that decade, Argentina could not eliminate the fiscal deficit even in periods of relatively high real growth.

The absence of fiscal equilibrium during booms and even when terms of trade are favorable can in part be attributed to the fact that public spending is normally repressed by a financial constraint that, once relaxed, generates an expansion in outlays similar to the increase in revenues. This behavior partly is the result of financial programs making the fiscal deficit a key target in the framework of macroeconomic consistency when in reality the deficit is an endogenous variable. Instead, macroeconomic programs should be based on such exogenous variables as the level of nominal public expenditures or statutory tax rates. The International Monetary Fund's programs emphasize the ex ante coincidence of fiscal, monetary, and external sectors but do not pay enough attention to the endogenous nature of some of the variables for which ceilings are established. Sound fiscal institutions should restrict quantitative targets to tax rates and nominal public expenditures and should not use them for fiscal deficits.

The financial repression of expenditures reflects the weakness of budgetary processes. Budgets are in principle estimated in nominal terms. However, growth is often deliberately overestimated to avoid showing a planned cut in spending; when more growth does occur, this leads to higher spending and thus to a higher correlation of taxes and expenditures than would result from a more rational budget. This problem becomes even more acute in recessions, given inflexible debt-service and social security payments. In the past, this was less significant because high inflation allowed flexibility in real public expenditures, by cutting real wages. When reduced growth results from an external shock, rather than a normal business cycle, the problem is further aggravated because it may be necessary to boost interest rates.

Supply shocks can reduce—sometimes in a dramatic way—the potential output of an emerging-market economy. These shocks can take the form of a drastic drop in the terms of trade in goods or in the quantity of services (e.g., in economies heavily dependent on tourism), or a rise in the real interest rate in economies that rely heavily on external savings. The impact of these shocks is magnified where the possibility of substitution between traded and nontraded goods is small, which is sometimes due to high protection having made naturally tradable sectors become nontradable or of low tradability outside the borders.[4]

Under these conditions, a shock has a very different impact than in very open economies. If exports have a large component of natural resources, are concentrated in a few sectors, or depend on regional (quasi-domestic) markets, the required (market-clearing) change in relative prices is very large because the elasticity of supply of exports is usually small. Alterna-

4. Argentina, Brazil, and India are examples of economies that are relatively closed to foreign trade.

tively, the corresponding recession or contractionary adjustment in quantities is very significant if the exchange rate regime is rigid and (together with rigidities that may be amplified by policy) does not allow prices to be rapidly corrected. This explains why external events can have sizable effects even if trade shares are relatively small.

To minimize these costs, following a prudent fiscal policy is very important. One way of implementing this policy is to recognize that any abnormal excess of domestic absorption over national income causes tax revenues to be overestimated in relation to their equilibrium level, at which the current account of the balance of payments is in a steady state. This is because tax revenues are largely levied on, and therefore determined by, aggregate (i.e., tradable and nontradable) expenditures.

A useful rule of thumb is that, in the presence of an above-normal external deficit, fiscal policy should seek a surplus equivalent to the product of the abnormal deficit times the marginal tax rate. This is a "gross" estimate of the increase in tax revenues that a higher-than-normal external deficit would produce, and that needs to be saved to maintain government expenditures in the years of below-normal capital inflows. In no case should the surplus be less than 35 percent of the external disequilibrium.[5]

This rule would ensure that expenditures are not increased unsustainably in response to a temporary capital inflow. Fiscal institutions need to be powerful enough to avoid twin deficits and to ensure that a fiscal surplus is achieved under favorable external conditions. This is a fundamental necessity of macroeconomic design to avoid capital inflows that create conditions for a serious crisis when the cycle reverts. For countries whose fiscal revenues significantly depend on commodity exports, the need to purchase this "fiscal insurance" is magnified during a boom.[6]

A safe policy is to seek a systematic reduction of the public debt, assuming that interest rate spreads are at their average level of recent years. If one sets public expenditures around their intertemporal equilibrium level (the level that makes the present value of the flow of expenditures equal to the present value of the expected flow of tax revenues), the reduction in the ratio of public debt to GDP would result from the joint and exponential contribution of the real growth rate and the external rate of inflation.

---

5. The 35 percent is a rather arbitrary figure, but it tries to address the situation of countries with low tax rates.

6. It is possible to refine this rule of thumb to take into account the sustainability of the country's public and external debt. However, we emphasize a simpler rule for several reasons: (1) Debt sustainability exercises require defining a ratio of sustainable public or external debt to GDP, and governments and the private sector tend to be optimistic about them in the years of abnormally high capital inflows. (2) These ratios need to be carefully defined so as to include the impact of changes in the real exchange rate and the fiscal impact of natural catastrophes.

What this requires for the purpose of fiscal planning is that the growth trend be corrected by the deviation of the terms of trade and the international interest rate from their respective historical or expected values. This would avoid allowing an unsustainably favorable situation to lead to a dangerously high level of public expenditures. The limit of indebtedness within the cycle should recognize the so-called golden rule, whereby the fiscal deficit should at most reach the level of public investment. One must not forget that public expenditure accounts are based on flows and do not incorporate depreciation allowances, which implies that the level of current expenditures is underestimated and therefore the level of public savings is overestimated.

It would be worth setting a Maastricht-type debt limit of about 30 percent of GDP once reasonable levels of indebtedness are reached. This is only half the level the Europeans have set in the Maastricht agreement, but that reflects Latin America's narrow domestic capital markets, higher interest rates, and lower revenue shares relative to GDP. This would further reinforce the pressure to increase public savings and therefore weaken the vulnerability associated with a fragile fiscal position. The rule would also help to avoid an exaggerated expansion of current expenditures and private consumption, which in turn would reinforce private savings.[7]

A rule of avoiding twin deficits would result in additional capital inflows, leading automatically to a lower interest rate. If the inflow nonetheless continues, debt management policy should complete the arsenal of stabilizing measures by changing the composition toward domestic debt until the capital flow reverses.

These rules are particularly important in the context of fixed or rigid exchange rate regimes. During the preannounced regimes in the late 1970s and early 1980s in Argentina and Uruguay—and in Argentina, Mexico, and Brazil during their periods of convertibility and crawling exchange rates, respectively, in the 1990s—public expenditures went to clearly unsustainable levels. Sooner or later, the truth was uncomfortably revealed by external shocks.

Summing up, destabilizing, procyclical fiscal policy afflicts most Latin American economies. More intriguing, even when countercyclical budget rules would clearly improve welfare, they do not emerge. This points to problems of political economy. In fact, certain models explain procyclicality as an equilibrium between the interaction of political pressures to increase expenditures during booms and the optimal response of an executive branch concerned with deficits and distortions.

In some of these models (see Talvi and Vegh 2000), the inability to restrict public spending gives the economic authorities an incentive to reduce taxes in expansions so as to avoid additional spending—but this

7. See, e.g., López Murphy and Navajas (1998) for the relation between public savings and private consumption and savings in Argentina during the early 1990s.

serves to make fiscal policy even more procyclical. Nevertheless, we believe that the so-called procyclical problem arises, in many instances, simply as a result of a very bad reading of the fiscal problem by the economic authorities.

The key point of the agenda to eliminate procyclicality developed above is that current and capital expenditures should be based on an institutional framework that sets stringent debt targets and aims to balance the budget along the projected potential growth trend. This effort will mean adjusting actual revenue by a correction reflecting external conditions, notably the terms of trade and capital inflows.

In practice, this agenda will be affected by the degree of openness of the economy and the history and nature of fiscal institutions; more open economies with exports based on more elastic supplies will be better able to adjust to facilitate macroeconomic corrections, which will give slightly more latitude to take risks with the proposed countercyclical policy. Conversely, the importance and significance of these rules should be accentuated if the monetary (exchange rate) regime is very rigid, in which case fiscal policy must follow a path consistent with the numeraire of the economy and the fact that it is the only instrument left available to cushion the impact of external shocks.

Making Hidden Debts Explicit

A recurrent problem in fiscal management in emerging-market economies has been the existence of implicit debts that have not been incorporated into fiscal accounts, for various reasons. Some examples are the outcomes of judicial processes, losses from operations of the central bank (more important in the 1980s and known as quasi-fiscal deficits), debts resulting from losses in the financial system and more commonly in official banks, and government guarantees that are called and have not been computed in the fiscal accounts. Such "skeletons" have increased public debts substantially in some cases. For example, in Brazil the Fernando Henrique Cardoso administration cleaned up "skeletons" worth about 10 percent of the GDP in the period 1993-2001, and there are estimates that in the subsequent 6 years something above another 5 percentage points may be added (Goldfajn 2002).

Another significant issue arises in reforming a pension system from pay-as-you-go to fully funded. This reform does not result in any net expansion of debt, but rather in an explicit recognition of debt. The intertemporal impact on the fiscal accounts is neutral if the reform is designed to maintain preexisting conditions. But in most of Latin America, pension reform has been designed to improve the actuarial balance of the pension system, because in most countries the so-called implicit pension debt is very large (see table 4.2). The wide range of estimates shown in the

Table 4.2 Range of estimates of implicit pension debt in selected Latin American countries in the 1990s (percent)

Country	Ratio of debt to GDP
Argentina	55 to 305
Bolivia	40
Brazil	188 to 213
Chile	130
Colombia	59 to 88
Mexico	37 to 118
Peru	37 to 45
Uruguay	187 to 289
Venezuela	30 to 37

Sources: Kane and Palacios (1996), Bravo and Uthoff (1999), FIEL (1998a), Grandolini and Cerda (1998), and Von Gersdorff (1997).

table comes from different methodologies, assumptions, and macroeconomic conditions at the time of the exercises, and it is fair to say that some of them are more simulations than actual estimates.[8] But the point is that a pay-as-you-go system implies debt that is hidden in the fiscal accounts, while this gradually becomes explicit after pension reform. These explicit debts have to be financed voluntarily by capital markets.

The first issue that arises with regard to hidden debts is transparency. Acknowledging potential liabilities may influence expectations and affect capital markets. Making fiscal accounts, projections, and estimates more transparent is fundamental both in the presentation of budgets and in fiscal reports; it narrows uncertainties and avoids private-sector hypotheses that are exaggerated, lack an empirical base, or embody fears that the government will behave in an inconsistent or opportunistic manner. Transparency is crucial to motivate commitment in fiscal policy. This commitment, in turn, is fundamental to the development and efficient working of capital markets, particularly when liabilities of the government need to be processed and calculated as a stream of payments in the future.

A second issue is the macroeconomic impact on aggregate spending of recognizing the debts. One case involves debts that are unregistered and illiquid (the "skeletons"). This is different from the case of debts of the central bank or public-sector financial institutions. But in both cases, it is

8. E.g., for Argentina, studies like FIEL (1998a) have estimated an implicit debt of 55 percent of GDP at the time of the reform, whereas Bravo and Uthoff (1999) estimate a potential figure almost six times greater. In fact, almost all the upper-bound estimates in table 4.2 come from Bravo and Uthoff's simulations—except for Mexico, for which they estimate 37 percent while Grandolini and Cerda (1998) report 118 percent before the reform; for Colombia, the range is taken from Bravo and Uthoff (1999).

appropriate to compute the debts at the moment they are transformed into explicit debts, and to fully internalize their macroeconomic impact. Part of their impact may indeed have been felt before the moment they accrued, but to assume that there was no impact at that time also requires assuming that economic agents are perfectly informed, even when the debt process is uncertain, and have full access to capital markets to finance the anticipation of expenditures.[9] This is not likely to be the situation in emerging markets, where agents are normally liquidity constrained and markets are narrow and lack financial guarantees.

This latter point is important, because ad hoc treatment of these liabilities can give rise to an incorrect reading of the fiscal situation and mislead about the type of debt instrument that should be used to cancel these obligations. Where the deficit is measured on a cash basis, the impact should be allocated at the moment when the instrument of payment is created, which will avoid underestimating the deficit that is being faced. This procedure could substantially change the reading of the size of fiscal disequilibria that some emerging-market countries have faced in recent years.

The transition from a pay-as-you-go to a fully funded pension system is one example of newly generated liabilities being made explicit and creating an immediate burden on the government's borrowing requirement. If a country's fiscal position is tight, this can add significant pressure on capital markets. It is true that if the change is equivalent—or positive—in actuarial terms, the funds accumulated in the new system should by definition finance the transition. However, the evidence suggests that in emerging markets one cannot assume that the financing of the transition cost is guaranteed simply because the actuarial balance has improved with reform.

The objectives of developing capital markets and of reestablishing incentives through a fully funded system suffer if the effort to make debts explicit is not supported by a greater fiscal effort. The idea that future fiscal surpluses are fully incorporated into the demand for public debt, even though it is attractive theoretically, is too optimistic to furnish a rule for sound financial programming.

This is not to say that principles of intertemporal accounting based on optimizing behavior should not be used to guide fiscal decisions; rather, appearances can also matter in economies that are subject to sudden stops of external financing. More prudence will strengthen the performance of economies that have a tradition of low domestic savings. In the case of hidden debts that stem from judicial decisions, such as claims by retirees, public employees, or government suppliers, the beneficiaries should receive debt with a very long maturity, to avoid more short-maturity debt disrupting thin capital markets and debt management.

9. Argentina during the 1990s was a good example of a country with debt increases that could not be fully explained by cumulated deficits.

The resulting agenda can be summarized as follows. First, in the case of as yet unregistered debt pending judicial resolution, fiscal institutions should make potential liabilities more explicit and predictable, and they should clearly state the nature of the potential "skeleton." Second, in the case of debt originating in financial institutions, reports should establish a clear accountability of the origin of the liability so as to make overall fiscal policy and public finances less difficult to evaluate.

Third, in the case of pension system reform, it is important to clarify both the details of past deficits and the actuarial change that is taking place, to facilitate structural change in public finances. Moreover, the need to augment public savings in an environment of volatility suggests that current revenues should cover a great part of the financial gap created during the transition from a pay-as-you-go pension system to a fully funded one.[10] Fourth, in the case of unregistered debt coming from the resolution of judicial disputes where the government becomes a debtor because of concessions to private agents granted by law, it is convenient that debt be issued at long maturities and with low interest in the intermediate decades. These rules should be applied to all levels of government, and debt statistics should make the consolidation process transparent.

Controlling Tax Expenditures

Tax expenditures are hidden subsidies to business. They constitute one of the major challenges for fiscal policy and fiscal institutions in emerging-market economies. They introduce distortions, usually increase the inequality in income distribution, promote rent seeking, hinder transparency, impede regional economic integration, and bias fiscal accounts toward deficits. A correct reading of the magnitude of public spending requires making tax expenditures explicit. Transparency in this area, like that just discussed, will facilitate choosing fiscal options with realism and accountability.

These hidden subsidies have generally been biased in favor of capital (by reducing taxes on capital) or in favor of capital-intensive sectors such as manufacturing, and have rarely benefited labor. Moreover, to the extent that they increase the fiscal deficit, they put extra pressure on country risk and thus depress net-of-tax wages in small, open economies. They complicate tax administration and create many loopholes, and promote movement toward untaxed sectors or regions. The quasi-tariffs they often cre-

10. The optimal proportion of tax financing of the cash deficit created by pension reform will depend on the magnitude of the gap, the size of the preexisting public debt, and the nature of the country. For poor countries with low country risk premiums on government debt, it may be sensible to finance a larger share of the transition cost of pension reform through debt financing.

ate hinder regional integration, for the reactions of trading partners are often hostile. This is particularly serious where regional integration is a first step toward wider integration.

These mechanisms are sometimes presented as a way to avoid the growth of traditional public spending (explicit subsidies) or as a way of forcing countries to set a limit on business taxation. We believe this viewpoint is wrong in general, and especially so in emerging-market economies. Good economic performance requires similar rules for all participants (i.e., a level-playing field). The distortion of prices and signals, as well as their unpredictability, harms economic efficiency and thus growth.[11] This problem is compounded in the context of weak tax administration and a public sector that chronically runs a deficit.

The costs of tax expenditures are magnified by the proliferation of rent-seeking activities. These waste additional economic resources beyond the traditional estimates of deadweight loss. There is ample evidence that, in countries such as Argentina, tax expenditures give incentives for rent seeking and have contributed to fiscal deficits.[12] In most emerging-market economies, where governance and efficient political processes are still weak, rent seekers focus on tax expenditures, particularly in decentralized and heterogeneous countries.

These considerations add some important points to our fiscal agenda. Ideally, tax expenditures should be abolished. Any political goal can be better handled through explicit subsidies in the budget. If tax expenditures are maintained, fiscal institutions should make a transparent account of these expenditures, distinguishing between old and new measures and estimating their impact on current and future fiscal budgets. And an economic report on the subsidies should make explicit those cases where tax expenditures exceed the capital stock or payroll of the subsidized firms (because these are typically justified as employment promotion). Moreover, these subsidies should be explicitly compared with annual budget allocations to social sectors such as education and poverty reduction.

11. The evidence on the regional subsidies to firms granted by some US states and by the European Union proves this point. Incentives were not effective in augmenting growth or creating more jobs. See Artana (1996) for a summary of the empirical evidence.

12. See, e.g., FIEL (1988) on the industrial promotion regime in Argentina, which was designed to give exemptions from national tax obligations to sectors located in certain regions. The provinces had incentives to seek these subsidies because the rest of the country financed them, while pressure groups promoted legislative action. This kind of competitive externality (a variety of the "problem of the commons") concerning tax expenditures is described in Heymann and Navajas (1989) for the Argentine case. The political resistance in favor of the status quo proved to be very difficult to change during the 1990s, even though the national authorities were more committed to a reform. Estimates of the fiscal costs of this regime gave figures of about 1.5 percent of GDP (World Bank 1993), with the traditional welfare cost (without considering rent-seeking activities) constituting only about 25-50 percent of this cost (FIEL 1988).

Making Fiscal Decentralization Compatible with Macroeconomic Stability

Fiscal decentralization has a clear policy logic, for it brings decisions on the provision of public and social goods closer to the affected parties. However, vertical imbalances between national and subnational governments are a stylized fact,[13] particularly in emerging markets, which poses the problem of how to make transfers across jurisdictions.

Intergovernmental transfers create incentive problems because they break the link that exists when a public agency makes expenditure decisions and finances all of them with its own-source revenues. The problem becomes more acute when intergovernmental transfers are used to redistribute income from richer to poorer regions. Another issue is whether transfers are based on a formula as opposed to discretion, which may be inefficient and poses dangers of political manipulation.

In this chapter, we are mainly interested in macroeconomic issues.[14] When GDP is growing at a much higher rate than the potential growth rate, the government receives more revenues than when in the steady state. A sound fiscal policy requires that these surpluses be saved so as to ensure that enough resources will be available during the bust, when tax revenues diminish and expenditure needs usually increase. Intergovernmental transfers that are specified as a fraction of federal tax revenues give more money during booms to subnational governments, which are likely to increase their expenditures unless there are constraints on subnational spending, thus exacerbating the federal difficulty in stabilizing the economic cycle. This problem is more severe in countries that are more exposed to changes in capital inflows or in the terms of trade.

Another problem that arises concerns the issuance of debt by subnational governments. Even if there are no intergovernmental transfers, subnational governments may "undo" the effects of the macroeconomic policy of the federal government if they face no restrictions on the issuance of debt. In some industrial countries, there are restrictions on the volume of debt that subnational governments may issue. Alternatively, the federal government's prior authorization may be required for provinces (states) or municipalities to issue new debt; or else one may rely on the credit-rating process of the capital markets to limit debt issues.

But this raises some problems. Will these restrictions be credible when the risk of a federal bailout exists and is higher than for private firms that

13. Although the most onerous expenditures are best decentralized (national public goods like external defense represent today a much lower share of total expenditure in peaceful countries), constraints like factor mobility or administrative problems prevent the decentralization of many taxes to the provincial or municipal level.

14. See, e.g., FIEL (1993), Artana and López Murphy (1995, 1996).

issue debt?[15] Moreover, for public agencies, the problem of incentives is more acute than for private managers; there are similar agency problems, but the intertemporal restrictions are weaker than those faced by private managers because politicians usually remain in office for a relatively short time. The fact is that subnational indebtedness has often appeared again and again (e.g., in Argentina, Brazil, and Colombia), and bailouts finally occurred. Controls on domestic indebtedness can be subject to political manipulation and moral hazard.

We propose a five-point agenda that seeks to strike a balance between decentralization and macro stability. First, we favor implementing the basic principle of public finance that calls for the same authority to be responsible for spending and for raising the marginal revenue to finance those expenditures. Specifically, reduced intergovernmental transfers should be compensated for with more tax decentralization, as administratively feasible.

Second, procyclical elements in the design of transfer rules should be eliminated. Rather than being based on a percentage of federal revenues, transfers should be calculated as lump-sum amounts that may change every year on the basis of variables that are independent of the economic cycle (e.g., population growth).

Third, the principles of budget balancing that guide fiscal policy at the national level should be extended to subnational levels. These measures should emphasize increasing capital expenditures in bad times and building up stabilization funds in good times.

Fourth, the debt policies of subnational governments must be coordinated by the central government. Debt volume caps are one method of coordination; the requirement of a minimum rating to be able to issue new debt is another. The rating process has the advantage of making the information about the finances of subnational governments more transparent and reliable.[16]

15. There has been a hot discussion about the need to restrict the access of the private sector to international capital markets, based on the postulate of a positively sloped marginal cost of foreign funds for the country as a whole. Each individual borrower ignores the additional cost he or she imposes on other borrowers by increasing his or her foreign debt, which may suggest a case for taxing borrowing (as Chile did during the 1990s) or imposing more stringent prudential regulations on the banking system (as Argentina did in the mid-1990s). We do not take sides in this discussion, but we want to stress that for public debt of the subnational governments, the problem is aggravated because the risk of a federal bailout is higher than for a single private firm, and this may make the credit rating process less severe (if ultimately the lenders are expected to collect the loan from the federal collateral). Moreover, the process is more likely to be politicized, e.g., because a provincial default may trigger a negative externality to other public and private borrowers.

16. Guillermo Perry suggested to us that developing and applying adequate bankruptcy procedures for subnationals (as in the United States and Hungary) might be the only efficient long-term solution.

Fifth, it is not desirable for subnational governments to have their own financial institutions, especially if these bypass prudent bank regulation. Such institutions have often been a source of soft budget constraints.

Tax Design and Administration

Emerging-market economies' tax systems have several characteristics that make them different from those of industrial countries. Usually, total tax revenues expressed as a fraction of GDP are lower, and the share of consumption taxes in total tax revenues is larger. In Latin American and other emerging-market economies, income taxes and property taxes account for a much lower fraction of GDP than in countries that belong to the Organization for Economic Cooperation and Development (OECD) (see table 4.3).[17]

There are three principal reasons for this situation, all of which point toward policy recommendations. First, the size of government tends to increase with GDP per capita, which implies that emerging-market economies require lower revenues than industrial countries. Figure 4.1 shows a positive correlation between tax revenues measured as a fraction of GDP and per capita GDP.[18] Moreover, the inflation tax, which is often an important source of revenue in emerging markets, is not included in tax revenue statistics. Recent stabilization attempts have increased the need to raise tax revenues from sources other than inflation.

Second, in emerging-market economies, income distribution is worse than in industrial economies, informality in the labor market is higher, and tax administration is weaker. Therefore, the income tax base is lower; income taxes fall on only a small fraction of the population,[19] many individuals pay hardly any tax at all, and the tax evasion rate is usually higher for taxes on income (which rely on self-declaration for many taxpayers) than for consumption taxes (which often have cross-checks built in, e.g., in the case of the value-added tax, or VAT).

Third, in many countries, foreign savings are very important (either because remittances from their citizens abroad are high or because they benefited from high capital inflows to emerging markets during much of the

17. Data for each country have been weighted by the total GDP calculated using the Atlas method of the World Bank.

18. Tax revenues were obtained either from the IMF's *Government Finance Statistics* or from IMF country reports, which usually provide a fuller account of the tax revenues raised by subnational governments. The regression does not change appreciably if oil-producing countries are excluded.

19. Sometimes this is explained by very high exemption levels in the personal income tax. Note than in the 1940s, when the United States had very high exemption levels, the Internal Revenue Service collected about 2 percent of GDP in personal income taxes, a fraction that is similar to that now observed in many emerging economies. See FIEL (1998b) for more details.

Table 4.3 Average composition of tax revenues, various country groups, 2001

Group	Taxes on income, profits, and capital gains	Social Security contributions and taxes on payroll workforce	Property tax	Subtotal: Taxes on income and property	Taxes on goods and services	Other taxes	Total
Percent of GDP							
OECD[a]	12.4	9.7	2.4	24.5	7.7	0.3	32.5
Latin America[b]	4.7	3.8	0.3	8.8	8.9	3.4	21.1
Other emerging-market countries[c]	6.5	0.8	0.2	7.5	8.3	3.4	19.2
Percent of total tax revenues							
OECD[a]	38.2	29.8	7.3	75.3	23.8	0.9	100.0
Latin America[b]	22.1	18.1	1.4	41.6	42.1	16.2	100.0
Other emerging-market countries[c]	33.9	4.2	1.0	39.1	43.2	17.8	100.0

OECD = Organization for Economic Cooperation and Development

a. Excludes Mexico.
b. Latin America includes Argentina, Brazil, Colombia, Chile, Guatemala, Ecuador, Mexico, Paraguay, Peru, Uruguay, and Venezuela.
c. Includes India, Indonesia, Malaysia, Russia, Singapore, Thailand, and Ukraine.

Sources: Own estimates based on OECD, *Revenue Statistics 2001;* IMF, *Government Finance Statistics;* and IMF country reports to complete data for subnational governments.

Figure 4.1 Average tax revenues (percent of GDP) **compared with per capita GDP** (average 1997-2000)

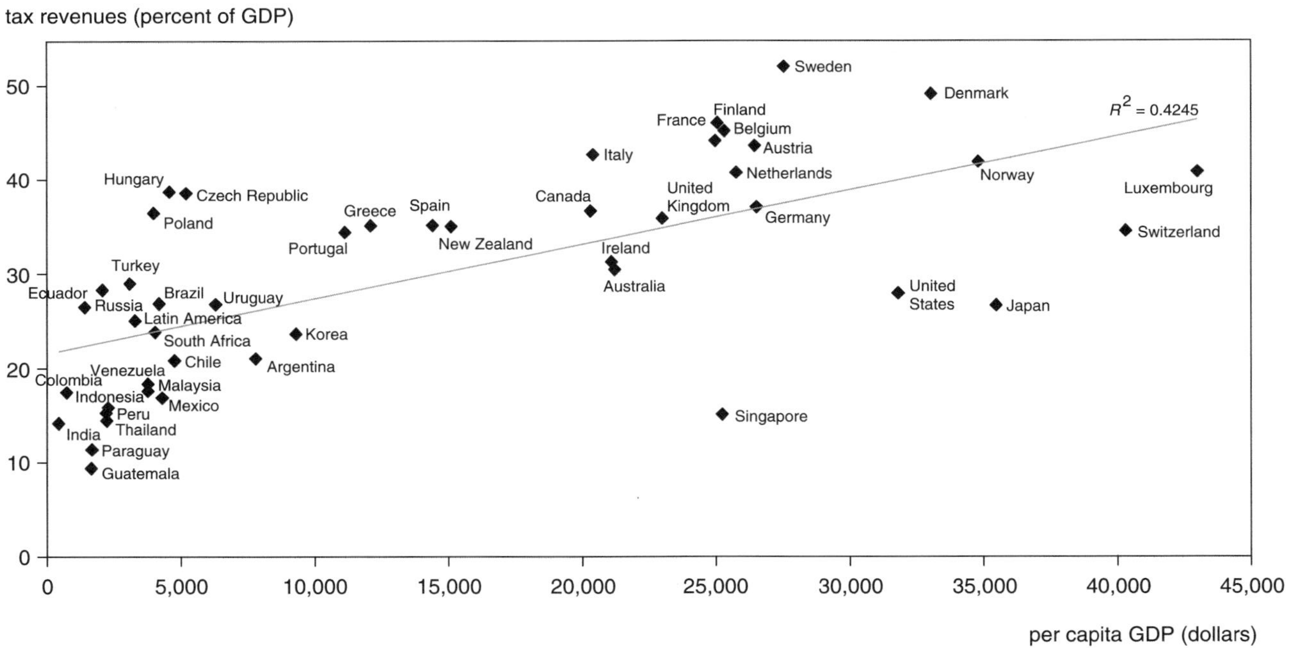

Note: Per capita GDP is determined using the method of the World Bank's *Atlas*.

Sources: FIEL, based on OECD *Revenue Statistics* and *IMF Country Reports*.

Table 4.4 Evasion rate for the value-added tax, selected Latin American and other countries, 1992 (percent)

Country	Evasion rate
New Zealand	5.1
Sweden	5.4
Israel	7.8
Portugal	14.0
South Africa	14.6
Canada	23.0
Chile[a]	23.3
Spain	26.0
Uruguay	27.0
Honduras	35.4
Colombia	35.8
Hungary	36.3
Mexico	37.1
Ecuador	38.2
Philippines	40.8
Bolivia	43.9
Argentina[b]	46.5
Guatemala	52.5
Panama	53.5
Peru	68.2

a. Data are for 1994.
b. Data are for 1996.

Source: Silvani and Brondolo (1993).

1990s). Therefore, the base of consumption taxes is relatively enlarged in comparison with countries that are net exporters of capital. In some extreme cases, consumption is close to 100 percent of GDP.

Informality and Tax Evasion

In emerging-market countries, high tax evasion rates and labor informality are serious problems. For example, Silvani and Brondolo (1993) estimated the evasion rate for the value-added tax for 20 countries in the early 1990s and found rates ranging from 5 percent in New Zealand to 68 percent in Peru (see table 4.4). Most Latin American countries have rates higher than 35 percent.

Tax evasion and labor informality create a dual economy with substantial differences in productivity whereby informal producers are able to compete with formal firms because they avoid paying the tax that the others pay to the government. This is also aggravated by the tendency to conduct many transactions in cash.

Tax evasion and labor informality have a serious impact on both efficiency and equity. The traditional method used in industrial countries to improve the distribution of income, a progressive personal income tax, is itself liable to be a source of serious inequity when evasion rates for taxes on income or property are 50 percent or even higher. One consequence in emerging-market economies with pervasive evasion is that social programs must rely more on targeted social expenditures than on the tax system.

The limited level of redistribution that can be achieved through the tax system and weak administrative capabilities in public agencies together suggest that propoor policies in emerging-market economies should put a special emphasis on incentives. For example, policies that rely on self-assessment of the beneficiaries of assistance are better than those that rely on selection by government officials (especially where local governments are too weak to handle the delivery of social policies).[20] Social expenditures that disproportionately benefit rich families should not be free of charge, or might even be privatized. In Latin America, this rule is not always followed; the clearest example is tuition-free public universities, where a large majority of the students usually come from rich or high-middle-income families.

Evasion is usually very high for taxes on labor; in many cases, the individual is not registered for social security. This occurs not only for some labor services performed by individuals but also in firms, where some employees are not declared to the social security system. Lowering taxes on labor has the advantage of encouraging the formalization of more workers and securing wider coverage of the social security network. Low labor taxes would also help to reduce unemployment. A deepening of formal financial intermediation, so as to capture those firms that have a closer integration with formal ones, would also help to reduce labor informality, as well improving controls on money laundering.

Small and medium-sized firms in emerging-market economies tend to enter into arrears for the payment of taxes because this is often a cheap way of accessing credit when the degree of financial intermediation is low and capital markets are underdeveloped. The preservation of the fiscal interest requires a penalty rate above market interest rates, and that rate may need to be very high in real terms to deter small and medium-sized firms because the spread between the borrowing rate of high-grade corporations and small firms is usually much higher in developing countries than in industrial ones. In other cases, the government forces firms to advance working capital to the government, even though this conflicts with normal commercial practices.

High tax evasion rates and weak tax administration have encouraged governments of emerging-market countries to obtain tax revenues from the consumption of some goods whose supply is concentrated and easy to control (e.g., fuels, cigarettes, soft drinks) or to extend the network of withholding devices much more than is the norm in industrial economies.

---

20. E.g., workfare programs for the unemployed look better than unemployment insurance. The role of government officials is less important in the first type of welfare program for the unemployed and individual's moral hazard is also better addressed.

There is, of course, an economic rationale for special taxes on fuel, cigarettes, and alcoholic beverages, because they create negative externalities. Most countries therefore apply higher tax rates to them than to other consumption goods.

However, the high tax rates levied by many emerging-market economies on goods that create no negative externality (e.g., soft drinks) suggest that governments have tried to ensure substantial tax collections from these sectors simply because they are easier to monitor. Although this may be sensible, its potential is limited by smuggling and round-tripping of exports, which have increased the proportion of illegal sales of many of these goods. This constrains attempts to extract revenues from these sectors.

Finally, labor informality is largely an endogenous phenomenon. When the benefits of being formal (access to credit, security, social security, avoiding penalties) are not large compared with the costs (red tape, high taxes), many firms and workers opt for informality. Thus, reducing informality requires a multifaceted approach, including effective enforcement, reduction of red tape and some tax rates, and improvements in transparency and the quality and equity of tax policy and administration, public expenditures, and public services.

Volatility in Tax Revenues

In economies with high resort to external savings and a large fraction of tax revenues coming from consumption taxes, abrupt changes in capital inflows create major stress on tax collections. Consumption taxes tend to have lower payment lags than income or property taxes, and an important fraction of tax revenues comes from durable goods (because these have a relatively concentrated supply), whose consumption is relatively volatile. Thus there are several potential sources of high volatility in tax revenues. This strengthens the need to have budget stabilization funds in emerging-market economies.

Incidence of Taxes

Small, open economies with capital mobility cannot "export" taxes to the rest of the world. In particular, capital will tend to bear the same burden as it bears in the country of origin of the investment because of the pressure for net-of-tax returns to be equalized. If capital is taxed more heavily, investors in the long run will move their investment to those countries where net returns (adjusted by differences in country risk) are higher. The same rule applies to domestic investors given their access to the capital markets of industrial economies.[21]

21. Tax havens and exemption of interest income accruing to foreign persons in some industrial countries, such as the United States, magnify the difficulty of taxing domestic residents.

This implies that there is a limit to the tax rate that can be imposed on capital; there is not much room to have tax rates higher than those prevailing in the industrial countries from which the capital came. Labor taxes, in contrast, will usually be borne by workers, except perhaps for the highly skilled who compete in a global market. Consumption taxes (most obviously those on tradable goods, whose price is fixed in the world market) are largely borne by consumers.

Policy Recommendations

A suitable tax system for the central government of an emerging-market economy should be based on a generalized VAT of the consumption type, a progressive income tax with few exceptions and moderate marginal tax rates, a uniform duty on imports, and special excise taxes on goods that create negative externalities (e.g., cigarettes, alcoholic beverages, and fuels) and perhaps on luxury goods (Shome 1995). Subnational levels of government could rely on taxes on property and on a provincial VAT, calculated on the same tax base as the federal VAT. This tax system should be biased toward savings, so as to reduce dependence on foreign savings.[22] One way of doing this is to allow the expensing of investment, although this has a substantial fiscal cost because it de facto eliminates the business income tax at the margin.

Countries rich in natural resources have another important potential source of revenue. If reserves are relatively well known, it is efficient and transparent to rely on a system that tries to capture the rent of exhaustible resources in a competitive auction (e.g., the "bonus bidding" used by the US government for offshore oil leases) and to subject firms to the same tax treatment as that for other sectors of the economy (plus a small royalty).[23]

Tax administration can be strengthened by encouraging, or even requiring, firms to use the formal financial system (e.g., by obliging firms to pay wages and salaries through the banking system). Replacement of labor taxes by high excises (except perhaps on fuels, which are an important input in many tradable activities) is another reform worth exploring, provided the risk posed by smuggling and round-tripping in exporting countries is not severe.

Summing up, the key reforms in this area are improved tax administration; the promotion of domestic savings through greater dependence

22. Tanzi and Zee (1998) found that higher taxes in general reduce household savings in OECD countries, but that income taxes have a much higher impact than consumption taxes.

23. When reserves are not known, the government might find it helpful to use a battery of instruments so as to reduce uncertainty about the value of a field. One alternative is to auction exploration leases with clear requirements of reversals of part of the area; another is to have sliding royalties linked to the size of the discovery, although this creates a distortion in the net price faced by the company.

on the VAT than in industrial countries; more scope for property taxes levied by subnational governments; and a lowering of labor taxes, to encourage the formalization of labor and reduced unemployment.

Budget Mechanisms and Critical Public Spending

We turn now to a discussion of the budget mechanism, including the design, incentives, and monitoring of public spending in critical areas. The budget is a process that coordinates spending decisions, provides a macroeconomic framework, and establishes public policy credibility. But beyond this, certain areas of government spending are especially crucial for emerging-market economies—because they involve functions that only the government can provide, tackle severe problems of social policy, or are fundamental to increasing aggregate productivity. The goals are to design efficient, cost-effective programs, and to avoid corruption and political rent seeking. Privatization has provided a way to delegate expenditures that in industrial economies are in some cases provided by the state, which has shifted resources from the explicit budget. But privatized industries have had mixed results in some emerging-market countries.

Many things could be said on these issues, but we limit our remarks to a few points. First, program evaluation and accountability need to be based on a measurement of output (preferably in physical terms) and costs. This is one of the bases of a system of well-ordered budgetary decisions, spending procedures, registry, disbursement and control, and debt management. Such a system is crucial for orderly and effective fiscal performance, which is important to provide transparency to both domestic and foreign observers, and therefore to achieve access to financing on reasonable terms.

Experience points to the desirability of a legal framework that both covers in an integrated manner the financial management of the country and also establishes a timeline for the delivery of the budget in due time and form. This requires setting guidelines for the presentation of the budget, and describing the financial and macroeconomic hypotheses on which it is based. The legal framework should require that the message accompanying the budget include a careful assessment of the current fiscal year, as well as a comparison with the new budget and with the trend from the past 5 years or so.

In the elaboration of the budget, use and explicit mention should be made of the national accounts projections, of the monetary program, of the balance of payment accounts, and of the 5-year forecast implied by current policies. Also, as stressed in previous sections, explicit estimates of the implicit or contingent debts as well as of tax expenditures should be included in the presentation. A very useful rule that is part of the budget legislation of some emerging-market countries is that initiatives on the level of public expenditures can be taken only by the executive power, leaving the national legislature with the right to accept or reject, but never increase, spending.[24] This avoids incentives for opportunistic or demagogic behavior that are common in many contexts.

These criteria should be applied to subnational governments as well. It is desirable to avoid a proliferation of nonbudget operations, which weaken information and management systems.

It is crucial that budget limits be set so that they cannot be changed, after an executive or legislative initiative, except within the framework of a comprehensive budget amendment. The budget must be elaborated with provisions to accommodate unexpected events. The level of spending should not change if tax revenues increase above the projected level. It is very important to set penalties for noncompliance with the budget, which should be communicated annually to the corresponding authorities, as is enshrined in the laws of many countries.

Emerging-market countries need to improve the productivity of resources devoted to areas of exclusive public spending, such as the provision of justice and legal services.[25] By their very nature, public goods or social goods with multidirectional externalities lack a market reference for the prices or values to be used in a cost-benefit analysis. This makes evaluation of provision and spending a difficult task, especially because the measurement of quality is tricky for many public services. Problems of asymmetric information, transaction costs, and weak property rights are all present and make it difficult to find a solution through either the market or the government. International experience during the 1990s showed important efforts to decentralize and outsource activities[26] as well as to introduce user charges designed to limit severe cost inefficiencies and waste of resources.

Other efficiency mechanisms include benchmarking, multiyear budgets for comparative purposes, and the use of physical units and of explicit costs of provision. In this task, the precise definition of goods, services, and processes is crucial for establishing standards from which to define cost-effectiveness and to facilitate monitoring and control. Here, the agenda is very large and important for emerging-market economies. In the past, high inflation rates and the difficulties of fiscal management in such an unstable scenario weakened efforts to properly monitor expenditures.

---

24. The ministry of finance should be in charge of the consolidation of budget authorizations and may even have a veto power inside the executive branch.

25. Costs in these areas are often high, which acts as a tax on real activity and depresses investment and employment. In Argentina, studies have found high costs in relation to performance at the federal level (see Artana, Cristini, and Urbiztondo 1995) and more serious quality problems at a state level.

26. This is true even of the auditing process in the case of New Zealand.

In some emerging-market countries, services may be provided through regulations that in industrial countries are provided through public spending and financed with contributions earmarked for that purpose. For instance, in some countries unemployment insurance comes in the form of labor regulations that establish compensation for being fired.[27] This is not registered in public-sector accounts, but it should be included when budgets are being compared.

Another important issue is the focalization of social expenditures to avoid undesirable leakages to sectors, households, and regions. This is important for both budgetary and distributive reasons. Here is where it is most important to compare the cost of public provision with the mechanism of subsidizing demand. Education and health sectors are the prime examples of the potential of the latter.

Summing up—given a long list of reasonable points in this area—we stress three topics. First, program evaluation and accountability require mechanisms that incorporate the measurement of physical units and the cost of provision. Second, delegated expenditures in the form of private-sector provision, which usually is done with new regulations and bypasses budget processes, need to be incorporated into the assessment and control of fiscal policy. Third, the demand-subsidy approach seems the best way to tackle problems of efficiency, cost-effectiveness, and corruption in most social programs.

National and Supranational Institutional Frameworks

One of the main contributions of the analysis of fiscal policy and fiscal institutions in the past decade has been the characterization of the incentive problems that exist in weak institutional settings, where decentralized decisions without proper rules or procedures create incentives for overspending and a bias toward deficits. This is the so-called common pool problem, a term borrowed from the literature on competitive or multidirectional externalities that exhaust natural resources. The point is that individuals or actors perceive the full benefit of their action, but common property dilutes the costs among all participants.[28]

27. Of course, unemployment insurance and severance payments are not equivalent in allocative or welfare terms. The point here is that regulations are in some cases a substitute, albeit an imperfect one, for spending programs. E.g., in Argentina in 2000, the equivalent of 1.5 percent of GDP was spent on these alternatives to unemployment insurance.

28. See the volume edited by Poterba and von Haguen (1999). For Latin America, Heymann and Navajas (1989) provided an early formalization of the argument for Argentina, and a vast research program has subsequently emerged, with substantial contributions by, inter alia, Alesina et al. (1996) and Stein, Talvi, and Grisanti (1998).

In the context of fiscal policy, this cost-benefit asymmetry implies that an absence of rules or coordinated procedures creates a bias toward spending by decentralized decisions that do not fully internalize the costs, leading to inefficient fiscal outcomes. Thus there is a need for institutional and procedural arrangements to eliminate or at least constrain such bad incentives. Explicit fiscal rules or budgetary procedures that lead participants in the budgetary process to internalize the costs of budget deficits will lead to more efficient fiscal outcomes.

The implications of the common pool approach are clear enough regarding the need to change incentives and solve coordination failures among different participants. But the approach leaves open the question of how to achieve the desired change. One way is to design explicit rules intended to restrict outcomes. Another is focus on the design of the budget process. Recent studies have still not definitively answered this question. The preference for explicit (constitutional or statutory) fiscal rules (e.g., debt ceilings, balanced-budget rules, and expenditure limits) is based on the view that designing constitutional rules is difficult and political transaction costs make them difficult to enforce.

However, recent studies—such as Kennedy and Robbins (2001)—have argued that rules are not a necessary condition for good fiscal outcomes; these can be, and have been, attained in contexts without explicit fiscal rules.[29] Kennedy and Robbins use evidence from many industrial countries to compare the performance achieved with and without fiscal rules, and they cite Canada as an example of a country that has achieved fiscal consolidation without explicit rules at the federal level.[30] They argue that the real test of rules (a recession) has not occurred in some cases (e.g., the United States) or has given rise to reversals (e.g., Japan). They do not say that rules cannot be useful, but they question the view that rules are sufficient to ensure good fiscal outcomes.

We do not see this as an argument for not using rules, but rather conclude that efforts to improve institutional design may also be worthwhile, if there is a need for improvements in this dimension. The distinction between explicit rules and procedural design is not a debate on the merits of centralization (for they both attempt to resolve a coordination failure) and does not challenge the evidence in favor of a strong executive role that is stressed in the literature. The relevant question is not so much rules versus procedures as whether countries with given institutions and budget procedures can improve fiscal outcomes by introducing explicit rules. In many cases, the answer seems to be positive.

29. Braun and Tommasi (2002) make a similar argument against the "simplistic view" that numerical limits on fiscal variables provide a solution for fiscal profligacy by subnational governments.

30. In fact, Canada has balanced budget rules and expenditure limits at the subnational level, but the brunt of the fiscal consolidation efforts of the 1990s fell on the federal government.

Countries have established or proposed a variety of different mechanisms intended to nurture more balanced and predictable fiscal policies: a variety of fiscal responsibility laws, in some cases extended to subnational levels; debt targets; balanced-budget requirements; and expenditure evaluation programs. In some cases, explicit penalties for noncompliance have been a part of the legal framework; but evidence suggests that commitment is a major problem in the presence of external shocks.

In other cases, supranational agreements have sought to improve fiscal institutions (e.g., the Maastricht Treaty and the complementary European Union Stability and Growth Pact, with the penalties they foresee in case of deviations from the established criteria concerning fiscal deficits). Such fiscal limits are intended to constrain during the adverse phase of the business cycle, and it is therefore expected that countries will achieve a lower deficit than the limit or a surplus in better-than-normal times.

There are also ceilings on public debt that are intended to force a considerable effort in the future to reduce deficits. In all cases, the intention is to provide a transparent and long-term focus for budgeting so as to facilitate parliamentary and public scrutiny and assessment of economic and fiscal plans. They should in turn reinforce the credibility of fiscal policy, reduce risk, and create conditions for more durable stability.

An unusual aspect incorporated into the European Union's Maastricht Treaty is the requirement during the preliminary phase that the rate of interest on public bonds be no more than 1.5 percent above that of the most stable countries. This limits the acceptable spread between countries, a concept similar to the country risk premium concept for emerging-market economies. Its inclusion as a criterion is very significant, because it involves private-sector evaluation of public policy and judgment of the consistency of fiscal plans. Even more, the "price" of public spending, which in the end is no more than a bundle of investment projects, is the same rate of interest on debt issues by which public-sector activities are financed. If enough attention had been paid to this last point, many emerging-market countries would have anticipated the risks of a future crisis and might therefore have avoided the excessive debt buildup so common in the past decade.

Our view is that the promulgation of this legal framework would be an extremely valuable component of an agenda that seeks public policy credibility and facilitates the development of capital markets, thereby fostering macroeconomic stability and growth. It would be even better if such a framework were embodied in international treaties that included agreements on measurement standards for public accounts.

We offer one final comment on how to make new fiscal institutions credible. In emerging-market economies, credibility in public policies and laws is often a scarce resource. Clear "exit costs" for abandoning the rules are key. There is no unique answer to this problem. Depending on the history of each country, the independence of its judicial system, and the quality of the electoral process for the national legislature, different solutions are possible. In some cases, a law might be enough; in others, it might be necessary to amend the nation's constitution; and in extreme cases, it might be necessary to "buy" that credibility from other countries. Bilateral or multilateral agreements with other countries, analogous to the Maastricht agreement, are a possibility if it is clear what is at stake if a country violates the rules.

Concluding Comments

This chapter has presented an agenda of reforms that we believe would contribute to creating a transparent and predictable fiscal environment. It would not only consolidate a country's public policy management and performance; it would also achieve better integration into world markets, thus improving the country's opportunities for growth.

The discussion has taken advantage of treatments in previous analyses of fiscal policy in Latin America. We have recommended an agenda for action intended to further a wide-ranging process of institutional reform undertaken by emerging-market economies seeking to overcome the acute difficulties of the 1980s and the very volatile environment of the 1990s.

It needs to be noted that many of the reforms included in the agenda have in fact already begun to be implemented, as part of the macroeconomic stabilization of the 1990s. This move toward stability brought a reward: the end of the previous debt crisis and renewed access to capital markets, leaving behind the financing mechanisms of the 1970s that were based on commercial and multilateral credit and syndicated loans from multinational banks.

It is important to stress that the proposals made here are complementary—particularly concerning the procyclicality of fiscal policy, the recognition of debts, the control of public expenditures, the reconciliation of macroeconomic stability and decentralization, the correct design of the tax system and its administration, the budgetary mechanism and its incentive and monitoring elements, and the various initiatives for institutionally controlling fiscal policy. Such an agenda is feasible in view of the widespread recognition that fiscal policy is at the center of economic performance in emerging-market economies.

5

The Financial System

PEDRO-PABLO KUCZYNSKI

Periodic financial crises have characterized the economic history of Latin American countries. Relatively low rates of saving and their corollary, a high dependence on foreign capital inflows, create the conditions for financial crises. An external or internal event, such as an impending debt default or a bank failure, creates a lack of confidence, which in turn puts pressure on bank deposits—especially those in local currency—and on the foreign exchange markets, so that domestic credit gets squeezed. The room for central bank action is limited, because any countercyclical moves are interpreted as putting more pressure on international reserves. As a result, financial crises tend to be prolonged, with costly negative effects on economic growth.

The period of economic reform since the late 1980s should have been followed by a lessening of the frequency and duration of financial and banking crisis, but this has not been the case. In the 1990s alone, there was a major banking crisis in Venezuela in 1994; the so-called tequila devaluation-cum-banking crisis in Mexico in 1995, when GDP fell about 6 percent; and the large devaluation followed by some bank failures in Brazil in 1999. In addition, there were serious strains in the banking systems of Colombia, Ecuador, Peru, and even to some degree of Chile; in these countries, the late 1990s was a period of credit disintermediation and drought for most companies other than the largest. Hardly any country escaped some kind of serious financial and banking problem in the course of the decade. To be sure, most of these problems were the result of, or were closely intertwined with, macroeconomic disturbances—particularly devaluation. But that was not always the case (e.g., Peru 1999-2000 and Venezuela 1994).

The notable fact is that these financial crises and problems took place at a time when most Latin American economies enjoyed foreign capital inflows as never before, at least since the 1920s. For the 1990s, foreign capital inflows averaged almost 4.5 percent of GDP annually, fairly steadily throughout the period. So what has been the cause of financial instability?

Low Domestic Savings Rates and Their Consequences

A central theme in any analysis of capital markets in Latin America is that of domestic savings. The main difficulty in discussing the performance of savings is whether savings rates are simply an outcome of other variables, particularly of the growth of income, or whether savings as such affect income and capital formation. The literature on the subject is not conclusive.[1] Various correlations over relatively short periods are not fully convincing because domestic savings rates move slowly over long periods. Despite these conceptual difficulties, the fact remains that in emerging-market economies higher savings rates have been associated with higher rates of economic growth and vice versa, at least over long periods. Attempts to push up domestic savings may be futile—and may in fact slow growth—but it seems clear that dynamic economic growth does not survive for long unless it is accompanied by a strong performance of savings.

The fact is that gross domestic savings in Latin America are in general quite low. For a reasonably representative sample of countries, gross domestic savings averaged about 20 percent of the GDP during the 1990s (see table 1.3 above), with a slightly declining trend as a result of the recession at the end of the decade. Particularly notable was the fall in the savings rate in Chile, the high-end saver of the region, from about 28 percent of GDP in 1990 to 22 percent in 2000, in large part reflecting the decline in the price of copper.

Savings rates are notoriously hard to measure and are usually calculated as a residual item so that estimates can be inaccurate. Despite the difficulties of calculation, because most Latin American countries are relatively low savers, they are especially dependent on foreign capital inflows to finance their capital formation. These reached an extraordinarily high level during the 1990s; the fact that the bulk of these inflows came from foreign direct investment, a somewhat more stable source than portfolio investment, does not necessarily make them more buoyant in the long run. The turmoil and decline in financial markets in 2001-02 casts

1. E.g., see the review by Gavin, Hausmann, and Talvi (1997).

serious doubt on the sustainability of foreign investment inflows in the immediate years ahead. The obvious result is that Latin American economies may find it difficult to recover and then sustain higher levels of economic growth until the inflows of foreign savings and especially the level of domestic savings starts to recover.

The crisis in Argentina, which blew up in December 2001 with the collapse of the government and the default on the public debt, has further dampened the prospects for foreign direct investment in the region. This deterioration is the result of poor growth in the region, of the financial problems in major countries such as Brazil and Argentina, and especially of the huge write-offs foreign investors have had to make in Argentina. These in turn were the result of the asymmetrical treatment of peso and dollar assets and liabilities (probably $10 billion or more in write-offs for banks) and of tariff freezes on utilities (another similar amount in write-offs for companies in generation, transmission, and distribution of gas and electricity, and also telephones). These losses were so large that they affected the ability of the companies involved to make new investments, not just in Latin America but in some cases also elsewhere. It is a new type of "contagion."

The collapse in private-sector finances in Argentina was preceded by a gradual but persistent deterioration in public finances. Even though the public-sector deficits were not all that large (in the range of 3.5 percent of GDP during the period 1996-2001), the fact that there were few domestic sources of savings to finance the deficit forced the government to go abroad increasingly to borrow at ever higher rates of interest. The ensuing crisis of confidence eventually became untenable in 2001, because the premium Argentina had to pay (over the US Treasury benchmark rate) rose as high as 20 percent and even 50 percent in the final days of crisis. In the end, the Argentine crisis was therefore as much a crisis of inadequate domestic savings as of the public deficit itself, which was exacerbated by the perennial deficits of regional governments.

A key component associated with growth is thus not just overall savings but in particular public-sector savings. It is true that over short periods a rise in public savings induces the private sector to save less (Gavin, Hausmann, and Talvi 1997, 8), but it also seems intuitively true over long periods that if the public sector is a dissaver, it is sending a message that dissaving is acceptable. That message, in financial terms, gets translated into an overly large presence of government borrowing in the domestic capital market, a problem for some of the larger Latin American economies in recent years, Argentina and Brazil in particular. The domestic public debt is relatively high in Brazil; for example, it reached 60 percent of GDP at the end of October 2000. The result—even recognizing that there are other causes of the large pressure of governments in the capital market—is a tilt of the domestic capital market toward government debt, which is tax exempt in most countries. Even though the private sector generates the bulk of domestic savings, in domestic financial markets it is governments that dominate on the borrowing side.

In order to remove obstacles to the formation of domestic savings, it is probably essential, as a first step, to build a solid foundation for public-sector savings—which rely heavily on social security systems in a number of countries—and at the same time to improve the outlets for existing domestic savings. This last point means streamlining and making more efficient banking systems and capital markets, to improve the returns on savings and thus provide an incentive for their buildup.

The performance of Latin American banking systems and capital markets in the past decade has by and large been poor. After a period of high growth in 1989-94, local equity markets went into hibernation in the wake of the tequila crisis; from compounded annualized rates of return of about 25 percent in 1989-94, returns fell to next to nothing in 1995-2000, a period of boom in US and European stock markets.[2] Returns on bank capital more or less followed the same trend, as banking crises followed after Mexico in Brazil and Argentina, and also in Chile, Colombia, Peru, and Ecuador, as well as Venezuela earlier. Domestic debt capital markets were somewhat less erratic but still suffered serious difficulties. Overall, the financial returns on savings have been low, a factor that obviously discourages the transformation of savings into financial assets.

Pension Systems

Pension systems are a major potential source of savings. At the same time, if they are not properly managed, they can become a big source of dissavings when the systems are underfunded and then have to rely on large budgetary transfers. This has already happened inter alia in Argentina, Brazil, and Colombia. In Colombia, for example, the present value of future government pension liabilities is 200 percent of present GDP and social security pension payments are more than 20 percent of the public-sector budget. For most countries, pension reform is an urgent priority, not only for obvious budgetary reasons but also to avoid major pressure toward dissavings in the future.

In addition, there are demographic reasons for pension reform. Because of dramatic progress in health and longevity along with a dramatic drop in birthrates, the aging of populations, especially in South America, is no longer an academic question but rather a reality that is beginning to spread northward from the countries of the Southern Cone (Argentina, Chile, and Uruguay) (see the discussion of demographic data below).

Fortunately, one of the most positive trends of recent years, in the sense of creating channels for financial savings and thus for credit, has been the

2. Data obtained from the International Finance Corporation.

strengthening of pension systems in many countries of the region. This evolution has taken three forms. The first has been the replacement—partial or complete—of government pension systems by private ones administered using efficient financial criteria. The second has been the reform and simplification of several of the surviving state social security and pension systems. The third has been the insertion of both private and public systems into the financial markets of their respective countries and also into international investment markets.

The Chilean pension reform of 1981 was the pioneer in the field and is therefore the most imitated, at least in part. The genesis of the pension reform was a report by a private group of economists in 1972, in the middle of the Salvador Allende administration, that analyzed the serious flaws of the public system. As of the mid-1970s, that system consumed 21 percent of government outlays, with a bewildering variety of benefits and systems. These were replaced by a privately administered system with a number of approved pension fund administrators. The transition from the government system to the private one was initially quite costly in fiscal terms because older workers stayed with the public system while younger ones moved en masse to the private system and took their accumulating contributions with them. In the initial transition years, the social security deficit rose from about 1.5 percent of GDP in the late 1970s to 7.5 percent in the early 1980s, after the new system was in place.

Despite the initial fiscal cost of the switch, there is little doubt that over time the new system contributed substantially to strengthening domestic savings. To arrive at a judgment on the effect of the new system on national savings, one needs to distinguish between the enormous swings in the business cycle in the early 1980s—30 percent unemployment in 1982 would have created a social security deficit anyway—and the long-term trend of savings in the economy in the 1980s and 1990s. By the early 1990s, after several years of growth from the mid-1980s onward, Chile's gross domestic savings rate was the highest in Latin America—27 percent of GDP. This level was close to that of the most successful Asian economies of the time.

That high level of saving in Chile cannot be attributed solely to pension reform, but rather to the whole panoply of measures and liberalizing reforms that made possible rapid growth. The accumulated assets in the private pension system—about $41 billion in 2001, or the equivalent of 60 percent of GDP—did make one very major contribution to the growth and efficiency of the economy in Chile, namely, the creation of a lively and liquid domestic market for long-term corporate bonds and also for corporate equity.

This achievement enabled Chilean companies, especially the larger and more solid ones, to finance themselves in the domestic market at long-term and reasonable cost, in sharp contrast to comparable companies in other Latin American countries, where there has been little in the way of a domestic bond market or long-term domestic financing. By the early 1990s, private pension funds owned about 60 percent of the corporate bonds outstanding. More than anything else, the attempt to create a stable source of domestic long-term finance has been one of the two main motivations for other Latin American countries—especially Argentina, Colombia, Mexico, and Peru—to copy Chilean social security reform. The other motivation has been, of course, to eliminate a big drain on the budget.

The basic features of the new Chilean pension system are simple. All those with a salaried job must make a tax-free contribution of 10 percent of their salary (for the first $1,500 per month[3]) to a pension fund; they have the right to select an approved pension fund manager (*administradora de fondos de pensión*, or AFP), and they have the right to switch the AFP as often as they like (but not before 4 months with the new AFP). A special government agency regulates the investments that AFPs can make and the fees they can charge, within a range; upon reaching the mandatory retirement age of 65 years for men or 60 for women, the pensioner can choose to convert his or her AFP assets into a life policy purchased from an insurance company (the choice for most) or take the risk that the pension will cut off at death (with half the benefits going to the surviving spouse). The system is not a defined-benefit one but rather a defined-contribution one, although the pension fund must meet a certain minimum pension; if it is unable to do so, the government provides a small guaranteed minimum pension, although in fact this guarantee has not been used.

The Chilean pension scheme has both benefits and disadvantages. The fiscal benefits are obvious, as is the major contribution it has made to the development of the capital market, despite the tight regulations governing investments. Only "AFPable" investments are allowed, rated by local credit agencies, and there are limits on each category of investments—such as domestic corporate bonds; rated domestic equities (company shares are rated in Chile); up to 15 percent in rated and liquid foreign securities; and so on. The major advantage for beneficiaries is the portability of pension benefits, a big plus for labor mobility in an economy where the majority of the labor force is employed in medium-sized and small businesses that are likely to change or fold within the lifetime of a worker. Tight supervision of the AFPs avoids abuses of the type that have sometimes occurred in other settings. In the United States, for instance, there have been over the years—despite the provisions of ERISA[4]—well-documented raids of corporate pension fund assets by less-than-reputable corporate managers.

Conversely, returns were poor or negative in the late 1990s. In real terms, the average return for the system was a cumulative total of 3.8 per-

3. Up to 60 *unidades de fomento* (UFs) can be saved monthly through an AFP, tax exempt. A UF is worth about $30 at present.

4. The Employee Retirement Income Security Act of 1974.

cent for the 3 years ended June 1998, or just above 1 percent a year.[5] Before that time, the pension funds had failed to diversify sufficiently, and then in 1998 they pushed hard to increase their investments abroad rapidly, putting pressure on the Chilean peso.

The main criticism leveled at the pension system is its cost, which at about 1.5 percent of assets under management is broadly comparable in percentage terms to that of United States defined-benefit corporate pension plans, but at a significantly lower level of income and benefits.[6] To avoid a price war in financial services, the pension fund legislation limits price competition among AFPs; to attract clients, therefore, the AFPs employ an army of salespeople (18,000 in 1998). Turnover of clients is high—about once a year per client—and sales expenses represent about 15 percent of AFP costs (plus advertising), arguably a questionable use of resources. As long as the domestic bond and equity markets were buoyant, the issue of cost was not important. But the weak performance of the domestic market in the late 1990s pushed to the fore a discussion not only of costs but of portfolio diversification. If the weakness of the domestic capital market continues, the movement abroad of $4 billion to $6 billion of AFP assets could become a destabilizing force in the Chilean balance of payments, a point of concern to the central bank.

The Chilean private pension system has been one of the country's most successful exports, although as an intellectual export it has yielded few returns other than satisfaction for its creators. Today Argentina, Bolivia, Colombia, Costa Rica, El Salvador, Mexico, Peru, and Uruguay all have pension systems patterned in one way or another on Chile's, whereas Brazil has a number of large individual company pension funds, along the lines of the defined-benefit plans in the United States. These countries followed the system of independent specialized pension fund managers, the portability of pension contributions from one manager to another (a key feature of the Chilean system), and the regulation of permissible investments by a special authority. Most countries did not follow the Chilean example of a sunset for the state system, although a few—such as Peru—are gradually legislating a shift of most workers to the private system.

The results of the implementation of the Chilean system have been highly favorable in helping to develop the local bond market and in forcing state systems to straighten out their finances. The outlook for the pension fund management industry in Latin America appears to be buoyant for a decade or two while populations are still relatively young—although not for much longer—and provided participation rates in the formal labor force start to rise again as more females go to work in the formal sector. The obstacles are well known: delinquencies by workers in paying up their retained contributions, the desire of legislators to give more up-front

5. Superintendencia de Administradoras de Fondos de Pensiones (1998).

6. See Diamond and Valdés-Prieto (1994, 259-61).

benefits to workers before the savings accumulate—as was attempted in Colombia in 2000—excessive regulation of investments (Mexican retirement funds, known as AFORES, are still not allowed to invest in equities).

The worst danger comes from governments trying to stuff their bonds into pension funds, as happened in Argentina in the late 1990s and in the period 2000-01, thereby effectively bankrupting the pension system once the government defaulted on its public debt at the end of 2001. The outlook for the pension system—both public and private—in Argentina is at best guarded because, even if the state resumes service on its debt in some form at some point, a probably irreparable breach of trust has occurred. Pensioners have longer memories than bank lenders, because they do not have lenders' write-offs.

Projections by observers of the field (the principal one of whom is José García-Cantera at Citibank/Salomon Smith Barney) show that the assets under management of the main Latin American private pension funds are expected to rise rapidly, from about 20 percent of GDP in 2001 to 38 percent in 2015 (table 5.1). The projections for Argentina are obviously highly uncertain. Even leaving out Argentina, the assets under management would reach about $700 billion, or 39 percent of the GDP of the countries involved.

The evolution and improvement of pension systems is perhaps the most important development in Latin American financial development since the scrapping of interest controls and differential reserve requirements in the 1980s. In a sense, it was high time these improvements took place. Because population growth rates are falling off sharply everywhere, especially in southern South America, there is a danger—if nothing is done—that Latin America could become the region of the world that grows old before it grows up. It is estimated that in 2050, 22 percent of the population of Latin America will be 60 years of age or higher, compared with 8 percent today. More telling, that percentage compares with 16 percent in North America today. Although today 11 working-age persons support 1 person 65 or older in Latin America, that ratio is expected to be 4 to 1 in 2050—a major deterioration. Pension fund reform is therefore a high priority if pension systems are to be viable.

To maximize the benefit for capital market development of growth in the next two or three decades, pension systems—today mostly private systems—must secure better integration of pension management, life insurance, and credit systems. The link between the first two is already developing, as potential pensioners take out life insurance annuities in lieu of pension benefits. But the third variable really needs to be developed; the pool of contributors to pension funds is potentially one of the most reliable groups of potential recipients of credit that exists. Yet banks, many of which are direct or indirect owners of pension management companies, have so far made only limited efforts to harness this pool of potential borrowers. Once they do so, there could be a revival of consumer and mortgage credit on a far more solid footing than existed in the 1990s.

Table 5.1 Projected assets of private pension funds, selected Latin American countries, 1999-2015

	Assets under management (billions of US dollars at current prices)				Assets as a percent of GDP			
Country	**1999, actual**	**2001, estimate**	**2005, projected**	**2015, projected**	**1999**	**2001**	**2005**	**2015**
Argentina	16.8	26.1	55.2	181.4	5.9	8.7	16.4	34.6
Bolivia	0.6	1.7	4.3	9.0	7.6	17.1	34.1	44.7
Brazil	68.3	87.0	118.4	282.0	13.2	13.9	16.0	24.5
Chile	34.5	40.8	59.5	126.8	51.4	56.2	68.7	98.9
Colombia	2.9	5.0	11.7	58.3	3.4	5.9	11.9	37.9
Mexico	18.4	38.6	67.0	196.5	3.8	6.4	9.8	21.4
Peru	2.4	3.7	7.8	27.5	4.7	6.9	12.3	29.4
Uruguay	0.6	1.0	1.8	5.1	2.9	4.4	7.2	13.4
Total/average	**144.6**	**203.8**	**325.9**	**886.5**	**19.8**	**20.0**	**24.4**	**37.7**

Source: Salomon Smith Barney, *Private Pension Funds in Latin America, 2000 Update.*

Banking Systems

If savings are a key—but only partially explained—symptom of macroeconomic health, then a sound and dynamic banking system is a crucial—if not the only key—ingredient of financial health. At one end, capital markets cannot exist without banks to finance their operations; at the other, medium-sized and small businesses, which provide the bulk of employment, cannot thrive unless they have access to credit at a reasonable cost and at a maturity which is realistic for them.

Unfortunately, on both these counts but especially on the second one, Latin American banking systems have failed dismally, with few exceptions. The basic reason for this failure has been the behavior of governments, which nationalized banking systems (Mexico in 1982) or put in regulations and controls that amount to nationalization (Argentina, 2001; Peru, 1987; Chile, 1982; and Ecuador, 2000). The result has been a culture of risk aversion, which banks try to protect through oligopolistic behavior. Competition among banks is limited, except for top corporate clients. For other clients, it is rare to see major competition, especially after the disasters in a number of countries in the 1990s in what were once seen as potential growth areas, such as consumer credit.

The building up of a competitive and dynamic banking system is a long-term task that requires a series of pedestrian steps such as better-informed banking supervision, credit information, changes in regulations (which discriminate in favor of holdings of government paper), and other steps reviewed below. This is not a glamorous agenda. In the meantime, the central problem of banking systems in Latin America other than Chile and Uruguay is low coverage; in Argentina, for example, even before the crisis only 10 percent of the adult population had a bank account.

On the asset side, commercial banks focus on the larger companies. The forays into consumer finance during the boom years of the mid-1990s ended with big losses in the late 1990s in countries as diverse as Argentina, Chile, and Peru. In Mexico, mortgages, credit cards, and consumer credit essentially shut down after 1995 for several years, for default rates reached more than 90 percent after the devaluation.

A key ingredient in widening the credit and deposit base is lower inflation. Most countries in Latin America have made significant progress here in recent years (table 5.2), but some inflationary expectations persist in the wake of the Argentine crisis. Lower inflation brings down nominal interest rates and thus tends to improve the creditworthiness of borrowers, especially because inflation tends to reduce the real incomes of poor people and of smaller enterprises that have no pricing power.

If lower inflation is combined with improved confidence in the political and economic outlook, the decline in interest rates can be dramatic. In Peru, for example, once the political outlook clarified for a time after the

Table 5.2 Inflation in selected Latin American countries, 1995-2002 (average annual percent change in consumer price index)

Country	Average for 1995-99	2000	2001	2002, estimate
Argentina	0.8	–0.9	–1.1	40.0
Brazil	9.0	7.0	6.8	7.3
Chile	6.0	3.8	3.6	2.8
Colombia	17.9	9.2	8.0	6.5
Mexico	24.2	9.5	6.4	4.7
Peru	8.3	3.8	2.0	0.9
Venezuela	51.7	16.2	12.5	24.9

Source: Country statistics, as shown in JPMorgan, *World Financial Markets*, fourth quarter of 2002 and earlier issues.

June 2001 presidential elections, interest rates plummeted. The interbank domestic rates went from 13 percent (in dollars) and 15 percent (in soles) to 2.5 percent at the end of that year, almost equivalent both for soles and dollars. This precipitous decline, combined with a shift away from dollars into local currency, gradually led to an improvement in the volume and cost of bank lending at the beginning of 2002.

Public confidence in banking systems in most economies of Latin America remains low. There are many reasons for this mistrust, but episodes of high inflation and even of hyperinflation (e.g., Argentina and Peru in 1989-90) are one of the main reasons. As a result, any major sign of political or financial trouble leads to significant deposit withdrawals. These withdrawals in turn lead to credit squeezes (Braun and Hausmann 2002), which tend to be deeper and more prolonged in Latin American economies than in other emerging markets. According to Braun and Hausmann, "credit crunch" episodes in Latin American economies in the 1980s and 1990s lasted longer (2 years) than in other developing countries (1.5 years) and were more intense (Braun and Hausmann 2002, tables 2 and 3). Even allowing for the fact that the debt crisis of the 1980s affected Latin America far more than other regions, the sharpness and duration of credit squeezes in Latin America is notable.

During the past decade, as foreign banks—particularly Spanish banks—sharply increased their participation in local banking systems, it was thought that this trend would give banking systems greater stability. Foreign banks have about half or more of total system assets today in Argentina, Mexico, Peru, and Venezuela, and almost half in Chile. The strengthening of local banking systems was assumed because of the high quality of the acquiring foreign banks, particularly Santander Central Hispano and Bilbao Vizcaya Argentaria of Spain, Hong Kong Shanghai (renamed HSBC) of the United Kingdom, and Citibank. The Spanish banks, in particular, thought that they could expand deposit and credit coverage

Table 5.3 Degree of effective protection for creditors, selected Latin American and Caribbean countries and comparator groups (scale: 0 to 1.0)

Group or country	Degree of protection
Latin America	0.14
Trinidad and Tobago	0.48
Panama	0.30
Bolivia	0.21
Chile	0.19
El Salvador and Venezuela	0.16
Brazil	0.11
Ecuador	0.08
Peru, Mexico, and Colombia	Less than 0.05
East Asia	0.47
Industrial economies	0.38

Sources: Inter-American Development Bank; estimates given in Galindo and Micco (2001) and La Porta, López-de-Silanes, and Shleifer (2000).

rapidly. Unfortunately, the foreign banks have faced a timing problem. They expanded in the mid-1990s, only to be promptly thrown into the recessions of the late 1990s.

The reasons that expectations have failed to materialize are thus partly macroeconomic—as in Argentina, Colombia, Peru, and Venezuela. They also reflect lack of progress in the basic legal underpinnings of banking systems and their supervision.

Creditors in a number of Latin American countries—notably Colombia, Mexico, and Peru—have a low level of legal protection. Recovering the assets underlying a mortgage can take 2 years or more; in 2002, Peru passed legislation sharply restricting the activities of collection agents, a major setback for the expansion of consumer credit. The lawmakers also imposed exaggerated limitations on credit documentation, such as eliminating blanket guarantees. Various studies suggest that creditors have a low degree of protection in several major Latin American countries;[7] this is particularly true of Brazil, Colombia, Mexico, and Peru. The degree of protection in Latin America is on average far below that in East Asia and in industrial countries (table 5.3).

The practical manifestation of this is legislation that protects those who do not pay, and inadequate information from credit bureaus, so banks are naturally inclined to lend only in situations where there are strong guarantees and where the guarantees are easily accessible in case of default. Clearly, most Latin American countries have to change credit legislation to make it more flexible if credit is to expand, especially toward smaller

7. These various studies, sponsored by the Inter-American Development Bank, include Galindo and Micco (2001) and La Porta, López-de-Silanes, and Shleifer (2000).

enterprise. Unfortunately, the legislative trend has been in the opposite direction in recent years.

Another important area is that of bank supervision. Although much progress has been made in strengthening bank supervisors, they are still slow and formalistic, and they are seldom assisted by the judiciary. For example, a bank that failed in Peru in December 2000 was still unsold in July 2001, when a new government came in and ordered its liquidation. The process of liquidation was interrupted by a judge on a technicality, which delayed the process and thereby accelerated the deterioration of the bank's loan portfolio, which hurt creditors and depositors alike.

At present, state-owned banks still account for almost 20 percent of banking system deposits and assets regionwide. The percentages are especially high in Argentina, Brazil, Costa Rica, and Uruguay. Recently, there have been divestitures of state banks, notably in Brazil, with the sale of Banespa (Banco do Estado de São Paulo) to Banco Santander Central Hispano in 2000. State-owned banks with commercial activities continue to be active inter alia in Argentina, Brazil, and Peru.

In Argentina, Banco de la Provincia de Buenos Aires is one of the largest retail banks, whereas Banco Nación is a large but inefficient farm lender whose functions extend well beyond its treasury and paymaster role for the government. Banco do Brasil, the largest bank in that country, performs well below its commercial peers. And in Peru in 2001, the functions of Banco de la Nación, basically a state treasury, were extended to granting retail loans to government employees.

Although these incursions of the state into commercial activities are usually justified by the lack of banking facilities in remote areas, the inefficiencies of these state banks and the diversion of state resources into activities that could be performed commercially by others suggest the need for a different approach, which would emphasize incentives for banks to spread to poorer and remote areas in exchange for government deposits, for example. As part of the process of reform, state-owned commercial banks should gradually disappear and have their commercial functions taken over either by commercial banks or by state treasuries.

The various difficulties faced by banks in Latin American economies—inflation, lack of standardized credit information, legal difficulties in collection, competition by state banks—mean that the risk premium for loans is high, anywhere from 5 to 15 percent above the cost of deposits, and that loan maturities are very short, usually no more than 1 year except in the limited cases where mortgage loans are possible (Chile, Colombia and, to an extent, Mexico and Peru). Maturities are usually quite unsuited to the purpose of the loan, such as capital investments in agriculture and industry that may take several years to mature.

The short maturities induce borrowers to borrow from Peter to pay Paul, causing debt costs to rise and greatly increasing the risks of default. These risks have led to the creation of specialized lending vehicles, such as leasing companies and industrial and agricultural banks, as well as specialized banks for small borrowers (on the model of the Grameen Bank of Bangladesh or Banco Sol in Bolivia). The record of these institutions has been mixed; for state-owned "development" banks, it has been weak, though leasing companies and specialized banks for small borrowers have a stronger track record.

In the end, the only solutions that can promote lower-cost and longer-term credit from financial institutions are those that tackle the causes of financial insecurity: inflation, poor credit information (which accompanies tax avoidance and poor tax records), and excessive protection of borrowers' rights. In addition, greater competition in the provision of credit is also a necessary ingredient—and that is best provided through the development of active and transparent securities markets, especially domestic bond markets.

Domestic Bond and Securities Markets

With declining inflation, except in Argentina and Venezuela, the prospects for developing local bond markets are improving. The ability of domestic borrowers, at least the stronger ones, to raise funds locally outside the banking system is fundamental so as to create a competitive credit market. Unfortunately, in the past, regulators paid too little attention to the local bond markets and too much to local equity markets, which are much more difficult to develop, given the culture of nondisclosure that is ingrained in what are essentially privately held companies. Other than the major banks and utilities, as well as a few major industrial companies such as cement producers, the vast majority of firms in Latin America are privately controlled. Raising equity capital through the public markets is therefore a difficult option, because it dilutes the controlling shareholders, who are permanently tempted to limit the rights of the minority public shareholders.

For these reasons, developing the domestic bond market is an essential first step in the construction of a local securities market. High levels of commercial and political risk in a number of countries mean that investors, whether private or institutional, are more likely to buy bonds than they are to buy shares, which in general are considered speculative. The basic ingredients needed to build up a domestic bond market are well known. As in banking reform, the five necessary steps are rather pedestrian but difficult to organize successfully.

The first step is *low inflation*. High and unpredictable rates of inflation introduce too much uncertainty, even if indexation can partially mitigate their effect. In Peru, for example, as inflation stayed at about 1 percent in the period 2000-02, the domestic bond market—which had been dormant for years—revived rapidly both for the major corporations and for the government. This heightened competition for the banks gradually spurred them to revive credit.

Table 5.4 Selected Latin American domestic bond markets, 2001

Country	Outstanding domestic public debt as a percent of GDP	Daily trading volume (millions of US dollars)	Tax treatment
Brazil	53	400-500	15 percent withholding on interest and capital gains
Chile	7	Negligible	4 percent withholding on interest
Mexico	11	2,000	No withholding; some exceptions

Source: JPMorgan.

The second step is *credible and uniform accounting standards*. There is still far too much leeway in the reporting of basic financial information about the financial health of companies, which makes informed credit judgment difficult. The many subjects that need to be addressed include the rules for consolidation of subsidiaries, the accounting of leasing obligations and of contingent liabilities, and the role of treasury stock (often used as an undisclosed mechanism of control).

The third step is *a level regulatory and tax playing field among competing financial instruments*. In some countries, interest on government bonds is tax exempt to the recipient, increasing the cost of credit (on an equivalent after-tax basis to the lender) for private-sector borrowers. Other distortions include both preferential or discriminatory tax treatment for foreign holders and also regulations (modeled on the Basel standards) governing permissible holdings, which also often discriminate against private-sector issuers and give the illusion that government bonds are safer, when in fact in some cases (e.g., Argentina) the opposite may be true.

The fourth step is *motivated investors*. Here the most important development is private pension funds, which were discussed above. But other investors need to be encouraged by more modern investment regulations; this is particularly the case for insurance companies and for government surplus funds, which sometimes let their funds languish in savings accounts.

The fifth step is *liquidity*. This is a fundamental requirement, but it is hard to achieve in what are essentially small markets (table 5.4). The problem is sometimes exacerbated by a multiplicity of instruments: Brazil, for example, has five different types of short- and medium-term government notes, with a wide variety of maturities. In smaller markets, the lack of a benchmark government bond or note that is widely traded and recognized is an impediment to liquidity and tradability. Withholding taxes are also a deterrent to the development of bond markets, especially if they are high (table 5.4).

Table 5.5 Major Latin American equity markets, 1995 and 2001

Country and market	Dollar index, December 31, 2001 (December 31, 1995 = 100)	Average trading volume (millions of dollars per day)	
		1995	2001
Argentina, Merval	56.9	19.2	20.4
Brazil, Bovespa	132.4	209.2	220.4
Chile, IPGA	71.4	44.6	21.5
Mexico, IPC	192.5	137.7	152.7

Source: Economática, various issues.

If developing a domestic bond market is a challenging and complex task in Latin America, it is doubly so in the case of domestic equity markets (table 5.5). From 1989 to 1994, the heyday of Latin American financial recovery after the debt crisis, the main equity markets in the region averaged a compound annualized rate of return of about 25 percent, as noted above. From 1995 to 2001, however, the growth rate was negative, depending on how it was measured (an overall cumulative decline of 24 percent from May 1997 to May 2002—according to Bloomberg data).

Domestic bond markets in this latter period had a very low average annual return of 2.5 percent (Bloomberg data), partly because of financial crises in various countries; excluding Argentina, the return rises to about 8 percent, still a low number in relation to country risk. The paradox then is that equities showed low or no return but high risk; bonds, conversely, had lower risk and higher returns. The result has been a massive flight from Latin American equities by international investors, which in the early 1990s accounted for the bulk of trading and liquidity in domestic equity markets. Foreign portfolio investors had not returned as of 2002. Only one initial public offering of size has taken place locally in the past 5 years—that of Embraer, the Brazilian aircraft maker.

The depressing trend in the equity markets mirrors that of GDP, which grew only about 2 percent a year in the period 1995-2001, compared with about 4.5 percent in 1989-94. Only a sustained period of growth and especially the prospect of sustained growth—since the perception of the future is the key variable in equity markets—can brighten the gloom in local equity markets. Other changes would also help, particularly much greater transparency in the way companies deal with minority shareholders.

Despite much talk of minority rights and transparency, stock markets and their regulators in Latin America are known for their opacity and arcane rules. A lack of disclosure and insider trading are common occurrences. Such a setting is a major deterrent to international institutional investors, most of which are fiduciary institutions (with obligations to others, such as pensioners, shareholders, and endowments). Without institutional investors, it will be very difficult to restore vitality to domestic equity markets. This is where the development of domestic pension systems can over time play an essential role.

Foreign Direct Investment

Most Latin American economies can expect to continue to be capital importers for a long time to come. But for some, particularly Chile and Mexico, their dependence on foreign capital is likely to decline fairly rapidly; their past problems of external debt are long gone. In both cases, interest payments on the external debt are just 7 percent of annual exports of goods and services. But for most of the other major economies, external debt is still a problem. In Brazil, for example, interest payments are 25 percent of exports of goods and services; the ratio of interest due in Argentina is even higher, at 38 percent. Other countries, such as Colombia and Peru, have more manageable debt-service burdens but still face heavy repayment maturities that reflect past fiscal deficits.

The bulk of the external debt of Latin America, about two-thirds of it, is owed by the public sector, much of it for deficit financing with no measurable impact on productivity or growth. The private-sector debt, other than self-liquidating trade lines, in large part reflects borrowing to finance specific investment projects, sponsored both by domestic and foreign investors. There is thus a significant amount of double counting in the debt and foreign direct investment statistics, because a part of the latter is financed by external borrowing. Unlike the public debt, however, the private debt is directly linked to cash flows that permit servicing the debt. In that sense, foreign direct investment, which acquired increasing importance in the 1990s (table 5.6), and the debt that partially finances it may well be more desirable than general-purpose public borrowing.

Latin America has had cyclical booms and busts in foreign direct investment, following trends in the world economy, in commodity prices, and in other factors during the 1990s, particularly privatization and the opening of trade. The 1920s was a period of record inflows, followed by drought in the 1930s and a new boom beginning with World War II that was followed by the heyday of import-substitution investment in the 1950s and 1960s. The 1970s was a period of record debt inflows, followed by a drought of loans and direct investment during most of the 1980s until the debt crisis started to recede in the late 1980s. Then in the 1990s foreign direct investment picked up strongly, stimulated by reforms in Argentina and Mexico, then by the impending accession of Mexico to the North American Free Trade Agreement, and finally by the large-scale privatization effort of Brazil in the second half of the decade.

Over the years, foreign domination of parts of the economy has been a subject for hot debate in a number of countries. From the 1950s to the

Table 5.6 Trends in foreign direct investment in selected Latin American countries, 1992-2001 (billions of US dollars at current prices)

Country	1992	1994	1996	1997	1998	1999	2000	2001[a]
Argentina	3.2	2.5	4.9	4.9	4.2	22.0	10.5	3.5
Brazil	1.9	2.0	11.7	18.6	29.2	28.6	30.5	19.0
Chile	0.5	1.7	3.4	3.4	1.8	4.4	–1.1	0.9
Colombia	0.7	1.3	2.8	4.9	2.4	1.1	2.1	1.8
Dominican Republic	0.2	0.2	0.1	0.4	0.7	1.3	1.0	0.9
Mexico	4.4	11.0	9.2	12.8	11.3	11.6	13.2	24.5
Panama	0.1	0.4	0.4	1.3	1.2	0.6	0.6	0.3
Peru	0.2	3.1	3.2	1.7	1.9	2.0	0.6	1.0
Venezuela	0.5	0.1	1.7	5.0	4.2	2.0	4.4	2.5
Total for Latin America	**12.5**	**23.7**	**39.4**	**55.6**	**61.6**	**77.0**	**64.8**	**58.3**

a. Preliminary estimates.

Source: Economic Commission for Latin America and the Caribbean, *Statistical Yearbook 2000* and *Preliminary Overview of the Economies of Latin America and the Caribbean*, 2001.

1970s, most foreign-owned utilities were taken over by the state, partly for nationalistic reasons but also for practical reasons—principally that the multilateral development banks did not lend to private-sector entities, a policy that was broadly followed by international commercial banks in the lending boom of the 1970s and early 1980s.

The contribution of foreign direct investment to development and economic growth has been questioned, although often on unconvincing assumptions that fail to take into account other variables that also affect economic performance.[8] Certainly, despite the very high levels of foreign direct investment in the 1990s (averaging about 4 percent of GDP in the second half of the decade), economic performance was poor almost everywhere except Mexico.

But what would have happened if foreign direct investment had been sharply lower? Or is there some way, so far not explained, in which the effort of foreign investors somehow relieves locals promoting their own entrepreneurship? So far, these questions are in the realm of speculation.

For the immediate years ahead, however, there is little doubt that foreign direct investment will continue to be viewed as a key barometer of economic dynamism, whether as a cause or a reflection of it. There is also little doubt that a number of events will tend to depress foreign direct investment. First, the slow economic growth of most Latin American economies will be a damper, and a significant turnaround in growth will be nec-

8. A recent example of this discussion is Carkovic and Levine (2002). Also, the World Bank and other organizations sponsored a conference with the theme "Financial Globalization: Blessing or Curse?" in Washington on May 30-31, 2002.

essary before perceptions improve. Second, the era of easy privatizations is over; a number of utilities overpaid for their Latin American assets in the 1990s, especially in telecommunications and electricity, and the remaining large potential privatizations are precisely in the utility field (generation in Brazil; generation and distribution in Mexico), where the major foreign players have mostly been badly burned. Third, the write-offs by foreign investors in Argentina (probably in the range of $20 billion to $25 billion, mostly in banks and utilities) are of such a magnitude that they have endangered the very survival of some of the companies involved, adding another major downward pressure on foreign direct investment.

To palliate the downward trend of the immediate years ahead, governments will need to do the same things to encourage foreign investment as they must do to promote domestic investment. The requirements are very much the same in both cases. Labor costs (see chapter 9) must become much more competitive internationally, by reducing the large burden of extra costs (particularly severance costs) that are not matched by corresponding levels of productivity. The same goes for infrastructure costs, although they have significantly improved, and credit costs, which the threat of inflation and a lack of competition keep high in several countries. Corruption, especially of administrative officials and judges, is also a major obstacle. Without lower costs and higher productivity, most Latin American economies cannot hope to be more than marginal players in the international economy.

6

Monetary Policy and Exchange Rates: Guiding Principles for a Sustainable Regime

LILIANA ROJAS-SUAREZ

During the past three decades, experiments with alternative exchange rate regimes have not been in short supply in Latin America. Mexico typifies this "search for an optimal regime." Since the beginning of its 1987 International Monetary Fund program, Mexico has moved from a peg, to a crawling peg, to a widening band and, after the tequila crisis of 1994, to a flexible exchange rate system. Brazil is another good example. In the 1990s, the country has tried a peg, a crawling band and, in January 1999, moved to a flexible exchange rate system. Both Brazil and Mexico complemented their move toward increased exchange rate flexibility with inflation targeting. Moreover, in the context of one of the deepest financial crises in recent Latin American history, in early 2002 Argentina abandoned its 10-year-old currency board and moved to a managed floating regime.[1]

Liliana Rojas-Suarez is a senior adviser at the Inter-American Development Bank and a nonresident fellow at the Center for Global Development. *This chapter has benefited from the excellent research assistance of Trond Augdal and Josh Catlin, which is greatly appreciated. The remaining errors are, of course, my own.*

1. In 2002, two other Latin American countries, Venezuela and Uruguay, moved toward increased flexibility in their exchange rate systems; the latter did so following the contagion effects in its financial system from the crisis in Argentina.

This is not to say that all countries have moved in the direction of increased flexibility. Indeed, after trying a variety of pegs, multiple exchange rate systems, and the like during the 1980s and 1990s, Ecuador took the ultimate step in abandoning flexibility: in 2000, the country adopted the US dollar as its medium of exchange. And in 2001, El Salvador joined another Central American country, Panama, and dollarized its economy.

Table 6.1 illustrates the evolution of exchange rate systems in a number of Latin American countries. As the table shows, the region has moved through the entire spectrum of exchange rate regimes from 1970 to 2002. It is noteworthy, however, that while in the 1970s and the 1980s most countries followed a form of peg, the number of countries that are reported by the IMF to be "floaters" has increased significantly during the early 2000s.[2]

Throughout the region, most cases of drastic changes in exchange rate regimes have been accompanied by severe exchange rate crises and (with a few exceptions) severe banking crises.[3] Two interesting questions arise from this fact. After a major devaluation of an exchange rate that had become unsustainable, what led to changing the regime? How was the new regime chosen?

Two main factors appear to explain the choice of a new regime. The first is related to the evolving constraints imposed on Latin American policymakers by international capital markets. The second is the disillusionment with the effectiveness of the existing regime in achieving domestic objectives—in the late 1980s and early 1990s, disillusionment with the performance of central banks in achieving price stability, and in the late 1990s, disillusionment with the capacity of Latin American governments to prevent speculative attacks on their currencies.

The well-known proposition of the Impossible Trinity (i.e., the impossibility of simultaneously fixing the exchange rate, setting domestic interest rates, and having perfect capital mobility) can help to explain the

2. Recent empirical evidence shows that there are significant differences between the exchange rate regime officially reported by countries and the actual system that dominates transactions in foreign exchange (see Calvo and Reinhart 2002; Reinhart and Rogoff 2002). E.g., during the 1980s, in a number of countries classified as having pegs, a large fraction of foreign exchange transactions took place in the parallel exchange rate market. Likewise, in the 1990s, a number of countries that were classified by the International Monetary Fund as having flexible exchange rate regimes displayed significant "smoothing" of exchange rate fluctuations either through central bank intervention in the foreign exchange markets or through the use of interest rate policy. However, though Latin American countries may be "less clean" floaters than industrial economies, in my view the recent movement away from a precommitted exchange rate (or band) has helped countries in the region to avoid speculators' "safe bets" against their currencies.

3. The most important exceptions are Colombia and Chile. Both countries moved from exchange rate bands to flexible exchange rate systems in 1998 without either a currency or a banking crisis. In addition, El Salvador's dollarization in 2000 did not follow an exchange rate crisis. Brazil's devaluation in 1999 was not accompanied by a banking crisis.

Table 6.1 Evolution of exchange rate systems in selected Latin American countries, 1970-2002

	1970-74	1975-79	1980-84	1985-89	1990-94	1995-99	2000-02
Argentina	Peg	Crawling peg	Adjustable peg	Managed float	Peg; currency board	Currency board	Currency board; managed float
Bolivia	Peg	Peg	Peg	Managed float	Managed float	Managed float	Managed float
Brazil	Exchange rate indexed to inflation (real exchange rate targeting)	Exchange rate indexed to inflation (real exchange rate targeting)	Mini devaluations based on price differentials	Mini devaluations based on price differentials	Managed peg	Band; float	Float
Chile	Peg	Crawling peg; peg	Peg; crawling peg	Crawling peg	Crawling peg	Crawling band; float	Float
Colombia	Crawling peg	Crawling peg	Crawling peg	Crawling peg	Crawling peg; exchange rate band	Crawling band	Float
Ecuador	Dual exchange rate system	Dual exchange rate system	Multiple exchange rate markets	Multiple exchange rate markets	Dual exchange rate system	Dual exchange rate system	Dollarization
Mexico	Peg	Peg	Peg; managed peg	Managed peg	Crawling peg; float	Float	Float
Peru	Peg	Peg	Peg	Peg	Float	Float	Managed float
Venezuela	Peg	Peg	Peg	Multiple exchange rate markets	Managed peg	Peg; bands; crawling band	Crawling band; managed float

Note: System reported is the predominant one during the period considered.

Sources: IMF, *International Financial Statistics Exchange Arrangements and Exchange Restrictions* (various issues); Frieden and Stein (2001).

Table 6.2 "Typical" evolution of monetary policy in Latin America

Time frame	Domestically determined monetary policy	Fixed or managed exchange rates	"Freer" capital mobility
1970s debt crisis to mid-1980s	Yes	Yes	No
Late 1980s to mid-1990s	No, in most countries	Yes, in most countries[a]	Some (Brady Plan)
Late 1990s to early 2000s	Many as intermediate target	No	Yes, extensive use of private and public bond issuance in the international capital markets; elimination of restrictions to foreign direct investment, etc.
	No	Dollarization, and Argentina's currency board (abandoned in 2002)	

a. Peru is a notable exception. Departing from the "Latin American consensus" of the early 1990s, the authorities adopted a flexible exchange rate system in 1990. Bolivia adopted flexibility as early as 1985.

evolution of exchange rate regimes and their corresponding monetary policy frameworks (table 6.2).[4] Through the debt crisis of 1982 and up to the implementation of the Brady Plan in 1989-90, a number of countries had in place stringent and comprehensive capital controls on a variety of foreign flows. These included, for example, restrictions on foreign direct investment in domestic banking systems and other sectors of the economy, as well as strict limitations on the investment of domestic residents in foreign assets. A number of other controls on capital outflows during part of the 1980s also attempted to limit the sharp pressures on the exchange rate that developed in the context of inconsistent macroeconomic policies. During this period, fixed exchange rate regimes (or managed pegs) coexisted with domestically determined monetary policies.[5]

However, independent monetary policies—namely, the ability to set domestic interest rates without being restricted by the behavior of international interest rates—by no means implied independent central banks. Indeed, a typical feature of the 1970s and 1980s was the bad management of monetary policies that implied the monetization of fiscal deficits. Although monetary policies were not constrained by the international capital markets, they were slaves of the fiscal authorities. The well-known result was long and repetitive episodes of high inflation or hyperinflation and unsustainable exchange rate parities.

4. Of course, I am using this framework only as an analytical tool to organize stylized facts.

5. See Mathieson and Rojas-Suarez (1993) for a comprehensive discussion of issues related to the liberalization of capital accounts in developing countries.

The Brady Plan, aimed at ending the "paralysis" in Latin America that followed the 1982 debt crisis, imposed new constraints on the region. As part of the newly designed programs to revitalize the region's economies (starting with Mexico in 1989), structural reforms included financial market and capital account liberalization. With renewed access to international capital markets facilitated by the securitization of their external liabilities, many (but not all) countries decided to accept the restrictions of "freer" capital mobility.[6] This meant that a government could no longer have both an independent monetary policy and a fixed exchange rate system.

For many countries, the choice of exchange rate regime in the late 1980s and early 1990s was not difficult (it was even obvious to many). On the basis of the argument that monetary anchors had failed to achieve price stability, the exchange rate was perceived as the best (and only) anchor for inflation. The central idea was that lacking credibility on its own, a central bank could "borrow" the credibility of the currency to which it was pegging.[7] The popularity of exchange-rate-based stabilization programs during the 1980s and early 1990s (i.e., pegs, crawling pegs, and bands) followed.

Conquering inflation (the median inflation rate for the region declined from 32 percent in 1990 to 14 percent in 1994), however, did not prevent the eruption of exchange rate crises and the emergence of significant disturbances in domestic banking systems in the mid- and late 1990s.[8] The severe consequences of the so-called twin crises, in terms of fiscal costs and output losses, led to renewed disillusionment about the ability of policymakers to prevent speculative attacks on announced exchange rate regimes.

Once more, many countries had to rethink the right combination of policies. As the region had become increasingly dependent on portfolio capital inflows, countries discarded either reverting toward (for those who had eliminated them) or increasing (for those who had some in place) capital controls.[9] In the context of continuous developments in securitization tools and techniques, policymakers in Latin America made extensive use of "financial technology" in the international capital markets during the 1990s to actively manage the maturity and currency structure of their external liabilities. In this environment, there was a new

6. Notice that the two countries most cited in Latin America as representatives of the benefits and costs of capital controls are Chile and Colombia; these countries did not have a "Brady Plan."

7. Theoretical papers to support this argument abound. For a discussion on the dynamics of economic activity after the implementation of an exchange rate anchor, see Calvo and Vegh (1999). Central banks in many Latin American countries implemented the prescription; e.g., see Carstens and Werner (1999).

8. During this period, the four larger economies in Latin America experienced a severe exchange rate and/or banking crisis: Mexico, 1994-95; Argentina, 1995; Venezuela, 1994; and Brazil, 1999. For a comprehensive analysis of banking crises in Latin America, see Rojas-Suarez and Weisbrod (1995) and Hausmann and Rojas-Suarez (1996).

9. Even Chile began gradually to dismantle capital controls.

dilemma: How could a country continue advancing with a credible anti-inflationary policy while avoiding speculative attacks? Not much was left in the policymakers' toolbox; the monetary-based anchor had failed in the early and mid-1980s, and the exchange rate anchor proved unsustainable in the mid- and late 1990s.

Facing this realization, this time around, countries did not follow a common prescription. Instead, two polar views emerged in the region. The first view encompassed those who believe that the answer rests in directly targeting the final objective (inflation) while letting the exchange rate fluctuate: the so-called inflation targeters.[10] The second view was held by those who believe that the best way to avoid inflation and speculative attacks is to get rid of the domestic currency altogether (i.e., dollarization). At the time of this writing, the inflation targeters included Brazil and Mexico, the two largest economies in the region, as well as most medium-sized economies. The dollarizers included smaller countries (Ecuador, Panama, and El Salvador).

From 1990 to 2001, there was also a third group, whose only member was Argentina. It chose a currency board, implying that the solution was to get rid of monetary policy but preserve the circulation of the domestic currency together with US dollars. Regardless of the merits of such a regime, the dramatic collapse of Argentina's currency board in early 2002 in the midst of a severe economic, political, and financial crisis (which might rank as the deepest and most costly in Latin American history) essentially has eliminated this regime from the viable alternatives for the region.

But can either of the remaining current regimes be sustainable? Has not the experience of Ecuador since 2000 demonstrated that dollarization is no panacea? Did not the sharp deterioration of Brazil's international creditworthiness in mid-2002 show that increased exchange rate flexibility cannot fully insulate a country from external shocks? Because external and domestic conditions evolve continuously, an exchange rate regime that works in one country at a certain time may prove inappropriate in another country or at a different time.

The central issue is not whether there is an *optimal monetary/exchange rate regime* for all countries in Latin America *at all times*, because there is none.[11] Instead, the relevant question is to identify the regime that is most appropriate at a certain time, given the constraints faced by the country. Identifying constraints on the sustainability of an exchange rate regime is thus the key. Implementing policies to eliminate these constraints would

10. By construction of the framework, inflation targeting along with increased flexibility of exchange rates implies that the central bank is allowed to intervene to control drastic changes in the exchange rate if those changes are deemed to conflict with the targeted inflation rate (or range).

11. This, of course, means that I agree with Frankel's (1999, 1) statement that "no single currency regime is right for all countries or at all times."

increase a country's set of feasible regimes and would prevent the sudden and disruptive forced abandonment of the chosen regime.

The rest of this chapter deals with these issues and provides policy recommendations,[12] in three steps. First, it identifies how the constraints imposed by international capital markets set limits on the effectiveness of alternative monetary and exchange rate policy regimes in Latin America. Second, it identifies the necessary preconditions to make alternative regimes sustainable. Third, policy recommendations are offered, on the basis of whether countries in the region meet the requirements for regime sustainability.

Understanding the External Constraints Facing Latin America in Conducting Monetary Policy

As was stated above, the process of international securitization of government (and private, but to a much more limited extent) debt that started in the late 1980s with the emergence of Brady Bonds has had important consequences for the choices of monetary and exchange rate regimes in Latin America. It is important to note that the process of international "securitization" is explicitly being emphasized here, rather than the more general process of "financial integration." Although reference to the latter is often used to describe the depth of countries' participation in a wide variety of cross-border flows as well as "structural" processes (e.g., the role of foreign banks in the region), increased securitization refers to countries' growing usage of the international bond market rather than more traditional loans from international banks for their financing needs.

Two basic differences between international bank loans and international bonds are key to understanding the influence of the process of international securitization on the conduct of monetary policy. First, in contrast to unsecuritized bank lending, there is a well-developed secondary market for international bonds. Second, in contrast to internationally active banks, there is no syndication or other concerted arrangement among bond holders to deal with collective action problems in case of sovereign default.[13] The first feature of the international bond market implies that

12. A comprehensive analysis of the pros and cons of alternative exchange rate regimes in emerging markets is contained in Goldstein (2002).

13. However, recent default events in some Latin American countries, such as Ecuador and Argentina, have led private creditors in the international capital markets to endorse the general adoption of collective action clauses (CACs) in bond contracts. By imposing a majority rule on bond creditors, CACs would solve the collective action problem that arises when a government decides to default on its debt payments. This problem translates into holdouts by a minority of creditors that can delay debt resolution and prevent sovereign debtors from regaining access to international capital markets. See European, Japanese, Latin American, and US Shadow Financial Regulatory Committees, *Joint Statement: Reforms in the Process of Restructuring International Sovereign Debt*, October 7, 2002; www.claaf.org.

any type of news affecting investors' perceptions of a country's capacity or willingness to service its debt is reflected immediately in the spread between the yield from bonds issued by that country and the yield from US Treasury bonds of corresponding maturity. Because both bonds are denominated in US dollars, the spread is free of exchange rate risk and is considered a typical measure of the "country" or "default" risk. The second feature implies that there could be sharp increases in the spread following deteriorated perceptions of a country's ability to service its debt obligations because collective action problems may impose an additional significant cost that translates into higher spreads.

When investors' perceptions of risk deteriorates significantly for a given country, the spread increases sharply, raising the country's external financing costs and severely limiting the availability of external sources of finance. Because an increase in spreads constitutes a market signal of the increase in the risk of assets issued by a government, higher country risk quickly translates into higher domestic rates. Because the entire financial system is dominated by short-term instruments, domestic interest rates at all existing maturities are affected. This transmission mechanism is reinforced by the very limited supply of domestic sources of finance in Latin America, which cannot offset severely curtailed external finance.[14] Therefore, in countries with "freer" capital mobility, it is likely that domestic interest rates will be strongly influenced by the behavior of spreads on external bonds, namely, by international perceptions of country creditworthiness. Some evidence of this relationship is given below.

The discussion above serves to illustrate how "default" risk can interfere in the conduct of monetary policy by affecting the behavior of domestic interest rates. My argument is that country or default risk matters—quite a bit. However, not everyone agrees that default risk is important. Indeed, one can argue that defenders of fixed and of flexible exchange rates can be divided according to the relative importance they attribute to default risk relative to exchange rate risk in determining domestic interest rates.[15]

14. At a given point in time, a given stock of debt (both domestic and external) becomes riskier if the capacity of the country to roll over maturing debt decreases sharply. If, following a sudden adverse shock, increased perceptions of default lead to an increase in spreads and a severe reduction in market access, the country's overall capacity to service its existing obligations decreases. Domestic interest rates increase as domestic holders of the country's liabilities perceive the deterioration in its capacity to meet payments. Notice that this transmission mechanism of default risk into the domestic interest rates is valid even if the economy follows a flexible exchange rate system. The reason is that even a large depreciation of the exchange rate cannot generate external resources quickly enough to offset a sharp decrease in the availability of foreign sources of finance. This problem is, of course, exacerbated the larger the stock of debt and the shorter the maturity structure.

15. In analyzing why flexible exchange rates have not been able to insulate emerging markets' policy from changes in international interest rates, Frankel, Schmukler, and Serven (2000) recognize that a proper understanding of this empirical finding needs to focus on the separate impact that changes in international rates have on country risk and exchange rate risk.

The proponents of the extreme case of fixity, the dollarizers, argue that default and exchange rate risks are highly correlated. From their perspective, an increase in the risk of large exchange rate depreciations leads to higher default risk. That is, exchange rate risk is the key variable keeping domestic interest rates high. Their argument is based on the so-called structural currency mismatch between the assets and liabilities of the private sector in Latin America (Hausmann 1999). Thus, due to the long history of exchange rate instability in the region, especially sharp devaluations, domestic investors are willing to lend long term only if the contracts are denominated in US dollars.[16] Because many long-term projects are directed to the domestic market, where transactions take place in local currency, the structural currency mismatch ensues. The existence of this mismatch causes extensive corporate bankruptcies if the exchange rate depreciates significantly. As investors become aware of this effect, their perceptions of default risk increase.

While agreeing that default risk and exchange rate risk are correlated, I believe that the causality runs in the opposite direction from that suggested by the defenders of dollarization. The problem with the dollarizers' argument is that it ignores the initial source of the problem, which rests on the presence of domestic policy inconsistencies. In a number of recent emerging-market crises, large stocks of short-term debt (either domestic or external), sometimes inherited from previous administrations and sometimes fueled by large government deficits, raised doubts about the capacity of these countries to service their debts.[17] As perceptions of default deteriorated, countries found it more difficult to roll over maturing external debt.[18] Large net external amortization payments followed, calling into question the sustainability of the exchange rate and thus deteriorating perceptions of exchange rate risk.

Dollarization does not prevent the deterioration of country risk arising from these policy inconsistencies, because dollarization per se cannot gen-

16. Fears of a sudden sharp depreciation of the exchange rate are also often cited to explain the lack of development of capital markets denominated in the domestic currency. As expectations of large changes in the exchange rate emerge, liquidity in local-currency securities dries up quickly.

17. Notice that a large inherited stock of debt is a problem in itself, even if the government is running fiscal surpluses. The reason is that a sudden adverse shock, by impairing the country's capacity to service its obligations, may require further fiscal adjustments to avoid a deterioration in creditworthiness. If the needed fiscal adjustment is significantly large, the market may believe that it is unlikely that the country will make those adjustments. The Brazilian experience in mid-2002 is a case in point.

18. The problem of overindebtedness cannot be solely attributed to the government. In a number of cases, the problem originated in private-sector debt. However, the experience also shows that, in Latin America, private debt can be considered a contingent liability of the government because, in cases of severe difficulties by the private sector, governments have often "absorbed" private-sector liabilities into the public-sector accounts.

erate additional resources to restore confidence in a country's capacity to service its debt. Moreover, a "dollarized" economy cannot print dollars. In contrast, in some crisis episodes, such as Mexico 1994 and South Korea 1997, depreciating the exchange rate was part of the solution as improved competitiveness allowed for an increase in exports and consequently in needed resources. While exchange rate depreciation was essential, however, it was certainly not enough (see footnote 14). A crucial component of crisis resolution was the large financial packages made available to these countries by multilateral organizations. The immediate availability of liquidity provided assurances to external investors that debt obligations could be met on a timely basis. Perceptions of default were, therefore, contained.

To illustrate the role of default risk, figure 6.1 shows an (albeit casual) indicator of the importance of default risk on the behavior of domestic real interest rates in Argentina, Brazil, and Mexico.[19] The figure suggests a key feature of the relationship between these two variables, namely that in all three countries, domestic real interest rates and yields on sovereign external debt tend to converge.[20] While the domestic real interest rate "jumps" at times of large expected changes in the real exchange rate (mostly led by expected changes in the nominal exchange rate), these deviations seem to be transitory. In other words, drastic changes in the perception of exchange rate risk do affect domestic real interest rates and, at times, may become the dominant explanatory variable, but these effects appear to be temporary. In contrast, perceptions of default risk appear to maintain a more stable and permanent relationship with domestic real interest rates. The three countries in the sample clearly exemplify this observation. Of course, these observations are only illustrative because they are based on casual observations derived from a graphic relationship. Definite conclusions would need more strict statistical analysis.

Yet two important lessons can be derived from the casual relationships depicted in figure 6.1. The first is that the importance of country risk on the permanent behavior of domestic real interest rates does not seem to depend on the exchange rate regime. The convergence of the two variables is apparent in Argentina, where a fixed exchange rate system (currency board) was in place during the period considered, as well as during the flexible exchange rate periods in both Mexico (throughout the entire period) and Brazil (after early 1999).[21] As was discussed above, temporary deviations occurred in periods of high pressure on the exchange rate

19. Real interest rates are defined on an ex ante basis; i.e., nominal interest rates minus expected inflation. One-period-ahead realized inflation was taken as a proxy for current-period expected inflation.

20. Strictly speaking, the interest arbitrage condition implies that: domestic real interest rate = yield on sovereign debt + expected rate of change of the real exchange rate.

21. Favero and Giavazzi (2002) formally demonstrate the effect of spreads on external bonds on domestic interest rates in Brazil.

Figure 6.1 Domestic real interest rates and sovereign yield for selected Latin American countries, 1997-2001

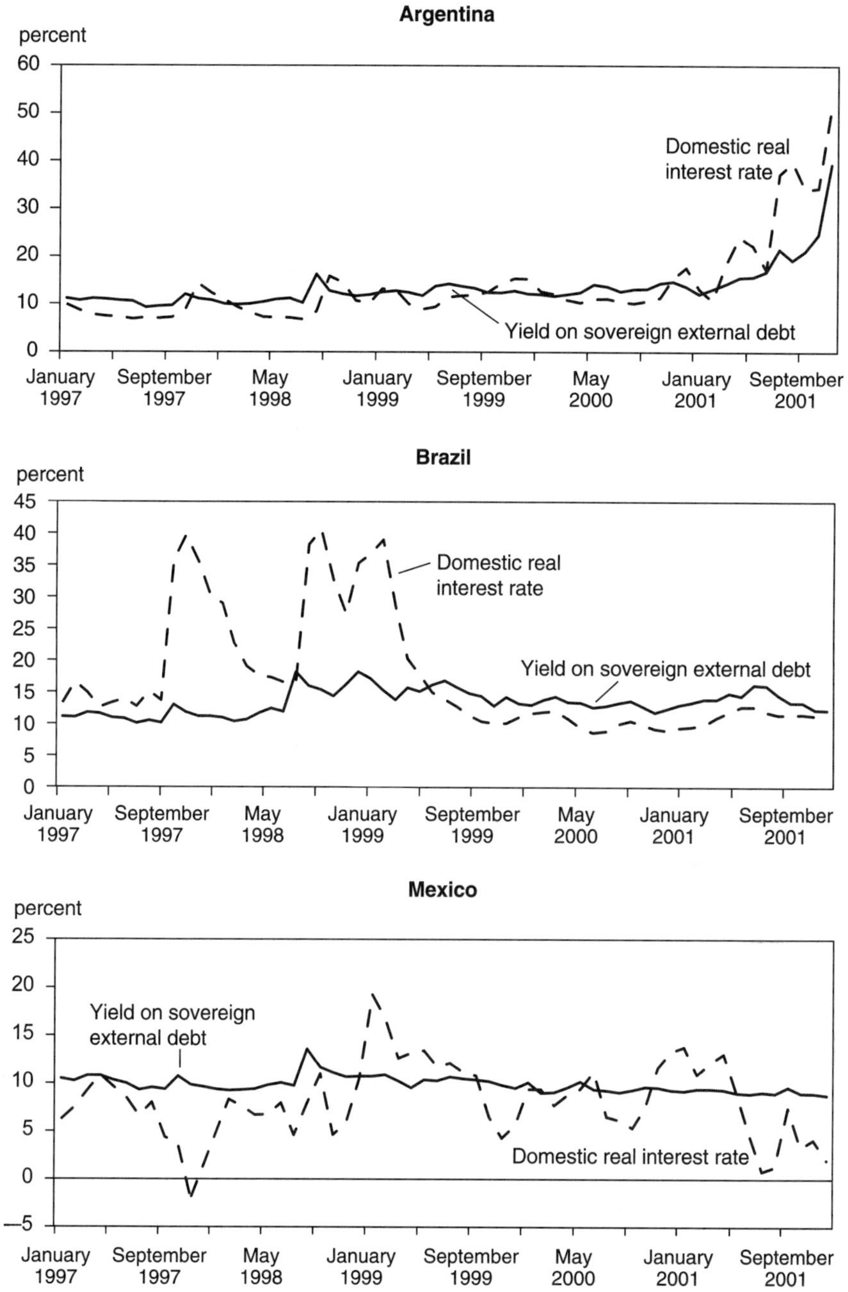

Source: Bloomberg Professional Services.

(Argentina in late 2001; Mexico after the Brazil crises; and Brazil following the East Asian crisis in late 1997, the Russian crisis in mid-1998, and Brazil's own change in exchange rate regime in early 1999).[22]

The second lesson is that, on the basis of Argentina's experience, a currency board does not bring about the expected convergence between domestic interest rates and US rates. Real (and nominal) interest rates in Argentina remained well above those in the United States throughout the entire period under consideration.

In a nutshell, therefore, the effectiveness of interest rate policy in Latin America is strongly influenced by international perceptions of country risk. The main reason is that, in contrast to industrial countries, liberalizing the capital account has not meant continuous access to international capital markets. Sudden and frequent stops of capital inflows are a well-known feature of the region.

Latin American Features That Further Constrain the Choice of Exchange Rate Regimes/ Monetary Policy

Having identified investors' perceptions of default risk as a central external constraint on the behavior of interest rates, it is important to ask what additional features of the Latin American economies need to be taken into account when considering alternative monetary and exchange rate regimes.[23] Two features deserve particular consideration. The first is that many countries in the region are subject to large terms of trade shocks. The second is that the region is not free of "stock problems," as manifested in either actual or contingent liabilities of the public sector. Let us look at each of these features in turn.

In some countries, large and long-lasting terms of trade shocks reflect countries' dependence on commodity exports. To the extent that these shocks bring about a sudden reduction in the net transfer of real resources from abroad, the adjustment to the shock requires an adjustment in relative prices, implying a reduction in the price of nontradable goods relative to the price of tradable goods; namely, a depreciation of the real exchange rate. This adjustment can take place via depreciation of the nominal exchange rate (in a more flexible exchange rate system) or a slowdown or recession of economic activity (in a system with fixed or quasi-fixed ex-

22. The case of Mexico is clearly interesting and deserves further analysis. In spite of the significant volatility of real interest rates, the variable seems to fluctuate "around" the yield on sovereign debt.

23. This chapter focuses only on unilateral decisions of countries to adopt alternative exchange rate systems. Currency unions, which imply policy coordination among a group of countries, are not discussed here.

change rates or one that is dollarized). Which adjustment is more costly? In theory, there is no single answer.[24] However, on the basis of the analysis developed in the previous section, the most costly response is the one that, following the shock, causes international perceptions of a country's capacity to repay its obligations to deteriorate.

Consider first the adjustment to a long-lasting adverse terms of trade shock in an economy under a fixed exchange rate or dollarized system. If the exchange rate cannot adjust, the adjustment will take place by contractions in output and employment and/or reductions in real wages. Consistent with my view that country risk is the most important factor determining investors' attitudes toward emerging markets, long and deep recessions do nothing but exacerbate the perception of a country's reduced capacity to service its debt.

By contrast, in a more flexible exchange rate system, the needed adjustment following the shock can take place through nominal depreciation of the exchange rate. This could at least partly increase competitiveness, mitigating the negative impact on output and employment. This is the well-known "shock-absorber" advantage of flexible exchange rates.[25]

The more open and trade diversified an economy, both in products and markets, the greater its ability to choose among alternative exchange rate regimes. This is because the greater the degree of trade diversification (especially on exports), the less vulnerable will the economy be to terms of trade shocks. In addition, the more open the economy, the smaller the needed depreciation of the real exchange rate to compensate for the shock.

To illustrate this further, consider an economy that has a flexible exchange regime and suffers an external shock to trade (either through a decrease in the demand for its exports or an adverse change in relative prices). The needed nominal exchange rate depreciation to correct for the shock will be lower the more open and trade diversified the economy.[26] Likewise, if the economy has a fixed exchange rate, the impact of a shock

---

24. Some researchers have argued that, due to wealth effects, a sharp depreciation of the exchange rate is recessionary in emerging markets (e.g., see Edwards 1986). From that perspective, a severe adverse shock will be followed by a recession in both a fixed and a flexible exchange rate regime, reducing the differences in adjustment costs between the two regimes. In addition, some researchers have argued against large exchange rate depreciations in open economies with weak independent central banks. The argument is that large exchange rate depreciations may result in an important pass-through into the domestic price level. E.g., if pressures to increase nominal wages develop (to avoid a sharp decease in real wages), the government may force the central bank to increase the rate of growth of the money supply. A cycle of inflation-devaluation-inflation may develop, rendering the initial exchange rate depreciation inefficient and extremely costly.

25. For further discussion of this issue, see Sachs and Larraín (1999).

26. With a larger and more diversified set of exports and imports, the net revenue elasticity of an exchange rate depreciation would tend to be larger.

to the terms of trade will be lower the less dependent the economy is on a small set of export products (especially commodities). Once again, this implies that the necessary adjustment in terms of output and employment would tend to be lower the more trade diversified the economy. Trade openness and diversification, therefore, may help countries alleviate the constraints that limit their choice of exchange rate regime.

The second feature of Latin America that affects countries' choice of exchange rate regimes is what I call "stock problems." In many countries, a large stock of domestic debt and/or a weak banking system (implying contingent liabilities to the government) impose important constraints on the choice of exchange rate regime.[27] Under any kind of managed peg, speculators would perceive a "one-sided bet" when pressures on the exchange rate develop. The bet is that governments will eventually choose to abandon the announced parity (be it fixed or managed) rather than defend it by keeping interest rates very high for a prolonged period. This is because the defense would aggravate existing fragility in the banking sector or increase the fiscal cost of servicing the existing large stock of domestic debt (or both).[28] As a result, speculators exacerbate the attack on the exchange rate when governments attempt to defend the parity.

Will stock problems be less severe if the economy is fully dollarized? This is unlikely. Although no bet against the exchange rate is possible, unexpected shocks that reduce a government's capacity to service its debt and/or deal with a banking problem (e.g., a sharp, adverse, long-lasting terms of trade shock leading to a reduction in output growth) will increase investors' perceptions of default even more than in a nondollarized economy as investors assume that the government lacks sufficient tools (i.e., changes in the exchange rate) to generate the needed additional resources to deal with the shock.

Among stock problems, the issue of liability dollarization deserves special attention. To some analysts, liability dollarization lies at the origin of the problem of currency mismatch discussed above.[29] A number of analysts have claimed that, in highly (but not fully) dollarized economies, the

27. Mexico (in both the 1982 and 1994 crises) is a good example of the restrictions imposed by a weak banking system on the conduct of monetary policy.

28. This is also true if most of the debt is external. Increasing the interest rate to defend the parity would lead to reduced economic activity, aggravating the risk of default. Speculators—aware of the dilemma—exacerbate the attack on the exchange rate, betting that the country would prefer to abandon the parity than be forced to default.

29. Liability dollarization refers to the public's preference to keep a large proportion of its deposits (a bank's liability) in dollars. To avoid a currency mismatch between assets and liabilities in their balance sheets, banks receiving deposits in dollars also lend in dollars, often to borrowers with revenues denominated in the domestic currency. Some analysts argue that though the currency mismatch on banks' balance sheets can be prevented, the overall economy's currency mismatch is much more difficult to prevent. As I explain below, there are certain policy tools available to deal with this problem.

currency mismatch between bank loans (dollars) and borrowers' sources of revenues (domestic currency) calls for avoiding depreciation of the exchange rate because it would aggravate the capacity of borrowers to service their dollar-denominated obligations. Although it is true that depreciation will exacerbate the mismatch, it is not clear that the non-devaluation strategy can do something to improve borrowers' capacity to service their obligations.

Consider a situation where an adverse shock calls for a depreciation of the real exchange rate. Assume that such an economy chooses not to depreciate the exchange rate, but instead goes the recession-deflation route. Is the economy better off? Not likely! Recession will decrease even further the capacity of borrowers to service their debt. The situation will get even worse if the country is facing large external obligations as recession leads foreign investors to also perceive a deterioration of the country's capacity to service its external obligations. As was explained in the previous section, this will keep domestic interest rates high, further aggravating the recession.

Does this story sound familiar? Yes—it is the story of Argentina, which, after a long period (3 consecutive years) of recession, in late 2001 found itself unable to generate additional sources of funding and defaulted on its debt obligations. Shortly thereafter, in January 2002, it officially abandoned the convertibility law it had adopted 10 years earlier.

My view is that many analysts have not focused on the true problem generated by the presence of liability dollarization. Having a fixed exchange rate regime while maintaining policy inconsistencies (e.g., large and unsustainable external debts) is equivalent to the government extending an underpriced guarantee that induces banks to take excessive risks when lending to the nontradable sector. The reason is that the guarantee (i.e., the promise of a fixed exchange rate) discourages banks from internalizing the risks associated with lending in dollars to the nontradable sector. The risk is that were the government to devalue (in spite of its promise not to), the exchange rate risk would be transformed into a credit risk in the nontradable sector.

Because the banking system will attribute the consequent balance sheet problem as generated by unfulfilled government promises, it will de facto exercise the guarantee, demanding the use of fiscal resources to solve the banking difficulties. That is, the combination of a fixed exchange rate and policy inconsistencies in economies facing the liability dollarization problem implies the accumulation of fiscal contingencies that will materialize if the government is forced to abandon the promised parity. At the time of this writing, the Argentinean government was facing precisely this problem.

For semidollarized economies that are willing to maintain the circulation of both dollars and domestic currency, the right issue is how to induce banks to correctly price the ex ante risk of lending to the private sector and avoid offering free guarantees. Although liability dollarization can certainly become a problem and place additional constraints on policymakers, this does not need to occur if banks correctly internalize the risk of their exposure to the nontradable sector.

Can full dollarization help in the situation described above? Dollarization ex post can help to prevent a bank run but cannot solve the fundamental problem of excessive indebtedness because it cannot generate the additional resources needed to restore creditworthiness.[30] In the last section, I offer a proposal to deal with the problem of liability dollarization that focuses on bank regulation and other alternatives.

Pairing Constraints and Countries: What Works Best for Latin America?

The discussion above has identified important constraints limiting a country's capacity to choose among alternative monetary and exchange rate systems. In particular, the analysis suggests that there are strong preconditions for any form of managed peg to work on a sustainable basis. The most important are a strong banking system, the absence of an actual or potential government debt problem, and limited dependence on commodity exports.

The first part of this section provides a preliminary assessment of whether a selected group of countries in the region satisfies conditions for engaging in managed pegs, or even dollarization. The second part considers alternative monetary systems involving more flexibility in exchange rate management for those countries that do not satisfy the necessary conditions for a peg (in any of its forms). The obvious candidate, and an increasingly popular one these days, is the combination of floating or managed floating exchange rates with inflation targeting.

Do Countries Satisfy Conditions for Managed Pegs or Dollarization?

To provide a tentative answer to this question, I divide the countries in two categories: the large and medium-sized economies in South America plus Mexico, and the small economies in Central America and the Caribbean. Empirical evidence for the large and medium-sized economies is provided in table 6.3 and figures 6.2, 6.3, and 6.4. Table 6.3 and figures 6.2

30. One can draw a parallel between the prescription of "dollarization" and "full deposit insurance." By now, it is well known that badly designed deposit insurance "invites" rather than "avoids" a banking crisis. However, when a systemic banking crisis hits, most countries choose to offer a full guarantee to minimize bank runs. Similarly, liability dollarization becomes a problem when it is associated with a free guarantee (the promise of a fixed exchange rate system) offered by the government. This guarantee, however, is risky because the probability of a devaluation remains. As in the case of deposit insurance, when the probability of a systemic crisis increases significantly, full dollarization is proposed as a way to avoid bank panics.

Table 6.3 Direction of trade of Latin American countries, 2000 (as percent of exports of country listed in left column)

Exporting country	Partner country: Argentina	Bolivia	Brazil	Chile	Colombia	Ecuador	Mexico	Paraguay	Peru	Uruguay	Venezuela	Central America	Caribbean countries	United States	Canada	Rest of the world
Argentina	—	0.79	26.30	6.38	0.37	0.42	1.08	1.89	0.48	2.64	0.50	0.25	0.11	15.67	0.80	42.32
Bolivia	13.31	—	19.54	7.54	8.26	3.53	1.54	0.21	5.58	0.13	0.12	0.08	0.02	16.36	0.73	23.04
Brazil	11.66	0.44	—	1.96	0.82	0.13	2.15	1.03	0.50	1.22	1.88	0.35	0.39	23.46	1.49	52.51
Chile	10.06	0.56	6.55	—	1.27	1.16	4.07	0.33	1.96	0.35	1.33	0.49	0.15	18.38	2.11	51.23
Colombia	0.82	0.99	3.20	1.81	—	3.16	3.15	0.02	2.09	0.09	9.10	2.05	1.68	42.80	1.79	27.25
Ecuador	2.23	1.10	1.72	4.17	8.32	—	2.03	0.05	2.42	0.12	3.73	3.54	0.32	34.87	1.62	33.76
Mexico	0.16	0.01	0.70	0.39	0.21	0.05	—	0.00	0.11	0.06	0.27	0.60	0.25	80.36	2.17	14.65
Paraguay	24.37	0.14	30.44	2.73	0.13	0.11	0.29	—	0.29	2.50	0.27	0.01	0.01	12.86	0.13	25.71
Peru	1.81	1.01	3.87	5.59	3.52	1.58	2.56	0.09	—	0.33	3.35	1.59	0.46	28.83	2.20	43.20
Uruguay	21.64	0.06	20.77	2.00	0.25	0.22	2.19	1.69	0.36	—	2.87	0.26	0.35	9.22	1.45	36.66
Venezuela	0.56	0.01	3.90	0.86	3.90	0.69	1.86	0.02	1.36	0.14	—	1.70	0.00	46.05	1.41	37.54

— = not relevant

Source: IMF, *Direction of Trade Statistics,* December 2001.

Figure 6.2 Commodity exports as a percent of total merchandise exports, selected Latin American countries, 1990 and 1999

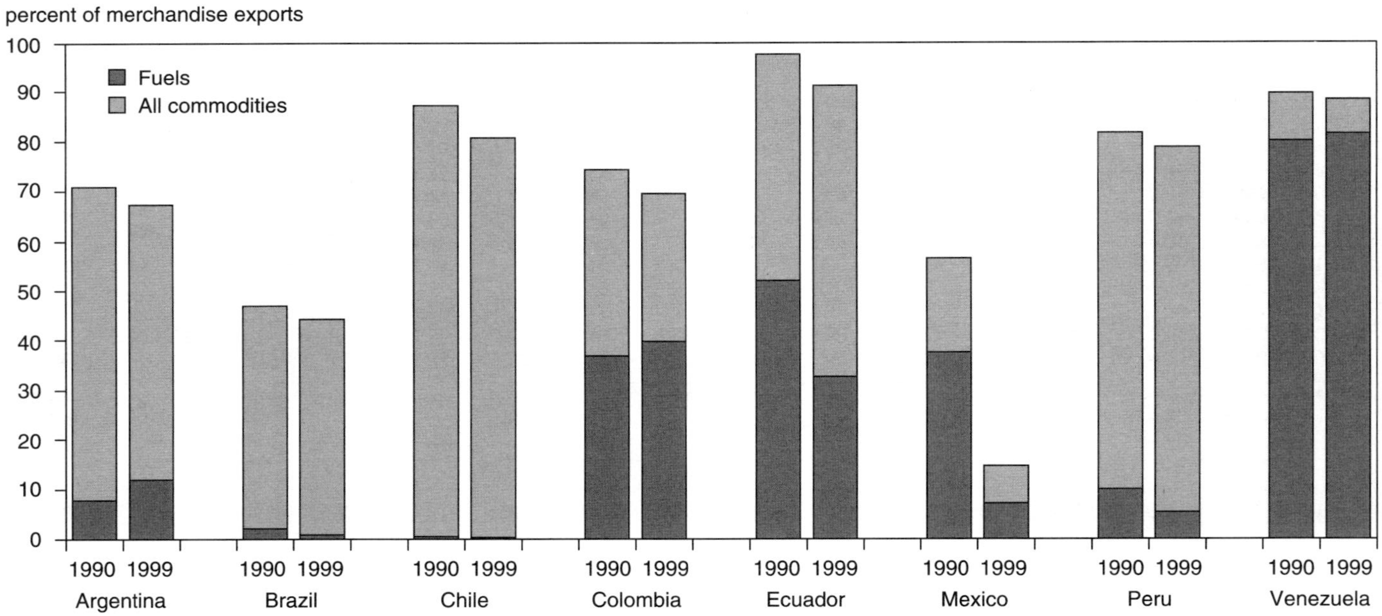

Source: World Bank, *World Development Indicators* (2001).

Figure 6.3 Trade openness of selected East Asian and Latin American countries, 2001 (exports and imports of goods and services as a percent of GDP)

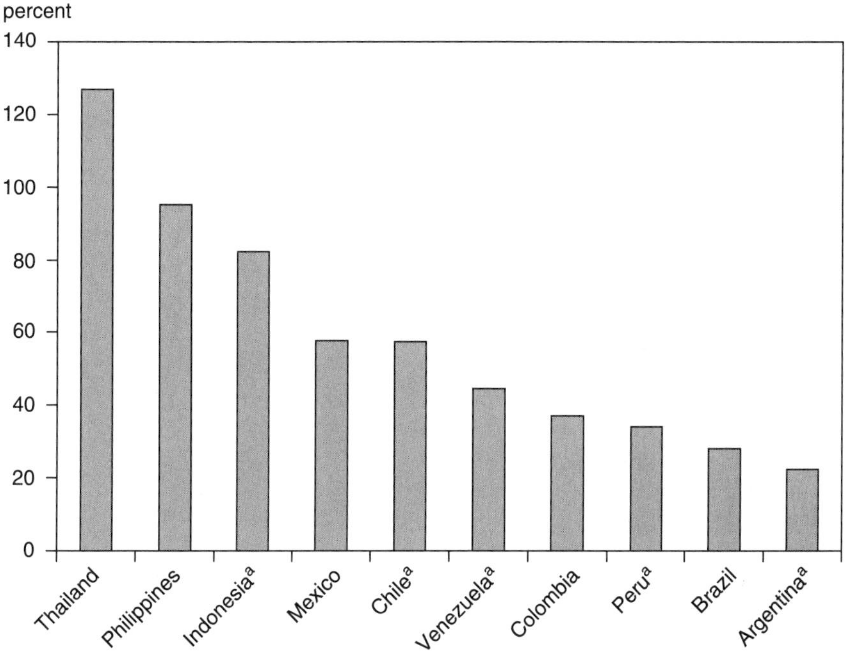

a. For 2000.

Source: IMF, *International Financial Statistics*, June 2002.

and 6.3 deal with trade features: the direction of trade, dependence on commodity exports, and degree of openness. Figure 6.4 deals with the recent evolution of external debt.

With respect to the direction of trade, it is evident from table 6.3 that trade patterns vary significantly between countries. For example, trade between the Mercosur partners (Argentina, Brazil, Chile, Paraguay, and Uruguay) is quite significant. Moreover, for this group of countries, trade with Europe has a larger share in total trade than trade with the United States. In contrast, trade between countries in the Andean Community (Bolivia, Colombia, Ecuador, Peru, and Venezuela) is very small (less than 10 percent of total trade in the community takes place between partners). The bulk of trade of these countries is with Asia, Europe, and the United States. Mexico stands out as the country in the region with the most concentrated trade pattern: its trade with the United States is 80 percent. Moreover, the share of Latin American countries in Mexico's total trade is less than 5 percent.

Analyzed solely from the perspective of the direction of trade, most countries do not qualify for an exchange rate system in which the domes-

Figure 6.4 Short-term external debt for selected Latin American countries, 1995, 1997, and 2000 (percent of international reserves)

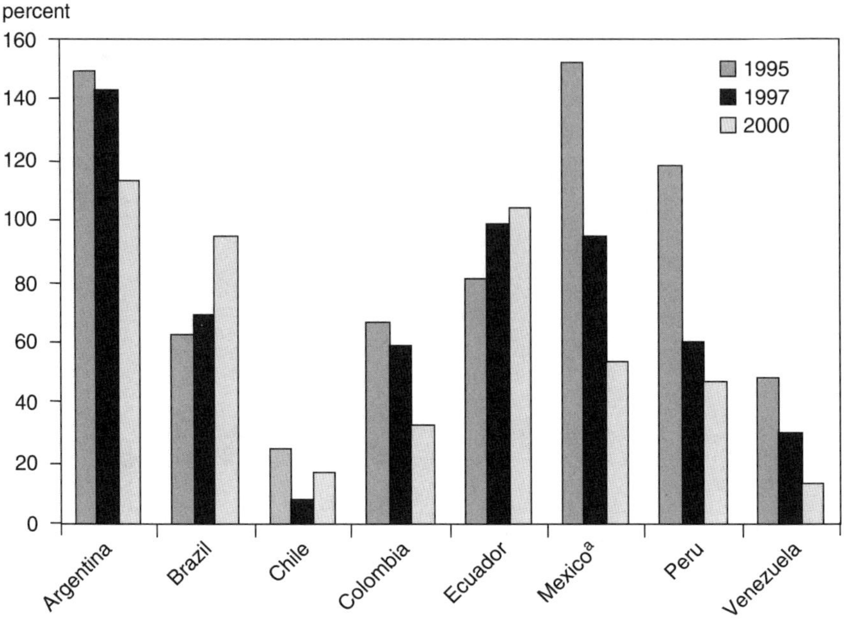

a. First column: 1996, not 1995.

Source: World Bank, *Global Development Finance, 2002.*

tic currency is pegged to the US dollar or for dollarization. The reason is that changes in the exchange rate of a major trading partner relative to the dollar might bring unexpected and undesirable changes in the domestic real exchange rate. The best illustration of this issue is Argentina in the late 1990s, when a convergence of adverse shocks hit Argentina. Two of these shocks are strictly related to the issue at hand. First, the Argentinean peso, pegged one to one to the US dollar, experienced a large real appreciation when the dollar appreciated relative to European currencies (and since 1999 to the euro). This hurt Argentina's competitiveness with Europe, its major trading partner. Partly due to the loss of international competitiveness, Argentina entered a recession and domestic investment declined significantly.

Second, in the midst of Argentina's recession, Brazil devalued against the US dollar. This devaluation implied that Brazilian consumers found imports from Argentina relatively more expensive, while Brazilian products became relatively cheaper to Argentinean consumers. Because Brazil is Argentina's most important trading partner, the Brazilian devaluation hit Argentina by further curtailing its sources of growth and exacerbating its recession. These factors argue against the maintenance of the Argentinean peg to the US dollar in the late 1990s.

Indeed, focusing on the direction of trade statistics, Mexico seems to be the only country that would qualify for a form of peg with the US dollar. However, it is not sufficient to look at direction of trade data to reach any significant conclusion about the appropriateness of a given exchange rate regime. As was discussed above, other key features of the current and capital accounts of the balance of payments also need to be considered. We now turn to these features.

First, consider the sensitivity of the group of countries under analysis to large terms of trade shocks. Clearly, the greater a country's dependence on commodity exports, the larger its exposure to variations in terms of trade. Figure 6.2 reveals two important stylized facts. The first one is that many large and medium-sized countries are extremely dependent on commodity exports. In some countries, such as Ecuador and Venezuela, the ratio of commodity exports to total exports is close to 90 percent. The second fact is that Mexico is the only country in the region that has significantly reduced its dependence on commodity exports during the past decade. Indeed, with a ratio of about 15 percent, Mexico is now much less vulnerable to terms of trade shocks than it was in the early 1990s.[31]

This first observation suggests that most countries in this group are quite vulnerable to terms of trade shocks. Depreciating the real exchange rate will, therefore, be a desirable part of the adjustment process. Given the discussion in the previous section, this indicator calls for more rather than less flexibility in the design of exchange rate systems.

However, can these countries fully exploit the benefits of exchange rate depreciation following an adverse terms of trade shock? Figure 6.3 provides a mixed answer. Certainly, no country in this group can benefit as much as some of the East Asian countries, where the degree of openness (measured as the ratio of exports plus imports of goods and services to GDP) reaches or exceeds 100 percent. However, Mexico and Chile stand out as the two Latin American countries in the sample that have achieved important successes in their efforts to open their economies to trade. By 2001, the ratio of exports plus imports to GDP was close to 60 percent in these two countries. It is expected that this ratio will rise even further given these two countries' current aggressive initiatives toward bilateral and multilateral trade agreements.

The conclusion so far is that although there are good reasons, from the trade side, to prefer more rather than less flexibility in exchange rate systems, few large and medium-sized countries in the region are ready to

31. These conclusions do not change significantly if commodity exports are calculated as a ratio of total exports of goods and services (rather than as a ratio of merchandise exports). This is because merchandise exports constitute the bulk of total exports in most Latin American countries (an average of 84 percent for the countries shown in figure 6.2).

exploit the benefits of such flexibility. Countries should, therefore, follow the example of Mexico and Chile in their efforts to achieve a higher degree of trade integration.

Next, let us consider the extent of stock problems by analyzing the short-term indebtedness of the region's large and medium-sized countries. Figure 6.4 shows short-term external debt as a percentage of international reserves. This ratio is illustrative of a country's capacity to service its immediate obligations.[32] Once again, the results are mixed. On the basis of this ratio, Chile is in better shape to choose among exchange rate regimes.[33] Mexico has achieved impressive progress toward reducing the ratio, and therefore it has gained more freedom to choose between exchange rate systems.

In contrast, Brazil's increasing short-term indebtedness does not allow room for fixed exchange rates and instead supports flexibility in exchange rate management. As recent experience has already shown, Argentina's high level of external debt did not serve the country well in maintaining its currency board. The country now follows a managed float. From the perspective of short-term indebtedness, the current situation in Ecuador does not lend support to the country's decision to dollarize its economy.[34]

Although more extensive analysis is needed, a safe preliminary conclusion is that few large and medium-sized countries in the region fully satisfy conditions for successful pegs or dollarization. Increased flexibility appears to be the sensible (and only?) choice because any form of fixity may be quite vulnerable to a sudden loss of credibility. Indeed, the only country that seems to be able to choose between exchange rate systems in a sustainable and credible way is Mexico, which (1) has significantly reduced its dependence on commodity exports, (2) has dramatically opened its economy to trade, and (3) has made important progress toward reducing the fragility of its external debt profile.

Let us now turn to the small countries in Central America and the Caribbean. Some empirical evidence is summarized in table 6.4. With respect to the direction of trade data, this group of countries trades more on average with the United States than do the large and medium-sized countries in Latin America. The smallest countries, especially those in the Caribbean, are also highly open to trade, with indicators of openness sim-

32. This, of course, does not mean that countries with a long-term debt structure are protected from default risk. Indeed, Argentina had a long-term debt structure before its default in early 2002.

33. Although Venezuela's ratio of short-term to international reserves was low in 2000, the Venezuelan situation deteriorated in the 2001-02 period, when the country lost a significant amount of reserves and the government considerably increased its financial needs. According to market estimates, short-term external debt as a proportion of GDP would reach more than 30 percent by the end of 2002, a ratio almost twice as large as the one attained in 2000.

34. Debt ratios for Ecuador did not improve in 2001 and remained high in 2002.

Table 6.4 Trade and debt indicators of small Latin American and Caribbean countries, 2000[a]

Country	**Commodity exports** (percent of merchandise exports)	**Total trade** (percent of GDP)	**Trade with United States** (percent of total trade)	**Short-term external debt** (percent of international reserves)
Barbados	48.3	105.8	36.8	n.a
Belize	87.3	107.3	39.7	40.7
Costa Rica	34.4	100.9	41.5	72.5
Dominican Republic	20.2	69.3	68.5	186.9
El Salvador	51.6	61.7	48.9	55.5
Grenada	86.6	125.4	32.7	44.8
Guatemala	68.0	46.4	43.6	73.9
Honduras	67.3	99.6	61.6	28.4
Jamaica	27.2	107.4	42.2	71.2
Nicaragua	92.2	122.3	35.2	201.0
Panama	84.1	74.2	36.5	64.1
Saint Kitts and Nevis	26.8	118.1	50.1	4.9
Saint Lucia	81.2	126.2	22.8	86.0
Saint Vincent and Grenadines	87.1	122.8	12.4	56.9
Trinidad and Tobago	71.2	93.4	50.6	61.3

a. Or closest year available.

Sources: World Bank, *World Development Indicators 2002;* World Bank, *Global Development Finance 2002*; IMF, *Direction of Trade Statistics*, October 2002.

ilar to those of East Asian countries. This is, of course, not surprising because the sheer size of these economies makes it infeasible for them to function as closed economies.

However, many of the smaller countries display a relatively high dependence on commodity exports. The picture is less clear when analyzing their debt situation, because some countries show very low short-term external debt ratios and others present ratios as high as those prevailing in the large Latin American countries that have recently defaulted on their external obligations. It is therefore not possible to reach a uniform conclusion for all countries in this group regarding the sustainability of exchange rate alternatives.

Some countries in the group, such as Panama and El Salvador, have chosen to dollarize their economies. For their dollarization to be sustainable, they need to improve their debt ratios and diversify their export baskets. On an overall basis, however, the indicators suggest that El Salvador will be better able than Panama to sustain dollarization.[35]

35. Does the case of Panama count as a successful experience of dollarization? It is difficult to say. On the one hand, this regime has been kept in place for a long time. On the other hand, Panama is the country with the largest number of IMF programs during the past 20 years (13 in total!). Is the choice of a regime sustainable if it depends on continuous transfers of resources from multilateral organizations?

More Flexible Exchange Rates and Inflation Targeting: Fad or Sensible Alternative?

When considering alternatives involving more flexibility in exchange rate systems, it is still essential to keep in mind a major constraint facing Latin American countries: in contrast to industrial countries, open capital accounts have not meant continuous access to international capital markets. For many countries in the region, opening the economies to capital flows has involved excessive indebtedness in "good times" (when economic growth has improved international perceptions of creditworthiness and spreads thus have been low) and a sharp reversal of inflows in "bad times" (when adverse shocks caused severe deterioration of international perceptions of creditworthiness).

In spite of the economic and financial volatility associated with the behavior of capital flows to Latin America, most countries in the region have not chosen to restrict the movement of capital. The clear exception has been Argentina in the midst of its massive 2002 financial crisis. A noteworthy feature about Argentina is that from 1990 to 2001 it was classified as one of the region's most financially open economies. Whether this experience will induce countries to rethink the desirability of free capital mobility remains to be seen. We will examine this issue further in the next section.

The restrictions imposed by the volatility of capital flows to the region imply that a *pure* flexible exchange rate system cannot adequately contribute to economic and financial stability. A major reason is that if inflows were to suddenly cease, a sharp depreciation of the exchange rate would not be able to generate sufficient resources quickly enough to meet due external amortization and interest payments. Without sufficient ex ante accumulation of foreign exchange reserves, both in the public and the private sectors, as well as access to additional sources of liquidity, sudden stops of capital inflows can result in defaults on external obligations and deep economic crises, even if the exchange rate is allowed to float freely after the shock to the capital account.[36]

Because of the need to manage the availability of foreign liquidity, managed floating is a better alternative than pure floating for most countries in Latin America. This of course implies a certain degree of discretion, but this is inevitable in countries that lack continuous access to international capital markets. To be exact, the policy involves a combination of rules and

36. The benefits of accumulating foreign liquidity as a buffer to unexpected shocks need to be balanced against the cost of holding these assets, which are characterized by low returns. Indeed, an important problem showing in the consolidated government and quasi-government balances (including the central bank) of a number of countries is the large interest rate differential between their debt liabilities and their liquid assets. Choosing the optimal level of liquidity is, therefore, no simple problem because it entails important public costs.

limited discretion. An important rule is that central banks cannot intervene to continuously smooth exchange rate fluctuations.[37] The discretion is that, sporadically, central banks can intervene—either directly in the foreign exchange market or through changes in interest rates—to manage their international liquidity position.[38] This policy prescription has been advanced and fully developed in Goldstein (2002). Consistent with the discussion above, it is important to stress that, in addition to the foreign exchange reserves at the central bank, large holdings of liquid foreign assets are also necessary for those institutions that may be required to "show liquidity" at times of difficulty. They are usually banks and the government.

In addition to the problem of volatile capital flows, many countries in Latin America face additional constraints that prevent the achievement of an independent monetary policy in the context of flexible exchange rates. Two of these constraints, generally absent in most industrial countries, are (1) the "effective" lack of independence of most central banks from political interference and (2) significant (albeit lesser than in the 1970s and 1980s) pass-through effects from changes in the exchange rate to the inflation rate. In the face of these constraints, a small but increasing number of the region's countries have chosen to combine more flexible exchange rate regimes with inflation targeting.

As was mentioned above, a regime involving more flexibility in the management of exchange rates and inflation targeting was chosen to send a credible message of central banks' commitment to keep inflation low while avoiding speculative attacks on the exchange rate. The choice of inflation targeting has the advantage of dealing with both the central bank independence problem and the pass-through problem.

With respect to the absence of adequate independence of central banks, this feature constitutes an important limitation on the credibility of any announced monetary/exchange rate policy. Inflation targeting helps be-

---

37. Continuous intervention would be inconsistent with a managed floating regime.

38. A number of analysts argue that an important cause of speculative attacks against the exchange rate has been large and sustained misalignments of the real exchange rate (sharp deviations of the real exchange rate relative to its long-run "equilibrium" level). In this regard, avoiding such misalignments is viewed as an important role of monetary/exchange rate policy. Supporters of this view argue for some form of announced foreign exchange intervention to prevent real exchange rate disequilibria; see Williamson (2000).

It would certainly be beneficial for Latin American countries to prevent significant exchange rate misalignments. However, I believe there are a number of reasons that do not support the implementation in the region of a policy aiming at keeping the real exchange rate at or around its equilibrium level. To give two of these reasons: First, estimates of the "equilibrium" real exchange rate for countries in the region have varied widely across empirical studies; see Edwards and Savastano (1999) for an analysis of the difficulties in estimating equilibrium real exchange rates in emerging markets. Second, because of the problems associated with identifying the true value of the equilibrium real exchange rate, the policy lacks the credibility and transparency needed by central banks in the region.

cause by posting the inflation target directly, central banks' decisions become more transparent and central bankers gain more "power" to justify their policy actions.[39]

With respect to the pass-through problem, this feature still remains important in a number of countries. This element favors a managed floating exchange rate regime over pure floating. The reason is that letting the exchange rate fully float at all times could conflict with achieving the inflation target. The framework of inflation targeting allows for some exchange rate intervention when indicators of "expected inflation" signal a significant deterioration arising from exchange rate depreciations. As was indicated by Svensson (1999), the inflation targeting framework allows central banks to exercise "constrained discretion": while goals for monetary policy are clear and transparent, the framework gives central banks the freedom to choose what instrument to use and when to use it to reach the target.

The degree of pass-through varies significantly among countries. Figure 6.5 shows some casual evidence of selected episodes of exchange rate devaluations and the accompanying behavior of inflation. The figure, which of course serves only for illustrative purposes, indicates that during the 1980s and early 1990s, there was a close association between sharp devaluation and high inflation in most countries. A feature of the late 1990s is that crisis periods were characterized by much smaller exchange rate depreciations. Notwithstanding, pass-through continued to be important in most countries, albeit to a lesser degree, as the crises in Brazil (1999) and Argentina (2002) demonstrated.[40] Even if declining, pass-through is significantly higher in Latin American countries than in industrial countries and in other emerging markets, as has been confirmed by recent statistical analyses.[41]

The experience with inflation targeting in (an increasing number of) Latin American countries has been extensively examined in a number of academic and policy papers.[42] So far, the group of countries that call themselves "inflation targeters" are Brazil, Chile, Colombia, Mexico, and

39. I think that Brazil's 1999-2002 period illustrates this situation clearly. By targeting inflation at low levels, the president of the Central Bank was able (most of the time) to conduct a tight monetary policy, even at times when political pressures demanded an easing of monetary policy. Inflation targeting increased the de facto independence of the central bank.

40. Brazil was a noticeable exception at the beginning of 1999, when the country sharply devalued its currency. In mid-2002, however, there were concerns about the "revival" of pass-through problems.

41. See Carstens and Werner (1999), Goldfajn and Werlang (2000), Gonzalez-Anaya (2000), and Mihaljek and Klau (2001).

42. E.g., see Eichengreen (2002), Truman (2002), Goldstein (2002), Mishkin and Schmidt-Hebbel (2001), Schaechter, Stone, and Zelmer (2000), Bernanke et al. (1999), and Cottarelli and Giannini (1997).

Figure 6.5 Exchange rate pass-through: Exchange rate depreciation, and inflation during the 12-month period after a significant exchange rate depreciation, selected Latin American countries, selected periods

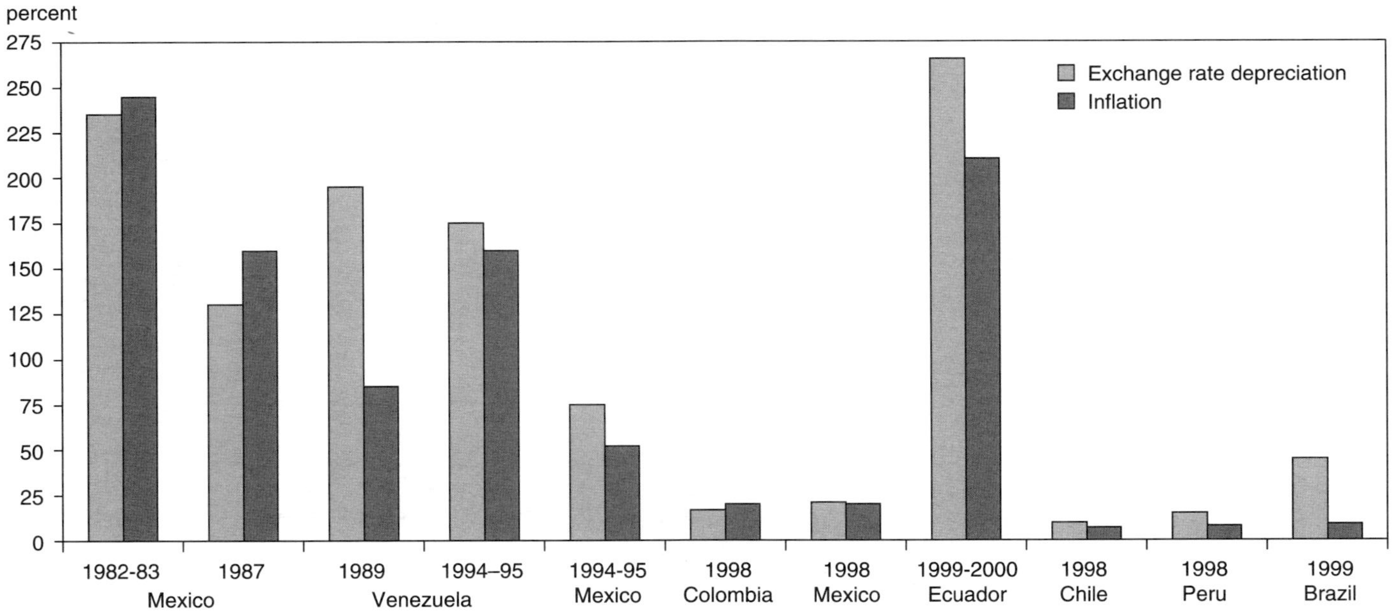

Source: IMF data.

Peru (a small number of countries, but together they account for more than 60 percent of the region's GDP). Although the experience with inflation targeting in industrial countries is generally assessed to be successful, the Latin American experience is still too recent to allow definite conclusions (see Truman 2002).

To summarize the conclusions thus far: Most Latin American countries face serious constraints in implementing their monetary and exchange rate policies. A lack of continuous access to international capital markets, a lack of central bank credibility, and a history of significant pass-through from exchange rate changes to the inflation rate together call for a combination of policies that involve both managed floating and inflation targeting and a balance of rules and discretion. The rule is that the inflation target becomes the main goal of the central bank. The discretion is that the central bank can intervene in the foreign exchange market (including indirectly, through changes in the interest rate) when changes in the exchange rate conflict with the inflation target (or, sporadically, to increase its holdings of international liquidity).

Further Policy Recommendations

Let us return to the question implied in the title of this chapter: Is there an optimal monetary/exchange rate system for Latin America? An analysis of the evidence leads us to conclude that "one size does not fit all," but that with the exception of a few countries, more rather than less exchange rate flexibility is desired. However, facing a set of constraints particular to Latin America, "pure flexibility" is not the right choice. Inflation targeting combined with managed floating, involving clear and limited instances for intervention in the foreign exchange market, appears to be an appropriate choice for most of the region's countries, at least in the short run. Accumulation of foreign liquidity in the banking sector and in government-managed funds is also a necessary complement.

The true long-term challenge, however, lies in removing the constraints that limit the options of viable exchange rate regimes. Not doing so may bring about yet another bout of disillusionment with exchange rate management. As has been noted, Latin American countries need to deal with two broad sets of constraints. The first includes the external constraints imposed by the volatility of capital flows. The second comprises structural and policy-determined constraints related to the independence of central banks, the degree of trade openness, the concentration of exports in commodities, the fragility of banking systems, and the extent of external indebtedness.

With respect to the first set of constraints, Latin America in general has chosen a path toward freer capital mobility. However, at the time of this writing, discontent with this choice has been increasing. By mid-2002, the brutal crisis in Argentina, the increasing problems with debt sustainability in Brazil, and the high cost and volatility associated with the access of most countries in the region to international capital markets were fueling these concerns. Indeed, a new impetus toward finding a more stable motor of growth is developing in the region. Proposals for renewing efforts toward the development of domestic sources of finance (e.g., domestic capital markets) as well as an emphasis on trade integration arrangements (bilateral and multilateral) are being considered as a complement to the instability of sources of funding provided by international capital markets.

What about capital controls? Highly volatile capital flows justify the imposition of some controls on the inflows to those countries in the region that have inadequate systems to appropriately assess risks. For example, financial systems that do not have adequate risk management systems (including capabilities to assess, manage, and supervise financial risks) may not be able to efficiently and safely intermediate large inflows of capital. The experience of Chile during the 1990s provides an excellent example of how a sequential approach to liberalization of the capital account can prevent the emergence of severe debt problems.[43]

In line with the discussion above concerning the limitations on monetary/exchange rate policies imposed by international perceptions of country risk (i.e., perceptions of default), overindebtedness by both the public and private sectors needs to be avoided. Well-defined capital controls on inflows combined with prudential regulations in the financial system can go a long way to prevent the overindebtedness (and its devastating consequences) that has infected many Latin American countries during the past three decades.[44] Indeed, as long as deficiencies in assessing financial risks (particularly credit and market risks) remain in banks, corporations, and the government, capital controls on inflows can be an effective temporary countercyclical tool when the supply of inflows is "too large" (relative to

43. Chile's experience with capital controls has been widely analyzed in the literature; e.g., see Agosin and Ffrench-Davis (2001); De Gregorio, Edwards, and Valdés (1998); and Williamson (2000). Capital controls on inflows during the 1990s in Chile took two forms. First, a nonremunerated 20 percent reserve requirement to be deposited at the central bank for 1 year on liabilities in foreign currency for direct borrowing by firms. The rate of reserve requirement was raised to 30 percent in 1992, and in 1998 it was lowered first to 10 percent and then to zero. Second, foreign direct investment (FDI) was subject to a minimum stay in the country. Until 1992, the requirement was a 3-year minimum stay; the stay was then reduced to 1 year. There were no restrictions on the repatriation of profits from FDI. Further analysis on the effects of capital controls in other emerging markets can be found in Reinhart and Smith (1998).

44. Capital controls in a number of countries have taken a variety of forms, including taxes, reserve requirements discriminating against short-term deposits denominated in foreign currency, and quantitative restrictions.

what the economy could have safely absorbed if there had been no deficiencies in the valuation of risks).[45]

It is appropriate to recommend temporary controls on capital inflows to countries that can use such a policy as a prudential device to avoid the intermediation of large quantities of short-term capital inflows through banking systems that do not adequately assess and manage risks. But it would not be advisable to control capital outflows, especially when they are imposed in the midst of financial difficulties. Controls on capital outflows amount to default because they impose nonmarket losses on holders of assets in the domestic financial system. The experience in Latin America is full of examples when the imposition of controls on capital outflows brought sharp disintermediation from domestic financial systems.[46]

We now turn to structural and policy-determined constraints.[47] With respect to the trade constraint, the policy prescription is quite straightforward. To gain freedom in their choice of monetary/exchange rate arrangements, countries in the region need to open and further diversify their trade patterns. But this goes beyond unilateral reductions in tariffs and other nonprice restrictions to imports. An aggressive approach to both bilateral and multilateral trade integration is urgently needed.

As was discussed above, avoiding a path toward unsustainable external indebtedness is central to allowing countries greater freedom in their choice of viable and sustainable monetary and exchange rate systems. Although temporary capital controls to the inflows can help, the policy is certainly by no means sufficient. The key to preventing debt sustainability problems is the buildup of fiscal institutions that ensure the maintenance

45. The emphasis on the temporary nature of capital controls to the inflows is because this device should be in place only as long as the true deficiencies to avoid overindebtedness—including a lack of adequate mechanisms to correctly assess risks by banks, corporations, and the government—remain in place. This is so because capital controls to the inflows also bring costs to society as they prevent the optimal allocation of external resources into profitable domestic investments. Having said that, however, it is important to recognize that it could be a long time before countries in the region establish and utilize effective risk management practices. In the foreseeable future, therefore, it is a good idea to have in place a mechanism of capital controls for the inflows. Chile's decision to keep the reserve requirements associated with capital controls in place, but equal to zero (in the current adverse international environment with limited access to international capital markets), was an excellent policy choice.

46. Some cases of sharp financial disintermediation associated with capital controls for the outflows are Argentina, Peru, and Mexico in the 1980s and Argentina in the early 2000s.

47. I will not expand further on the constraint imposed by the lack of independence of the central bank because (1) it is largely a political decision and (2) the discussion above illustrates how inflation targeting may be a mechanism to gain greater de facto central bank independence.

of fiscal discipline.[48] It is especially important to avoid contingent liabilities to the fiscal sector. Hidden problems in the banking sector and underpriced government guarantees eventually lead to large fiscal expenditures.

In this regard, we now come back to the problem of liability dollarization discussed above. This feature of many countries in the region has led a number of analysts to one of two extremes. Some argue for full official dollarization of the economy because no currency mismatch can occur if all transactions (real and financial) take place using the dollar. Others, however, argue for exactly the opposite prescription: dedollarize the economy to avoid the problem. My view is that regardless of the government's decision about the circulation of dollars in the domestic economy, important regulatory measures can be taken to minimize the problems associated with liability dollarization. Indeed, this problem is aggravated because of a lack of adequate bank provisioning systems.

The problem of liability dollarization presumes that a sharp depreciation of the exchange rate brings about a reduction in the capacity of the nontradable sector to service its dollar-denominated loans. This is correct; the evidence substantiates this view. The evidence also reveals that sharp depreciations of the exchange rate are a recurrent feature of many markets.

Taken together, these two sets of evidence seem to imply that, ceteris paribus, expected losses from loans to the nontradable sector would tend be larger on average than those resulting from loans to the tradable sector.[49] Exchange rate risk is transformed into credit risk for the nontradable sector. Why, then, do banks in emerging markets not have distinct provisioning requirements for these two kinds of loans? The main reason is that emerging-market countries do not have clear regulations about provisioning, and certainly no risk-based regulations.

This example needs to be taken simply as an illustration of the severity of the problem associated with inadequate loan loss reserves in Latin America. A proper analysis needs to estimate the probabilities of default for different categories of loans in various countries. By providing information about expected losses, the mean of the frequency distribution of loan losses for separate classes of loans should guide the appropriate design of provisioning requirements. The key message, however, is that the problem of liability dollarization can be alleviated by adequate provisioning rules that reflect the risks specific to Latin America.

48. Moreover, comprehensive tax reforms, including establishing institutional changes that minimize tax evasion, are badly needed in many countries in the region. This and other central aspects of fiscal reform are discussed in chapter 4 of this volume.

49. Likewise, a sharp appreciation of the real exchange rate hurts the tradable sector. However, these appreciations tend to occur at times when foreign capital is flowing into the economy and therefore a financing constraint to the tradable sector is not binding. The central message is that provisioning needs to take into account the expected risk features of different sectors of the economy. This involves different provisioning for different sectors.

However, what about the proposal for dedollarization as a way to solve the liability dollarization problem?[50] Is it desirable to induce a dedollarization of financial assets? In considering this question, it is important to clarify that I am discarding forced dedollarization. The experience of Argentina with forced pesofication should provide sufficient arguments against such a policy alternative.[51]

In contrast, creating nondistortionary incentives for increasing the demand for assets denominated in domestic currency needs to be considered seriously. This, however, is not an easy task. In many Latin American countries, creditors are only willing to lend long term if the assets are denominated in US dollars and depositors are only willing to save in US-dollar-denominated instruments.

Two factors affecting countries in the region have contributed to this attitude. The first is the long history of sharp depreciations and episodes of high inflation or hyperinflation in many countries. The second and more recent development is related to the establishment of foreign banks. There is a common belief that, in difficult times, the region's subsidiaries of foreign banks will find it easier than domestic banks to access funds in dollars because of their links to the center.[52] That is, holding dollar-denominated deposits in foreign banks is viewed by depositors as protection against both exchange rate (inflation) risk and default risk.

It may take a very long time before economic agents perceive assets that are denominated in domestic currency as safe assets. The challenge for the short and medium terms, therefore, is to create incentives for savers to diversify their portfolios by increasing their holdings of assets denominated in domestic currency. Alternatives to consider include inflation-indexed deposits and the development of local capital markets with transparent laws on bankruptcy and on minority bond holders. Incentives for offering inflation-indexed bonds may be considered once an adequate, well-functioning capital market is established.

---

50. I have already discussed extensively the opposite alternative, i.e., full dollarization (see the chapter's second and third sections).

51. Although some argue that the problem with forced pesofication in Argentina was that it was asymmetric (i.e., that the conversion of dollar assets into pesos took place at a less favorable exchange rate than that applied to the pesofication of liabilities), I would argue that any form of forced pesofication would have been disastrous for the financial system because it involved a default on preestablished contracts. Indeed, another experience of forced pesofication (without asymmetries), that of Mexico in 1982, ended in a severe banking crisis and in the nationalization of private banks.

52. The validity of this belief needs empirical research. Although the crisis in Argentina brought doubts about the behavior of foreign banks during trying periods, this experience cannot be taken as a representative example of foreign banks' attitudes because the Argentinean government imposed a number of measures that forced foreign banks into decapitalization.

Issues related to the development of capital markets are examined extensively in chapter 5 of this volume. Here, however, it is essential to emphasize that capital markets cannot develop in Latin American countries where uncertainties regarding the soundness of banks persist—for two reasons. The first is that banks, through their access to the central bank's discount window, are the ultimate providers of the liquidity that enables capital markets to function. The second is that bank deposits need to serve the function of "safe" assets relative to the riskier assets traded on capital markets. As in industrial countries, savers need to feel confident that if capital markets become turbulent, they can "flee to quality" by shifting their funds toward bank deposits.[53] If safe deposits need to be denominated in US dollars, so be it. It may be precisely the existence of such safe assets that allows for the expansion of riskier currency-denominated assets.

53. In a sound banking system with fractional reserve requirements, the shift into dollar-denominated deposits implies that the central bank would have to increase its dollar-denominated liabilities (the central bank item: banks' deposits in dollars). Immediately, this transaction reduces the central bank's net holdings of foreign exchange reserves. The final extent of the reduction of net foreign exchange reserves would depend on the degree of flexibility of the exchange rate. For a detailed explanation of the changes in banking system balance sheets following a shift of wealth into dollar-denominated deposits, see Rojas-Suarez and Weisbrod (1995).

7

Making Trade Liberalization Work

ROBERTO BOUZAS AND SAÚL KEIFMAN

Since the early 1990s, the Latin American and Caribbean countries have made remarkable progress toward more open foreign trade regimes. Applied tariff rates have fallen sharply, many nontariff barriers have been removed, and multilateral disciplines have become integral parts of national trade policy regimes. In the context of more outward-oriented trade policies, preferential agreements have had a significant impact on trade flows and protection. Although the depth and stability of trade policy reform has differed from country to country, the general trend is indisputable: The region's trade has been significantly liberalized, particularly when compared with initial conditions and with other developing regions of the world.

Overall, trade policy reform led to only slightly faster real export growth (aggregate export volumes increased at a 9 percent annual average rate in the 1990-99 period, as compared with 7 percent in 1980-90 and 6 percent in 1970-80). Aggregate economic performance was also disappointing. Except for Chile, faster export growth failed to translate into rapid expansion of output, productivity, and employment. Output growth accelerated relative to the 1980s, but it was still disappointingly low and below the rates recorded in the developing economies of Asia.

Roberto Bouzas is a professor at the University of San Andrés and a senior research fellow at the National Science Research Council. Saúl Keifman is a professor of economics at the University of Buenos Aires and chair of the master in economics program at the same university. *The authors thank Federico Jelinski and Santiago Wright for their valuable research assistance.*

There is also little evidence of faster growth of total factor productivity or of overall labor productivity. In the aggregate, employment growth was concentrated in the services sector, even in countries whose manufactured exports increased rapidly (e.g., Mexico). In this context, it is not surprising that unemployment, poverty rates, and income inequality did not decrease.

Latin American countries need to sustain rapid export growth to reduce their reliance on foreign savings and lay the foundation for more resilient and faster economic growth. Trade policy reform has helped to reduce the worst inefficiencies of inward orientation, thus raising the growth potential. There is no doubt that a reversal of trade policy would be very costly. But translating faster growth potential into better economic performance requires complementary policies. Past experience shows that the benefits of trade liberalization can be partly counterbalanced by policies that work against sustainable outward orientation. Chile until the mid-1980s and Mexico during the 1990s showed that even strong export growth does not guarantee fast expansion of output.

This chapter assesses the trade policy record and foreign trade performance of Latin American countries during the 1990s, drawing policy recommendations for the future. These recommendations do not constitute a set of ready-made prescriptions. Instead, they aim to draw attention to policy issues that will need to be addressed if trade liberalization is to contribute to better economic performance.

The Consensus on Trade Liberalization and Outward Orientation Before Reform

The aim of trade policy reform in Latin America during the past 15 years has been to abandon inward orientation. The two main ingredients of successful outward-oriented policies are a competitive exchange rate and elimination of the antiexport bias characteristic of import substitution. A competitive and unified (at least for trade transactions) exchange rate is a prerequisite for rapid growth in nontraditional exports. Export expansion needs to be fast enough to "allow the economy to grow at the maximum rate permitted by its supply-side potential, while keeping the current account deficit to a size that can be financed on a sustainable basis" (Williamson 1990, 14). Because there is of course a trade-off between a competitive exchange rate and keeping inflation under control, the use of the exchange rate as a nominal anchor is prudent only when its prospective cost in lower competitiveness is tolerable.

In Latin America, trade liberalization has been frequently accompanied by capital account liberalization. However, the two are conceptually distinct; one can be pursued without the other. Moreover, liberalization of capital outflows is not a main objective, because developing countries should be capital importers and retain their own savings for domestic investment. Indeed, Southern Cone stabilization plans in the late 1970s showed quite dramatically that liberalization of the capital account could result in large capital movements with undesired effects on the real exchange rate.

The first step in eliminating the antiexport bias characteristic of import substitution was to replace quantitative restrictions with tariffs. This would also serve to discourage corruption and to transfer rents from importers to the government. The conventional recommendation was to reduce tariffs over time to a 10 to 20 percent range. Most countries also chose to avoid levying taxes on imported inputs used to produce exports. The general rule was that "the domestic resource cost of generating or saving (one) unit of foreign exchange (should be) equalized between and among export and import-competing industries" (Williamson 1990, 14).

Views varied about the optimal speed of trade liberalization, within a range of 3 to 10 years. The timing of liberalization could even be determined by the state of the balance of payments (as in the European experience of the 1950s) or the economic cycle. These timing recommendations synthesized widespread views about the optimal process of trade liberalization and were shared by many Washington insider analysts and practitioners as well as by Latin American scholars, policymakers, and institutions disenchanted with import-substitution industrialization (ECLAC 1995).

By the early 1990s, there was little dispute about the superior growth record of export promotion as opposed to import substitution. The standard explanation for this contrasting performance was offered by Bhagwati (1987), who argued that export promotion was potentially less distorting than import substitution. Export promotion would help "to get prices right" by, first, preventing antiexport bias and, second, ensuring that budget constraints limit deviations from laissez faire.

However, empirical evidence indicated that the static distortions caused by import substitution were quantitatively too small to account for the strikingly superior growth performance of export promoters. One candidate to account for the difference was better exploitation of scale economies, which were more likely to be accessible under export promotion than under import substitution (Balassa 1982). The combination of outward orientation with industrial and technology policies may encourage greater exploitation of dynamic scale economies in the presence of market failures in technology, international trading information, and financial markets, thus helping to explain the superior growth performance of East Asia vis-à-vis Latin America (Stiglitz 1996).

In sum, since the late 1980s there was widespread agreement that the antiexport bias of Latin America's postwar trade regimes hindered growth and efficiency and distorted the policy process, stimulating rent-seeking practices and corruption. Similarly, there was little dispute over the growth superiority of openness as measured by trade shares in GDP.

However, there was no robust evidence on the channels and policies through which this linkage occurred (Edwards 1993b). The East Asian experience suggested that moving an economy onto an outward-oriented growth path required more than trade liberalization.

Similarly, there was enough evidence that the results of the trade policy reform process would partly depend on whether it was led by import liberalization or export expansion (Agosin and Ffrench-Davis 1993). Despite this broad consensus, however, the predominant policy mood in the region relied too much on straightforward and simplistic policy recommendations that placed excessive emphasis and expectations on a single policy instrument: trade liberalization.

The Extent of Trade Policy Reform

During the past 15 years, trade liberalization in Latin American countries has proceeded through the elimination of nontariff barriers (NTBs), the reduction of applied tariff rates, the enforcement of multilateral disciplines, and the forging of more substantive and encompassing preferential trade agreements (PTAs). These four ingredients combined to produce a significant shift toward more open trade regimes.

NTBs—by far the most distorting device used during the era of import substitution—deprived trade regimes of transparency and created incentives for rent seeking and corruption. In countries such as Argentina, Brazil, and Mexico, nominal tariff rates were largely irrelevant; typically, published rates and the duties that were effectively collected bore little relation to each other, because trade regimes were a compound of ad hoc measures, exemptions, and special treatments. The removal of NTBs during the 1990s was quite remarkable, making Latin American countries on average more moderate users of NTBs than other developing countries (Michalopoulos 1999). Remedial protection became more widespread in the 1990s, but with the possible exception of Mexico, it was less intense than in some industrial countries.

Parallel to the removal of NTBs, applied tariff rates fell markedly. At the turn of the century, Latin America was the most open developing region in the world (as measured by applied average tariff rates) and the one with the highest ratio of bound rates to total tariff lines (table 7.1). According to Laird and Messerlin (2001), by the end of the 1990s, average and maximum tariff rates (as well as other indicators of nominal protection, e.g., the standard deviation and the coefficient of variation of tariff rates) for a sample of six Latin American countries (Argentina, Brazil, Chile, Colombia, the Dominican Republic, and Mexico) compared favorably with a group of East Asian countries (Indonesia, South Korea, Singapore, and Thailand) and European economies that were in transition or developing (Poland, Romania, and Turkey).

Table 7.1 Tariff averages in developing economies, about 1999 (percent)

Region or group	Number of economies	Bound tariff rate[a]	Applied tariff rate[b]	Unbound tariff lines[c]	Coefficient of variation[d]
Latin America and the Caribbean	13[e]	38	13	0	28
East Asia and Pacific	6[f]	30	17	28	155
Sub-Saharan Africa	12[g]	74	20	42	30
Middle East and North Africa	4[h]	47	25	34	40
South Asia	4[i]	64	39	70	33
Higher-middle-income economies	12[j]	35	14	8	82
Lower-middle-income economies	13[k]	42	20	20	32
Low-income economies	14[l]	74	24	54	28
All developing economies	39	51	20	28	50

a. Simple average bound rate at the end of the implementation of the Uruguay Round agreement.
b. Simple average applied rate (latest year available).
c. Share of total tariff schedule.
d. Simple average of country tariff coefficients of variation, where a country tariff coefficient of variation is the standard deviation for applied tariff lines divided by the applied tariff.
e. Latin America and the Caribbean: Argentina, Bolivia, Brazil, Chile, Colombia, Costa Rica, Dominican Republic, El Salvador, Mexico, Paraguay, Peru, Uruguay, and Venezuela.
f. East Asia and Pacific: Fiji, Indonesia, Malaysia, Philippines, South Korea, and Thailand.
g. Sub-Saharan Africa: Benin, Cameroon, Côte d'Ivoire, Ghana, Kenya, Mauritius, Nigeria, Senegal, South Africa, Uganda, Zambia, and Zimbabwe.
h. Middle East and North Africa: Egypt, Morocco, Tunisia, and Turkey.
i. South Asia: Bangladesh, India, Pakistan, and Sri Lanka.
j. Higher-middle-income economies: Argentina, Brazil, Chile, Costa Rica, Malaysia, Mauritius, Mexico, South Africa, South Korea, Turkey, Uruguay, and Venezuela.
k. Lower-middle-income economies: Bolivia, Colombia, Dominican Republic, Egypt, El Salvador, Fiji, Morocco, Paraguay, Peru, Philippines, Sri Lanka, Thailand, and Tunisia.
l. Low-income economies: Bangladesh, Benin, Cameroon, Côte d'Ivoire, Ghana, India, Indonesia, Kenya, Nigeria, Pakistan, Senegal, Uganda, Zambia, and Zimbabwe.

Source: Authors' calculations based on Michalopoulos (1999).

The enforcement of multilateral rules also led to more transparent trade regimes and bound countries to implement new disciplines in areas other than trade in goods. Since 1986, 15 Latin American countries have joined the General Agreement on Tariffs and Trade and its successor, the World Trade Organization, including some of the largest economies, such as Mexico and Venezuela. This wave of new accessions occurred at a time when the demands and conditions for membership were being made stricter and more binding. In addition, policymakers frequently used multilateral commitments to lock in unilateral trade reforms. This partly accounts for the fact that Latin American countries display one of the highest ratios of bound to total tariff lines in the developing world (often 100 percent).

Last, more substantive and encompassing PTAs contributed to an increase in the exposure of national economies to foreign competition. The "new regionalism" included more detailed liberalization commitments, a broader exchange of concessions, automatic tariff phase-out calendars, and a relatively high degree of reciprocity (Devlin and Estevadeordal 2001). In addition, many PTAs covered issues other than trade in goods, such as services trade, treatment of foreign investment, protection of intellectual property rights, government procurement, and sanitary measures. A major trait of the new regionalism was the emergence of reciprocal North-South arrangements, such as the North American Free Trade Agreement and the free trade agreement between Mexico and the European Union.

Many Latin American countries continued to use conventional export-promotion instruments (e.g., import-duty drawbacks, export-processing zones, and marketing and insurance support) to offset the antiexport bias of residual protection and to address failures in some key markets (e.g., information and finance). Except for Chile and Mexico, however, these policies did not achieve the expected results (Macario 2000). Since the mid-1980s, Chile has used a series of instruments to promote exports aggressively: "simplified tax rebates," temporary admission of imports, tariff deferrals, exemptions on exporters' capital goods imports, and corrections of informational market failures (Díaz 1995; Agosin 1999; Silva 2001). Mexican policies have deviated significantly from laissez faire as well, as indicated by the extensive use of measures such as the *maquila* regime, generous temporary admission programs (e.g., PITEX), and other incentives (e.g., the ALTEX program and Bancomext export finance; Ten Kate, Macario, and Niels 2000).

Foreign Trade Performance

Trade policy reform was accompanied by faster growth of export values. During the 1990s, Latin American countries' exports rose at a rate double that of the previous decade (table 7.2). However, this was far from an export boom; the region's exports increased at a rate slightly lower than that of all developing countries. Faster Latin American export growth was to a large extent the result of higher sales to the US market and a sharp recovery of intraregional trade flows, in turn stimulated by more substantive PTAs reinforcing unilateral liberalization.

Aggregate figures mask heterogeneous export performances across countries. In fact, the higher growth rate of Latin American countries' exports is largely accounted for by the exceptional performance of Mexico and the Central American economies, whose exports respectively increased

Table 7.2 Performance of export values in Latin America (average annual percent growth rate)

Country and group	1980-2000	1980-90	1980-85	1985-90	1990-2000	1990-95	1995-2000
Mercosur	5	5	4	6	6	10	3
Argentina	6	4	1	8	8	11	5
Brazil	5	5	5	4	6	8	3
Paraguay	9	13	3	24	5	25	–12
Uruguay	4	5	–4	15	3	5	2
Andean Community	3	0	–4	5	7	5	8
Bolivia	1	–1	–8	6	4	5	3
Colombia	6	6	–2	14	7	8	5
Ecuador	4	1	3	–1	6	10	3
Peru	3	–2	–5	2	8	11	5
Venezuela	3	–1	–6	4	6	2	12
LAIA	7	4	2	7	10	11	9
Chile		6	–4	17	8	14	3
Mexico	12	8	8	9	15	14	16
CACM	6	–1	–5	3	13	16	10
Costa Rica	9	3	–1	8	16	21	11
El Salvador	5	–5	–9	–1	16	21	12
Guatemala	4	–2	–7	3	9	12	7
Honduras	4	0	–1	2	9	10	7
Nicaragua	2	–3	–7	2	8	8	8
Total[a]	7	4	1	7	10	11	9
Total (excluding Mexico)	5	3	–1	6	7	9	5

CACM = Central American Common Market
LAIA = Latin American Integration Association
Mercosur = Mercado Común del Sur (Southern Cone Common Market)

a. For 17 Spanish-speaking countries, plus Brazil and Haiti.

Source: Authors' calculations, based on data from the UN Economic Commission for Latin America and the Caribbean.

at 15 and 13 percent average annual rates (well above the 10 percent regional average; see table 7.2). Behind rapid Mexican and Central American export growth is the performance of sales to the US market. Indeed, Mexico was the only Latin American country (except Venezuela, which benefited from higher oil prices) that did not experience a slowdown in the rate of export growth during the second half of the 1990s. If Mexico is excluded, the region's countries saw their export growth in the 1995-2000 period nearly cut in half, from 9 to 5 percent (only slightly higher than the average growth rate recorded in the 1980s).

This poor performance was fully accounted for by adverse price trends; export volume growth increased slightly, from an annual average rate of 9 percent in the 1990-95 period to 10 percent in 1995-2000 (table 7.3). The adverse price performance was a consequence of the fact that Latin Amer-

Table 7.3 Performance of export volumes in Latin America (average annual percent growth rate)

Country and group	1980-99	1980-90	1980-85	1985-90	1990-99	1990-95	1995-2000
Mercosur	6	7	9	4	6	6	6
Argentina	7	7	7	7	7	7	6
Brazil	6	6	10	2	5	5	6
Paraguay	9	13	11	15	5	21	–10
Uruguay	5	5	1	10	5	4	6
Andean Community	5	4	0	8	5	6	4
Bolivia	3	3	–7	13	3	5	3
Colombia	6	7	0	14	5	5	4
Ecuador	6	6	7	6	6	12	0
Peru	5	2	3	1	9	7	10
Venezuela	4	3	–1	8	5	6	4
Chile	9	8	5	12	10	10	10
Mexico	15	15	16	14	14	13	15
Total[a]	8	7	7	8	9	9	10
Total (excluding Mexico)	6	5	5	6	7	7	6

a. For 17 Spanish-speaking countries, plus Brazil and Haiti.

Source: Authors' calculations, based on data from the UN Economic Commission for Latin America and the Caribbean.

ican countries (except Mexico and the Central American Common Market, or CACM) continued to rely on commodity exports, which are characterized by wide price fluctuations. Between 1989 and 1999, the share of manufactures in total exports of the region's countries increased from 30 to 57 percent, largely as a result of structural changes in the commodity composition of Mexican and Central American exports. In 1999, manufactures accounted for 84 percent of total Mexican exports, as compared with just 27 percent one decade earlier. In the case of CACM, the share of manufactures in total exports increased from 39 to 54 percent during the same period.

The contrast in the performance of imports between the 1990s and the previous decade was far more striking than in the case of exports. The average annual growth rate of import values jumped from 1 percent in the 1980s (when imports were repressed by the external debt crisis and international credit rationing) to 12 percent in the 1990s. Again, the highest rate of growth of imports was recorded during the first half of the decade, pushed by import liberalization and, in some countries, a sizable real appreciation of domestic currencies. Mexico emerges again as an exception; in contrast to the rest of the region, the growth of its import values accelerated during the second half of the 1990s (recording a remarkable 18 percent average annual increase, although that was pushed up by the rebound from the crisis of 1994-95).

The rapid expansion of Latin American countries' foreign trade flows during the 1990s led to a significant increase in tradability. Between 1990 and 2000, the ratio of foreign trade (exports plus imports) to GDP rose by more than 50 percent (from 22 to 36 percent). Mexico experienced the largest increase, followed by Brazil and Argentina. However, a much higher proportion of the rise in Mexico's ratio of foreign trade to GDP was accounted for by increased exports than was the case for Brazil and Argentina.

Growth, Employment, and Income Distribution

The performance of growth, employment, and income distribution during the 1990s was disappointing. Trade liberalization in itself was not enough to significantly improve performance, and in some areas (e.g., income distribution) it may have actually contributed to worsening it.

The record of an early reformer, Chile, confirms that strong export growth is not a passport to faster output expansion, because the benefits of trade liberalization can be partly counterbalanced by policies that work against sustainable outward orientation. In fact, during the period of trade liberalization-cum-real exchange rate appreciation of the late 1970s and the crisis that followed, Chile's GDP per capita failed to rise. It was only in the late 1980s that a rising trend in real output was firmly established, partly as a result of the contribution made to outward orientation by other policies, such as preventing a real appreciation of the domestic currency. Total factor productivity increased by 3.9 percent a year during the period 1990-98 (Hoffman 1999).

Mexico is another case of a country that experienced rapid export expansion during the 1990s, but it had a much more modest growth performance (Mexico's previous output peak was overtaken only in 1999). Part of this modest growth can be attributed to the policy of exchange-rate-based stabilization in the early 1990s, which led to a significant currency appreciation until the tequila crisis (Ros 2001). Mexico's trade liberalization-cum-market integration strategy has been successful in many respects, turning the country into one of the major world trading nations and exporters of manufactures.

However, Mexico's rapid export growth has taken place pari passu with deepening dualism. The *maquiladora* regime and the extensive use of temporary admission programs (that benefit around two-thirds of non-*maquila* exports) have reconciled rapid export expansion (from sectors and firms that have access to state-of-the-art technology and inputs at international prices) with a significant presence of backward sectors (Clavijo and Valdivieso 2000). This may account for the failure to achieve rapid productivity growth despite the fast growth of manufacturing exports.[1]

Before 1999, Argentina was usually cited as the country whose economic growth had seen the strongest rebound in parallel to trade liberalization. Between 1990 and 1998, output per head increased at a spectacular 4.4 percent annual rate. However, part of that growth was made possible by the enormous economic slack prevailing at the beginning of the period.[2] Between 1990 and 1998, manufacturing output per hour also increased at a remarkable 7 percent annual rate, but again, a cyclical component accounts for a large share of it. The post-1998 recession and the crisis that led to the collapse of the currency board in early 2002 dramatically worsened Argentina's growth performance, providing a new example of how exchange rate and macroeconomic policies can work at cross-purposes with trade liberalization in the quest for outward orientation.

Employment figures were also disappointing in many countries. In Argentina, in spite of fast economic growth until 1998, unemployment spiraled. Two-thirds of the fall in the number of full-time workers during the decade was accounted for by the loss of manufacturing jobs due to fast growth in output per worker and higher tradability (Frenkel and González Rosada 2000). Employment figures in Brazil performed equally poorly (although Brazil's output growth rates were much lower than those of Argentina).

Moreira and Najberg (1999) studied the employment cost of adjustment during the trade liberalization period in Brazil and found that job destruction was largest in capital-intensive sectors (as should be expected). But they also found labor shedding in labor-intensive and, more surprisingly, natural-resource-intensive sectors. The employment performance in Mexico was much better; while the urban unemployment rate rose from 2.6 percent in 1991 to 6.8 percent after the tequila crisis, it went down afterward to reach 2.2 percent in 2000 (underemployment also diminished significantly). However, despite the rapid increase of manufacturing exports, services made the largest contribution to employment growth.

In most of the countries analyzed, poor employment performance had a negative effect on income distribution. Frenkel and González Rosada (2000) studied the evolution of inequality in Argentina and found that the Gini coefficient for those employed rose from 0.42 in the 1991-94 period to 0.46 in 1998. Unemployment, income distribution, and poverty indicators also performed poorly during the initial stage of trade liberalization in Chile. However, unemployment and poverty (but not income distribution) performed considerably better after the late 1980s. In Mexico, de-

1. Total factor productivity increased by 0.7 percent a year during the period 1990-98 (Hoffman 1999).

2. In 1990, real output per capita was at a 22-year low.

spite better employment performance, income distribution and poverty indicators continued to lag behind (Lustig 2001).

The poor performance with regard to poverty and income distribution, which is related to the disappointing evolution of either employment or the skill premium among workers (and sometimes both), deserves a special comment because of the standard prediction that trade liberalization will result in a combination of higher wages and higher employment for unskilled labor in developing countries. Unfortunately, this is an incorrect generalization for most Latin American countries. The classic studies of Leamer (1984) and Bowen, Leamer, and Sveikauskas (1987) show that the abundant factor in most countries of the region is not unskilled labor but rather some natural resource, and that labor skills in the region rank at an intermediate level on a world scale.

Policy Issues for Trade Liberalization

Latin American countries need to sustain rapid export growth to reduce their reliance on foreign savings and to lay the foundations for faster economic growth. Earning foreign exchange through higher exports and foreign direct investment rather than volatile portfolio capital will make the region more resilient and less vulnerable to foreign shocks. This will ultimately improve economic performance. However, to put the region's countries on a sustainable outward-oriented growth path, more than trade liberalization is needed. Trade liberalization raises the growth potential, but translating that potential into reality demands a complementary set of policies. Moreover, trade liberalization in the region may not necessarily have positive effects on income distribution, which poses the need for policies to make trade liberalization both sustainable and compatible with equity.

The policy recommendations that follow do not constitute a set of ready-made prescriptions. Rather, they point to critical issues that will need to be taken into account in policy design, paying due attention to national circumstances. We have classified these policy issues in three broad categories: macroeconomic and exchange rate policy, market access, and competitiveness.

Some of the recommendations that follow are beyond the discretion of the region's policymakers, such as ensuring adequate market access to third-country markets. Others demand institutional capabilities that may not be readily available, such as fostering competitiveness or dealing with the adjustment costs of trade liberalization. Finally, some may involve significant trade-offs with other policy objectives (e.g., the tension between controlling inflation and securing a competitive real exchange rate). Yet they will need to be addressed as a coherent whole to enable countries to fully reap the benefits of international specialization. No quick fixes will do the job.

Macroeconomic and Exchange Rate Policy

The experience of Latin America in the 1990s shows the critical role of macroeconomic policy and exchange rate management in making trade liberalization sustainable and part of an effective progrowth strategy. Many Latin American countries implemented trade liberalization policies as a part of economic stabilization programs in which the exchange rate was used as a nominal anchor.

Although there is an obvious conflict between exchange-rate-based stabilization and trade liberalization, many governments chose both. This suggests either that the temptation is too strong, or that there is a poor understanding of the long-term trade-offs, or that there is not much of a choice. It appears that there is some sort of political inertia at work: once a government launches an exchange-rate-based stabilization program, it usually takes a crisis to persuade it to change course.

The costs of real appreciation should not be underestimated, particularly in a context of rapid trade liberalization. A successful trade reform program needs to raise two relative prices: the price of exportables relative to importables, and the price of exportables relative to nontradables. Tariff cuts and the removal of nontariff barriers achieved the former, but the latter depends on the evolution of the real exchange rate. This means that if the domestic currency experiences a real appreciation pari passu with trade liberalization (as a result, e.g., of capital account liberalization cum stabilization), one relative price (exportables relative to nontradables) would be shifting in the wrong direction. This would stimulate an inefficient and unsustainable allocation of too many resources to the production of nontradables.

It is hard to disentangle the effects of trade liberalization, currency appreciation, and capital account liberalization—and even of foreign shocks. But the contrasts between the experiences of Argentina and Chile help to draw some useful lessons.

Argentina started its trade liberalization process in the late 1970s in the context of an exchange-rate-based stabilization program that included full capital account liberalization. This policy mix led to a significant real appreciation of the domestic currency, spiraling current account deficits, a threefold increase in the external debt, and eventually a foreign exchange and financial crisis.

The Argentine trade liberalization-cum-currency board implemented in the 1990s showed similar fragility; given structural vulnerability to terms of trade, interest rate, and contagion shocks, after an initial period of strong growth, lack of flexibility led to protracted stagnation and eventually a full-fledged crisis. In the process, new distortions—such as dual foreign exchange markets, targeted tax exemptions, and volatile trade policies—made a comeback, as policymakers sought desperately for something to do the job of the exchange rate. Eventually, both trade liberalization and economic performance suffered.

Chile, as the oldest and most successful case of free-market reform and trade liberalization in Latin America, displays a revealing contrast between the 1973-82 period of trade liberalization-cum-domestic currency real appreciation and the post-1982 phase. The first period ended in a major economic crisis that included a 14 percent contraction of real GDP and a collapse of the financial system (Agosin 1999; Ffrench-Davis, Leiva, and Madrid 1993).

However, Chilean policymakers learned their lessons. After the financial collapse of the early 1980s, the most dramatic departure from earlier policies was the exchange rate. The domestic currency depreciated continuously in real terms during the 1982-88 period by means of a crawling peg combined with occasional discrete jumps. In contrast to the previous phase, the authorities implemented foreign exchange controls that led to the development of an informal foreign exchange market.

During the 1990s, Chile's real exchange rate suffered the pressures of large foreign capital inflows. To discourage short-term inflows and prevent an excessive appreciation of the domestic currency, the authorities enforced tax and reserve requirements on foreign credits and deposits. The central bank also intervened frequently to limit the extent of currency appreciation, and the (crawling) peg was switched from the US dollar to a basket of currencies to further discourage capital inflows.

Nevertheless, by 1997 the Chilean currency had appreciated by 21 percent as compared with 1990. This was partly reversed by capital flight triggered by the East Asian crisis and financial turmoil in the neighboring Mercosur countries. The experience of Chile demonstrates that managing exchange rate policy to secure the right relative prices is a difficult challenge, particularly in a world of volatile global finance. In such circumstances, countries may need to resort to capital controls to achieve the stated goal, preferably to discourage undesired inflows rather than to constrain capital outflows in times of crisis (when they are least likely to be effective) (Eichengreen 1999).

A stable macroeconomic regime requires conditions that are addressed in other chapters of this book. Most relevant are those concerning fiscal policy and, particularly, the growth of public-sector debt. A large public-sector borrowing requirement or rapid debt growth raises the vulnerability to "sudden stops" in capital flows or other (e.g., terms of trade) external shocks. The impact of these shocks is magnified when public- and private-sector debt is denominated in foreign currency.

Experience has shown that these crises can lead to policy reversals or bring progress toward trade liberalization and outward orientation to, at best, a temporary halt. The Argentine crisis of 2001 and 2002 shows the vast negative spillover effects that macroeconomic turmoil can have on trade policy. But sudden stops in foreign finance and terms of trade shocks are long-standing features of Latin America's integration with the world economy. One may wonder why analysts and policymakers tend to forget these lessons at the crest of the wave.

Market Access

During the 1990s, the Latin American countries' drive toward more open trade regimes was not matched by reciprocal liberalization in industrial-country markets. The exception was preferential North-South agreements, such as the North American Free Trade Agreement (NAFTA), which provided better market access to some countries at the expense of negative discrimination against the rest. The record of Mexico during the 1990s clearly demonstrates the potentially significant effects of improved market access on export growth.

Indeed, asymmetrical liberalization may not have been very costly in the past, when Latin American countries' trade regimes were strongly inward oriented. However, in the context of more open trade policies, having adequate access to industrial-country markets has become critically important. North-South PTAs—such as the Free Trade Area of the Americas—may partly compensate for the effects of asymmetrical multilateral liberalization. But for them to do so, a number of conditions will have to be met.

South-South PTAs provide an additional avenue to better exploit the benefits of international specialization and more deeply integrated markets. However, these agreements are vulnerable to external shocks and national institutional fragility. For this reason, a multilayered, mutually reinforcing approach that targets better market access at global and regional levels will offer the best promise for positive results.

Making Doha a True Development Round

Although the Uruguay Round of Multilateral Trade Negotiations carried strong commitments and new disciplines for developing countries, the industrial economies offered modest trade liberalization in areas vital to developing countries' export growth. One possible exception was textiles, but even there transition periods were extremely long and concessions were postponed toward the end of the period.[3] The consequence was that significant trade barriers remained virtually untouched in sectors of

3. Some fear that the elimination of textile quotas by 2005 may be compensated for with more aggressive enforcement of trade remedies.

prime interest for Latin America, challenging the reciprocity principle that should provide the basis for these multilateral negotiations.

Developing countries' exports to industrial markets face tariff peaks and significant tariff escalation. Tariff peaks are frequent for agricultural staple foods, and they actually increased as a result of the "tariffication" of quantitative restrictions. Tariff peaks are also common in cotton and tobacco, fruits and vegetables, processed food products (including fruit juices, canned meat, peanut butter, and sugar confectionery), textiles and clothing (already quantity restrained by the Agreement on Textiles and Clothing), footwear and leather products, and some automotive and transport-sector products (Michalopoulos 1999).

Similarly, although some reduction was agreed on in the Uruguay Round, tariff escalation continues to be a major feature of industrial countries' protection in sectors such as processed foods, clothing, leather, and wood products. The Uruguay Round reduced the incidence of conventional nontariff measures such as quotas, voluntary export restraints, and nonautomatic licenses, but tariff rate quotas are still common in agriculture.

The use of nontraditional trade barriers is more difficult to evaluate, but they have become more important as border protection has waned. Contingent protection has been on the rise and has become more sophisticated, especially targeting developing countries. Moreover, technical and sanitary standards can act as new barriers to trade if concepts such as the precautionary motive or practices such as mandatory labeling are eventually adopted. The multifunctionality of agriculture and the link from market access conditions to environmental and labor standards have also become major causes of concern for developing countries.

One result of the Uruguay Round was to make export and production subsidies subject to stricter disciplines. But these disciplines are not even-handed; the kind of domestic aids most frequently used by industrial countries (e.g., regional development funds or environmental protection assistance) were left largely untouched. Moreover, agricultural subsidies were made legal and, in spite of the shift toward less price distorting mechanisms, the volume of funds allocated to domestic aids has hardly fallen. Considering where comparative advantages lie, and the severe budget constraints and low per capita income of developing countries, this is a major and legitimate grievance.

The Doha Round must be a true development round if trade policy reform in Latin America is to be sustainable and help the region to fully reap the benefits of specialization. Strong political-economy forces oppose the liberalization of sensitive sectors in industrial countries. These forces will not be counteracted easily. This is why the region should aggressively pursue a strategy of market opening in the Doha Round, supporting initiatives such as the elimination of tariff rate quotas, "peak for peak" tariff negotiations, and a significant reduction of agricultural export and production subsidies (including the closure of loopholes, e.g., the "blue box"). Maintaining negotiations as a "single undertaking" offers the best way to help address the backlog of market access issues that interest the developing world.

Negotiating a Balanced FTAA

One of the novel features of regional integration during the past 15 years has been the emergence of North-South preferential trade agreements in the Western Hemisphere. Given a fixed level of multilateral liberalization, PTAs can be cost-effective as a negotiating strategy, particularly if better market access serves to attract foreign direct investment and stabilize expectations (thus adding to traditional Vinerian considerations; Ethier 1998). These incentives were to a large extent behind Mexico's decision to negotiate NAFTA with the United States and Canada.

It is now well established that NAFTA was a key successful ingredient in Mexico's foreign trade strategy during the 1990s. In effect, NAFTA gained Mexico contractual preferential access into the huge US market (in 1993, the United States accounted for 75 percent of Mexico's total trade in goods). It also helped to stabilize expectations (lessening the risk of future policy reversals) through the enforcement of new disciplines in areas such as foreign investment, services, intellectual property protection, and standards (Lopez-Cordova 2001). The familiar domino effect of trade discrimination (particularly when a large trading partner is involved) led other countries to try to compensate for the negative effects of being left behind. Given the reluctance of the US administration to enter into new bilateral deals, Mexico became—much to its benefit—a hemispheric trade and investment hub.

The ongoing negotiations to create a Free Trade Area of the Americas (FTAA) are an outgrowth of NAFTA. An FTAA will create new opportunities for Latin American countries and become a powerful development tool for the region. It can also become a significant source of economic, political, and strategic benefits for the United States. However, the size of net gains and an even distribution of costs and benefits will require a prospective FTAA to meet certain conditions.

First, the FTAA should be implemented on the basis of reciprocal concessions, taking into account differences in size and levels of development. As was discussed in the previous subsection, reciprocal liberalization among industrial and developing countries made limited progress during the Uruguay Round. Perhaps, by making it possible to focus more clearly on market access gains, preferential negotiations may help to achieve bigger gains than have so far proved possible multilaterally.

However, in areas where there are entrenched domestic interests (e.g., textiles or agriculture) or where policies are deeply intertwined with those of third parties (e.g., agricultural subsidies), substantial progress on a preferential basis will not be easy. Although "defensive considerations" may make nonparticipation too costly and membership almost inevitable (even if these issues are not fully or adequately addressed), this would make an unbalanced agreement and an uneven distribution of costs and benefits more likely. Creative initiatives—such as the adoption of a joint approach and common procedures to combat extraregional agricultural subsidies—could offer a path toward a more balanced deal.

The likelihood of an equitable bargain will be influenced by the dynamics by which the FTAA is negotiated and enforced. Trade discrimination tends to exacerbate the mercantilist bias implicit in trade negotiations. FTAA negotiators must openly face this risk. Given the significant prevailing disparities in the Western Hemisphere in economic size, factor endowments, and levels of development, North-South bilateralism will reduce the likelihood of a balanced deal.

Political-economy considerations suggest that the selection of partners will be influenced by the size of transition and adjustment costs, as well as by the tractability of the bilateral trade agenda. A strategy of "choosing and picking up" partners parallel to the FTAA process (particularly by the United States) will most likely lead to a further unlevel negotiating field. The recently concluded free trade agreement between the United States and Chile and the launching of negotiations between the United States and Central America confirm that the FTAA process will move forward as a bilateral or quasi-bilateral exercise. This does not bode well for the prospect of a balanced agreement that takes into consideration the interests of all parties involved.

To be sustainable, an FTAA should also pay special attention to the issue of transition and adjustment costs. Economic integration among countries with significantly different factor endowments offers the promise of large efficiency gains. However, these benefits will accrue only in the long term, whereas sizable adjustment costs will have to be borne during the transition period. The key role that adjustment assistance played in the passage of Trade Promotion Authority by the US Congress in 2002 confirms that this remains crucial in domestic debates on trade liberalization. Different degrees of economic openness and size mean that the impact of dislocations will be highly asymmetric across countries. Differences in per capita incomes and levels of development imply that the financial resources available to cope with them will also differ greatly. Consequently, if the issue of adjustment and transition costs is not addressed explicitly, other policy alternatives may have to be sought (e.g., sufficiently different calendars for tariff phaseouts).

Latin America will be able to fully reap the benefits of an FTAA only if countries have created the required structural conditions to take advantage of free trade. One of these conditions is a propitious macroeconomic environment. Countries subject to periodic external shocks and volatile capital flows are unlikely to be able to cope with sustained liberalization. Although an FTAA may help to diversify exports and raise foreign direct investment and thus increase the resilience of smaller economies, a healthy macroeconomic environment must go hand in hand with trade liberalization. This means that there must not only be fiscal prudence—which might be encouraged by indicative or mandatory hemispherewide targets—but also the introduction of financial mechanisms geared to cope with unexpected shocks and disturbances.

There is no doubt that NAFTA helped Mexico overcome the tequila crisis, but so did the prompt financial assistance made available by the US government and the international financial institutions. Considering the criticism that the IMF has received in recent years for its handling of developing countries' crises (the last episode of which is Argentina), a regional approach may both be timely and give Latin America a sense of ownership. Over the longer term, this might even include some sort of exchange rate arrangement aimed at limiting exchange rate volatility.

Structural conditions for benefiting from free trade also include the effective capacity of countries to take advantage of the opportunities opened by trade liberalization. The risks of "polarization" between countries and regions trapped in virtuous circles of economic growth and vicious circles of economic decay or stagnation must be addressed.

Thus, the FTAA should explicitly consider initiatives aimed at laying the institutional and structural preconditions to benefit from freer trade, overcoming the reluctance to establish new mechanisms or strengthen existing ones. If NAFTA needed a regional development bank or fund, then the rest of Latin America surely will too. At the FTAA level, a stronger Inter-American Development Bank could do the job, provided that part of its activities are explicitly targeted at smoothing regional disparities (particularly in what concerns the availability of public goods).

Increasing the Effectiveness of Preferential Agreements

South-South preferential trade agreements will remain part of Latin America's foreign trade strategies in the future. If the FTAA fails, the region's countries will continue to trade preferentially with each other under the stimulus of geographic and cultural proximity (Frankel, Stein, and Wei 1997). South-South PTAs can also help to deal with distributional concerns inherent to trade liberalization, exploit gains from intraindustry trade, and raise members' bargaining capacity vis-à-vis third parties.

In effect, under standard assumptions, trade liberalization would lead to a *potential* Pareto improvement. Yet an *actual* Pareto improvement would require transfers that involve a great deal of information and quite sophisticated institutions (including fiscal ones). Because few developing countries appear to have the institutional capacity to cope with the adjustment costs associated with trade reform (especially the private costs incurred by displaced workers), a strategy of preferential liberalization—as opposed to unilateral liberalization—may enable them to pick trade partners and smooth the costs of adjustment over longer periods of time, keeping them at more manageable levels. And because participating countries tend to be more similar in per capita income and relative factor endowment, adjustment costs may be lower.

Similarity in factor endowments also lays the basis for intraindustry trade, creating an incentive to reap benefits from increasing returns. The fact that intraindustry trade has risen significantly in agreements such as Mercosur suggests that the gains from increasing returns in South-South agreements are not negligible (Fanelli, González Rosada, and Keifman 2001). South-South agreements can also contribute to raising a region's bargaining capacity vis-à-vis third parties.

But even if there is an FTAA, some regions or groups of countries may wish to engage in deeper integration agreements, such as a customs union (which will, among other things, eliminate the need for rules of origin on intraregional trade). Yet the challenges of South-South integration remain monumental. Even if intraregional trade flows expand rapidly (as they did within Mercosur between 1991 and 1998) their share in total foreign trade will remain modest, limiting the incentives to coordinate. Limited incentives to coordinate and the lack of a focal point for convergence (most likely to be the case in agreements among developing countries) will hinder the sustainability of South-South trade pacts, for trade liberalization and market integration may be reversed during crises.

Other constraints (e.g., weak domestic institutions) may also conspire against the enforceability of agreements (Bouzas 1999). Mercosur offers a good example both of the potential accomplishments of South-South regional integration and also of the policy challenges posed by low but rising regional interdependence in a context of macroeconomic and exchange rate turmoil (INTAL 2001). Given this fragility, a balanced FTAA could provide an anchor and an umbrella for deeper and more effective South-South regional integration agreements.

Competitiveness

An open trade regime is a necessary condition for an efficient economy. However, in a world characterized by market failures, other complementary policies also are needed to reap the benefits of international specialization and the dynamic gains from trade liberalization. The empirical evidence collected in the literature on both trade and growth shows the existence of large international differences in production functions (Clark and Feenstra 2001; Trefler 1993, 1995; Easterly and Levine 2001), underscoring the fact that technology is not a public good and that the process of acquiring technological capabilities is not automatic.

Moreover, there is evidence that trade and output tend to grow more slowly in countries with rich natural resource endowments than elsewhere (Sachs and Warner 1997; Ros 2001; Sala-i-Martin 1997), a result that seriously challenges Latin American policymakers. Consequently, fostering economic development requires designing a comprehensive strategy to improve competitiveness on the basis of three pillars: (1) building adequate infrastructure, (2) diversifying the productive structure, and (3) developing and strengthening national innovation systems.

A lack of adequate infrastructure is a major factor behind foreign trade repression. Many goods are not traded simply because high transport costs constitute an insurmountable barrier, reducing the set of regional goods and repressing trade. Argentina and Chile, for example, are still connected by only a single paved road, which is occasionally closed in wintertime due to snow storms. Mercosur countries have been largely unable to implement integrated customs facilities because of budget constraints. The high cost of foreign trade services reduces the incentive to spread production across countries, lowering the scope for intraindustry trade. Foreign official assistance could significantly contribute to upgrading trade-related infrastructure by focusing on regional projects or national projects with regional spillovers.

Export policy can help to diversify production. In this regard, an active commercial diplomacy geared to securing market access, identifying new opportunities, and counteracting trade restrictions can help to expand exports. This demands a highly trained foreign trade bureaucracy (a resource in short supply in part of Latin America) able to cooperate with the private sector and supply information on opportunities offered by trade agreements to potential exporters. There is a place for export promotion focused on providing information, supporting marketing abroad, and facilitating access to export finance and insurance.

Many of these instruments are already in use in Latin America, but implementation is frequently poor. Upgrading institutional capabilities to make better use of resources already channeled to these areas is therefore necessary, and successes such as ProChile confirm that this is quite possible. A neglected but valuable idea would be to establish a mechanism to channel venture capital to new exporting firms. World Trade Organization disciplines still leave some (much-reduced) leeway for subsidies, in such forms as regional aids, research and development (R&D) activities, and direct subsidies under a de minimis clause. Export subsidies have been used widely in the past, but with limited success. This suggests that such subsidies as remain should be moderate, temporary, and subject to regular review.

A familiar element of export policy is to allow exporters access to imported inputs at international prices (through temporary admission or duty drawbacks), something already in place in most Latin American countries. One problem with this policy is that it discriminates against domestic suppliers of inputs for exporters. To correct that, such suppliers should also be allowed to recover tariffs and other indirect tax expenses. This would have the merit of reinforcing backward linkages and spreading the benefits of outward orientation. A tax system based on a value-added tax (VAT) that enables export-oriented production to be exempted from the financial burden of "cascading" indirect taxes can also increase the incentive to export, especially if VAT reimbursements are expedited.

Given the pervasive failures that exist in markets for technology, credit, and human capital, policies geared to fostering productivity are the best recipe for improving export performance over the long run. Although the Uruguay Round prohibited nonagricultural export subsidies, it gave a green light to other forms of domestic assistance widely used in industrial countries (e.g., R&D assistance). Three dimensions seem critical to closing the gap in the use of state assistance between Latin American countries and countries that belong to the Organization for Economic Cooperation and Development (OECD) (CEPAL 2002; OECD 1999).

First, forward and backward linkages need to be stimulated, so as to overcome the dualism of dynamic exporting sectors amid a stagnant overall economy and to foster spillovers to the rest of the economy. The provision of public infrastructure and coordination between the government and private firms aimed at strengthening productive clusters might help (CEPAL 2002).

Second, government agencies should assist firms, especially small and medium-sized businesses, on issues of technology diffusion, innovation, and the promotion of human resource development. Government should seek to nurture a strong scientific and technological infrastructure, provide incentives for R&D, and coordinate innovation efforts among universities, research institutes, and business firms. According to the OECD (2001b), the links between technology and science have a strong national component, even for small countries.

Third, because the share of GDP invested in R&D in industrial countries is five times that in Latin American countries, governments should consider offering incentives for private R&D. The public sector should foster links between the university science and technology system, development banks, public and private R&D laboratories, and the business sector.

Conclusions

During the past decade, trade liberalization has proceeded rapidly in most Latin American countries, leading to a significant increase in tradability (as illustrated by the three-fourths rise in the ratio of foreign trade to GDP). Both exports and imports have expanded more quickly, but import growth has by far outpaced the rate of export expansion. This imbalance was made possible by foreign direct investment and portfolio capital inflows, partly stimulated by liquid international capital markets. However, this growth pattern has maintained (indeed increased) the vulnerability of Latin American countries to foreign shocks. Making their countries more resilient is therefore one of the major challenges faced by policy-makers. Faster-growing exports and a more diversified export base can make a significant contribution to meeting this challenge.

Although aggregate export performance improved during the 1990s, the record across countries was very heterogeneous. The growth in export values accelerated as compared with the previous decade, but mainly as a result of favorable prices during the first half of the 1990s. During the later years of the decade, export values (excluding Mexico's) increased at a meager 2 percent a year. Export volumes, in contrast, performed roughly in line with the past record.

Exports have remained concentrated in commodities, leaving export earnings vulnerable to wide price fluctuations. Only Mexico and the nations of Central America moved toward a higher share of manufactures in total exports (particularly labor-intensive ones). Intra-Latin American trade diversified toward a higher share of manufactures, but it still accounts for a relatively minor share of total trade. The rise in the share of manufactures in total Mexican and CACM exports was a result of improved (preferential) access to the US market.

Except for Chile, even instances of rapid export expansion failed to translate into high growth of employment, productivity, and output. Although Mexico and Central American countries exhibited a performance superior to the rest of the region (basically due to rapid employment growth in export-processing activities), even their record was far from remarkable. Overall, employment growth was concentrated in services, even in countries (e.g., Mexico) whose manufactured exports increased rapidly. Total factor productivity or overall labor productivity gains have also been limited. Even when measured manufacturing productivity rose, that seems to have been caused by labor shedding, outsourcing, imported inputs, and new labor-saving capital goods. In this context, it should come as no surprise that unemployment rates, poverty incidence, and income inequality did not decrease satisfactorily regionwide.

Trade liberalization made a significant contribution to correcting the grossest inefficiencies of Latin America's past trade regimes. However, lower protection has not been a panacea for better economic performance. The experience of the 1990s indicates that complementary policies are needed. Specifically, countries need better access to international markets, not just lower tariffs on their part; policies to increase competitiveness; and an exchange rate and macroeconomic policy regime consistent with outward orientation.

A Free Trade Area of the Americas could make a decisive contribution to promoting outward orientation in the region—provided it takes the form of a balanced agreement that respects the interests of all its members, helps countries deal with transition and adjustment costs, is enforced in a transparent and balanced manner, and promotes a sustainable macroeconomic environment. These demands pose a big challenge to policymakers in Latin American countries, as well as to the rest of the international community. Although many of the issues outlined will not be easily addressed, an oversimplified policy agenda is no substitute. Insisting on such an inadequate approach would most likely backfire, at the expense of sustainable economic reform and better economic performance.

8

Education and Training: The Task Ahead

LAURENCE WOLFF AND CLAUDIO DE MOURA CASTRO

This book is about economic policy in Latin America during the next decade. It has a chapter on education and training. It does not have a chapter on the environment, on agricultural development, on infrastructure and roads, or on health. Why, then, does this book on economic policy have a chapter on education?

The answer is that it is a response to the three overriding economic changes in the world during the past 20 years—globalization, the growth of the knowledge economy, and the information and communications revolution. Globalization involves integration across national boundaries in such a way as to create a single world market. The knowledge content of traded goods and services is increasingly important, while in contrast traded primary goods are an increasingly marginal component of international trade; therefore economic development is more and more linked to a nation's ability to acquire and apply technical knowledge. Finally, rapid progress in electronics, telecommunications, and satellite technologies is resulting in the quasi abolition of physical distance, which will lead in the near future to near-zero costs for communication among people, institutions, and countries. That allows businesses increasingly to locate anywhere that offers good-quality human resources at a competitive price.

Laurence Wolff has been a consultant at the Inter-American Development Bank since 1998. Claudio de Moura Castro is president of the advisory council of Faculdade Pitágoras in Brazil.

Knowledge, and knowledge-induced technological change, is more than ever driving economic growth. The entire system of knowledge creation, dissemination, and usage is encapsulated in the idea of "national innovation systems"—the set of interrelated agents, institutions, and practices that constitute, perform, and participate in the process of technological innovation. By 1999, knowledge-based industries'[1] share of GDP in industrial countries was already above 50 percent (Melo 2001). Within this area, information and communications technologies constitute the core of the knowledge-based economy. At the same time, the knowledge content of all types of industry and services—ranging from soybean growing to banking to manufacturing items from (robotic) toys to automobiles (with hundreds of computer chips in each car)—is growing.

These changes in the world economy require increasing numbers of workers with higher-level skills who need to update their knowledge and skills on a regular basis. "Higher-order learning"—involving methodological knowledge as well as skills such as creativity, communication, and the ability to work in teams—is increasingly valued relative to the learning of facts. In many other places throughout the world, just as in Latin America, the increased value of knowledge is resulting in a decline in the wages of unskilled or semiskilled workers compared with those of skilled workers (Heckman 2001). These changes in the relative value of skilled workers increase the potential for divergences in income distribution within countries. Political and economic modernization, as well as rapid changes in society, has also led to another set of goals that can be furthered by education: the development of a civic culture that stresses tolerance, cooperation, and a broader sense of national community.

Globalization and the information and communications technologies revolution are transforming higher education. The difference between "virtual" and "in-person" education is disappearing. Virtual higher education and training courses are among the most rapidly expanding internationally traded services, and there are now promising pilot projects in providing virtual instruction at the secondary education.

Although the progress in many Latin American countries is impressive, the region still remains behind others in human resource development. Inadequate human resources continue to be a major impediment to economic growth. Young workers in the region on average enter the labor force with fewer years of education than workers in East Asia, and the gap was still widening through 1999 (figure 8.1). Enrollment ratios in most countries are lower than would be expected by the standard of countries at similar levels of development. It has been estimated that, if the region's educational achievement were equivalent to that of countries in the Far

1. These are defined as high and medium-high technology manufacturing industries and services, e.g., finance, insurance, and communications.

Figure 8.1 Average years of schooling of the labor force, Latin America and other regions, 1960-99

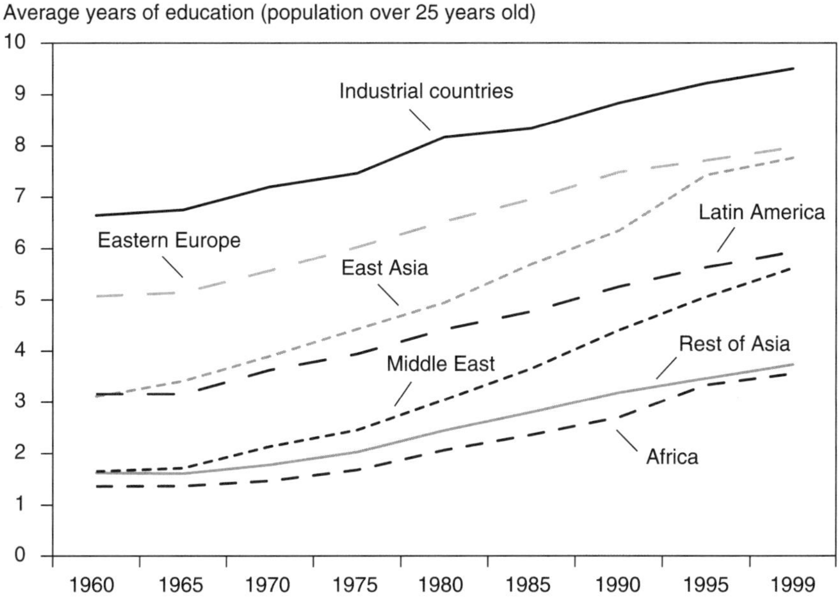

Source: Adapted from Barro and Lee (1999).

East, per capita income could grow 0.5 percent a year faster (Birdsall 1999). Quality, in terms of learning achievement, is low. Latin American students included in international test comparisons consistently score near the bottom.

As is documented in this book and elsewhere, income inequality in Latin America—the difference between the income of the richest and poorest members of society—is among the highest in the world. This inequity reflects and also perpetuates disparities in educational opportunities. The region's richest 10 percent of people 21 years of age or above average about 11 years of education, compared with about 6 years of education for the poorest 30 percent (table 8.1).

Indirect measurements of the impact of education on the economy also show that the region is lagging behind. For example, productivity growth has been half the world average since 1973 (IDB 2000a). Patent applications, the share of high-technology exports to OECD markets, researchers per thousand workers, and linkages and external interactions by business all are lagging (Melo 2001). And while the region's Internet connections are increasing rapidly, it still has only 2.6 per 1,000 people, compared with 177.3 in industrial countries and 10.4 in East Asia and the Pacific (Chong and Micco 2001).

Table 8.1 Average years of education for people 25 years of age and above, selected Latin American countries, 1994-96

Country	Richest 10 percent	Poorest 30 percent	Difference
Uruguay[a]	11.9	6.3	5.6
Venezuela	10.8	5.0	5.8
Chile	12.8	6.7	6.1
Argentina[b]	13.6	7.4	6.2
Nicaragua	8.5	2.3	6.2
Peru	10.8	4.3	6.5
Bolivia[a]	13.1	6.6	6.5
Costa Rica	11.5	4.8	6.7
Paraguay	10.7	3.6	7.1
Honduras	9.6	2.3	7.3
Ecuador	11.8	4.3	7.5
Brazil	10.5	2.5	8.0
El Salvador	10.3	2.1	8.2
Panama	13.6	5.3	8.3
Mexico	12.1	3.0	9.1

a. The surveys for Bolivia and Uruguay include only urban areas.
b. The surveys for Argentina include only greater Buenos Aires.

Source: Inter-American Development Bank, *Economic and Social Progress 1998-99*, appendix table 1.2.III, education. Based on household surveys conducted from 1994 to 1996.

Four Challenges: Access, Quality, Equity, and Technology

The region has made significant progress during the past decade in improving education and training. Nonetheless, the task ahead remains formidable.

Improving education is a long-term endeavor. There are no quick fixes or simple solutions. The successful implementation of change in education requires a systematic approach and constant feedback, tinkering, and revision. Nor will the same prescriptions be valid for every country in a region as varied and vast as Latin America. Each country must design its own educational goals in accordance with its own level of educational development and economic resources.

Increasing Access to Education

In the region as a whole, 82 percent of those 17 to 20 years of age now report that they have completed at least 6 years of primary education.[2] Students enter and remain in the school system for longer periods of time

2. This was based on household surveys. Estimates using reconstituted flow rates suggest lower completion rates.

Table 8.2 Primary school completion rates for people 17-20 years of age, selected Latin American countries, various years

Country	Year	Percent completing 6th grade	Year	Percent completing 6th grade
Argentina	—	—	1999[a]	98
Bolivia	1990[a]	86	1999	77
Brazil	1988	49	1999	68
Chile	1990	93	1998	96
Colombia	1990[a]	86	1999	76
Costa Rica	1989	85	2000	88
El Salvador	—	—	1999	54
Honduras	1992	69	1999	70
Mexico	1989	83	2000	88
Nicaragua	—	—	1998	60
Panama	1991	92	1999	94
Peru	1991	96	2000	95
Uruguay	1992[a]	97	1998[a]	96
Venezuela	1989	87	1999	90

— = not available

a. This includes only urban areas. Enrollment ratios in the two time periods for Bolivia and Colombia are not comparable because they are for urban areas only in about 1990 and for the country as a whole in about 2000.

Note: Primary school completion is defined as completing at least 6 years of school.

Source: Social Information Service, Research Department, Inter-American Development Bank, based on household surveys.

and are able to advance more quickly to higher-level courses now than in 1990. Brazil has made especially significant progress; 68 percent of its youth reported that they had completed 6 years of education, compared with only 49 percent in 1990 (however, this figure is still among the lowest in the region). Other countries have had much less spectacular increases in completion rates (table 8.2), with an average improvement of only 4 percent during the past decade. In only Chile, Argentina, Uruguay, and Peru do 95 percent or more entering children complete 6 years of primary education.

Much progress has been made in reducing repetition, from 29 to 16 percent during the decade, yet the "culture of repetition" still leads teachers to require large numbers of students to repeat grades, resulting in many youths of 18 and above who are still seeking to complete primary school. Repetition rates remain higher than in other regions (it costs an estimated $4.6 billion a year to educate these repeaters).

The region's average gross secondary education enrollment ratio has increased significantly, from 54 percent in 1990 to 62 percent in 1997 (table 8.3). Again, Brazil has had the greatest increase. Its gross enrollment ratio in the 3-year secondary school system rose from 38 to 62 percent of the secondary school age cohort. The region's higher education gross enroll-

Table 8.3 Gross school enrollment ratio per country, Latin America and the Caribbean, 1990 and 1997 (percent)

	Preschool		Primary		Secondary		Higher	
Region and country	**1990**	**1997**	**1990**	**1997**	**1990**	**1997**	**1990**	**1997**
Central America and the Caribbean								
Bahamas[a]	—	9	102	98	94	87	—	—
Barbados[a]	—	—	93	—	—	—	27	29
Belize[a]	24	27	112	121	41	49	—	—
Costa Rica	61	74	101	104	42	48	26	30
Cuba	101	88	98	106	89	81	21	12
Dominican Republic	—	33	—	94	—	54	—	23
El Salvador	21	40	81	97	26	37	16	18
Guatemala	26	35	81	88	23	26	—	9
Haiti	34	—	48	—	21	—	—	—
Honduras	13	14	108	111	33	—	9	10
Jamaica	78	—	101	100	65	—	7	8
Mexico	64	73	114	114	53	64	15	16
Nicaragua	12	23	94	102	40	55	8	12
Panama	53	76	106	106	63	69	22	32
Trinidad and Tobago	9	—	97	99	80	74	7	8
South America								
Argentina	50	56	106	111	71	73	38	36
Bolivia	32	—	95	—	37	—	21	—
Brazil	48	59	106	125	38	62	11	15
Chile	82	98	100	101	73	75	21	32
Colombia	13	33	102	113	50	67	13	17
Ecuador	42	59	116	127	55	50	20	—
Guyana[a]	69	89	98	96	83	75	—	11
Paraguay	27	61	105	111	31	47	8	10
Peru	30	40	118	123	67	73	30	26
Suriname	—	—	—	—	52	—	9	—
Uruguay	43	45	109	109	81	85	30	30
Venezuela	41	44	96	91	35	40	29	—
Simple average for the region	**44**	**54**	**99**	**106**	**54**	**62**	**17**	**19**

— = not available

a. Data are for 1996.

Sources: UNESCO World Education Report 2000; World Bank, *World Development Indicators 2001.*

ment ratio increased from 17 to 19 percent. Preschool enrollments increased from 44 to 54 percent of the target population (as defined by each country, usually children ages 4-5). An unknown but certainly increasing number of youths and adults are attending a wide variety of formal and nonformal training programs.

Let us now look at expenditures. In the region as a whole, public expenditures on education as a percentage of GNP increased from 4 to 4.6 percent in the period from 1990 to 1999 (table 8.4). Nearly every country increased this percentage. Adding private and nonformal expenditures on

Table 8.4 Public expenditures on education in Latin America and the Caribbean, 1990-99

Region and country	As a percent of GNP 1990	As a percent of GNP 1999	As a percent of government expenditure 1990	As a percent of government expenditure 1996
Central America and the Caribbean				
Bahamas	4.3	—	17.8	13.2
Barbados	7.9	6.4	22.2	19.0
Belize	4.8	5.4	18.5	19.5
Costa Rica	4.6	5.5	20.8	22.8
Cuba	—	7.7	12.3	12.6
Dominican Republic	1.4	2.6	8.9	13.8[b]
El Salvador	2.0	2.4	16.6	16.0[b]
Guatemala	1.4	1.7[a]	11.8	15.8
Haiti	1.5	—	20.0	—
Honduras	4.1	4.2[c]	—	16.5
Jamaica	5.4	6.3	12.8	12.9
Mexico	3.7	4.6	12.8	23.0
Nicaragua	—	4.0	—	8.8[b]
Panama	4.9	6.3	20.9	16.3[b]
Trinidad and Tobago	4.0	4.0	11.6	—
South America				
Argentina	3.4	4.7	—	12.6
Bolivia	—	5.8	—	11.1
Brazil	4.5	5.2	—	—
Chile	2.7	4.3	10.0	15.5[b]
Colombia	2.5	4.4	16.0	19.0
Ecuador	3.1	2.5	17.2	13.0
Guyana	4.8	4.6	—	10.0
Paraguay	1.1	4.8	9.1	19.8[b]
Peru	2.3	3.5	—	19.2
Suriname	8.3	6.7	—	—
Uruguay	3.1	2.8	15.9	15.5
Venezuela	3.1	5.2[a]	12.0	22.4
Simple average for the region	4.0	4.6	15.1	16.0

— = not available

a. 1995 figure.
b. 1997 figure.
c. 1998 figure.

Source: UNESCO Statistical Yearbook 2002.

education and training would increase this percentage significantly.[3] Expenditures per pupil as a percentage of GNP per capita also went up in the region as a whole. The greatest increase in per-student expenditure was in secondary education, which went up from 14.5 to 16.2 percent of GNP per capita. Public and private investment in science and technology

3. If these elements were included, it is estimated that Brazil could be spending up to 10 percent of GDP on education and training (Wolff and Castro 2000).

Table 8.5 Research and development expenditures in selected Latin American and other countries (as a percent of GDP)

Country	1990	1991	1992	1993	1994	1995	1996	1997	1998	1999
Latin America										
Bolivia	—	—	0.37	0.39	0.39	0.37	0.33	0.32	0.29	0.29
Brazil	0.46	0.46	0.38	0.48	0.69	0.76	0.76	—	—	—
Chile	0.51	0.53	0.58	0.65	0.66	0.65	0.66	0.65	0.62	0.63
Colombia	—	—	—	—	0.37	0.39	0.41	0.41	—	—
Costa Rica	0.73	1.05	1.23	1.42	1.23	1.25	1.13	—	—	—
Cuba	0.72	0.65	1.13	0.93	0.82	0.77	0.61	0.70	0.87	0.83
Ecuador	—	—	—	—	—	0.08	0.09	0.08	0.08	—
Mexico	—	—	—	0.22	0.29	0.31	0.31	0.34	—	—
Panama	0.38	0.38	0.34	0.36	0.37	0.38	0.38	0.37	0.33	—
North America and Iberian Peninsula										
Canada	1.45	1.51	1.56	1.60	1.65	1.62	1.57	1.59	1.61	1.50
Portugal	0.54	—	0.66	—	—	0.56	—	0.62	—	—
Spain	0.85	0.87	0.91	0.91	0.85	0.85	0.87	0.86	0.89	0.90
United States	2.62	2.69	2.61	2.49	2.39	2.48	2.52	2.55	2.59	2.67

— = not available

Source: Red Iberoamericana de Indicadores de Ciencia y Tecnologia, *Indicadores de Ciencia y Tecnologia*, Buenos Aires, 2000, www.ricyt.edu.ar.

as a percentage of GDP has increased significantly in Brazil, Chile, and Mexico (table 8.5). Average primary student-teacher ratios have declined from 30:1 to 28:1, and 80 percent of primary teachers are now formally qualified (table 8.6).

The quantitative challenge is to increase enrollments and completion rates at all levels to meet both labor market and social demand. Some illustrative goals could include ensuring that all children in the region complete primary education (recommended as part of the UN Millennium Development Goals for 2015); increasing secondary enrollment ratios to 75 percent in 2010 (recommended by the participants in the Quebec Summit of the Americas); and increasing higher education enrollment ratios from 19 percent to perhaps 25 percent by 2010. The costs would be significant. For example, the target increase in the enrollment rate in secondary education would cost an estimated additional $11 billion in capital costs and $5 billion in annual recurrent costs. Public expenditures on education would likely increase from 4.6 percent of GNP in 1997 to at least 5 percent to meet these goals and to approach industrial countries' efforts.

The current environment in the region offers a window of opportunity, in the form of declining "dependency ratios" (i.e., the ratio of those outside the labor force to those in it). Through 2015, an increasing percentage of the population will be in the labor force. The secondary education level-age

Table 8.6 Changes in measures of inputs to primary education in Latin America, 1990-92 and 1997-99

Measure	1990-92	1997-99
Percent enrolled in preschool (15 countries)	29.3	40.1
Student-teacher ratio (12 countries)	30 to 1	28.3 to 1
Percent of trained teachers (13 countries)	76.0	80.0
Public expenditure on primary education as a percent of GDP (13 countries)	1.3	1.7
Expenditure per student as a percent of GDP per capita (20 countries)	9.5	9.8

Sources: UNESCO, *Informe Regional de América Latina de EFA*, 2000, for all items except expenditure per student, which is from the *UNESCO Statistics Report*, 2001.

population will grow a total of only 6 percent from 1995 to 2010, from 46 to 49 million. The overall school-age population will actually remain stable (figure 8.2) and children as a percentage of total population will decline from over 30 percent now to 20 percent by 2040 (figure 8.3).

This window provides the opportunity for increased savings and therefore faster economic growth, and it likewise gives the opportunity to increase education spending per school-age child without prohibitive cost. At the same time, expenditures on adults for training and skills upgrading will have to increase. Of course, finance ministers will have to provide the needed funding, whenever adequate education policies are proposed to them, if the region is to take advantage of this window. In any event, especially at higher levels of education, the private sector will need to be encouraged to cover a major share of increased costs. This is already happening, because private higher education accounts for 65 percent of current higher education enrollments in the region.

Improving the Quality of Education

In about 1990, the academic achievement of Latin American students, as measured in the few available comparative tests, was far lower than that of students in the OECD countries as well as most East Asian countries. There is now a richer body of learning indicators comparing Latin America with the rest of the world. These indicators, some of which are summarized in box 8.1, confirm the poor performance of the region's students.

The qualitative challenge (raising educational standards) is, in many ways, more difficult to deal with than the quantitative one. It has to contend with the low educational attainment and literacy of parents, which makes

Figure 8.2 Projected population of 6 to 18-year-olds in Latin America and the Caribbean, 1960-2050 (millions)

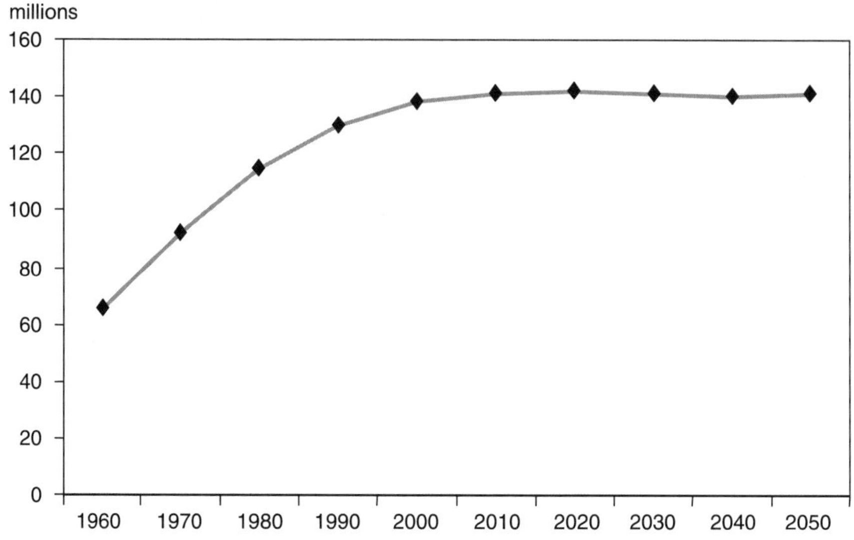

Source: World Bank estimates, 1998.

Figure 8.3 Children (aged 6 to 18 years) **as a proportion of the total population of Latin America and the Caribbean, 1960-2040** (percent)

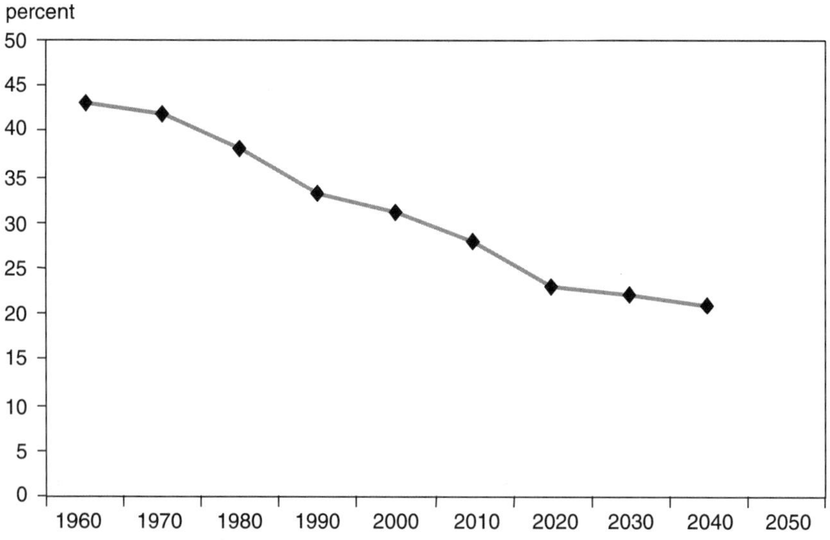

Source: World Bank data, 1995; United Nations data, 1996.

Box 8.1 Evidence on the quality of education

In 1995 Colombia—the only Latin American country to participate in the Third International Mathematics and Science Study (TIMSS) of the International Association for the Evaluation of Educational Achievement (IEA)—placed 41st out of 42 countries, higher only than South Africa. Mexico participated in the study, but at the last moment it did not authorize publication of the results. In 2002, Mexico's results, published by a news magazine, showed that its students had done worse than those of Colombia.

In 1999, Chile participated in a similar study named the TIMSS-Repeat, a replication of the test conducted in 1995. Chile, long considered among the regional leaders in educational achievement, scored ahead of only the Philippines, Morocco, and South Africa out of 38 countries, and comparatively no better than Colombia. Both Colombia and Chile scored significantly lower than countries at similar per capita levels of income. Chile also participated in an adult literacy study which found that 50 percent of its labor force was below the minimum level of reading to comprehend a simple text.

A UNESCO-Orealc study of learning in third and fourth grades in 11 countries in Latin America concluded that only in Cuba were children able to read and understand simple sentences and do arithmetical problems in a real-world context (UNESCO/Orealc 2000). Table 8.7 shows the scores of Latin American countries compared with the United States, which itself scores at the same level or below other industrial countries.

It appears clear that learning has increased modestly or not at all in the region during the past decade. Studies of learning in Chile, which have continued during a 10-year period, showed increases in achievement for the period 1990-97 but no statistically significant improvements since then. The latest studies, based on new curricula, and with better technical comparison of year-to-year progress, show no improvement in learning achievement. In Brazil, student achievement levels also did not change much during the period 1996-2000. The good news in Brazil is that repetition rates in primary education have declined dramatically, so that "internal efficiency" is improving.

the task of improving education a long-term endeavor. The additional students remaining in school are normally those who are most poorly prepared and have uneducated parents. Differential fertility rates mean that children from poorer families will be overrepresented in the educational system. It could therefore be considered some sort of a success if learning and achievement levels do no more than remain stable over the next 5 to 10 years.

A wide variety of efforts are being made to improve quality. There seems to be a growing regional consensus on the inputs and processes that are needed to improve the quality of education. This consensus includes high-quality teachers, who are paid relatively well in comparison with those in other professions; full-time teachers, open classrooms, and rigorous teacher evaluation; long school days; strong community involvement; universal preschooling; and quality in school inputs, including textbooks for all. Interestingly, Cuba (the country with by far the best educational attainment in the region; see table 8.7) has implemented all of these policies far more successfully than other countries in the region.

Table 8.7 Comparison of the results of international academic studies as a percent of US scores, selected Latin American countries, various years

	Tests, 1992				Tests, 1995-2000						
	IAEP, 1992: Grade 8		IEA, 1992: Grade 8	UNESCO, 1992:	TIMSS, 1995 and 1998: Grade 8[b]		UNESCO, 1997: Grade 4[c]		PISA, 2000: Age 15 years		
Country	Math	Science	reading	Reading[a]	Math	Science	Reading	Math	Reading	Math	Science
Argentina				66			83	79			
Bolivia				52			69	72			
Brazil[d]	67	79					82	79	77	68	75
Chile				67	78	82	84	78			
Colombia					77	72	78	76			
Costa Rica				70							
Cuba							103	104			
Dominican Republic				56			68	69			
Ecuador				55							
Honduras							70	68			
Mexico							74	75	83	80	84
Paraguay							74	73			
Venezuela			70	70			73	67			

IAEP = International Assessment of Educational Progress, Education Testing Service
IEA = International Association for the Evaluation of Educational Achievement
PISA = Progress in Student Achievement
TIMSS = Third International Mathematics and Science Study
UNESCO = United Nations Educational, Scientific, and Cultural Organization

a. The scores for the 1992 UNESCO study are expressed in relation to the US score in the IEA 1992 study, taking into account the fact that Venezuela participated in both studies.
b. The results for grade 7 in the TIMSS 1995 study are similar to those of grade 8 shown in the table.
c. The scores for the 1997 UNESCO study are expressed in relation to the US score in the TIMSS 1999 study, because Colombia and Chile participated in both studies.
d. Brazil's participation in the 1997 UNESCO study was restricted to the states of Rio Grande do Sul, Minas Gerais, and Ceará. Its participation in the IAEP study was restricted to the cities of Fortaleza and São Paulo.

Note: Blank cells indicate that the countries did not participate in the study.

Sources: For IAEP 1992, Education Testing Service; for IEA 1992, Elley (1992); for UNESCO 1992, Arancibia and Rosas (1994); for TIMSS, IEA (2000); for UNESCO 1997, UNESCO/Orealc (1998); for PISA, OECD (2001a).

Unfortunately, there is an immense gap between reaching a consensus on what needs to be done and actually doing it. For example, except in Cuba, Chile, Panama, and Uruguay, preschooling is rarely available to poor children, and even when it is, the providers are often virtually untrained.[4] As another example, while there is consensus on the importance of increased "time on task," constant teacher strikes rob many children of the opportunity to learn. In rural areas in countries such as Peru and Bolivia, students often attend class for only about 100 days a year, and engage in learning activities no more than 2 hours per day. Chile has recently taken the lead in vastly increasing the time students spend in school through the elimination of double shifting. This approach, though costly, will eventually need to be adopted throughout the region (but it will work only if *active learning time* is also increased).

The most crucial element in good education—well-trained and highly motivated teachers—is generally absent. Training is inadequate, standards are low, management is poor, accountability is almost nonexistent, teachers have little autonomy, and incentives for good performance are minimal. It is almost impossible to dismiss a teacher. In many rural areas, teacher knowledge of mathematics is not much higher than that of students, and teachers are often absent from class. Many teachers spend much of their time in routine matters, or in keeping discipline, with actual active teaching time a small percentage of classroom time.

Recognizing the importance of improving the quality of teachers, a number of countries are beginning to try to create better working conditions, increasing the care given to selecting candidates, and providing more intensive subject matter training. Efforts are under way to identify and disseminate best practices in the region. Some notable examples include Uruguay's system of intensive residential preservice training, Chile's practice of rewarding schools for superior performance, and the city of Bogotá's year-long "permanent training program for teachers." Chile has taken the lead in increasing salaries for primary school teachers, which are among the highest in the world as a ratio of GDP per capita (1.84).

Enlightened educators also recognize that providing incentives for teachers to work harder, such as higher salaries, rewarding them when students score better, dismissing them if students do poorly, and creating teacher salary ladders that reward competence, though important, need to be accompanied by a broad set of complementary policies and programs. Teachers must be given the opportunities to learn if they are to respond to sharpened incentives. This means a program to give the tools of

---

4. Although educators tend to focus on children of ages 4-6 years who could attend preschools, action to improve learning needs to begin at the prenatal stage, through good maternal nutrition and health care; for those from birth to age 3, multiple interventions (health, nutrition, social and cognitive development) are especially needed for at-risk children of poor families, especially where both parents have to work, or for single-parent families.

modern knowledge and pedagogy to new and current teachers, action to break down the isolation of teachers in their classrooms through creating within schools an environment for sharing experiences and learning, and giving teachers adequate time to prepare their lessons. Incentives or rewards given to schools and/or groups of teachers rather than individual teachers can encourage the teamwork and cooperation necessary for effective teaching.

There is also agreement, in principle, on the importance of coupling "standards-based reform" with teacher improvement. Unlike European educational systems, the region has few national achievement tests, and no country has implemented modern educational standards. Most assessment systems are weak and under the thumb of ministerial bureaucracies. The result (as was true in the United States until recently) is that there are no incentives at the classroom level to raise learning standards.

Standards-based reform seeks to define learning (and retention) goals that should be met by all children. To succeed, the tools to achieve these goals must be provided in the form of training, materials, time, and feedback. This type of reform focuses on what happens in the classroom—it seeks to measure and evaluate specific pedagogical practices and it measures learning increments. But setting standards is a complex process. They must be sufficiently detailed to be operationalized, yet not so detailed as to discourage innovation; they cannot be set so high that few students can reach them, nor so low that they offer no challenge to the average student. Recent developments in this area include a joint effort among Central American countries to agree on common standards, as well as programs under way in Chile and Brazil.

In most countries, enrollments in primary education will not grow during the next decade. This means that major capital investments in primary education will not be needed (unless other countries follow Chile's lead in phasing out double-shift schooling). It also means that there are likely to be many newly trained teachers seeking jobs in primary schools. The result could be a reduction in student-teacher ratios. There has been controversy elsewhere in the world on the extent to which lower class sizes necessarily have an impact on learning (see Ehrenberg et al. 2001). In Latin America, the smallest class sizes are often in rural areas with untrained teachers, so it is easy to see why a simple correlation of class size with educational attainment might lead to a perverse result. The most cost-effective approach might be a combination of selectively lowering class sizes for disadvantaged children in grades 1 to 3, encouraging the best teachers to migrate to these grades, and implementing in-service training programs to increase teacher subject matter knowledge and change teacher classroom pedagogy.

As growing numbers of youths have completed primary education, they have been flooding secondary schools, which have inadequate physical facilities. Large numbers of students (especially in Brazil) now attend night school, often in primary school buildings. Until recently, most secondary schools had little or no sense of identity, because it was common to have "taxi" teachers working in several schools and school directors with little authority. Teaching has been "lecture" style, and teacher knowledge and qualifications, especially in mathematics and science, have been inadequate. Repetition in secondary education is a more underappreciated problem than in primary education. The response to the explosion in the demand for secondary education has been belated. But in a number of countries, efforts are under way to update the curriculum, to create a sense of school "belonging" for teachers, and to strengthen the role of school principals.

Heckman (2001) has argued that cognitive skills as measured by achievement or IQ tests measure only one element of the skills needed in a modern economy. Social skills like self-discipline and creativity also help determine success in life. Informal on-the-job learning, as well as so-called tacit or implicit knowledge, is also critical for innovation in industry but is extremely poorly measured (Melo 2001). Latin America undoubtedly lags far behind on these more subtle measures of the quality of its human resources. International programs such as the OECD's Progress in Student Achievement and Adult Literacy and Life Skills Study are now beginning to measure these skills.

Throughout the region, there is increasing recognition that a good education includes the encouragement of trustful social relationships and an increased awareness of the basic rules of citizenship in a modern society. But there are no studies in the region on the impact of schools on long-term behaviors such as marriage stability, civic participation, reduced delinquency, and employment. The region likely has some good experiences—such as Fe y Alegría (Catholic schools located in slum areas, which are privately run but publicly financed, in a number of Andean countries), as well as *escuela nueva* in rural Colombia, with its emphasis on student participation and school democracy.

Increasing Equity in Education

The region continues to suffer from a grossly inequitable provision of educational opportunities. The greatest discrepancies by income can be found in Mexico, Central American countries, Brazil, and Ecuador (see table 8.1). An increasing awareness of this problem has led a number of countries to tackle the issue. For example, in the 1990s the Brazilian federal government changed its system of support to states to provide equal expenditures per student, which led to increased funds going to impoverished states in the Northeast. Chile has a 10-year-old program to identify and strengthen its poorest-performing schools. Mexico has a long-running program (Conafe) directed at at-risk students, especially indigenous populations in its southern states.

Argentina, Brazil, Colombia, El Salvador, and Mexico have programs that aim to help poor students remain in school by providing cash or in-kind payments to parents who keep their children in school (i.e., "demand-side" programs). Mexico's Progresa program has increased entry rates to lower secondary schools in rural areas by nearly 20 percent, as a result of which educational attainment is estimated to have increased by about two-thirds of a year (IFPRI 2000). Mexico's Telesecundaria, a 40-year-old television-based program, providing lower secondary education in rural areas, has been shown to increase retention and learning. Brazil's accelerated schools program targets children who have repeated for two or more years, and places them in classes with specially trained teachers and materials (Oliveira 1998).

In spite of this wide variety of new programs, the region needs to do far more to provide equitable access to educational opportunities. The focus should be on urban slums and rural and indigenous populations, providing a range of equity-enhancing policies. Increased preschooling targeted to the poor and to rural areas should be a priority. Other programs that deserve to be mainstreamed include demand-based programs, mass media programs directed at out-of-school, overage, or rural youth, and expanded need-based higher education student loan schemes.

Naturally, all such programs need to be carefully evaluated for their effectiveness. For example, while demand-side financing has been shown to increase school attendance in Mexico, a recent study of Argentina (Herran 2001) showed that youths who returned to secondary school because of monetary incentives were unprepared for the academic challenges and, without additional learning support, quickly became discipline problems, repeated, and eventually dropped out. A similar study of Mexico has yet to be done.

Lifelong Learning and Technology

The shift in the demographic pyramid and the growth of knowledge-based industry suggest that demands for lifelong learning will increase rapidly, as workers begin to require constant upgrading of their skills. As any casual big city observer can see, the private sector in Latin America has taken the lead in offering new training opportunities. Publicly supported training programs, once very effective in the region, are now reported to have become too costly and rigid (IDB 2001a). It is difficult to define public policy in this area because of the multiplicity of agencies involved. In any event, governments' role should be to provide an environment encouraging effective collaboration between education, training, and public and private sectors. Government should also provide an environment for the rapid development of virtual and distance higher education and training, which, interspersed with in-person guidance and collaboration, will likely be one of the main tools for out-of-school learning.

Another critical area of attention is that of access to and use of information technology. The digital divide—inequalities in access to understanding and utilization of information and communication technologies—is immense throughout the world. Such understanding is rapidly becoming part of the basic knowledge necessary for every citizen and worker. But half of US households own computers, compared with 5 percent in Latin America. A total of 78 percent of all Web sites are in English. Although attention is usually focused on the disadvantages of nonaccess to an individual, an equally important problem is the growing unattractiveness of underwired locations to business, which can lead to a concentration of poverty and a deconcentration of opportunity. At present, 96 percent of e-commerce sites are in English and 64 percent of secure servers are located in the United States. Moreover, inequalities in access to information and communications technologies may be as great within the countries of Latin America as they are across countries, although the statistics to prove this are not readily available. Fortunately, a number of countries in the region are rapidly increasing these technologies and Internet access.

Education and training can play a major role in helping to close the digital divide. While middle- and upper-class students have access to informatics at home, the school can introduce youths, probably at the secondary school level, especially those from poorer neighborhoods, to the basics of informatics—how computers work, how to use word processing and spread sheets, and how to use the Internet. Such knowledge increases students' interest in remaining in school and stimulates them to study technological subjects. Recent hardware cost reductions and evolving technology increase the feasibility of achieving this objective.

Many countries are also seeking to incorporate information and communications technologies into the secondary school curriculum, with Chile and Costa Rica taking the lead. Costa Rica's advances in educational technology are one of the reasons that it attracted a new Intel factory. Brazil now has an earmarked fund of more than $1 billion to incorporate information and communications technologies into schools. To help make schools supportive of these technologies, one policy ought to require that all new graduating teachers be computer literate.

There is a danger of overinvestment and misinvestment in technology in schools, because of the temptation to plump for politically appealing but expensive programs, such as wiring all schools to the Internet, before defining educational objectives and retraining teachers. Buying computers and installing Internet connections are not the only technology options for improving quality and increasing equity. It should also be understood that throughout the world, improving learning in secondary schools via computers on a massive basis is a promising but still unproven approach.

A wide variety of well-evaluated pilot programs in the use of computers to enhance learning are needed before firm conclusions can be drawn.

Older technologies, like radio and television, can be further exploited to improve learning and reduce inequities. Mexico's Telesecundaria and Brazil's Telecurso already reach millions of rural and out-of-school youth. Radio is being effectively used to improve learning in primary schools in Central America and in Venezuela and to train early childhood caretakers in Bolivia. Several mostly private institutions—including the Technological Institute of Monterrey, Mexico, the Escola do Futuro of the University of São Paulo, and TECSUP of Lima—are moving rapidly to introduce Internet-based learning in higher education. One underutilized but cost-effective approach in urban areas may be to use existing private-sector networks (e.g., kiosks), whose use is rapidly growing there, to provide the hardware for such instruction, rather than to burden schools with maintenance and security.

How to Meet the Challenge: The Smart State

Much of the focus of economic reform in the 1990s was on cutting back the bloated role that the state had assumed. Government had set itself up as producer of many goods and services that could be provided more efficiently by the private sector; government regulation of economic activity was oppressive, and government itself was far too centralized.

But cutting back government is not the same as ending the government's role in the economy. In fact, as the state pulls back from producing goods and services and from controlling and managing the economy, the public sector requires a "smarter" state with a far more competent (if smaller) cadre of public servants, resistant to the pressure of lobbies and aware of the subtleties and difficulties of encouraging elements such as competition, transparency, value added, and equity. The so-called second generation of reforms focuses on building the institutions that permit the state to perform effectively the tasks in which it clearly has an advantage over decentralized actors.

Education is one of those fields where the goal of improved performance demands changes in the role of the state. The state no longer simply finances and provides educational services. The "smart" state in education makes strategic investments to achieve its policy goals. It sets explicit targets for increased access, quality, equity, and response to technology, and then measures whether they are achieved. It becomes a knowledge generator and provider, and implements a wide variety of financial and other incentives to improve efficiency and effectiveness at all education levels. It plays a positive yet circumscribed role in encouraging technological innovation, establishing effective relationships with the private and nonprofit sectors in both the provision and the financing of education and related services, offering a strong, open, and fair regulatory framework, and wielding adequate financial tools to reach those goals.

Using information appropriately, through identifying and implementing cost-effective approaches, can help countries to achieve access, quality, equity, and technology goals, which in principle are not incompatible. For example, reducing repetition will lower the age of students and thus reduces the opportunity cost of remaining in school. Reducing repetition also will free funds with which to pay teachers more, while increasing their commitment to the learning process. Inadequate learning at each level results in repetition, dropping out, and inadequate learning at the next level. Some low-cost policies, such as encouraging the best teachers to work in the early grades, or reducing school-year teacher turnover, can have high payoffs. Increased private-sector financing will mean that public funds can be used more flexibly.

The past decade has seen a wide variety of efforts in this direction. Many of these efforts are promising, and several have had positive impacts on learning. Chile has certainly gone the furthest, while some countries, particularly the poorer ones and those troubled with political instability, have hardly begun. But most countries have a long way to go before they can boast of a smart state in education. The path toward the smart state is neither easy nor short. Three of the most critical roles of the smart state are the generation, provision, and use of information; the design and implementation of a more decentralized, autonomous, and accountable educational system; and the redesign of the state's role in higher education.

Generating, Providing, and Using Information

The smart state provides relevant "consumer information." It helps to generate new knowledge, and it disseminates information on the effectiveness of programs. Unfortunately, educational systems throughout the world are notorious for widespread implementation of new ideas and programs without adequate testing or evaluation. In the United States, for example, less than 1 percent of the Department of Education's budget is devoted to research. Latin America is no different when it comes to a lack of research on what works in education. Too many programs are implemented as "fads," and negative results are often suppressed. Although there has certainly been progress—there has been an increase in studies on "what works"—far more is needed. Areas of emphasis should include cost-effectiveness, measurement of the adequacy of teacher knowledge and pedagogy, continued analysis of factors affecting learning and achievement in school, an increased focus on the fit between schooling and labor market skills, and qualitative studies to identify effective school practices.

There has been progress in providing consumer information on learning. Seventeen Latin American countries now have programs to test and evaluate student learning and publish and utilize the results, compared with only four in 1990 (PREAL 2001). Chile, the states of São Paulo and Minas Gerais in Brazil, and some states in Colombia are testing all students in selected grades. Most other countries have undertaken sample surveys of learning and are publishing the results; and on the basis of test results, many are developing teacher-training materials and curriculum revisions. An increasing number of analytical studies seek to measure the impact of school policy initiatives on learning.

In some cases, quantitative studies of factors associated with learning are linked to qualitative studies designed to identify the school and classroom characteristics of "effective" schools. An increasing number of countries are participating in international assessments of student learning and are exchanging information on best practices in testing and utilization of test results. The groundbreaking 1997 study by the regional office of the United Nations Educational, Scientific, and Cultural Organization (UNESCO, Oficina Regional de Educación de la UNESCO para América Latina y el Caribe, or Orealc) compared learning and factors associated with learning in the third and fourth grades of 11 Latin American countries (UNESCO/Orealc 1998). The ministries of education of Brazil, Chile, and El Salvador have released frank and well-documented reports on the strengths and weaknesses of their educational systems and the challenges ahead. Both Mexico and Peru have released test results that were suppressed by the previous regime.

But the region still has far to go in the provision of relevant test information. And the utilization of test results is, to say the least, inadequate. For example, Colombia has reported test results in long technical reports, but until recently had not devised a useful way of reporting the results to teachers. The smaller, poorer countries do not have the specialized technical capacity to develop reliable tests. Technical weaknesses in assessments have led to potentially false conclusions. Brazil experienced unexplained variations from year to year on its standardized examinations. The improvement in scores in Chile from 1990 to 1996 cannot be confirmed because of a lack of comparability in test results from year to year. The informed public, parents, and many teachers still do not understand the value of testing. And the linkage between setting higher standards, measuring the extent to which they are being met, and providing the tools to meet them more adequately (i.e., "aligning" the official curriculum, the curriculum as it is "implemented" or not in the classroom; textbooks; and teacher training) is far from complete.

Decentralization, Autonomy, and Private Provision of Services

It must be recognized that well-managed centralized educational systems with high standards and strong accountability, such as those in Japan, Singapore, and South Korea, have yielded good results. But the "centralized" model has been an abject failure in most of Latin America, resulting in incompetent bureaucracies and counterproductive incentives. Paradoxically, this model, which is based on a complex set of "formal" controls, has led de facto to extreme decentralization at the classroom level, where there have been neither controls nor feedback.

Recognizing the ills of their own centralized school systems, many countries or states have implemented a wide variety of programs of decentralization and school autonomy.[5] What does research tell us about the impact of these efforts? In some cases, the impact has clearly been positive. Local school autonomy in Guatemala and El Salvador has led, at the least, to increased retention of students in rural areas. The long-running *escuela nueva* in rural Colombia, based on carefully prepared and tested teaching-learning materials, community participation, student democracy, and structured in-service training, has improved learning in rural areas and is being replicated in other countries. In fact, Colombia is the only country in the region where performance on standardized tests is higher in rural than in urban areas (UNESCO 2001b). In other cases, the results have been less promising. When the central government abandons its regulatory and monitoring role (as happened in Argentina and, until recently, in Peru), decentralization may be worse than the system it replaces.

To succeed, the "decentralized" state needs a cadre of "smart" bureaucrats to manage the new system. Unfortunately, the lack of motivated and competent staff in ministries of education is a decades-old theme. Although the revolving door of ministers of education has slowed down and there is increased continuity of policy, the number of technically competent staff throughout the region remains thin. Without good management, local elites can capture and/or politicize the educational process and local government officials may lack the expertise to manage an educational system. Intensive training programs for educational managers, coupled with incentives for them to remain in their posts, are needed.

Overall, the consensus is that decentralization and school autonomy, when linked to central government oversight, training, standards, achievement tests, strong parent involvement, and constant or increased financing, will have a positive impact on learning (Espinola 2001 and Wolff, Schiefelbein, and Schiefelbein 2002). Yet definitions, issues, and results with regard to decentralization vary dramatically between large federal states like Brazil and Mexico and small countries such as Honduras and Uruguay.

The smart state also turns to the private sector for educational services whenever the private sector offers advantages in costs, quality, diversity, or equity. A recent set of case studies on private provision of primary and secondary education provides a deeper understanding of public-private relationships (Wolff, Gonzalez, and Navarro 2002). These studies confirm

5. Decentralization of education is part of a larger political movement in the region of devolution of responsibilities to local and regional authorities and increased local democracy.

that private or communal programs such as PRONADE in Guatemala and Fe y Alegría in the Andean countries are cost-effective. However, government oversight of private education in a number of countries—including Argentina, Guatemala, Peru, and Venezuela—is sorely lacking in consistency and technical capacity. In Argentina, public subsidies have often gone to elite schools rather than to private schools serving poor communities. Private schools can constitute an unenlightened lobby; for example, private school directors in Guatemala have resisted publication of individual school examination results.

Chile's decades-old experiment in vouchers for primary and secondary education has induced some good research yielding important lessons. Private institutions now account for 45 percent of expenditures in primary and secondary education. The research has found that Catholic schools are cost-effective; and that private school costs are in general lower than those in public schools, which are still excessively constrained by bureaucratic rules. However, after controlling for social class, secular private schools in Chile do no better than public schools in achievement tests. There has been increased social stratification, with middle-class families moving to private subsidized schools while poor families remain in public municipal schools.

In short, private provision of educational services is an important, growing, and often positive option, but it is no panacea (there are *no* panaceas) for the ills of the region's educational systems. Transparent and consistent rules of the game, and thoughtful government oversight, are necessary if society is to benefit.

When all is said and done, publicly provided education will remain the norm, certainly for primary and secondary education, for the foreseeable future. Therefore, when the state does provide services, it must do so efficiently. The most promising approach is to give public institutions far more autonomy, linked to accountability, than they currently possess. And then the smart state needs to tackle the large numbers of "ghost" teachers, inflated bureaucracies, and counterproductive, often out-of-date, rules and regulations that remain throughout the region, as well as countering corruption in areas as varied as school construction and teacher selection.

The Smart State and Higher Education

The smart state faces a particular challenge in higher education. Perverse incentives, especially to public institutions, continue to encourage inequity and discourage innovation, cost-effectiveness, and linkages to the productive sector. Traditionally, upper- and middle-class students have attended free public institutions, while poorer students have had to pay for their schooling in private institutions. Public funds are now increasingly spread thinly among large public institutions, with consequent reductions in quality, which has promoted a trend to abandon these institutions by the classes that historically benefited from free tuition. Private higher education has expanded rapidly during the past two decades. Some private schools are of high quality, and many are more closely linked to the labor market; but too many are low-quality "diploma mills." Inadequate or counterproductive government oversight often has the perverse effect of encouraging corrupt practices and false advertising in the private sector.

It has been argued by some that the state has overinvested in higher education and ought to shift its funding toward lower levels. Although this may have been a compelling argument a decade ago, when higher education enrollments were lower and expenditures per student higher, today no generalizations can be made for the region as a whole. Appendix 8.1 provides a review of this question.

A more important issue is that of widespread perverse incentives in higher education policies in Latin America, which encourage low quality, inefficiency, and inequity, and result in the state not getting an adequate return for its higher education investments, which have been documented in countries as diverse as Colombia (Brunner 2002), Brazil (Wolff and Albrecht 1992), and Venezuela (Navarro 1999). Policies and financial incentives to make public institutions more flexible, cost-effective, and better linked to the private sector include financing schools on the basis of outputs (e.g., number of students trained) rather than inputs (number of teachers); varying financial provision with the extent to which an institution has a research as well as a teaching function; publishing information on the quality of higher education institutions; and establishing and/or strengthening competitive grant funding on the basis of transparent criteria.

The state also needs to ensure a critical mass, albeit small in relation to total enrollment, of high-quality research and training institutions and programs in areas important for economic and social development that are linked to each country's national innovation system. At the same time, cost recovery in public institutions, coupled with loans and scholarships, can boost equity, because most higher education students come from the high-income groups in society. Cost recovery can also improve governance and efficiency, because paying students are less likely to stay quiet when the quality of teaching falls or markets are saturated; and it can also provide extra resources for strained higher education budgets.

There has been some progress in higher education reform. Chile has a system of competitive grants to both public and private institutions based on quality measurements. Brazil has a long-running, well-managed grant program for graduate education and research and has set up an innovative system to test and publish the results of learning achievement in higher education institutions. El Salvador has developed a system for accrediting both public and private institutions. Many public institutions around the region have begun to diversify their programs and sources of income. Some state institutions in Mexico have increased tuition and established strong student loan programs. A regional student loan association provides technical assistance to 30 member institutions. But loans currently reach no more than 2 percent of all higher education students, so there is still scope for much expansion, provided student loan institutions are adequately financed, have competent staff, and are insulated from political pressures. Subsidized need-based student loans are probably the most cost-effective public investment in higher education, because, if well managed, such programs can simultaneously increase or improve equity, quality, and diversity and can also be targeted to areas with low private returns—such as teaching, nursing, and agricultural research—but that are critical for development.

The state also plays a key role in strengthening the overall national innovation system, which includes education and training. To strengthen science and technology, the state could devise tax incentives for research and development, directly fund precompetitive research performed by the private sector or in public-private consortia, build up a positive environment for venture capital, cofinance with industry technology diffusion and information centers, and provide incentives to link academic research institutions with the productive sector.

In the smaller and poorer countries, it would make sense to seek collaboration across national boundaries in areas such as the diffusion of technological information and precompetitive research in areas of common interest (e.g., "regional" public goods). However, state intervention to promote technological innovation can be counterproductive. When applied in the wrong institutional context, without flexibility and feedback mechanisms, it can open a Pandora's box of rent-seeking behavior and related abuses, which are difficult to reverse even when the economic environment changes (Melo 2001).

Several Latin American countries are implementing new policy approaches and instruments to promote technological innovation in the productive sector, including fiscal incentives, grants, and loans; incentives for new linkages between research institutions and the productive sector; and infrastructure for information and standards. Brazil, Chile, Mexico, and Venezuela have taken the lead. Small countries, such as Guatemala, El Salvador, and Panama, have begun to pay attention to the ways public policy can fortify their competitiveness, including strengthening regional and subregional research and development centers in areas such as agricultural technology.

The Political Economy of the Smart State

The backdrop for educational reform is the new public awareness of the importance of education. While in the 1980s economic crises kept the leadership of most countries from focusing on such long-term issues as human resource development, by the early 1990s there was an emerging political consensus on the importance of improving Latin America's performance in education. Leaders and the informed public became aware of the region's relative deficiencies in the educational attainment of its labor force.

Leaders in government and civil society throughout the region increasingly aver that education is a key to economic development, in fighting poverty, in reducing income inequalities and, beyond that, in incubating and safeguarding contemporary citizenship and democratic values. Constituencies including parents, students, teachers, governmental authorities, businesses, nongovernmental organizations, and the media are demanding more resources, new policies, and better decisions for the education sector; and they want these policies to be good enough to enable educational systems to address the economic, social, and cultural challenges of the global economy.

In many countries, educational issues are now front-page news. For example, the results of standardized achievement examinations in Chile have led to a national debate on why scores were not improving. Education ministers and secretaries in many countries are now political and opinion leaders, and in a number of cases are among the strongest cabinet ministers. Brazil and El Salvador each had the same minister of education for more than 6 years, until now an almost unheard of occurrence in the region. Although Chile has often changed ministers, the architects of its educational reform have remained in office and its education policy has been consistent. Alejandro Toledo, the current president of Peru, declared that he would be the "education president" and has a doctorate in the economics of education.

It is nonetheless true that, for the most part, the children of politically influential people attend private primary and secondary schools rather than public schools. Thus they do not directly feel the deficiencies of the public school system, because their interests are not directly and immediately affected by the success or failure of public schools. This reduces the sense of urgency that might otherwise lead influential parents to press decision makers to make tough policy choices, and makes it harder to put together a political coalition willing to pay the high political costs that come with making basic changes in public schools. In this respect, a far-sighted public education policy includes not only targeting resources to underserved and at-risk populations but also methods of attracting the upper middle class back to the public sector through "magnet" and other high-quality institutions.

Although the public debate is very important, education is always a part of the larger economic, political, and social environment. With good economic management a "virtuous cycle" can be created, because increased economic growth leads to demands for a better-educated labor force. A more educated labor force leads to higher productivity and increased economic growth, creating an increased demand for a more highly educated labor force. Education as much as any other sector depends on good economic management, including, as is discussed in this book, far more flexible labor market rules and regulations. Without economic growth, government will not be able to trade increased teachers' salaries and improved working conditions for increased responsibility and accountability.

Furthermore, political stability based on democratic processes is essential if politicians are to begin to take a longer view of the educational process. It is no coincidence that educational progress has been most rapid in countries such as Brazil, Chile, and El Salvador, which have been politically stable in recent years, but has been stagnant or even negative in Argentina, Guatemala, Peru, and Venezuela, which have been beset by continuing crises of political legitimacy.[6]

Public and opinion leaders must increasingly focus on consensus building if they are to achieve the collaboration of civil society and, in particular, of parents and teachers. Reforms will require transparency about the extent to which goals are being met, as well as effective feedback disseminated to the informed public so as to permit midcourse corrections. The feedback needs to focus on the critical outcome issues—how much children are learning, whether they are staying in school, and what kinds of jobs they are getting. Checks, balances, and incentives must encourage actors and stakeholders to behave in ways that strengthen the reform process. Opinion and business leaders must be convinced that the graduates of public institutions are those whom they are going to have to depend on for increased productivity.

Finally, key actors must have the capacity to implement reforms. This means effective training of administrators and teachers. Bad past practices, like the constant rotation of ill-prepared ministers of education (which continues in some but not all countries) and a plethora of multiple, usually short-lived "reform" programs with unclear objectives, need to end.

Education leaders and decision makers will need to convince finance ministers and officials that the educational system is effectively and efficiently managed if they are to press successfully for increased funding, especially in a time of overall fiscal constraints. At the same time, public funds should be forthcoming when effectiveness is demonstrated. Although many priorities, such as school construction and increased salaries, will require more funds, others will require mainly political courage and risk taking. Effective political leadership involves identifying and resisting rent-seeking behavior from wherever it may come, be it the productive

6. Brazil and El Salvador began the decade far behind their neighbors and have made significant progress. Argentina and Venezuela decades ago had relatively advanced education systems, which have since deteriorated. Peru has high enrollment ratios but among the lowest achievement levels in the region.

sector, stakeholders in public and/or private higher education, and/or middle- and upper-class parents.

One very important example concerns teachers' unions, which in most countries have antagonistic relationships to government. Many teachers' unions have been captured by small groups with political agendas unrelated to the teaching profession; and governments have often treated unions with contempt. The result has been an excessive number of long strikes, and inadequate interest in issues such as the quality of learning and the professionalization of teaching. For historical reasons, Mexico's unions control critical policy decisions, such as the selection of staff in teacher-training colleges. The aim should not be to "break" the unions, which usually is a self-defeating endeavor, but rather to make teachers' unions at all levels of education positive partners in reform, by encouraging a new generation of leaders concerned with promoting the learning process through the professionalization of teaching. An obvious, but nonetheless brave, policy change would be to end the widespread practice of continuing to pay teachers when they are on strike![7]

There are even more entrenched and articulate lobbies and pressure groups in higher education than at lower levels. The difficulties in implementing cost recovery in public institutions are symptomatic of this problem. In lieu of reform, the tendency has been for finance ministers to starve public institutions, which has had the perverse effect of destroying the few high-quality public programs but the positive effect of encouraging a wide variety of private-sector initiatives. Here, the debate needs to focus on the long-term social benefits of more flexible, results-based higher education financing.

Each country must design its reform package in accordance with its level of educational development and its economic resources. Using the United Nations Development Program's "education index," which is based on enrollment ratios and literacy,[8] the region's countries in the "lowest range" include Bolivia, most of Central America (with the exception of Costa Rica), and the Dominican Republic. One would expect their policies to focus on increasing access to lower secondary education, ensuring basic formal teacher qualifications, providing books to all students, targeted preschooling, and seeking cost-effective ways of encouraging some high-quality higher education.

For those countries in the "high" range, which include Chile, Argentina, Uruguay, and Costa Rica, the policies are likely to include giving an increasing proportion of their population access to 12 years of education

7. When asked why he continued to authorize payment to teachers while they were striking, a leading political figure in a Central American country answered that teachers were an important bloc of potential voters that he could not afford to alienate.

8. This index is imperfect because it does not reflect quality issues.

and subsequently to postsecondary education; seeking universal preschooling; and improving quality at all levels. In larger countries, there is a great need to reduce disparities between regions; for example, the average number of years of schooling of the adult population in the Brazilian Northeast is 4.1, compared to 6.2 in the Southeast.

International coordination and cooperation can advance the agenda of education reform. But idealistic statements and quantitative targets set at summits are of limited value because of the complexity of the educational process and the different starting points of countries. Perhaps the greatest value of international cooperation is to be found where regional public goods can be identified and countries are willing to work together on a common goal, especially when individual small countries lack a critical mass of human resources. Some areas for fruitful cooperation—which already is occurring on a small scale—include regional and subregional (e.g., Central American or Andean) research and development centers, testing and measurement programs, efforts to develop software for virtual education, and study tours across countries to observe successful innovations.

In education, leapfrogging and "magic bullets" are myths, and there are no shortcuts. Improving education is a long-term process requiring commitment, continuity, and consensus. Furthermore, progress in education, far from being an autonomous process, depends greatly on economic policies inducing equity-based growth and on political stability.

Appendix 8.1 Does Latin America Invest Too Much in Higher Education?

Some critics have argued that public expenditures in higher education in Latin America are "too high" and that funding should be shifted to primary education. Data recently collected by OECD help to clarify the extent to which this assertion is true. In six Latin American countries with available data (excluding Brazil), average expenditures per student in higher education are equivalent to 44 percent of GDP per capita. This ratio is higher than in the OECD countries but lower than in East Asia (table A8.1), suggesting that the effort that Latin America makes in higher education is comparable (neither too high or too low) to that of competitors.

These same Latin American countries spend an average of 13 percent of GDP per capita per student on primary education, compared with 19 percent in OECD countries (see table A8.1). Only Chile approaches the industrial countries in the ratio of unit expenditures for primary education to per capita income. The critics therefore appear to have some justification when they say that Latin American countries make an inadequate effort, relative to their resources, in spending per primary education student (in spite of recent improvements).

Brazil is a seventh Latin American country with data in the OECD tables, but it is an extreme outlier. Its per student expenditures—in public higher education institutions only—in 1998 were $14,618, or 210 percent of per capita income, higher in absolute terms than every OECD country except the United States and Switzerland. An unknown but very high proportion of these expenditures cover university hospitals, pensions for retired teachers, and other items that should not be included as teaching costs.[9]

One argument has been that the region should increase private-sector enrollment and expenditures. Again, using OECD data, the public sector in OECD countries accounts on average for 82 percent of expenditures (ranging from 99 percent in Austria and Switzerland to 52 percent in the United States and only 17 percent in South Korea; see table A8.2). In the six Latin American countries for which data are available, the public sector accounts for 67 percent of higher education expenditures (ranging from 100 percent in Uruguay to 31 percent in Chile). Overall, private higher education is relatively important in Latin America, especially compared with Europe, but less important than in some Asian countries. The tendency throughout the world has been for the private sector to increase

9. Brazil's high public expenditures per student, low percentage of enrollments in public institutions (less than 35 percent of total higher education enrollment), and lack of cost recovery have been regularly documented by researchers and the media. Efforts at reform have not yet been successful, although it is reported that unit costs have decreased since 1998.

Table A8.1 Expenditure per student in 1998 US dollars (purchasing power parity) **and as a percent of GDP per capita, selected regions and countries**

	Primary		Secondary		Higher		
Group or region and country	**In US dollars**	**As a percent of GDP per capita**	**In US dollars**	**As a percent of GDP per capita**	**In US dollars**	**As a percent of GDP per capita**	**Ratio of higher to primary**
OECD countries (29 countries), **of which**	3,940	19	5,294	26	9,063	44	2.3
Germany	3,531	15	6,209	27	9,481	41	2.7
Japan	5,075	21	5,890	24	6,356	41	1.3
United States	6,043	19	7,764	24	19,802	61	3.3
East Asia and Pacific	—	15	—	20	—	123	—
Indonesia	116	4	497	19	6,840	259	59.0
Malaysia	919	11	1,469	18	—	—	—
Philippines	689	18	726	19	2,799	75	4.1
South Korea	2,838	20	3,544	25	6,356	44	2.2
Thailand	1,048	19	1,177	21	6,360	116	6.1
Latin America (7 countries)	—	12	—	18		71[a]	—
Argentina (public only)	1,389	12	1,860	16	2,965	25	2.1
Brazil (public only)	837	12	1,076	16	14,618	214	17.5
Chile	1,500	17	1,713	20	5,897	67	3.9
Mexico	863	11	1,586	20	3,800	48	4.4
Paraguay (public only)	572	13	948	22	2,511	58	4.4
Peru	479	11	671	15	2,085	48	4.4
Uruguay	971	11	1,246	14	2,081	24	2.1

— = not available
OECD = Organization for Economic Cooperation and Development

a. The figure is 44 percent excluding Brazil.

Source: OECD, *Education at a Glance*, 2001, table B 1.1.

Table A8.2 Percent of public and private expenditures by level, selected Latin American and OECD countries, 1998

Country or region	Primary, secondary, and postsecondary Public	Primary, secondary, and postsecondary Private	Higher Public	Higher Private
OECD mean, of which:	91.3	8.7	82.1	17.9
Germany	75.9	24.1	92.1	7.9
South Korea	79.7	20.3	17.4	82.6
United States	90.8	9.1	52.5	47.5
Latin America				
(mean for 5 countries)	79.8	21.2	67.5	32.5
Argentina	89.4	10.6	74.3	25.7
Chile	68.7	31.3	30.9	69.1
Mexico	86.2	13.8	87.9	12.1
Peru	61.8	38.2	44.6	55.4
Uruguay	93.1	6.9	100.0	0

OECD = Organization for Economic Cooperation and Development

Source: OECD, *Education at a Glance*, 2001, table B 3.2.

its percentage of overall expenditures on higher education, as appears to be happening in Latin America. The increased social demand for higher education coupled with limited public funds is likely to further increase private-sector funding throughout the world.

On average, about 22 percent of the public education budget in 17 countries in Latin America goes to higher education (see table A8.3), a proportion that is roughly the same as the OECD average. The question of whether this amount is too high can only be answered after breaking down and analyzing, on a country-by-country basis, all the elements that go into it—the costs per student at all levels, enrollment ratios and school-age population at all levels, and public-private ratios; then estimating expected and/or desirable changes in these elements.

The knowledge economy is demanding increased higher-level skills and raising the rate of return for higher education; therefore, we can expect enrollment ratios in Latin America, which are currently 19 percent, to increase. Because capital markets in education are notoriously imperfect, the region will not be able to rely solely on more investment by the private sector in higher education. As more youths with disadvantaged backgrounds seek higher education, there will be a need for increased publicly subsidized student loan programs, as well as scholarships in cases of extreme need.

Higher education also has important elements, that require a strong public presence, including training teachers at all levels, supporting graduate education and research in areas important for economic development, encouraging the study and development of new technologies, and strengthening postsecondary nonuniversity training linked to the labor

Table A8.3 Percent of public education expenditure on higher education, selected OECD and Latin American countries, various years

Group or region and country	Percent
OECD average, 1998, of which:	22.1
Canada	29.1
Germany	25.8
Japan	13.4
South Korea	12.2
Netherlands	27.9
United Kingdom	19.6
United States	23.9
Seven Latin American countries, average, 1998	22.0
Argentina	23.6
Brazil	25.6
Chile	17.6
Mexico	20.6
Paraguay	21.4
Peru	22.5
Uruguay	23.2
Ten additional Latin American countries, average[a]	22.2
Bolivia, 1996	27.7
Colombia, 1996	18.8
Costa Rica, 1996	28.3
Dominican Republic, 1996	13.0
Ecuador, 1996	21.3
Guatemala, 1996	15.2
Honduras, 1995	16.6
Panama, 1997	26.1
Paraguay, 1996	19.7
Venezuela, 1995	36.2

OECD = Organization for Economic Cooperation and Development

a. Note that the information from these countries comes from the United Nations Economic, Social, and Cultural Organization rather than from the OECD and therefore is not strictly comparable.

Sources: For OECD and seven Latin American countries, OECD, *Education at a Glance*, 2002, table B 21b; for additional Latin American countries, *UNESCO Statistical Yearbook*, 2001.

market. Furthermore, higher education, unlike primary and secondary education, is an internationally traded service. The best teachers will migrate out of their country to other countries where salaries, teaching conditions, and opportunities for research are better.

Cost recovery and more private higher education certainly help to reduce the strain on public higher education budgets. But the increasing demands of the knowledge economy for more highly trained workers, the need for a minimum quality standard, research in areas critical for national development, considerations of equity, and the risk of losing the best higher education teachers and researchers to other regions all require the state's continued financial participation in higher education.

9

Labor Markets during the 1990s

JAIME SAAVEDRA

Market-oriented reforms became widespread in Latin America and the Caribbean during the 1990s. The expectations of reformers were that the shift toward a more competitive environment—with a change in the role of the state, so that markets would become the main determinant of relative prices and of resource allocation—would reduce inefficiencies, increase productivity, and spur growth. This would result in an increase in labor demand, which would absorb the increase in the labor force. Higher productivity would eventually lead to higher real wages and better jobs.

In turn, critics of the liberal reforms raised concerns about the possible negative impact that trade liberalization, privatization, and the reduction in the role of the state would have on employment, real wages, and earnings inequality—at least in the short run. To the extent that safety nets in many countries existed (and in many cases still exist) only on paper, some of those concerns were justified.

The lack of full recovery of employment and earnings after the macroeconomic crises of the late 1980s and unmet expectations are probably behind the negative perception regarding the impact of economic growth and structural reforms on the labor market. Employment performance was weak, and many analysts and the popular press voiced a perception

Jaime Saavedra is principal researcher and executive director of Grupo de Análisis para el Desarrollo (GRADE), a think tank based in Lima, Peru. *The author thanks Eduardo Nakasone for his superb research assistance.*

that even if there was economic growth, it was jobless growth. In addition, during the 1990s, macroeconomic stabilization and a more competitive environment induced by structural reforms, which in some countries included labor market reforms, might have changed the labor market adjustment mechanisms. And even though economic volatility was lower in the 1990s, Latin America is still a highly volatile region—as the developments at the end of the decade confirm—which has had an impact on the labor market.

The evidence shows that during the 1990s employment growth responded to economic growth. Where there was growth, there was employment creation, but the former was insufficient to absorb the increase in the labor force. Conversely, as most Latin American economies went into recession in 1997 or 1998, employment growth stopped. Moreover, lower inflation implied that adjustments through employment were more frequent than adjustments through changes in real wages. But the main problem in Latin America is one of low-quality jobs. The informal sector—understood as employment with no social benefits, unemployment protection, or compliance with occupational safety regulations—accounts for more than half the jobs in urban areas and the vast majority in rural areas, and has shown an upward trend, particularly at the end of the decade.

Labor legislation in the region was drafted with the intention of protecting workers and improving their bargaining position, on the understanding that they are the weak side of the labor relationship. Moreover, it was designed to regulate a relationship that was seen as one of intrinsic and permanent conflict between labor and capital. Labor market regulations in Latin America have a long tradition of reducing flexibility and protecting jobs—even at the cost of reducing the ability of firms to adapt to changes in demand. Firms in tariff-protected sectors, as well as public enterprises and the public administration, enjoyed high rents and were able to bear the risks of the high, quasi-fixed costs generated by regulation. An ever smaller group of workers in the modern urban sector were able to enjoy high-quality jobs, even if their productivity was not enough to cover those costs. With the dismantling of tariffs and the higher exposure to competition and integration, many of these jobs disappeared.

Labor market reforms were implemented in some countries, but legislative changes differed widely in depth and even direction. Despite popular perceptions, labor market reforms have been modest. In several Latin American countries not much happened, and in a few cases, labor market regulations were made even more stringent. Regulations are in most cases designed to provide the average worker with social benefits and job protection that are out of line with the average level of productivity. The high labor costs resulting from regulations are paid by high-productivity workers and those firms that are able and willing to finance these benefits, while others escape the regulations through informality. Since economies slowed down at the end of the 1990s, and with increases in nonwage costs in several countries, either unemployment or informal employment has increased.

This chapter reviews the employment performance of the region during the 1990s in the context of the structural reforms that many countries implemented, including in several cases labor market reforms. It is difficult to identify regularities common to all or most of the countries, although there are a few stylized facts that have characterized the evolution of Latin American labor markets during the past decade. Female labor force participation rates have increased steadily, the male-female wage gap has decreased, the share of manufacturing in total employment has fallen, and the informal sector has grown. Other factors seem to be common to many countries, but more empirical work is needed to confirm if these facts are transitory or structural changes. For instance, there is evidence of an increase in labor turnover and of higher returns from education.

As will be discussed in the second section of the chapter, in fact there was employment growth, at least until 1997 or 1998, in the context of a slowdown in the increase in labor force participation. At the end of the decade, there was evidence of increased unemployment in several countries. However, the main problem in Latin America seems to be the quality of the jobs available, including that of new jobs. The section reviews several indicators that serve as proxies for changes in job quality. According to almost all the different criteria that may be invoked to measure job quality, the region seems to be creating more low-quality than high-quality jobs. In most countries, the proportion of workers that do not have health or pension benefits has increased. The proportion of workers in the so-called informal or unregulated sector is increasing, regardless of the definition of informal jobs used. Within the formal sector, turnover—as well as the number of workers on temporary contracts—is increasing. Perhaps high job mobility can in principle be consistent with a highly flexible, dynamic, and healthy labor market. But where mobility is coupled with no social benefits and lower or at best stagnant real wages, a feeling of economic insecurity is inevitable.

As is shown in the third section, many of the changes observed in Latin American labor markets may be related to sectoral reallocations of output and employment induced by structural reforms. Trade reforms and financial reforms generated changes in relative prices, in particular an increase in the relative price of nontradables, that had an effect on the sectoral structure of output, and hence on the structure of employment. There is evidence of a reduction in the share of manufacturing jobs in total urban employment. In a simple theoretical framework, trade should have brought an increase in the output of unskilled labor-intensive goods and consequently an increase in the demand for, and the wages of, unskilled workers. However, liberalization, the increase in foreign direct investment, and exchange rate appreciation led to an increase in the incorporation of new technologies, which in turn generated an increase in the demand for skilled workers, in most cases for workers with a tertiary education.

Conversely, there was a clear increase in the share of services—both skill-intensive ones, as in the financial and business services sector, and unskilled-intensive ones, as in retail trade. The other important development in the structure of employment was the reduction in public-sector employment in the majority of Latin American countries, due to public administration downsizing and to privatizations.

We also review briefly who could have been winners and losers from the reform of labor markets. Even if we are still dealing with the short-run effects of reforms that have not always been completed, the lack of social safety nets for those who lost as a result of reform had important political economy implications for the sustainability of the reform process. The evidence shows that the proportion of workers with less secure jobs increased, and much of that change was among workers who used to belong to the middle class (those in the public sector, unions, public utilities, and in large manufacturing firms) and as such had more voice and more mechanisms through which they could manifest their discontent.

The chapter's fourth section reviews changes in labor legislation. Despite the popular perception that labor markets have been deregulated massively in Latin America, a review of the changes in legislation shows that changes have in general been modest. Even in such countries as Peru and Argentina, where there were noticeable changes from the extremely regulated labor markets of the 1970s and 1980s, changes have been erratic and postreform labor legislation cannot be considered flexible by any means. In certain cases, partial changes in regulations made things worse by generating distorted and inefficient outcomes. The increase in the use of temporary employment contracts is a good example.

The fifth section analyzes in detail the informal (or unprotected, or unregulated) sector, which is clearly related to the large prevalence of low-quality jobs in Latin America. A better understanding of its behavior and characteristics is crucial for determining what can be done to increase the number of workers with at least a minimum of social protection.

The sixth section reviews the main features of active labor market policies, which have a long tradition in Latin America. The final section concludes with a brief analysis of the policy changes that need to be implemented to improve the functioning of Latin American labor markets.

Employment and Unemployment during the 1990s

The elimination of distortions caused by import-substitution industrialization strategies was expected to spur sustained economic growth on the

Figure 9.1 Average GDP and employment growth rate of Latin American and Caribbean countries by decade, 1950s-90s (percent)

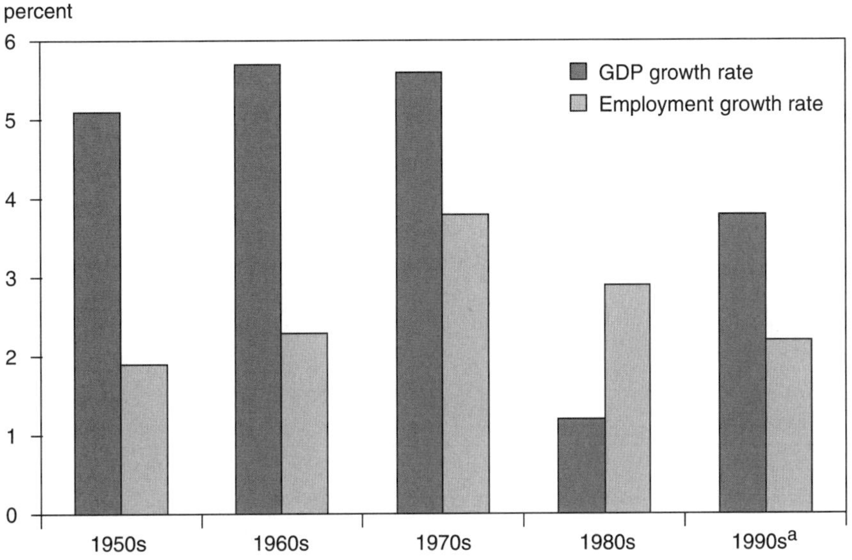

a. The 1990s include only the 1990-97 period.

Source: Weller (2000).

basis of a more efficient allocation of resources. This growth would generate employment and reductions in poverty rates. Furthermore, simple economic models predicted that trade liberalization would increase the demand for unskilled workers, because the relative abundance of unskilled workers would foster additional growth in sectors intensive in this factor. Therefore, reforms were expected not only to have a positive effect on overall employment, but to have an especially favorable effect on unskilled labor. Moreover, this bias toward unskilled labor was expected to substantially reduce poverty.

However, employment growth in Latin American and Caribbean countries during the 1990s was significantly smaller than in the 1980s. Despite the fact that economic growth was higher during the 1990s than the 1980s (3.9 vs. 1.1 percent), the rate of growth in employment was only 2.1 percent during the latter period, while in the 1980s it reached 2.9 percent (figure 9.1).

The research of Weller (2000) confirms the existence of a positive relationship between economic growth and job creation during the 1990s. Economic growth was not negative for employment; the problem was that job creation was small as a consequence of little growth. Stallings and Peres (2000), on the basis of statistics from Weller, argue that the employment-

Table 9.1 Female labor force participation rate, selected Latin American countries, 1986-99 (percent)

Country	1986	1992	1995	1999
Argentina	36.7	39.2	40.1	43.9
Bolivia	46.7	46.3	52.8	50.8
Brazil	44.4	50.1	51.3	52.6
Chile	31.6	36.9	39.0	41.4
Colombia	43.7	50.1	49.3	54.6
Costa Rica	39.3	37.3	40.7	44.9
Ecuador	41.3	—	48.2	53.7
Guatemala	—	—	—	54.3
Honduras	45.9	44.2	42.5	53.7
Mexico	29.6	35.6	38.0	42.8
Panama	39.7	43.4	46.9	51.5
Paraguay	52.4	50.7	60.1	—
Peru	—	—	—	62.1
Uruguay	40.3	46.0	47.3	49.6
Venezuela	33.6	39.4	43.3	47.9
Simple average	40.4	43.3	46.1	50.3
Weighted average[a]	39.5	44.6	46.3	50.0

— not available

a. Weighted average using working-age population by country.

Source: UN Economic Commission for Latin America and the Caribbean, *Statistical Yearbook*, 2000.

output elasticity during the 1990s was not significantly different from values found for the 1960s and 1970s. The 1980s were an outlier when, despite the disastrous economic performance, employment grew fast. Employment grew rapidly in the 1980s because the labor force was growing fast, and also because real wages could adjust downward easily in most countries, given the highly inflationary macroeconomic context. This mechanism was no longer available, given the macroeconomic stability achieved during the 1990s. Thus the jobless growth perception so in fashion, at least until 1998, was a consequence of insufficient growth reinforced by lower downward flexibility in real wages.

In part, the lower employment growth during the 1990s was due to demographic factors. As is pointed out by Duryea and Székely (1998), the rate of growth of the working-age population has begun to decline, falling from 3 percent per year in the 1980s to 2.5 percent in the 1990s. The increase in the labor force participation rate during recent decades can mainly be explained by the increase in female participation. During the 1990s, this rate increased sharply in all Latin America countries (table 9.1),[1] although there is evidence of a slowing down in this increase also.

1. The exceptions were Argentina and Uruguay, which witnessed an exogenous baby boom during the late 1960s and early 1970s, as is pointed out by Duryea and Székely (1998) and Kritz (2002).

The persistent increase in female labor force participation may be signaling structural changes in labor markets. It has increased, on average, by 6 percentage points, with the highest increases in Costa Rica, Colombia, Mexico, and Peru. Duryea, Cox-Edwards, and Ureta (2001) find that increases in female educational attainment explain only a third of the increase in participation. The increase within educational groups may be attributed to the reduction in fertility rates or to a change in females' social status (Berry and Mendez 1999).

Employment evolution is also dependent on the way the labor market adjusts. Despite country differences, lower inflation has meant that almost everywhere wages have stopped being an important adjustment mechanism. Gonzalez (1999) finds some evidence that in countries that carried out price stabilization programs (Argentina, Bolivia, and Chile in an earlier period) the response of employment to output shocks increased during the 1990s, while the wage response fell. The years of recession since 1997 have implied a reduction in employment rates in most countries, while wages have not always fallen at the same time. Instead, unemployment has risen in several countries.

In fact, using information compiled by the International Labor Organization (ILO), based on household surveys, we can see that employment rates (total employment as a percentage of working-age population) moved with the economic cycle (see figure 9.2). Excluding Brazil, employment grew faster than the working-age population, at least until 1997. In Brazil, even if employment growth was positive, it was slower than the growth of the working-age population. In all the other countries, the employment rate grew slightly or remained relatively flat until 1997 or 1998, and since then it has fallen in several countries. The exception was Argentina, where there was a reduction in the employment rate after the Mexican crisis. Thus, employment evolution benefited from the positive economic growth rates achieved following economic stabilization and structural reforms. But in the final years of the decade, employment was curbed by the international financial crises and the resulting lower economic growth rates.

Open urban unemployment has become an increasingly acute problem in Argentina, Colombia, Chile, and Venezuela (table 9.2). Current figures show that on average unemployment rates stand at a high 10 percent, despite the low rate in Mexico and the moderate rate in Brazil. Overall, unemployment rates are in most cases higher than they were during the 1980s. Part of the rise in unemployment seems to be related to the increase in labor force participation rates, but the increase may also be related to the smaller capacity of some economies to adjust to reductions in labor demand through lower real wages.[2]

2. De Ferranti et al. (2002) mention that increases in labor demand in the nontradable and construction sectors observed during the growth period disappeared by the end of the decade.

Figure 9.2 Urban employment rates for selected Latin American countries, 1990-2000 (percent)

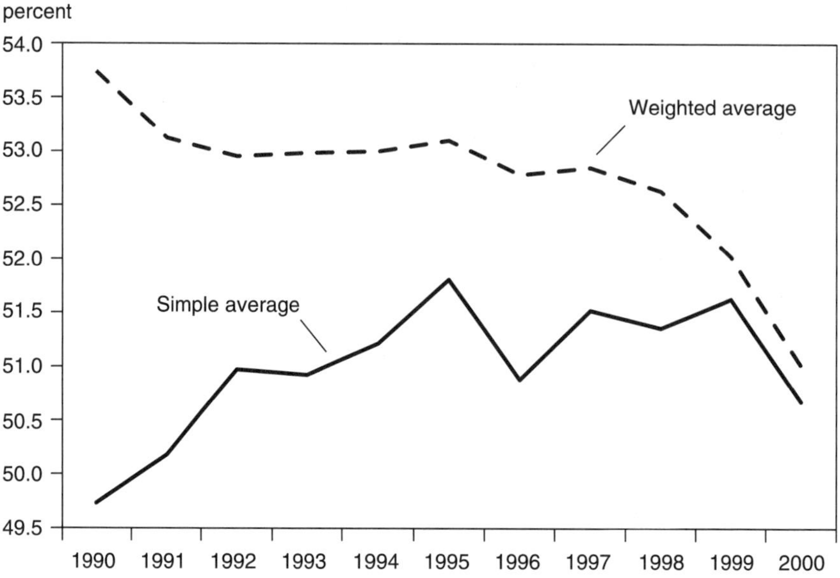

For all selected countries excluding Brazil

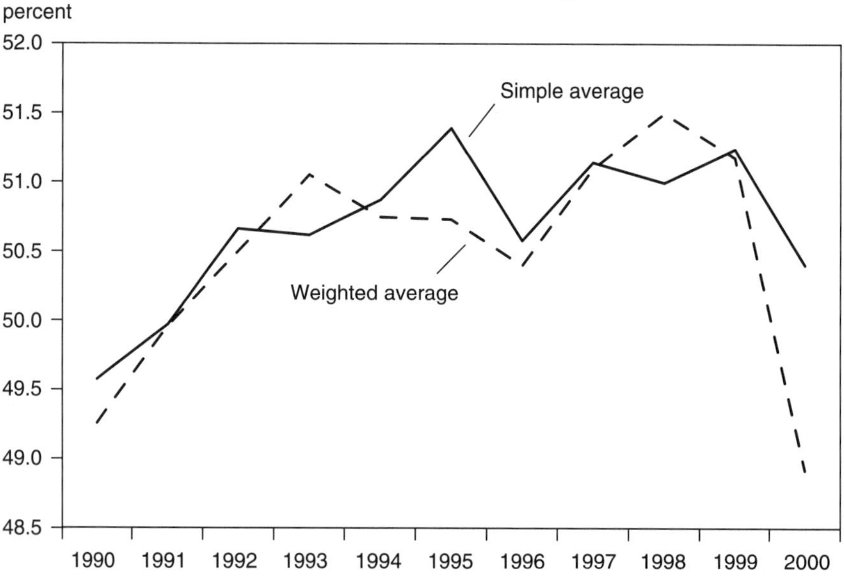

Note: The figure shows simple and weighted averages for Argentina, Bolivia, Brazil, Chile, Costa Rica, Ecuador, El Salvador, Honduras, Mexico, Nicaragua, Panama, Paraguay, Peru, Uruguay, and Venezuela. The weighted average was calculated using 1995 populations.

Source: ILO (2001).

Table 9.2 Unemployment rates, selected Latin American countries, 1990-99 (percent)

Country	1990	1993	1994	1995	1996	1997	1998	1999	2000
Argentina	7.4	9.6	11.5	17.5	17.2	14.9	12.9	14.5	15.1
Brazil	4.3	5.4	5.1	4.6	5.4	5.7	7.6	7.6	7.1
Chile	9.2	6.2	8.3	7.4	7.0	7.1	6.9	10.8	10.0
Colombia	10.5	8.6	8.9	8.8	11.2	12.4	15.3	19.4	17.2
Mexico	2.7	3.4	3.7	6.2	5.5	3.7	3.2	2.5	2.2
Peru	8.3	9.9	8.8	8.2	8.0	9.2	8.5	9.1	8.5
Venezuela	10.4	6.6	8.7	10.3	11.8	11.4	11.3	14.9	14.0

Note: Data may vary from country to country because of limitations in the available statistics. For Argentina and Mexico, unemployment rates include only urban areas. For Brazil and Colombia, data are, respectively, from six and seven metropolitan areas. For Peru, data are only for metropolitan Lima. For Chile and Venezuela, data are based on national statistics.

Source: UN Economic Commission for Latin America and the Caribbean, *Statistical Yearbook*, 2000.

In addition, evidence for Colombia suggests that rising unemployment, particularly among the less skilled since 1996, may be related to a sharp rise in nonwage labor costs (Kugler and Kugler 2001). Also, Bergoeing and Morande (2002), in the context of a growth model for Chile, relate the reduction in per capita output in 1999-2001 to a reduction in employment growth, which in turn may be explained by changes in real and perceived increases in hiring costs caused by labor legislation. But in Latin American economies, open unemployment has not always been the best indicator of how quantities are being adjusted and of the labor market situation in general. Given large differences in productivity across sectors, firms, and workers, the largest problem in the labor market is the large segment of the labor force that is in the informal sector or underemployed. The sizable heterogeneity that this implies for the quality of jobs is discussed in the next section.

The Problem of Low-Quality Jobs

Employment growth was biased toward specific groups of workers (as will be discussed in the next section), and there was an increase in the share of jobs that can be considered of low quality. In the early 1990s, the proportion of people who did not have any social benefits was already very high. In most countries, rates of informal employment, as defined by the ILO, were between 40 and 50 percent.[3] By the end of the decade, these

3. In the ILO definition, workers in the informal sector are those who work in small firms, either as wage earners or as microentrepreneurs, nonprofessional self-employed persons, domestic workers, and unpaid family workers.

Figure 9.3 Informal-sector employment in Latin America, 1990 and 2000 (percent of nonagricultural employment)

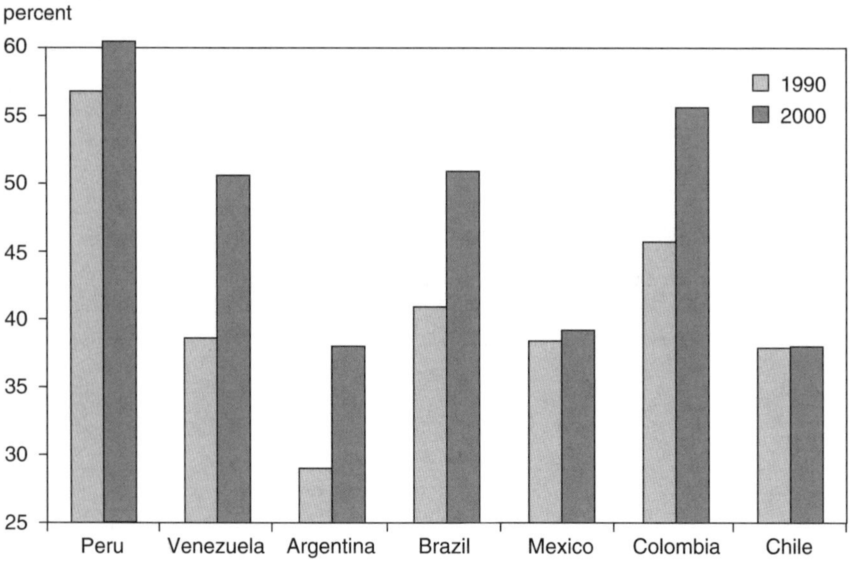

Sources: The data for Chile, Colombia, Venezuela, and Mexico use the International Labor Organization definition (ILO 2001). The data for Peru are from the National Household Survey (MTPS-INEI); for Argentina, from Gasparini, Marchionni, and Sosa-Escudero (2000); and for Brazil, from Ramos (2002). Informal-sector rates for Peru and Argentina are based on compliance with regulations and correspond to metropolitan Lima and greater Buenos Aires, respectively. The evolution in these cases roughly coincides with that calculated using the International Labor Organization definition. In Brazil, the informal sector includes salaried workers (*sem carteira*) and self-employed persons.

rates had increased in most countries, as is shown in figure 9.3. The share of jobs in the informal sector clearly increased in Argentina, Brazil, Mexico, Peru, and Venezuela. Using a different definition based on compliance with tax and labor regulations, or access to social benefits, changes in the rate of informal employment were similar. Only in Chile did the informality rate stay constant.

It should be noted that these estimates of the proportion of unprotected jobs are limited to urban areas. In countries that still have a large rural population, when this population is included, informal employment rates (or the proportion of unprotected jobs) may jump to the 60 to 70 percent range.[4]

4. Also, it should be noted that the definition of "informal" is arbitrary. When a legalistic definition is used, it is clear that there are small firms that operate formally, and there are also large firms that hire workers informally. Moreover, many firms are formal with the tax authorities while informal with the labor authorities.

Figure 9.4 Percentage of salaried workers with no access to social security, selected Latin American countries, 1990 and 2000

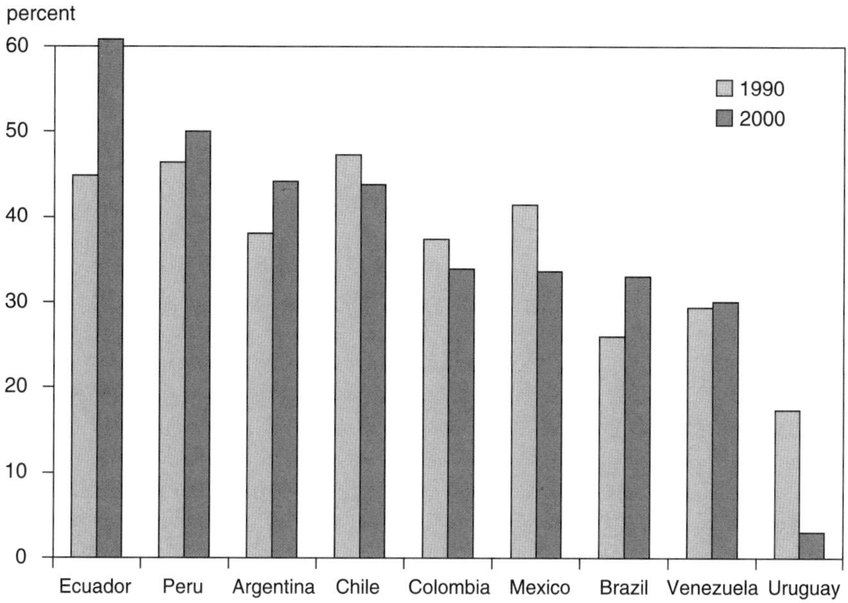

Sources: ILO (2001). Data for Chile are from Packard (2001) and correspond to the percentage of the economically active population with no contribution to social security. The final period corresponds to 1999.

As is shown in figure 9.4, the percentage of wage earners with no access to social security, either health or pension benefits, increased in most countries, with the exception of Chile, Colombia, Mexico, and Uruguay. In these countries, moreover, salaried employment decreased as a proportion of employment. This is also related to the high figure for self-employment and for the proportion of employment in microenterprises and small firms. Self-employment in countries belonging to the Organization for Economic Cooperation and Development (OECD) ranges between 5 and 15 percent of the labor force, and only Portugal, Spain, and Italy have rates between 15 and 25 percent. In Latin America, self-employment rates are between 25 and 45 percent. A minority of self-employed people own small firms or microenterprises that create salaried jobs, and most of them are self-employed in the nontradable sectors. Even if in some cases they are voluntarily in that type of job, high self-employment rates reflect low average productivity and wages.

There is evidence that job mobility has increased in several Latin American countries. Even for prime-age male workers, turnover increased, at least in Argentina and Peru (figure 9.5). Galiani (2001) shows that turnover

Figure 9.5 Job mobility in Peru and Argentina

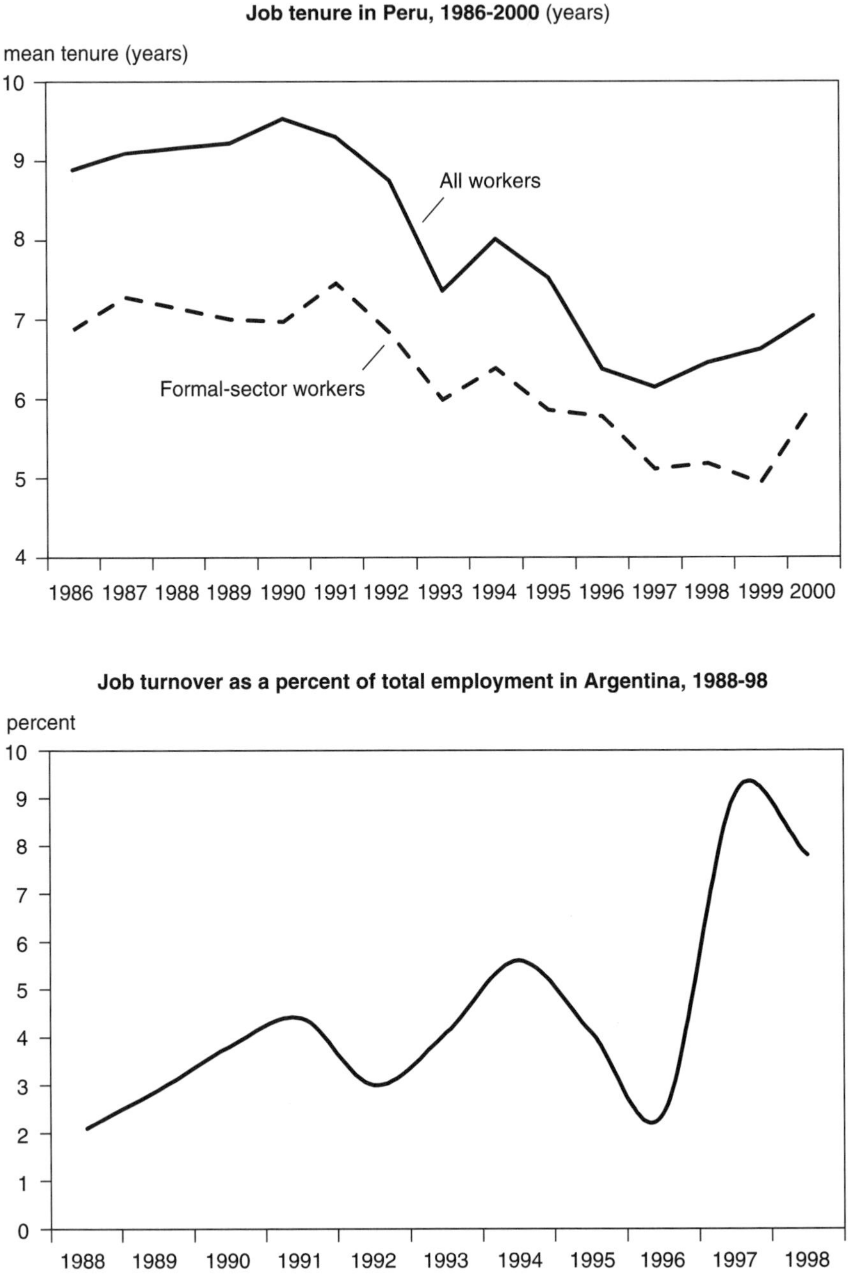

Sources: For Peru, National Household Survey (MTPS-INEI) for 1986, 1988, 1989-95, 1997-2001, metropolitan Lima only. For Argentina, Galiani (2001), calculated using household surveys for all urban agglomerations (25 urban regions surveyed between 1987 and 1998).

in Argentina increased dramatically by the end of the decade. In Colombia, there is evidence of an increase in turnover in the formal sector (Kugler and Cardenas 2003), while for Peru, Saavedra and Torero (2003) show that mean job duration among male salaried formal workers 25 to 65 years of age fell from 9.5 years in 1986 to 6.4 in 1997. Maloney (2001) reports that mean tenure—a proxy inversely related to turnover—is much lower in Mexico than in OECD countries.

This increase in job turnover may also be signaling a more intensive use of contractual arrangements that facilitate turnover, with an increase in the amount of risk that firms are able to transfer to workers. Even if this could be read as a positive development and reflect a more efficient reallocation of labor, it might still result in a reduction in welfare for currently working people.

Another summary indicator of the quality of jobs is the real wage. It is very difficult to find regularities regarding wages over the whole region. But except in the case of Chile, the increase in real wages (although positive in most cases in the 1990s) was not enough to recover from the reductions experienced during the 1980s. Another important fact is that, at least partly because of lower inflation, real wages seem to be less volatile than they were in the 1980s. Some of the data available for real wages are shown in figure 9.6. There is some evidence of small increases in real wages in the formal sector of the economy. They rose in Bolivia, Colombia, Ecuador, and Peru, remained relatively constant in Argentina, and fell in Venezuela.

In most countries, therefore, the past decade has brought increases in real earnings in the formal sector. This might be partly related to the increase in productivity observed in the modern sector, in particular in manufacturing. As is shown in figure 9.7, if data are pooled for Brazil, Chile, Colombia, and Peru, there was a clear positive correlation between productivity and real wages in manufacturing during the 1990s.

Nevertheless, no increase in productivity was observed in the informal sector.[5] Figure 9.8 reveals that earnings in the informal sector increased in Bolivia and Argentina, decreased in Colombia, Venezuela, and Ecuador, and remained fairly constant only in Peru. Simple comparisons of the evolution of wages in the formal and informal sector suggest that the benefits of economic recovery have not been spread uniformly. Increases in productivity were observed in certain sectors but not throughout the economy. Figure 9.9 shows that there was a clear increase in productivity in manufacturing in all countries except Venezuela. But in the tertiary sector (table 9.3), where most informal jobs are, and where most of the new jobs

5. Depending on how informality is conceptualized, informal workers and firms are in that sector precisely due to their low and stagnant productivity.

Figure 9.6 Evolution of real wages in the formal sector, selected Latin American countries, 1990-99 (index: 1990 = 100)

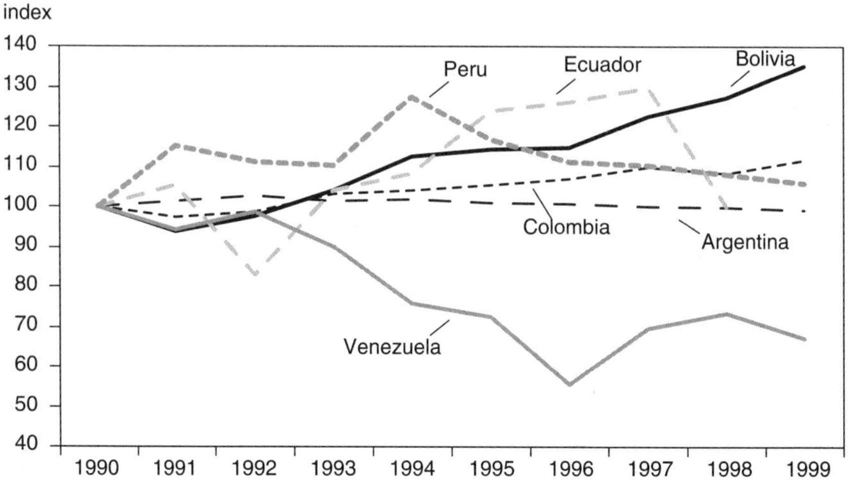

Note: Data for Argentina include only wages in manufacturing. Data for Bolivia include the private sector in La Paz. Data for Colombia include only blue-collar workers in manufacturing. Data for Ecuador include nonagricultural firms with more than 10 employees. Data for Peru include blue-collar workers in the private sector (for metropolitan Lima only). Data for Venezuela include blue-collar and white-collar workers in urban areas.

Source: UN Economic Commission for Latin America and the Caribbean, *Statistical Yearbook*, 2000.

were concentrated, labor productivity growth was much lower and was even negative at the end of the 1990s.

Finally, the quality of jobs is also related to economic insecurity. Even though at the macroeconomic level there was less volatility during the 1990s than in the 1980s in GDP growth, in consumption growth, and in labor market aggregates (De Ferranti et al. 2000), there is evidence that insecurity related to the operation of the labor market at the microeconomic level was on the rise. For instance, there is evidence in Argentina and Peru of more economic insecurity among workers in the formal sector. As was shown in figure 9.5, in these two countries turnover increased among formal workers, a phenomenon that is probably related to the increased flexibility needed by firms exposed to a more competitive environment, to the increase in employment in smaller firms, to the reduction in the bargaining power of unions, to the reduction in public-sector employment, and to changes in legislation.

Moreover, in Colombia and Peru more workers now have temporary jobs (figure 9.10)—jobs that in some cases not only explain most of the growth of formal employment but have even replaced permanent jobs. These changes have generated high employment uncertainty for seg-

Figure 9.7 Productivity and real wages in manufacturing, selected Latin American countries, 1990-99 (index: 1993 = 100)

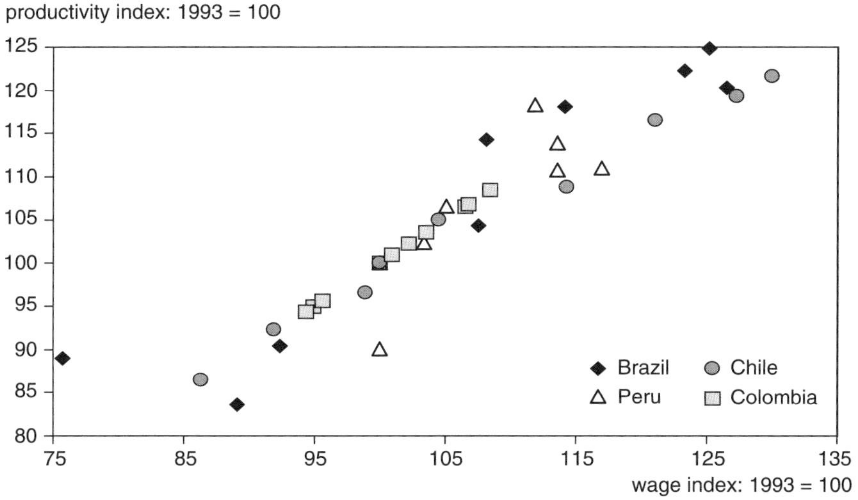

Note: Data for Peru include blue-collar workers in the private sector for metropolitan Lima only.

Source: UN Economic Commission for Latin America and the Caribbean, *Statistical Yearbook*, 2000.

Figure 9.8 Evolution of real wages in the informal sector, selected Latin American countries, 1990-98 (index: 1990 = 100)

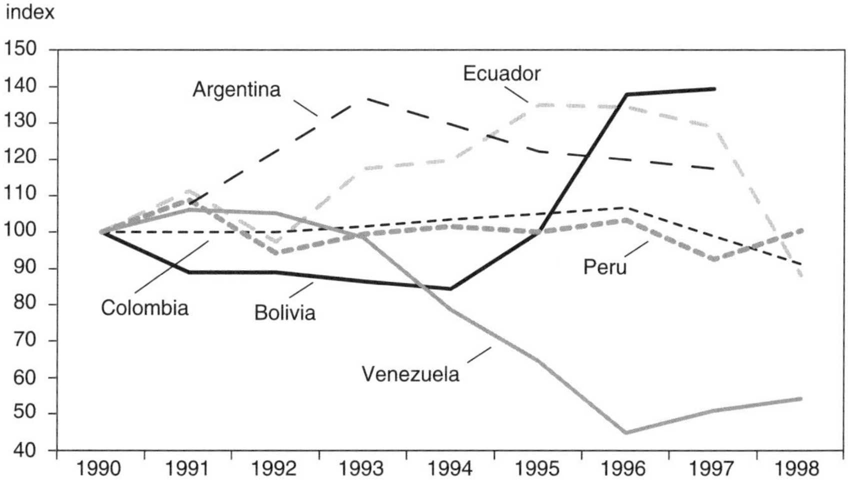

Sources: Data for Bolivia, Colombia, Ecuador, Peru, and Venezuela are from Egger and García (2001). Data for Argentina are from Arango and Maloney (2000).

Figure 9.9 Labor productivity in manufacturing, selected Latin American countries, 1988-2000 (index: 1993 = 100)

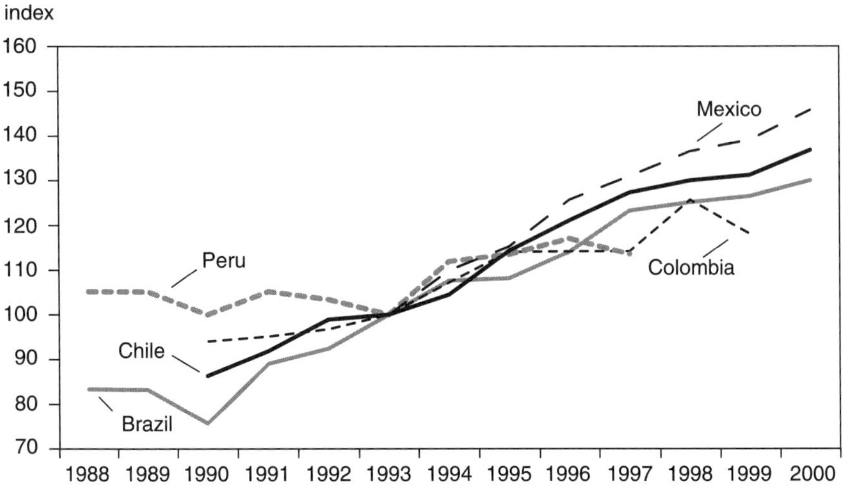

Sources: Due to the lack of a unique source for calculations of productivity, data are from diverse sources: for Brazil, Instituto de Pesquisa Econômica Aplicada; for Colombia, Reyes (2000); for Peru, National Household Survey, MTPS-INEI; for Chile, Chilean Central Bank; and for Mexico, Instituto Nacional de Estadística Geografía e Informática. For Colombia and Mexico, respectively, the coffee-processing industry and the *maquila* industry are excluded. For Chile, the average product per worker is taken as a proxy.

Figure 9.10 Temporary worker contracts in Peru and Colombia, 1990-2000 (ratios)

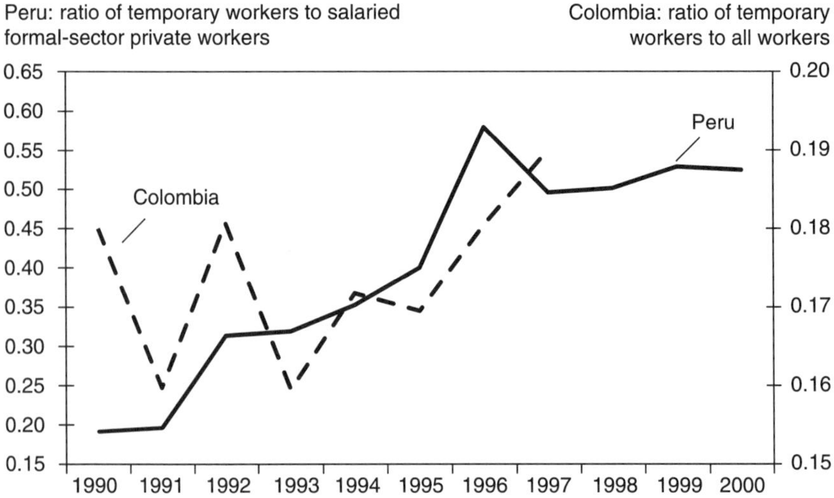

Sources: For Colombia, Reyes (2000). For Peru, MTPS-INEI data for metropolitan Lima.

Table 9.3 Labor productivity in Latin America by economic sector, 1970-97 (annual average percent growth)

Sector	1970-80	1980-90	1990-94	1994-97
Primary	1.8	2.4	3.2	5.6
Secondary	1.1	–0.6	3.6	4.0
Tertiary	1.5	–3.1	0.1	–1.7
Total	2.2	–1.3	2.0	0.8

Source: UN Economic Commission for Latin America and the Caribbean, *Estudio Económico para América Latina y el Caribe*, 1997-98.

ments of the employed population in the formal sector that have traditionally been shielded from fluctuations and that enjoyed job protection stemming from legislation, from working in high-rent sectors, or from working in the public sector.

The Labor Market's Winners and Losers from Structural Reform

The interaction of a set of structural reforms in Latin America had important effects on the operation of the labor market, even if many of the long-run effects are not yet clear. Market-friendly reforms, together with economic integration, influence modes of production, adoption rates of new technologies, human resource policies, and labor demand patterns whose long-term effects are not yet known. Yet even in the short run, trade reform, public-sector downsizing, privatization, and reductions in unionization have had large and profound effects on the labor market opportunities of specific demographic and occupational groups.

Even if the process of job creation and destruction led to a net increase in employment, some jobs were destroyed and some workers lost their jobs, while jobs were created in other sectors and for other workers. Overall, employment opportunities fell for older workers, particularly males. Pages, Duryea, and Jaramillo (2001) report that despite much larger unemployment rates among youth than adults, the gap has fallen in most Latin American countries because unemployment among adults increased more rapidly. Workers who lost their jobs in large manufacturing firms, in unionized firms, in the public administration, or in the public financial system may have dropped out of the labor force after remaining unemployed for a while, unless they found a job in the informal sector. An important regularity that may be crucial for reform's sustainability and political and popular support is that most of the burden of the labor reallocation was on the shoulders of the middle class and in some cases the upper-middle class.

Trade and Financial Liberalization

Labor markets were affected by trade liberalization, although probably less than many critics expected. One of the arguments of the opponents of an opening of the economy was that the manufacturing sector was going to be adversely affected, because the formerly protected industries would be unable to compete with imports. In fact, in several countries (e.g., Argentina, Brazil, Colombia, and Peru), there was an important transformation within the manufacturing sectors. Several manufacturing subsectors almost disappeared, and several capital goods sectors shrank. Manufacturing imports increased in most countries. Many large firms in such industries as chemicals and plastics turned to importing the same goods that they previously manufactured locally. At the same time, however, several other manufacturing industries that enjoyed some degree of natural protection grew (e.g., beverages, cement, and metallic products), as economies entered a period of fast growth between 1993 and 1998.

In countries such as Argentina, Brazil, and Peru, the capital inflows generated an increase in the prices of nontradables, which translated into an increase in the demand for labor in that sector, leading to an increase in employment in commerce and in services (Camargo et al. 2000; Pascó-Font and Saavedra 2001). In Colombia, employment in the nontradable sector increased, particularly in commerce, while manufacturing employment fell in absolute terms.

Although in some countries the decline in the level of manufacturing employment was short-lived, in all cases there was a reduction in the share of manufacturing in total employment, as is shown in figure 9.11. In most Latin American countries, services increased their share in total employment, both in such skill-intensive sectors as finance, insurance and banking, and business services, and in such unskilled-intensive sectors as retail and wholesale trade. In some countries, the increase was larger in the case of unskilled-intensive sectors. The reduction in the share of manufacturing is the continuation of a long-run trend, although it seems to have been more pronounced during the 1990s (figure 9.12).[6] The same pattern is observed in OECD countries.

Trade liberalization was also presumed to affect the structure of earnings. Goldberg and Pavcnik (2001) show that in Colombia relative wages fell in industries where tariff reductions were higher. In protected sectors, rents allowed for higher than market-clearing wages, which fell as rents disappeared. Tariffs fell more in sectors intensive in low-skill labor, so less educated workers were hardest hit by the liberalization.

---

6. Moreover, there is no evidence that trade liberalization has any relationship with unemployment, as shown by Maloney (1999). In cases where unemployment has increased sharply, particularly in Argentina and Colombia at the end of the decade, this occurred years after the onset of liberalization and seems linked mainly to macroeconomic conditions.

Figure 9.11 Changes in employment composition, selected Latin American countries, various years

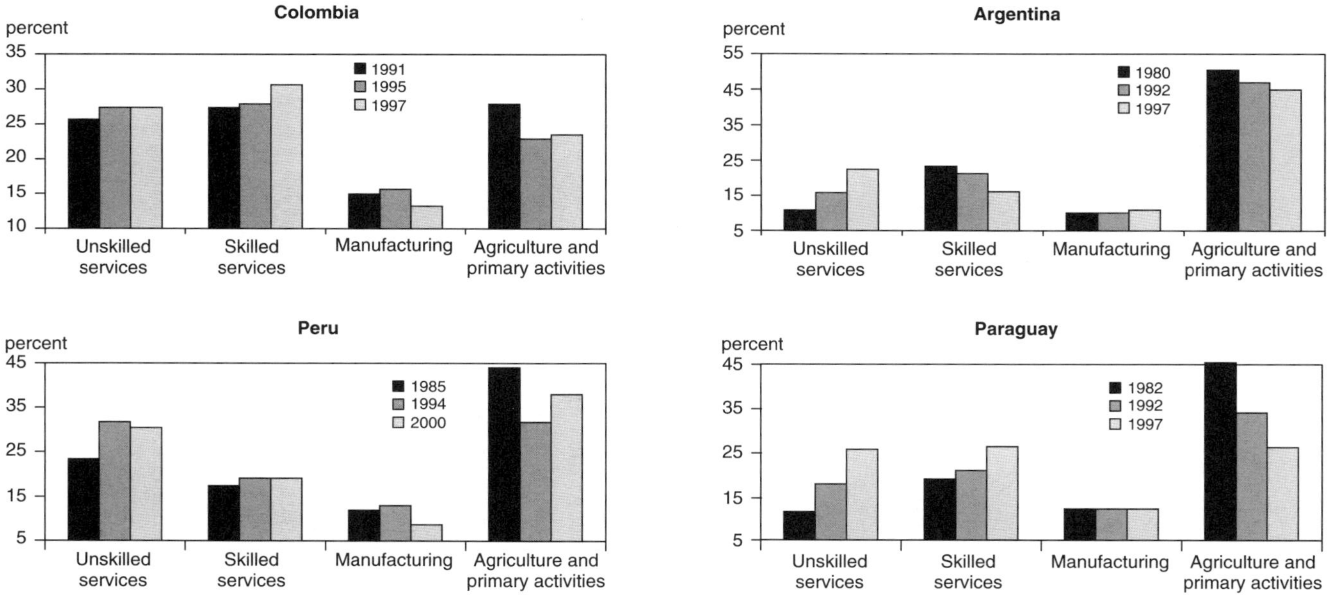

Note: For Argentina, unskilled services include trade, employment in restaurants and hotels, and transport and communications; skilled services include utilities, financial services, and other services. For Colombia, unskilled services include trade and communications; skilled services include financial services, utilities, and other services. For Peru, trade, restaurants and hotels, and transport and communications were included in the unskilled services category; financial services, public-sector employment, utilities, and other services were considered as skilled services. For Paraguay, unskilled services include trade and transport; skilled services include utilities, financial services, and other services.

Sources: For Argentina, data are from Frenkel and González Rosada (2001). For Colombia, data are from Ocampo, Sánchez, and Ernesto Tovar (2001). For Peru, employment composition was calculated using data from the World Bank's Living Standards Measurement Study for 1986, 1994, and 2000 (available at www.worldbank.org/lsms/). For Paraguay, data are from Gibson, Molinas, and Moli (2001).

Figure 9.12 Employment share of manufacturing, selected Latin American countries, 1980-2000 (index: 1980 = 100)

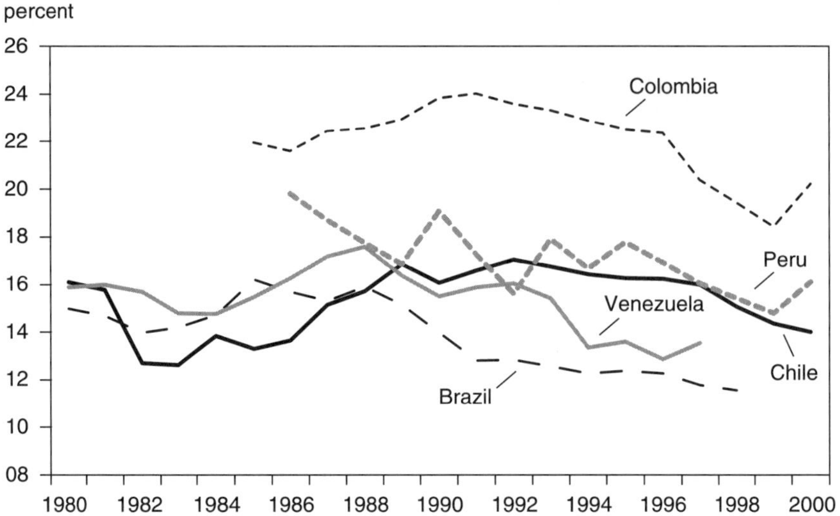

Sources: Data are from LABORSTA (http://laborsta.ilo.org) except for Peru, for which data are from the National Household Survey (MTPS-INEI) and include metropolitan Lima only.

In a simple Heckscher-Ohlin framework, trade should have brought an increase in demand for unskilled-labor-intensive goods and consequently an increase in the demand for and wages of unskilled workers. But there is evidence pointing toward the opposite result. Even if in most countries there has been an increase in the supply of skilled workers, there is evidence of an increase in returns to education, particularly tertiary education. Evidence consistent with this trend is presented by Blom, Holm-Nielsen, and Verner (2001) for Brazil; Contreras, Bravo, and Medrano (1999) for Chile; Cárdenas and Bernal (1999) for Colombia; Gindling and Robbins (1999) for Costa Rica; and Saavedra and Maruyama (1999) for Peru. Trade liberalization, together with a more favorable environment for foreign direct investment and exchange rate appreciation, facilitated the absorption of new technologies, which may at least be partially related to an increase in the demand for skilled workers.[7] Consistently, the earnings gap between skilled and unskilled workers increased in several countries, as is reported by Weller (2000) and shown in figure 9.13.

How much of these changes in the returns to education can be linked directly to trade is not clear. As is suggested by Behrman, Birdsall, and Székely (2000a), reform may have reduced the price of capital goods through a decrease in financial costs. Pascó-Font and Saavedra (2001) show that in

7. In most cases, the increase in educational differentials is concentrated on workers with tertiary education.

Figure 9.13 Wage of workers with tertiary schooling relative to wage of workers with 7 to 9 years of education, selected Latin American countries

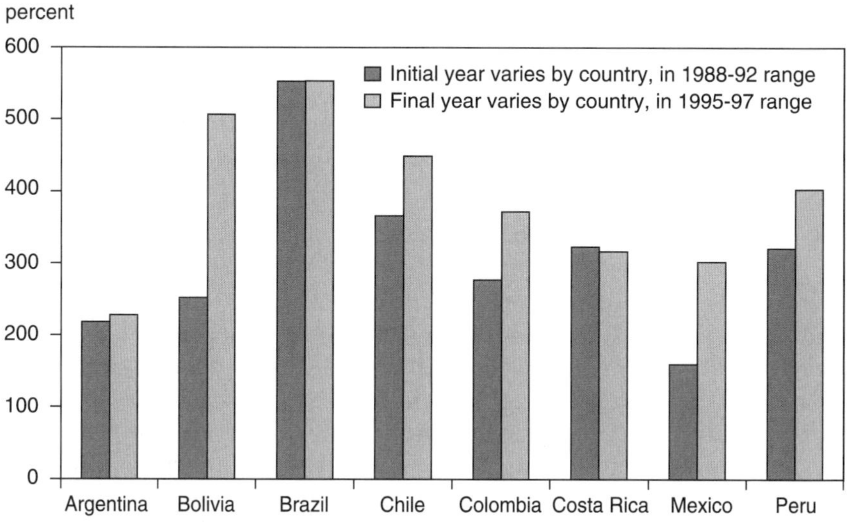

Sources: Weller (2000).

Peru there was a clear reduction in the relative price of imported machinery and an increase in capital goods imports. This may have induced substitution of the complementary factor of capital, skilled labor, against unskilled labor, with potentially negative effects on poverty and inequality. However, recent findings by Morley (2000) show evidence against this effect. Morley examines the evolution of the capital-labor ratio across several Latin American countries and does not find any clear pattern. Moreover, aggregate indices may be hiding within-country changes, and both financial liberalization and the increase in foreign direct investment that accompanied it may have had an effect on particular sectors.

Another, less optimistic interpretation of the increase in returns to education is that many countries in Latin America have experienced a deterioration of the quality of education. In a process that has not yet been well studied, firms may be hiring highly educated persons to perform tasks that in industrial countries are assigned to less educated people. As an example, many Latin American banks hire college graduates as tellers or administrative assistants, tasks that are performed by less educated workers in other countries.[8]

8. In that situation, education may pay from a private point of view, even though socially it just increases the dispersion of earnings around a stagnant mean.

Also, it should be noted that in most countries the increases in educational earnings differentials were concentrated in tertiary education. Secondary education premia over primary education fell in most cases. Gonzaga, Menezes Filho, and Terra (2002) conclude that in Brazil the reduction in the returns to secondary education may well be explained by the trade-related fall in the relative price of goods whose production is intensive in this type of worker. Overall, evidence points to a worsening in the relative economic position of workers with a secondary education and to an insufficient quantity and quality of more-educated workers.

Downsizing and Privatization

The short-run employment effect of privatization has not yet been well studied. Chong and López-de-Silanes (2003) report that using a large sample of privatized firms in Argentina, Brazil, Colombia, Mexico, and Peru, on average the change in employment in these firms is negative. However, contrary to popular opinion, there is some evidence that privatization had a positive effect on aggregate employment. Chisari, Estache, and Romero (1999), using a computable general equilibrium model, show that the increase in unemployment observed in Argentina in the mid-1990s was mainly related to the tequila effect and not to the privatization of utilities. Pascó-Font and Torero (2001) show that telecommunications privatization in Peru had a negative direct effect on employment but a total positive effect when indirect jobs, mainly through subcontracting, are taken into account.

Employment in the public sector fell in several Latin American countries, both as a consequence of privatization and because of public administration downsizing programs. As is shown in figure 9.14, in Argentina, Colombia, Mexico, Peru, and Venezuela, the share of public-sector employment in total urban employment fell by around a quarter. Only in Brazil and Chile was there an increase in public employment.

However, even if (and in some cases it is a big if) the net change in employment after privatization (or the downsizing of public administration) was positive, the quality of the jobs lost was higher than the quality of new jobs. Unfortunately, many of these high-quality jobs resulted from huge inefficiencies, for many of them were supported by quasi-rents appropriated by public-sector workers who had for a long time been used to higher-than-productivity wages, low effort, weak monitoring, lack of meritocratic promotion mechanisms, and job stability. Because few attempts were made to design appropriate compensation packages, downsizing and privatization implied huge welfare losses for specific demographic groups, whose possibilities of finding another job with similar wages and fringe benefits were very slim.

Figure 9.14 Public-sector employment, selected Latin American countries, 1990 and 2000
(percent of nonagricultural employment)

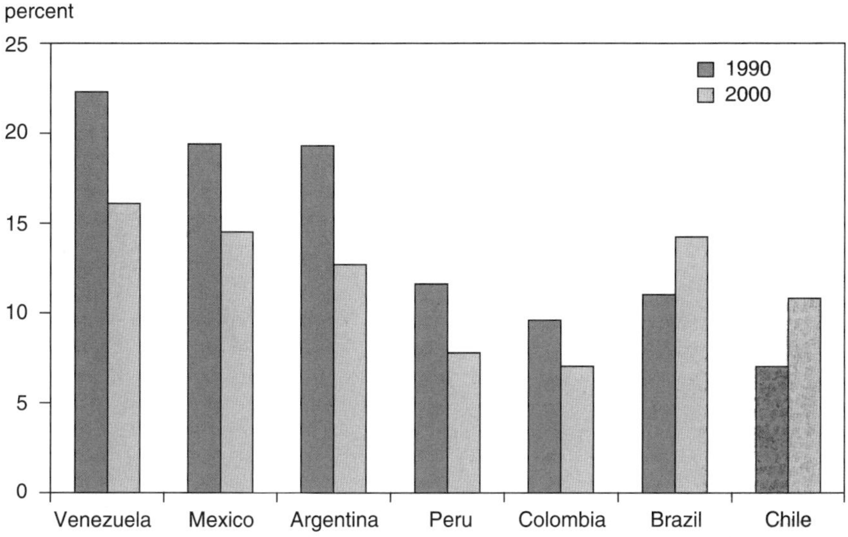

Source: ILO (2001).

Implications for Political Economy

The changes in employment patterns and the employment shocks suffered by specific segments of the population are behind the weak support for reform in Latin American countries. Reductions in public-sector employment meant that fewer of the jobs that have traditionally been shielded from economic fluctuations were protected. And many of those who lost such jobs were not able to find another job with the same level of protection, earnings, and social benefits—or were not able to find a job at all.

Privatizations were not (and should not be) designed to create jobs directly. Privatization is advisable as long as the private sector is better at providing a service than the public sector, provided it is appropriately regulated. Well-implemented privatizations should result in a more efficient provision of services, higher productivity, and eventually more jobs. However, privatization lost appeal due to both (1) a lack of transparency and in some cases blatant corruption, and (2) the direct negative effect on employment in the privatized firms. Even if it is true that many workers who lost their jobs had been extracting rents from the rest of the economy, from a political-economy and a social perspective countries should have offered them appropriate compensation packages.

These workers were playing by established rules not written by them, and changing the rules of the game for a worker in the middle of her career may lead to serious welfare losses. A large proportion of the workers who lost their jobs used to belong to the middle class, and as such had more voice and more mechanisms through which they could manifest their discontent. This was a radical shift from previous decades, when during macroeconomic downturns the middle class, even if not totally shielded from real wage losses, was at least shielded from losing a job.[9]

There is evidence of strong demand for job stability in Latin America. For instance, in Brazil in 1999 a million people queued for a total of 10,000 stable, formal jobs at the Banco do Brasil (Rodrik 1999). In Peru and Argentina, there is an excess supply of public-sector teachers, even though real salaries have been falling, because these jobs have almost total stability. Workers' willingness to accept lower wages in return for job stability seems to be very high in Latin America.

Changes in Labor Legislation

The United States started regulating its labor market at the federal level during the New Deal, while most European countries had started a few decades earlier (Lindauer 1999). Most Latin American countries started drafting labor legislation in the 1930s, despite their low level of economic development. Labor codes in the region were traditionally designed to protect workers and improve their bargaining position, on the assumption that they were the weak side of the labor contract. Moreover, they were designed to govern a relationship that was assumed, once an urban industrial labor force had emerged, to be one of intrinsic and permanent conflict between labor and capital.[10] In a more neoclassical interpretation, labor regulation was required to counter the existence of asymmetric information and free-riding problems.[11]

The institutions that were created in Latin America were a powerful tool to govern labor relationships in the modern sector of the economy,

---

9. See Graham and Pettinato (2002) for a discussion on how the reduction of well-being of the middle class may affect the political sustainability of economic reforms.

10. Interestingly, the chapter of the 1931 Chilean Labor Code that pertained to collective bargaining was titled "Collective Conflict" (cited in Edwards and Cox-Edwards 2000).

11. E.g., employers have more information than employees about occupational safety and the economic and financial situation of the firm. Workers may not be willing to save for retirement, assuming that the state or their offspring will support them when they are old. Capital markets are not willing to finance unemployment periods of low-skilled workers so they cannot insure themselves adequately. Finally, minorities and ethnic groups may suffer from labor market discrimination. All these market imperfections justify labor market regulations (Pages and Saavedra 2002).

but they left huge segments of the labor force totally out of the game. Latin American labor legislation is recognized as among the most restrictive, rigid, and cumbersome in the world, probably only behind that in India and West Africa (Rama 1998). In almost all Latin American countries, labor legislation favors permanent contracts, which limits the use of temporary contracts and other atypical contracts. However, permanent contracts carry high dismissal costs and very high nonwage labor costs, including health and pension contributions, occupational training taxes, payroll taxes, family allowances, vacations, and unemployment subsidies. Moreover, maternity and sick leave, annual bonuses, compulsory profit sharing, and occupational health and safety provisions are heavily regulated. The health and pension systems are plagued by special regimes and exceptions.

Labor market reforms were implemented in several countries, but legislative changes differed widely in depth and even in direction. Despite the popular perception that labor markets have been deregulated massively in Latin America, a review of the evolution of legislation shows that these changes have been diverse and generally modest. In several countries, not much happened, and in a few cases labor market regulations were made even more stringent. In some countries that opened their economies (e.g., Argentina, Colombia, and Peru), there were noticeable changes, particularly in comparison with the extremely regulated labor markets of the 1970s and 1980s.

In these liberalizing countries, job stability rules were made less stringent and firing costs fell. However, in Argentina, Colombia, and Peru, reforms of the pension system, including the use of individual retirement accounts, generated an increase in nonwage labor costs. In other instances where changes have been observed, partial changes in regulations actually made things worse by generating distorted and inefficient outcomes. In Brazil and Chile, labor reforms at the beginning of the 1990s were part of a response to democratization and involved a move in a more protectionist direction (Cook 1998; Amadeo, Gill, and Neri 2000). In Mexico, no major changes occurred, despite much debate. Changes in Bolivia, Paraguay, and Venezuela were small and tended to increase formal workers' rights. The main developments in this area are presented below.

Job Protection and Firing Costs

Most Latin American countries use severance payments as a mechanism to protect workers in the event of unemployment. They are usually calculated as multiples of the monthly salary, and they increase with tenure. These payments are liabilities of the firm that have to be paid if the worker is fired under a circumstance that is not considered a "just cause" by law. On the one hand, these resources allow the worker to smooth income.

Table 9.4 Changes in the job security index as calculated by Heckman and Pages between 1990 and 1999, selected Latin American countries

Direction of change of index	Country	
Increased	Brazil Chile Dominican Republic	
Remained constant	Argentina Bolivia Costa Rica Ecuador	El Salvador Mexico Paraguay Uruguay
Fell	Colombia Nicaragua	Peru Venezuela
Average for Latin America: 3.1 Average for OECD: 1.6 Average for Caribbean: 1.9		

OECD = Organization for Economic Cooperation and Development

Note: The job security index reported in Heckman and Pages (2003) takes into account advance notice, the discounted cost of severance payments adjusted by the probability of dismissal after different time periods and by the probability that economic difficulties of the firm are considered a "just cause," and payments to individual savings accounts. Figures are reported in average monthly wages.

Source: Heckman and Pages (2003).

They also act as a deterrent to firing. On the other hand, as is discussed below, these obligations increase labor costs and reduce the likelihood of hiring. A few countries—Brazil, Colombia, Ecuador, Peru, and Venezuela—in addition to severance payments, use some sort of individual savings accounts, from which funds may be withdrawn by the worker in the event of unemployment.

Heckman and Pages (2003) and Vega (2001) document in detail changes in dismissal costs and other forms of protection against the event of job separation. According to the data they compiled, dismissal costs are much higher in Latin America than in OECD countries, and the reduction during the 1990s was on average small. A summary of their calculations is presented in table 9.4. The small average change, however, hides many different stories. In Brazil, severance payments increased with the 1988 Constitution, and the fine for unjust dismissal was raised from 10 to 40 percent of the worker's FGTS account balance.[12] In Chile, 1990 labor re-

12. The FGTS is the Fundo de Garantia por Tempo de Serviço. It is an individual account held by the worker to which the firm contributes regularly. This fund may be used by workers who quit or are laid off.

forms increased the ceiling for severance payments from 5 to 11 monthly wages. Severance also included a 20 percent additional charge if no just cause of dismissal could be proved. In Ecuador, the severance payment profile was made steeper, increasing dismissal costs (figure 9.15).

In the other countries where changes were made, dismissal costs were reduced. In Colombia, there was a reduction in dismissal costs, as severance payment rules, tied to the monthly wage at the moment of dismissal, were replaced by individual savings accounts, with monthly payments tied to the current salary. Employers have to make compulsory deposits to their workers' accounts.[13] In Peru, the tenure-related severance payments schedule was made less steep, but the most important change in dismissal costs was the elimination of the obligation to reinstate a worker in his or her job if a labor court determined that the dismissal had no just cause. In Nicaragua and Panama there were also reductions in dismissal cost. Finally, in Venezuela, the requirement of "numerical stability" was eliminated, and in 1997, changes in the rules for the calculation of severance payments implied an effective reduction in dismissal costs. Overall, dismissal costs in Latin America are much higher than in OECD countries, despite lower levels of productivity and income.

The cost of dismissing a worker is also highly influenced by the specific motives that the law in each country accepts as just cause and by the attitudes of labor courts. In Argentina, Chile, Colombia, and Peru, dismissal costs were reduced through an increase in the array of causes that firms could claim for making lower severance payments, mainly the inclusion of economic factors as a just cause for firing. In Mexico, no formal changes to legislation regarding job dismissals have been made, but the attitude of labor courts has changed, leaning less toward preserving the jobs of specific workers (Calderon 2000). Edwards and Cox-Edwards (2000) also mention changing attitudes of labor courts as important sources of effective changes in dismissal costs in Chile, particularly during the 1980s. In Peru, labor courts were also more relaxed in allowing firings under the just-cause clause.

Heckman and Pages (2003) review a large set of studies and conclude that severance payments have an effect on turnover, average employment, and the composition of employment. Specifically, there is evidence for Colombia (Kugler and Cardenas 2003) and Peru (Saavedra and Torero 2003) that the reduction of job security increased turnover, particularly in the formal sector. Conversely, Paes de Barros and Corseuil (2001) find that the increase in job protection in Brazil reduced employment exit rates. In Peru and in Argentina (Mondino and Montoya 2002), there is evidence of a significant negative labor demand impact of dismissal costs in the formal sector. Kugler (2002) shows that the move in Colombia from severance

13. This implied a reduction in the sum that had to be paid by the firm in the event of a dismissal, but a higher nonwage labor cost.

Figure 9.15 Severance payments before and after labor reforms, selected Latin American countries, various years (in terms of months of wages)

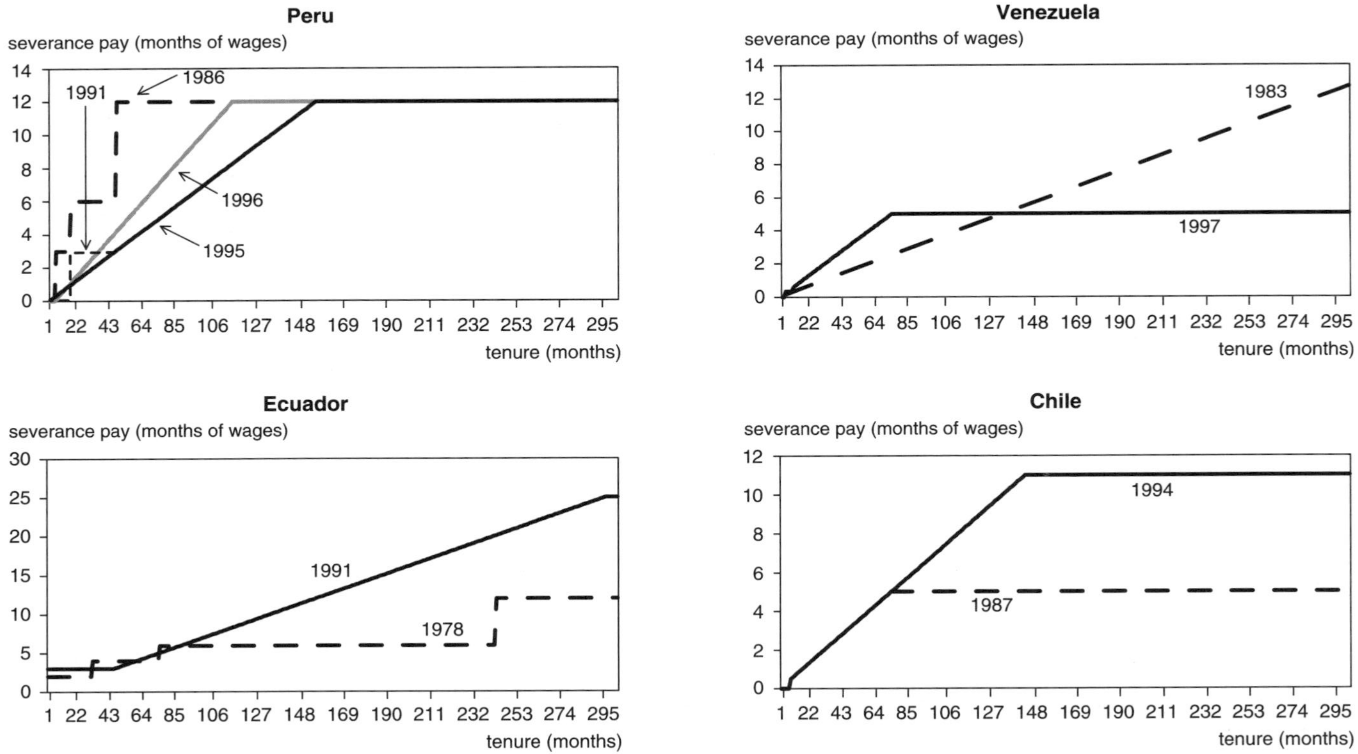

Source: Vega (2001).

payments to a system of individual accounts, whose costs could be partially shifted to workers, led to a reduction of unemployment rates of 1.3 to 1.7 percentage points. Finally, Montenegro and Pages (2002) provide evidence that in Chile job security policies were associated with substantial reductions in the employment-population ratio among young workers and an increase in the same variable among older workers.

Temporary Employment Contracts

As was observed in industrial countries during the 1970s, one way for firms to avoid high dismissal costs—and through which governments give firms an outlet from the high dismissal costs of permanent employment contracts—is to use temporary contracts. Usually, legislation that makes it easier to use temporary contracts encounters less political resistance than changes in severance payments or firing procedures.

In Argentina, after much political struggle, temporary contracts began to be allowed in 1991, but without much success. By 1995, conditions had changed significantly, and their use increased from 6 percent in 1995 to 17 percent in 1997 (Torre and Gerchunoff 1999). Temporary contracts (*modalidades promovidas*) were introduced for specific groups in the labor force, with lower severance payments, depending on the type of contract.[14] In 1998, however, these contracts were again eliminated. In Peru, the red tape required for the use of temporary contracts was greatly diminished, and the role of the administrative authority shifted from approval of these contracts to a mere registry. The main difference between temporary and permanent contracts was that the former carried no right to a severance payment. As is shown in figure 9.5 above, there was a sharp increase in Peru in the share of temporary employment within the formal sector.[15] This was also observed in Colombia. In Brazil, temporary and part-time contracts have been permitted only since 1998.

As is discussed in the last section, the easy way of trying to give firms the necessary additional flexibility in firing through use of temporary contracts is a second-best solution, given the political difficulties governments face in passing legislation that reduces firing costs under permanent contracts. However, this solution may have negative effects on productivity and also in nurturing perceptions of economic insecurity by

14. The *promoción al empleo* contract, for instance, had to be contracted with a registered unemployed person, and allowed a 50 percent reduction in severance payments. Youth contracts were related to training, and exemptions allowed 100 percent on both employers' contributions and severance payments (Pessino 2001).

15. In Peru, temporary contracts increased even after 1998, when absolute formal employment was falling. The implicit replacement of permanent by temporary contracts was in part a response to business expectations of a reversal of labor reforms that might lead to a reintroduction of job stability clauses in permanent contracts.

Box 9.1 Summary of payroll tax changes in selected countries

Colombia

Social security reform increased mandatory contributions for pensions and health gradually during the early 1990s. Pension contributions increased from 6.5 to 12.5 percent in 1995 and to 13.5 percent in 1996 for workers earning less than four times the minimum wage and to 14.5 percent for workers earning more than four times the minimum wage. Similarly, health contributions increased gradually, from 7 percent in 1994 to 8 percent in 1995 and to 12 percent in 1996 (Kugler and Cardenas 2002).

Chile

In Chile, payroll tax reform was introduced in the early 1980s. In 1980, a new reform reduced social security contributions from 33 percent on average to 20 percent (10 percent for retirement, 7 percent for health, and 3 percent for disability). Newly hired workers would contribute to the new private pension system, to be managed by private administrators. Old contributors could choose between the new and the old public pay-as-you-go system. In the case of health care, all workers were given the choice to opt out of the public system and to use their 7 percent contribution for a health care insurance provided by a private health insurer. A minimum pension, employment insurance, and family allowances were fully financed by the government (Edwards and Cox-Edwards 2000).

Mexico

Legislation introduced in 1997 reduced mandatory payments for health, disability, and death insurance by about 6 percentage points for the median worker (i.e., from 14.7 to 8.2 percent). The reform replaced a pay-as-you-go system by a retirement plan based on individual retirement accounts. Mandatory contributions for this retirement account increased from 2 to 6.5 percent for the median worker. Overall, total payroll taxes (including some minor payments besides health insur-

workers. For instance, Hopenhayn (2000) shows that the temporary contracts introduced in Argentina generated an increase in hiring, a reduction in long-term employment relationships, and an increase in turnover.

Nonwage Labor Costs

Nonwage labor costs (sometimes called the social wage) in Latin America include health and pension contributions, training contributions, family allowances, annual bonuses, vacations, unemployment subsidies, maternity and sick leave, occupational health and safety provisions, and more. In several countries, there were important increases in nonwage labor costs. In Colombia, mandated contributions increased between 1992 and 1996 by at least 12.5 percentage points, both due to increased health contributions and contributions to the newly created private pension system of individ-

Box 9.1 *continued*

ance and retirement fund contributions) were only reduced from 21.7 to 19.7 percent (Marrufo 2001).

Argentina

Between 1990 and 1995, payroll taxes represented approximately 60 percent of gross wages (32 percent for social security payments, 14 percent for health insurance, 7.5 percent for family assignments, and 1.5 percent for unemployment insurance plus other contributions). Since then, contributions have fallen. In greater Buenos Aires, total payments have reached 41.8 percent of gross wages. In 1994, the social security system was changed from a state reparto system to a mixed one, whereby workers could choose between remaining in the public system or switching to the private capitalization system. Health insurance, however, is administered by the union representing each firm. Since 1997, workers have been allowed to choose the health insurer of their choice, but within the union system (Pessino 2001).

Peru

Total nonwage costs increased sharply during the early 1990s as a consequence of changes in the calculation of individual retirement accounts (*Compensación por Tempo de Serviço*). In 1992, a parallel private pension fund system, based on individual accounts as an alternative to the state's pay-as-you-go system, was created. When commissions and other fees are included, the contribution was between 11 and 12 percent at the end of the decade. The health contribution was maintained at 9 percent throughout the 1990s but in 1995 the base for calculations was extended to include holiday bonus payments, thus increasing the effective rate. The National Housing Fund contribution, which in practice works as a plain payroll tax, underwent several changes based on fiscal needs and thus fluctuated between 6 and 9 percent. The base for calculation was also increased. (Saavedra and Maruyama 1999).

ual accounts (Kugler and Kugler 2001). In Peru, contributions increased due to increased pension contributions and changes in the established caps and minima (Saavedra and Maruyama 1999). In Brazil in 1988, nonwage costs increased due to the creation of a vacation bonus and increases in childbirth leave (Amadeo, Gill, and Neri 2000).[16] In Mexico, changes in both health and pension contributions compensated each other such that there was a very small reduction in 1997. In contrast, in Argentina contributions fell from the extremely high levels of the early 1990s to a range of 40-45 percent, still one of the highest in Latin America. Changes in nonwage costs in selected countries are summarized in box 9.1.

In Colombia and Peru, in addition to the increase in social security contributions, individual savings accounts that could be used upon dismissal operated as an additional nonwage cost. In Colombia, a severance pay-

16. Brazil also reduced the maximum number of hours per week from 48 to 44.

ment savings account was established, with amounts that had to be deposited by the employer periodically, a system that replaced the traditional severance payments system. In Peru, these savings accounts already existed (the Compensación por Tempo de Serviço), but in 1991 it was established that these savings had to be deposited in an account in the financial system.[17]

An important institutional change is that in a large group of countries (Argentina, Chile, Colombia, Peru, and later in the 1990s Uruguay, Mexico, Bolivia, and El Salvador), private individual-capitalization-account-based pension systems were introduced, either replacing or alongside old pay-as-you-go systems.[18] Except in Chile, the mandated pension contribution is now higher than it was in the pay-as-you-go system. However, the distortionary effect of this nonwage cost is probably smaller, for benefits are now linked to contributions. In that sense, increases in nonwage costs related to this institutional change might not have a negative effect on employment, at least for certain segments of the population. In the more mature systems, pension savings have increased significantly and constitute an important part of national savings (see chapter 5). However, except in Chile, there has been no significant overall increase in social security coverage, not even where the private system has almost completely displaced the former system.

In the case of health contributions, even where there was no increase in contributions, there is some evidence of a reduction in the quality of services provided, which again suggests that this contribution may be perceived as a tax, in particular by higher-income workers who prefer better-quality health services.

Increases in mandatory payroll contributions and other nonwage costs appear to have negative effects on employment or earnings (or both), according to recent empirical literature.[19] The effect of changes in mandatory contributions depends on the characteristics of labor supply and labor demand and on the specific structure of institutional settings. Edwards and Cox-Edwards (2000) find that in Chile 70 percent of social security contributions are shifted to workers. Marrufo (2001) finds a substantial shift of labor costs to wages in Mexico. Kugler and Kugler (2001) find that in Colombia, of the increase in 10 percentage points in payroll taxes in 1993,

---

17. Before the reform, the deposit could be kept in the accounting books of the firm. In practice, this meant that these resources were used as working capital by the firms. When firms went bankrupt, workers were not able to collect their funds.

18. In Bolivia, Chile, Mexico, and El Salvador, the public system has been closed.

19. Heckman and Pages (2003) provide a comprehensive compilation of recent empirical work on the effect of labor legislation over the labor market. In his presidential address to the Labor Economics Society, Hamermesh (2002) states that Latin American policy changes should be more exploited by the profession to reach a better understanding of the effect of labor legislation.

only about a fifth was shifted to workers as lower wages, and consequently there was a negative effect on employment. In their review of the empirical literature on this issue, Heckman and Pages (2003) conclude that a 10 percent increase in nonwage costs in Latin America has a negative impact on the employment rate, but there is a very wide variation in estimates of the quantitative effect, from 0.6 to 4.8 percent. Overall, nonwage costs in Latin American countries are high and in most cases have increased, and empirical evidence in the region points to negative effects of this cost on employment.

Unions and Collective Bargaining

In the highly regulated labor markets of the import-substitution era, unions played the role of protecting their members' jobs and negotiating for higher salaries and fringe benefits and better working conditions. In some countries, unions were part of a corporatist scheme and were heavily regulated by authorities; in others, unions developed more independently and were usually associated with political movements. During this period, high economic rents in modern sectors of the economy were generated by trade protection. Prolabor governments legislated complex labor legislation that provided generous nonwage benefits. The increase in social benefits for unionized workers, together with explicit profit-sharing schemes imposed by labor legislation, forced businesses to share these rents with workers.

Moreover, workers in sectors subject to soft budget constraints—the public administration and state-owned enterprises—and workers in nontradable sectors that also enjoyed economic rents due to oligopolistic structures, such as the banking sector, received salaries and benefits that in most cases went beyond what was justified by their productivity. In the 1990s, these rents fell in the context of the more competitive environment produced by trade liberalization, the elimination of price controls, privatization, and the downsizing of public administration.

Labor legislation regarding collective rights showed important changes during the past decade, although it is difficult to establish a general trend. The region as a whole has many different ways of organizing its labor relations and, despite somewhat similar economic pressures, countries have moved in different and contradictory directions (Cook 1998). Cook argues that countries that were in the process of democratization moved in a more protectionist direction, whereas countries that were implementing economic reforms moved toward "flexibilization." In Argentina, Colombia, and Peru, union density has fallen dramatically as part of a labor flexibilization process in the context of trade liberalization.

In the case of Argentina, however, the union movement maintained its political influence, given the restoration of collective-bargaining rights that

Figure 9.16 Trade union density, 1980 and 1990
(percent of nonagricultural labor force)

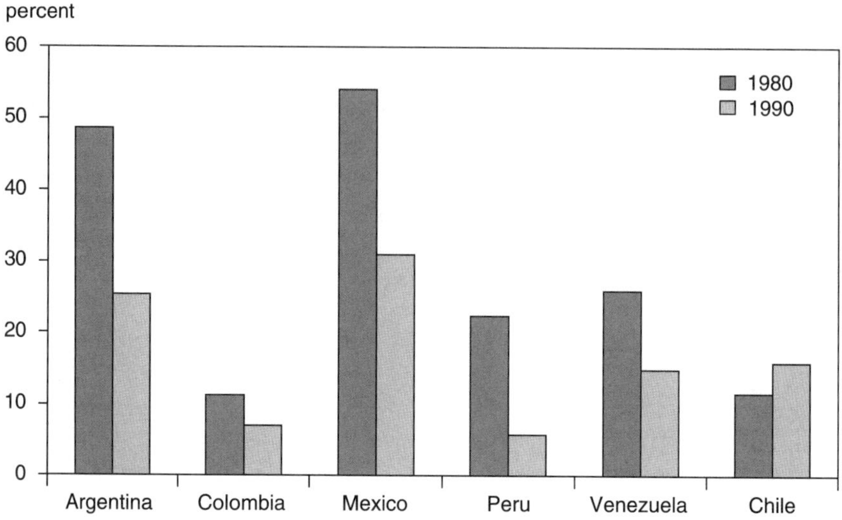

Sources: O'Connell (1999), except for Peru, for which data are from the National Household Survey (for metropolitan Lima only) and the unionization rate is calculated as a percentage of salaried workers.

came with the return to democracy in the late 1980s. The latter phenomenon was also observed in Brazil and Uruguay, and these countries tended to move to a more protectionist system. In Uruguay, however, there was a further move toward a less centralized system in 1993, with less intervention of the state and bargaining at the firm level. Chile has also moved toward more protective legislation, under which collective rights are promoted, although it is still more flexible than other Latin American countries.

During the 1990s, Argentina, Brazil, and Mexico maintained highly centralized corporatist systems, with strong state intervention and in most cases with bargaining at the sector level. In other countries, a wave of changes in collective bargaining moved countries toward a more decentralized bargaining model with limited involvement of the authorities.

In several Latin America countries, rates of unionization fell (figure 9.16), continuing a trend that had already started in the 1980s and that is also observed in industrial countries. A large part of the reduction in unionization is explained by the reduction in public-sector employment. However, there has also been a sharp reduction in union affiliation in the private sector.

Labor organizations in Latin America in general were not characterized as high-performance organizations and constantly maintained a belligerent position against firms, following the idea that profits are a pie that should be shared between firm owners and workers as part of a political process. Conversely, firm owners failed to develop a less adversarial relationship. In most countries, unions have managed to protect employment and also to obtain higher wages than those of comparable nonunionized workers, but it is not clear that these higher wages reflect higher productivity levels.

In Brazil, Menezes-Filho et al. (2002) have shown that unions have a negative effect on profitability. The relation between union density and productivity, employment, and wages depends on the extent of density. Some unionism has a positive effect on economic performance, but high levels of unionism have negative effects. In Peru, Saavedra and Torero (2002) find a negative impact of unions on profits for all firm sizes and that labor productivity is at best not influenced by unions. There is also evidence for Peru of a positive but diminishing union wage premium. In Uruguay, Cassoni, Allen, and Labadie (2000) find that during the period when bargaining was done at the industry level, unions were able to increase wages; after 1993, the union wage differential vanished in those industries that were exposed to international trade.

Minimum Wages

In some countries, minimum wages are not binding and do not have an important effect on the labor market. However, with the price stability achieved toward the middle of the 1990s, nominal minimum-wage adjustments were not easily eroded by inflation any more, and there was increasing evidence that minimum wages "bite." In Colombia, for instance, Bell (1997) finds negative effects of minimum wages on employment of low-skill and low-wage workers, whereas in Mexico the minimum wage is not binding. Maloney and Nuñez (2001) find that increases in the minimum wage have very significant positive effects on the probability of becoming unemployed, an effect that is stronger for workers with earnings in the neighborhood of the minimum wage. They find that on average a 10 percent increase in the minimum wage reduces employment by 1.5 percent.

Maloney and Nuñez (2001) demonstrate that the economic crisis in Mexico in 1994 required a fall in real wages, which was possible given a nonbinding minimum wage. In Colombia in the late 1990s, in contrast, a reduction in labor demand generated an increase in unemployment, for Colombia maintains a high indexed minimum wage. The informal sector does not easily absorb workers who are not employed in the formal sector, because the minimum wage is also used by the informal sector as a reference. In Brazil, there is evidence that the minimum wage affects not just the formal wage structure but also wage determination in the informal sector (the "lighthouse effect"; Amadeo, Gill, and Neri 2000).

Regulation and the Informal Sector

For many observers, it is a puzzle as to why employment growth was so sluggish if there was a reduction in labor market rigidities in Latin America during the 1990s. In a few countries, employment adjustments were facilitated by labor market deregulation, mainly through a reduction in firing costs and through the use of temporary employment contracts. However, movement toward a more flexible labor market was clear in only a few countries. Overall, employment grew only as long as there was economic growth, and labor legislation is still a hindrance to an expansion of employment in most countries.

The lack of growth of high-quality jobs—that is, jobs in which productivity is high enough to finance the social benefits mandated by law—is probably the more troublesome phenomenon. As discussed in Saavedra and Chong (1999), entering the informal sector, understood as noncompliance with regulations, is a decision that both firms and employees make on the basis of cost-benefit evaluations that are continuously revised. A firm's degree of compliance with regulations depends on how profitable it is for the firm to do so. That is, there is not a clearly segmented informal sector—in the sense of a formal sector with above-market-clearing wages and workers queuing for a formal job—but a continuum of economic agents repeatedly making decisions about whether and how far to comply with regulations. Moreover, the compliance decision is not a simple dichotomy between formal and informal, because firms may comply with some regulations and not with others. And some workers in a firm may be under formal contracts whereas others are not.

A firm faces monetary and nonmonetary costs of entering the formal sector: fees, licenses, taxes, payment of social benefits, compliance with health and safety regulations, and so on. And there is a cost of staying informal, given by the fines that the firm may have to pay if detected by authorities. Among microentrepreneurs, other key costs of becoming or staying informal are related to the restrictions on establishing commercial relationships with formally registered firms, the difficulty of exercising property rights, and the pecuniary costs of being caught not complying with regulations. This has to be balanced against the benefits of formality, in particular, the possibility of broadening the scale of production, establishing commercial relationships with bigger firms, and accessing credit in the financial markets. Benefits have to be higher than costs for informal-sector entrepreneurs to be willing to change their legal status. When benefits do not exist or are not valued, or when enforcement is weak, many individuals and firms will find it convenient to stay in or switch to the informal sector.

For wage earners, the choice between being formal or informal hinges on the choice of working in occupations with different characteristics. It is the firm offering the job that decides if it is expedient to comply with existing rules and regulations. Creating a formal job implies the inclusion of specific labor costs for the firm: taxes, nonwage costs, and administrative procedures. The firm will be willing to incur these costs if it is able to transfer at least part of them to workers in the form of lower salaries, or if it perceives that providing the benefits they finance will increase productivity. A firm might not be able to pass these costs on to workers if the labor market is tight, if there is a minimum wage, or if workers do not value the resulting benefits.

It is not strange that a majority of small firms choose to have informal employment relationships, both because their productivity is too low to be able to finance social benefits and because workers in the relevant market are not willing to receive lower salaries to cover these costs. Some workers also will choose informal jobs if they are not willing to pay for social benefits.

Maloney (1999) advances arguments on the same line. He claims that workers might prefer informal employment because of certain desirable characteristics, like the flexibility and independence of being self-employed, or the possibility of evading paying for certain nonwage labor costs that are not highly valued by low-productivity wage earners. This will be particularly likely where labor codes are inefficient and productivity differentials between the formal and informal sector are small. He argues that this is an alternative to the dualistic view of a segmented labor market in which workers queue for formal-sector jobs.[20]

In this framework, rises in productivity and reductions in labor taxes (either plain payroll taxes or legal benefits that are perceived as taxes) increase demand for formal salaried employment and reduce the profitability of operating as an informal self-employed person or microentrepreneur. The higher are taxes, the higher is the likelihood of it being profitable to run—or work in—an informal enterprise.

The central question is whether poorly designed institutions hamper the generation of higher-quality jobs, that is, jobs in which workers have at least a minimum of social benefits. In Latin America, the costs of formality are still too high compared with the perceived value of benefits, given productivity. If a formal job comes with a package of benefits that includes certain services that workers do not value, or that the firm's productivity is not high enough to pay for, then formal jobs will not be created. If the package of such benefits as vacations and dismissal costs is too

20. In fact, Cunningham and Maloney (1999) find that in Mexico, during a period of economic growth, 70 percent of those entering the informal sector did so to increase earnings or because they were lured by the higher flexibility. Robles et al. (2001) report that in Peru microentrepreneurs in textiles and metal mechanics who started their firms because they wanted independence would move to a permanent formal job if they were paid significantly more than what they received as entrepreneurs.

generous, given productivity levels, only a small number of workers will end up enjoying them. As long as workers are not willing to accept lower wages to pay for fringe benefits, or firms are not willing and able to finance them, they will find ways to avoid paying such benefits.

In many cases, workers are not willing to pay for these benefits because, at low levels of income, discount rates are too high and they value current consumption much more. Therefore, willingness to save for an old-age pension, for instance, is low, because they will perceive all or part of these payments as taxes. Something similar applies to health benefits, where they prefer to run the risk of not receiving proper medical care rather than paying premiums.[21] By the same token, firms may not want or are unable to invest in adequate occupational safety regulations. Moreover, long vacations, as are mandated by law in Brazil and Peru, are not observed by informal firms, and they act as a plain additional tax in larger firms, reducing labor demand. In many cases, workers in large and medium-sized firms, which force them to take vacations under the risk of being fined by the authorities, spend those days working in another job.

An interesting example of the way rigidities imposed by legislation have negative effects on welfare and productivity comes from the regulation of the number of hours worked. Many countries restrict the number of hours that can be worked, even paying overtime, or reduce firms' possibilities of changing schedules. Some multinational firms require Latin American subcontractors to limit the number of hours to just 8. However, given the market level of the hourly wage, workers would prefer working 10 or 12 hours. If the firm limits the number of hours to 8, they will work another shift in another firm, incurring unnecessary transaction costs. In such cases, the 8-hour limit does not benefit the worker but only reduces the firm's productivity and the worker's welfare.

Given this framework, why did informal employment increase during the 1990s? Or, why did the proportion of workers with access to social benefits decrease during the 1990s? The answer lies in a comparison between productivity and rents versus the benefits of being formal. When economies were closed, there were rents in oligopolistic sectors and in the public sector. As economies liberalized trade and deregulated goods markets, profits fell in many oligopolistic sectors, and soft-budget-constrained public enterprises and institutions disappeared or were downsized. Consequently, sectors that were inefficient but that maintained high-quality jobs financed by those rents shrank or disappeared.

In many cases, there is evidence of high productivity growth, but concentrated in certain manufacturing subsectors, public utilities (usually privatized), and business services, and employment creation in these sec-

---

21. In this case, for high-wage workers, health insurance might be perceived as a tax if the type of service they receive is of low quality and they prefer to contract additional health insurance from other—usually private—providers.

tors was meager. The number of jobs created in those high-productivity sectors was not enough to replace the jobs lost in low-productivity but formerly high-rent sectors. In the rest of the economy, there was employment creation, but in low-productivity jobs. In addition, within the informal sector, market niches that had been competitive with protection—for instance, informal manufacturing—were driven out of the market by cheaper imports.

During the 1990s, trade liberalization and greater exposure to competition in general forced firms to reduce costs. Yet nonwage labor costs were maintained at very high levels, or even increased in several countries. Conversely, job protection mechanisms were reduced in only a few countries. Because the evolution of productivity and the need to reduce costs was not compatible with the evolution of costs mandated by law, informal contractual regulations were a more frequent outcome. Despite heavy regulation, the labor market in most Latin American countries has undergone a de facto flexibilization process as some firms and employees have moved underground. In large parts of the region's labor markets, there is total flexibility, and wages, working conditions, and contracts are freely determined.

Finally, even though the labor code lays down how flexible or rigid the labor market is supposed to be, the extent to which these regulations affect the operation of the labor market depends heavily on the capability and willingness of the authorities to enforce regulations. The effect also often depends on unwritten rules that dictate the typical behavior of labor courts, in some cases with a prolabor bias and in other cases probusiness, usually depending on the political orientation of the government.

Active Labor Market Policies

Active labor market policies in Latin America have a long tradition in the areas of intermediation services and occupational training. In the 1990s, social investment funds and training programs directed to specific groups were added to the policy menu.

Labor intermediation services are intended to improve the quality and speed of the match between firms and workers looking for a job. They are slowly evolving from the monopolistic public employment services of the 1960s and 1970s into more modern and technologically savvy institutions that try to provide a more comprehensive array of employment services. This process of modernization has made progress in different countries at different speeds, but there have already been many interesting experiences throughout the region. Currently, labor intermediation services and job exchanges using computer-based systems are in place in Brazil, Chile, Mexico, and several Central American countries. In addition, countries are experimenting with different types of public–private alliances as a cost-effective way of increasing service coverage. Interesting but still limited experiences are found in Argentina, Guatemala, and Peru.[22]

Similarly, there is a long tradition of occupational and vocational training systems in Latin America. In most countries, large public training services, financed by payroll contributions, dominate the market. These institutions provide training services to youth as an alternative to higher education, and also to adults already in the labor force. Postsecondary training institutions expanded their coverage during the 1990s, but in many cases this happened at the expense of quality. However, the ability of this system to adapt to current requirements, together with its overall efficiency, has been questioned (Márquez 2002).

During the 1990s, training programs oriented toward increasing productivity and providing a labor market experience to specific groups—in many cases as a part of countries' poverty alleviation strategies—were developed. Projects targeted to unemployed youth, such as Chile Joven (started in 1992), Proyecto Joven in Argentina (1994), Opción Joven in Uruguay (1995), and Projoven in Peru (1996), were implemented with different degrees of success and on different scales.

These youth programs have several elements that should be part of a public strategy for occupational training. Training is financed by the government but is provided by public and private training institutions, which compete on a price and quality basis to provide the service. Institutions may only submit a tender if they can fulfill minimum quality standards established by the programs. Training courses have to be complemented by an internship arranged by the training institution. The structure of incentive implicit in these type of programs has led to an increase in quality standards and better coordination between firms and training institutions.

A few countries have implemented or continued programs aimed at reducing welfare losses due to economic shocks to provide market skills to displaced workers. Workfare programs—such as the Trabajar program in Argentina and the A Trabajar program in Peru—have been implemented. Also, social investment funds, which were heavily supported by multilateral development banks, have provided job opportunities in rural and urban marginal communities as part of the implementation of small-scale infrastructure projects. Programs oriented toward providing training and other support to adults displaced from shrinking economic sectors are scarce and generally have not been effective.

The Policy Agenda

The highly skewed income distributions in Latin America are related to an extremely unequal set of opportunities that workers face in finding

22. A review of current trends in Latin America regarding labor intermediation services and policy recommendations in this area may be found in Mazza (2001).

a high-quality job, given varying abilities and preferences. Inequality of opportunity in the labor market is related to several types of inequality of opportunity—opportunities to access high-quality education and health services, to get high-quality training, to find jobs that can provide basic benefits, and to use income-smoothing mechanisms. Some of these are prelabor market problems, but others may be subject to influence by labor legislation or active labor market policies

Education and Occupational Training

Education is probably the single most important factor that will determine productivity growth and the generation of higher-quality jobs. As is discussed in chapter 8, education faces formidable challenges in the region. Several policies aimed at promoting human capital investment also are part of the labor policy agenda, such as the provision of high-quality occupational training (both as a postsecondary alternative and for workers already in the labor force) and incentives for on-the-job training. Governments should try to shift their role from the direct provision of general training services to that of regulation and certification, with the objective of ensuring that all training institutions comply with minimum quality standards. The underlying objective should be to ensure that all potential trainees have the opportunity to access adequate training.

Training is in fact a very profitable investment, particularly among disadvantaged youth. The models of youth-training programs in which the government finances the training while providers are selected on a competitive basis should be expanded. Several public programs in the region are wisely combining direct training subsidies with monitoring and quality supervision of training institutions. The raising of quality standards for training has positive effects for program participants as well as for the occupational training market as a whole. Provided these courses are tied to a practical training period in a firm, they give trainees an opportunity to have a first exposure to formal salaried employment, increasing the probability of securing a better job match in the future.

Demand-side subsidies for training need to be accompanied by a more intensive use of mechanisms to monitor and certify the quality of the occupational training service, for the main problem in the market for occupational training in Latin America is not insufficient supply but an extremely heterogeneous supply and very scarce information for potential trainees about the quality of the service they are receiving. Helping parents and youth to distinguish between high- and low-quality training institutions will enable families to make better educational investments (which are huge, even among the poor), which will also foster more investment.

Increasing the quality of occupational training is crucial for two other reasons. First, a large majority of the Latin American labor force has already completed its cycle of basic education, and in many cases the quality of that education was very poor. Most of these workers will not go into tertiary education but will spend several decades in the labor market. For these workers, the only chance of strengthening their skills and increasing the possibility of securing a better job is occupational training. Second, rapid technological change and economic integration will require constant retraining of the labor force, independent of the amount of formal education already attained.

As well as subsidizing training in specialized institutions, governments should promote investment in training in the workplace, through direct subsidies that complement private contributions. Also, training programs for personnel of small and medium-sized firms and for workers displaced from shrinking sectors should be part of a public-private strategy for human capital investment. In the latter case, programs and subsidies directed to these displaced workers should be part of a social safety net oriented toward supporting workers hurt by unexpected shocks.[23]

Finally, countries should move toward schemes of public subsidies for training provided by private institutions. In general, private institutions have the potential to give higher-quality training, in particular if it is linked to the needs of private firms.

Information, Certification, and Intermediation Services

Governments should promote the provision of an array of information services regarding jobs, labor market conditions, skill requirements, and training opportunities, so as to improve the match between supply and demand for labor at all skill levels. Given the necessity of expanding the availability of these services, countries should try to use all the available resources in both the public and private sectors.

These services should also include the provision of information on the skill requirements for jobs, and on the availability of training opportunities to acquire the specific skills required by employers. Also, much progress is required in monitoring the labor market to provide information on current and future trends regarding occupations, skill requirements, training needs, wages, and labor demand. Such information, if properly disseminated, could help job seekers, training seekers, workers, employers, and training institutions. In addition, job placement and job search assistance and counseling services should be expanded.

A crucial institutional constraint is the lack of credibility and the poor reputation of public agencies among firms (Mazza 2001). For this reason,

23. It is not yet clear whether the highest social return is obtained from programs that attempt to retrain workers, from plain subsidies, or from subsidies directed to promote training of currently working older workers.

a complete restructuring of the institutional setting is required in many countries. Also, intermediation services usually cater only to firms in the formal sector; given that the majority of Latin American economies have an informal sector that surpasses 50 percent of the labor force, these services should also try to cover the firms in this sector.

A more efficient flow of information also is required on the skills and abilities of workers. Much learning and many skills are acquired through on-the-job training, experience, and other informal mechanisms. Programs aiming to provide certification of skills acquired outside formal training institutions are already in place in some countries, such as Chile and Mexico, but are incipient in most others. These programs require establishing institutional mechanisms to define competency norms, which should ideally be set jointly by firms, workers, and the responsible authority (usually a dependency of the ministry of labor). Once these norms are established, a body with a good reputation needs to certify that a worker is competent in a specific skill.

In the same way that firms should have at their disposal mechanisms that can allow them to know the specific abilities and competencies of workers, workers should have access to information regarding what they need to learn and where they can learn it. In most Latin American countries, information regarding the quality of training institutions is nonexistent, so much progress is needed in monitoring and supervising the performance of institutions and in providing this information to the public.

Labor Market Legislation

The reform of labor laws faces formidable challenges. More than ever, these laws must allow for the efficient operation of the labor market and at the same time create the right incentives for employers and employees to create job relationships that can ensure that workers feel secure and enjoy access to social benefits. Labor legislation thus should not be thought of primarily as either more rigid or more flexible; countries should aim for better regulation.

Most of the Latin American labor codes were written according to a legal doctrine that is based on the so-called fundamental rights of workers. However, these labor codes generally protect only those who already have a formal job and actually reduce the possibility of more workers being able to access a formal job. An important objective of labor legislation should be to create conditions in which most workers can have jobs with access to basic social benefits: health insurance, old-age protection, and income-smoothing mechanisms to cover episodes of unemployment. Legislation should not try to artificially protect workers by giving them rights that cannot be sustained by productivity. No matter how thoroughly the authorities enforce the legislation and unions monitor that the rights granted by legislation to their members are fulfilled, these rights will only apply to the most productive firms and will be purely mythical for a large part of the population.

Firing Costs

Many countries resort to the use of temporary employment contracts as a way to relax the rigidity imposed by dismissal costs. In European countries and in several Latin American countries, restrictions on the use of this type of contract have been reduced, by increasing the proportion of the payroll that can be hired under temporary contracts, the number of years for which they can be renewed, or the reasons for which their use is permitted. The reliance on temporary contracts is a second-best policy response to the political resistance to reducing firing costs in regular contracts.

These contracts probably leave workers and firms worse off, however, because their temporary nature may reduce productivity and salaries while increasing workers' perception of job insecurity. This is a case in which partial reform may be more harmful than no reform. Argentina, Colombia, and Peru allowed for increased use of these contracts during the 1990s, and in all cases labor turnover increased. When turnover increases due to technological, demographic, or organizational practices, countries should allow for smooth job-to-job transitions with the lowest possible short-term reduction in consumption for workers. Yet it does not make sense to induce higher turnover through legislation.

In 1998, Argentina moved toward prohibiting temporary contracts, but unfortunately without flexibilizing the use of permanent contracts. Temporary contracts helped increase employment in Argentina. Making it more difficult to use them would have been the right policy, if accompanied by a reduction in the cost of permanent contracts.

Countries should encourage firms to make permanent contracts, rather than trying to artificially enforce their use. For firms' use of these contracts to increase, they need to provide the flexibility required by the marketplace. If they are not flexible, they will only be used by a small group of firms; the rest will rely on temporary contracts, if available, or on part-time contracts or plain informal labor relationships.[24]

Firing costs should be designed as part of the income-smoothing mechanisms. In general, despite the reductions observed in some countries, firing costs are still very high and did not decrease substantially during the 1990s. Even if there are ways for firms to adjust to rigid regulation and incorporate more flexibility into their use of labor, it would be more efficient for all parties to have low firing costs. Both workers and firms would then know that their contractual arrangement has no definite termination date but will continue as long as is profitable for both parties.

---

24. With a reasonable cost structure for permanent contracts, temporary contracts should only be used when the labor requirement is for a specific time period.

Given the imperfection of capital markets, it is necessary to have mechanisms to smooth consumption and protect workers and their families during periods of unemployment. But that objective has to be attained without hampering the economy's ability to create jobs. Most current job protection mechanisms leave part of the labor force without the possibility of securing a job that carries social benefits in the formal sector, hamper efficient job mobility within the formal sector, and constitute an additional force that increases inequality.

Job Protection and Income Smoothing

Severance payments, individual savings accounts, and unemployment insurance have been the main mechanisms used by Latin American countries to reduce job turnover and give workers a way to finance periods of unemployment. As was discussed above, these mechanisms can have unfortunate effects on the operation of the labor market. Countries should choose institutions that provide effective protection without hampering job creation.

The application of unemployment insurance systems in Latin America is at best complicated, and they are not that common in the region. Where they exist at all, these programs are usually small and cover only a fraction of the formal sector. Given the huge informal sector in almost all Latin American economies, unemployment insurance systems can be too costly to be operated successfully, because keeping track of employment histories and job-search efforts is excessively complicated.

Severance payments are still popular in the region and are a simple way to provide workers with a way of financing unemployment periods. However, in most cases, they are still too high, and because they are tied to the most recent salary level they constitute a large contingent claim on the firm in bad times. Individual accounts, as in the Colombian scheme, allow for spreading out that cost in time, eliminate uncertainty, and make it possible to share part of the cost with workers, who will also internalize the cost of the insurance, thereby reducing disincentive effects.

Yet unlike unemployment insurance systems, individual accounts do not allow for risk pooling across workers. Countries with such schemes, such as Brazil and Peru, may improve them by restricting the size of the fund to that consistent with the median length of unemployment, avoiding an excessively large accumulation. This would also reduce the bias that such legislation generates against older workers, who were particularly affected during the 1990s.[25] Chile has recently adopted a mechanism that combines an insurance component with the accumulation of an individual fund and a severance payment by the employer. It is not clear yet whether this design is appropriate for the Chilean labor market, and even

25. Another possibility is to allow the use of part of these savings as collateral for mortgages or other exceptional uses.

less clear whether it would work in other Latin American economies with much larger informal sectors. However, it does aim to protect income and reduce welfare fluctuations, while simultaneously minimizing the employment-reducing effect of the typical job protection scheme and avoiding hampering the job mobility needed to maintain competitiveness in increasingly integrated markets.

Social Security Contributions

Nonwage labor costs are relatively high in most countries of the region, given productivity levels. Tax rates are in most cases relatively in line with international standards, although those rates may be too high to allow for an efficient operation of the labor market. Willingness to pay these contributions will increase with productivity, assuming that workers with higher earnings have lower discount rates and will thus give more value to future income (notably by valuing savings for an old-age pension more highly). By the same token, they will attach more value to health insurance.

Countries should continue moving toward tying contributions to benefits, as has already happened with pension contributions in Argentina, Chile, Colombia, Mexico, and Peru, all of which have introduced private pension systems. This reduces the potential negative employment effects of pay-as-you-go systems. However, the new system of individual capitalization accounts does not provide risk pooling across individuals, so extreme care has to be taken to regulate them properly so as to reduce risks with workers' savings.

In addition, minimum pensions should be established, in particular covering the transition period, for workers who were not confronted with the right savings incentives during a large part of their working lives. Another problem that many Latin American countries confront is that health and pension systems are plagued by special regimes, which generate small lobby groups with very high stakes in preventing required reforms.

Job quality is related to job security, earnings, and occupational safety. But in most of the region's countries, it is also linked to quality of life. If one loses a formal job, he or she loses health coverage and in most cases the possibility of access to a pension. We need to learn more about the possibility of de-linking these social benefits from labor status. At present, all good things come together: job protection, health services, savings for retirement. All are linked to labor status, so either one has the productivity required to pay for everything or one does not have anything.

Collective Bargaining and Industrial Relations

Better labor market outcomes can prevail if both firms and organized labor make the effort to create an incentive structure in which there is a balance between competitiveness and workers' rights. Agreements reached by firms' organizations and unions should take care not to end up excluding the large majority of the labor force from being part of a modern labor relationship. Countries need to design a model of labor relations in which unions work more in partnership with firms and do not adopt an exclusively confrontational relationship. Unions should establish programs and policies aimed at increasing productivity (training, work councils, and the like), transforming themselves into high-performance organizations that protect and promote their members' interests while simultaneously improving productivity. Although adversarial relations are inevitable at times and can be functional, they can become perverse if they lead unions and firms to ignore their common interests. High-performance unions will give great weight to cooperation and flexibility so as to raise productivity, not merely to pursue contracts, rules, and regulations (Saavedra and Torero 2002).

Governments should foster the adoption of modern human resource practices, the use of firm-based training programs, and voluntary worker participation in decision making and profits, all with the objective of increasing productivity. Labor laws should regulate both unions and business councils to ensure, particularly in the former, democratic decision-making processes, and at the same time avoid government intervention in their functioning. It seems inevitable that corporatist models—in which the state intervenes in management-union relations, in union registration, and in internal union affairs—end up being highly politicized. The state should remain the guarantor of the existence of appropriate bargaining mechanisms, but it should only intervene when called upon.

There are signs that the process of backward movement of unions has stopped. In Brazil, Chile, Mexico, and Peru, unions are taking a more important role in determining legislative changes. However, it is not clear how collective bargaining and industrial relations will evolve in each country. The challenge is to secure representation in the context of very large informal sectors.

Enforcement

Workers' rights granted by legislation are enforced in different degrees by labor authorities. In many countries, a lack of enforcement leads to noncompliance. In some cases, noncompliance can be corrected with a proper combination of low-cost enforcement, fines, and dissemination campaigns on the advantages of complying with rules on productivity and workers' welfare. However, none of these measures will ensure compliance if productivity is so low that firms cannot afford to pay the costs of complying with existing regulations. The latter situation is common in Latin America and is consistent with the existence of huge informal sectors where workers lack any protection.

In some countries, changes in the impact of legislation on the operation of the labor market have been related to changes in the ability and willingness of the authorities to enforce the law. This may be a consequence of shifts in the ideological orientation of the government. In other cases, the willingness to enforce is reduced when the economy goes into a recession. In Latin America, these de facto flexibilizations are not uncommon, particularly when small firms and microenterprises account for a large share of employment and their ability to comply with regulations is low and volatile.

These adjustment mechanisms, however, are inefficient both from economic and social points of view. Changes in enforcement standards introduce uncertainty and unpredictability that reduce profitability and investment. And a flexibilization of the labor market that stems just from weak enforcement may be perceived as an unfair attitude of the authorities, which are prepared to side with businesses regardless of what is legally established.[26] This type of flexibilization is politically unsustainable in the long run, so if firms make decisions based also on expected changes in legislation, it may not have the desired positive impact of a legal flexibilization.

Considerations for Implementing Reforms

The debate about labor legislation concerns who bears risks. Protective legislation has typically established that firms should bear the risks of economic fluctuations. Given economic shocks that may affect employment and salaries, legislation gave workers protection that had to be financed by firms; it obliged them to maintain salaries, using downward wage inflexibility clauses, and to maintain employment through steep severance payment rules.[27]

These practices were possible in Latin America in large firms that traditionally enjoyed tariff protection, were able to extract subsidies from corrupt or inept government officials, or were financed by a soft public budget constraint. Such rents have disappeared in most cases, so only large and highly productive firms can maintain this type of benefit. Consequently, firms are seeking ways to shift a larger part of the burden to workers. In some countries, this has been facilitated by changes in labor legislation; but as discussed above, changes in labor laws have not been that important. In most cases, this increase in flexibility has been met through the use of atypical contractual relationships, outsourcing, subcontracting, and, in the extreme, informal labor relationships.

---

26. Cook (1998) argues that protective legislation met little resistance from employers in El Salvador, Guatemala, and Paraguay because of de facto flexibilization.

27. Extreme examples were the *estabilidad numérica* in Venezuela, where firms could dismiss workers but had to maintain the same number of employees. Even worse was the Peruvian *estabilidad laboral absoluta*, whereby workers were practically owners of their posts.

Legislation needs to define the fair share of risk that workers and firms should bear to maximize society's overall welfare. Legislation may mandate that all the risk has to be borne by firms, but if that proves to be unsustainable, then compliance will only be partial. The challenge faced by labor legislation is therefore immense. It is senseless to continue making marginal changes in current laws as if more than half of the urban labor force—the informal sector—and most of the rural labor force in most countries did not exist. Countries must find ways to extend basic social benefits to a large part of the population.

But reform will always have winners and losers. During the transition toward a more market-oriented economy, for instance, safety nets that should have given specific groups of the population relief were precarious. Most governments, multilateral development banks, and international cooperative institutions were concerned to provide assistance to poor and extremely poor people, in a valid effort to target scarce resources toward the population with the lowest welfare levels. Much less importance, however, was given to specific groups that suffered large welfare reductions. Labor reform may harm a small group, even though it may be beneficial for the rest of the population. These negative effects on the welfare of specific groups that lose as a result of reform should not be neglected, and adequate and fair compensation needs to be treated as part of the cost of reform. Failure to do so may undermine the sustainability of reform.

Finally, the reform of labor legislation will have an important effect on the labor market only if it is perceived by economic agents as permanent. Moreover, the stability of rules is valuable in itself. Rules are more likely to be permanent if they are defined as part of a discussion and consultation process in which all relevant actors are involved.

Gender and Ethnic Discrimination

In most countries, the male-female wage gap has fallen dramatically, at least partly due to a reduction in the educational gap between males and females. In addition, female employment opportunities have increased significantly, and their employment rates have grown much more quickly than those of males. Despite these developments, Latin America still has one of the highest occupational segregation rates of any region of the world (meaning that the dissimilarity between male and female occupational structures is among the highest). Even if progress has been observed, active labor market policies should be oriented toward both eliminating the identification of specific careers with males or females and ending unjustified earnings differentials.

In the case of ethnic and racial discrimination, there is scattered evidence for such countries as Brazil, Guatemala, and Peru that there are unexplained earnings differentials even in urban settings among workers who are similar except for differences in ethnic or social background. In many Latin American countries, occupational segregation related to race and ethnicity is not a thing of the past. In many cases, it reflects prelabor market inequality of opportunities in education, health care, and access to social services; in other cases, it reflects plain consumer or employer discrimination. At least with regard to the labor market, the authorities should actively promote the eradication of discriminatory practices and should disseminate knowledge of the economic and social costs of discrimination to consumers and employers. They should certainly enforce the antidiscrimination laws that many countries have already enacted.

Concluding Comments

After the initial wave of market-oriented reforms and macroeconomic stabilization, most countries started a process of employment expansion that lasted until 1997 or 1998, when it was halted by economic crisis. But the increase in employment was not in general accompanied by an increase in productivity, so real wage growth was not significant and informality increased. Employment creation was much faster in low-productivity sectors. In addition, labor market-related economic insecurity was on the rise as turnover increased, and temporary contractual arrangements were more common. So the main problem in Latin America is of low-quality jobs.

Reforms had as a consequence the loss of jobs in the public sector, in state-owned enterprises, and in protected manufacturing industries. All these jobs commanded high wages and social benefits supported by the quasi rents that the previous protectionist and interventionist economic models generated. Reforms also produced an increase in productivity in some sectors, but it was not large, or general, or sustained. And employment creation in those sectors was meager.

An important proportion of workers who lost their jobs and were not able to find another salaried formal position used to belong to the middle class and as such had more voice and more mechanisms through which to manifest their discontent. If these workers, particularly older workers, were the losers during this period, women and youth, conversely, enjoyed greater employment opportunities. Also, relative wages of more educated workers showed a clear increase.

Reforms aimed at making the labor market more flexible were implemented in several countries, but overall, labor legislation has not changed dramatically, and it still hampers formal job creation. This, together with the increase in nonwage costs observed in many countries and the sluggish productivity growth, is behind the growth of informality. In most countries, the percentage of workers without social benefits has increased; and typically, still half the urban employed labor force works informally, as well as most of the rural labor force.

The challenges Latin American faces to increase productivity and generate better jobs are formidable. It needs to improve dramatically its educational and occupational training systems, promoting equality of opportunities in these markets. It should stimulate the development of efficient information systems regarding jobs, skill requirements, quality of training and educational institutions, labor market conditions, and the like to allow for better decisions of families, workers, and firms in the educational and labor markets.

Labor market reform is required to ensure the efficient operation of the labor market and at the same time create the right incentives for employers and employees to create job relationships that can facilitate workers' security and access to social benefits. Labor legislation needs to define the fair share of risk that workers and firms should bear to maximize society's overall welfare. It may mandate that all the risk has to be borne by firms, but if that is not economically sustainable, compliance will only be partial. Reforms in labor regulation thus should not be thought of primarily as either more rigid or more flexible; countries should aim for better regulation. And any labor reform that is part of a process involving all actors will more likely be seen as permanent, and consequently more likely to improve the functioning of the labor market and workers' welfare.

Finally, it is essential that a model of modern labor relations in which unions work more in partnership with firms—with the aim of increasing productivity rather than facing an exclusively confrontational relationship—becomes widespread.

10

The Politics of Second-Generation Reforms

PATRICIO NAVIA AND ANDRÉS VELASCO

What Does "Reform" Mean?

More than a decade after market-oriented reforms were launched in almost every Latin American country, the picture is not encouraging. Per capita growth reached almost 2 percent a year in the 1990s—a far cry from the dismal negative 0.7 percent during the "lost decade" of the 1980s—but hopes have been dashed nonetheless. Only Chile managed to achieve "Asian" rates of growth during the 1990s. In other countries—Argentina and Mexico are good examples—vigorous growth spurts have been followed by periods of stagnation or decline. Huge budget deficits and hyperinflation are a thing of the past (one hopes), but low investment and dismal public services are not. Income distribution has not worsened, but it has not improved either; Latin America remains the world champion of inequality. Prescriptions differ, but most observers agree that the time has come for a new round of policy reforms in the region.

Patricio Navia is the outreach coordinator for the Center for Latin American and Caribbean Studies at New York University where he also teaches Latin American politics and Latin American and Caribbean Culture. Andrés Velasco is Sumitomo-FASID Professor of International Finance and Development at Harvard University's Kennedy School of Government. *The authors thank the Center for International Development at Harvard University for generous support.*

What new policies could these be? The distinction between first- and second-generation reforms, originally made (to the best of our knowledge) by Naím (1994), still provides a useful way of organizing the discussion. Table 10.1, taken from Naím's paper, lists the reforms involved and their characteristics. First-generation reforms include the usual suspects: macroeconomic stabilization, tariff and budget cuts, privatization, and the like. Second-generation reforms are a motley crew, encompassing broad reforms of the state, the civil service, and the delivery of public services; of the institutions that create and maintain human capital (e.g., schools and the health care system); and of the environment in which private firms operate (more competition, better regulation, stronger property rights). In contrast to first-generation reforms, which were really statements about the instruments to be used and the inputs needed (reduce inflation by cutting money-supply growth and the budget deficit), many second-generation reforms are really statements of desired outcomes (e.g., civil service reform or improving tax collection), without a clear sense of policy design. This is not a failure in Naím's conceptualization; rather, it is a signal of our ignorance of how to achieve these goals.

First- and second-generation reforms overlap, but do not coincide entirely, with variations on Williamson's famous 1994 "Washington Consensus" (for a detailed discussion of the history and use of this term, see the appendix at the end of this book). Table 10.2, adapted from Rodrik (2002), contains the original 10 prescribed policies plus 10 more that originate in what Rodrik calls the "Augmented Washington Consensus." The extended list contains some items that are not new reforms in themselves but rather are changes that he argues are necessary to make the policies in the original list work, or to prevent some of those original reforms from failing. Examples are "financial codes and standards," "prudent capital account opening" and "nonintermediate exchange rate regimes," all intended to moderate the macroeconomic and banking instability brought by the initial round of financial reforms.

Other elements in the extended Washington Consensus are more properly second-generation reforms, involving legal, regulatory, and political institutions. Notice again that many are outputs and not inputs; poverty reduction is a lofty goal, but the Washington pundits are silent on how to achieve it. Indeed, a striking feature of second-generation reforms is their sheer technical difficulty. Any economist can tell you that curtailing inflation requires lower money growth; fewer are prepared to put forward a proposal for supervising operations in derivatives by banks and other financial institutions, or for solving failures in the market for health insurance.

Thorny Political Obstacles

Differences in the politics between the two stages are no less striking. With the important exceptions of import-competing industrialists facing

Table 10.1. The two stages of economic liberalization: from changing rules to changing institutions

Aspect	Stage 1: Launching	Stage 2: Consolidation
Priorities	• Reduce inflation • Restore growth	• Improve social conditions • Increase international competitiveness • Maintain macroeconomic stability
Reform strategy	• Change macroeconomic rules • Reduce size and scope of state • Dismantle protectionism and statism	• Institutionalization: creation and rehabilitation • Boost competitiveness of private sector • Reform health, education, and other public services • Create the "economic institutions of capitalism" • Build new "international economic integration"
Typical instruments	• Drastic budget cuts and tax reform • Price liberalization (including exchange and interest rates) • Trade and foreign investment liberalization • Private-sector deregulation • Creation of "social emergency funds" • "Easier privatization" (e.g., hotels, airlines, some manufacturing)	• Labor market reform • Civil service reform • Restructure government (especially social ministries) • Overhaul administration of justice • Upgrade regulatory capacities (for privatized utilities and other monopolies, antitrust, antidumping, financial sector, environment, labor, etc.) • Improve tax collection • Sectoral restructuring • Build export promotion • Restructure relations between state and federal governments
Principal actors	• Presidency • Economic cabinet • Central bank • Multilateral financial institutions • Private financial groups and foreign investors	• Presidency and cabinet • Congress • Public bureaucracy • Judiciary • Unions • Political parties • The media • State and local governments • Private sector
Public impact of reforms	• Immediate • High public visibility	• Medium and long term • Low public visibility
Technical and administrative complexity of reforms	• Moderate to low	• Very high
Nature of political response	• "Temporary corrections" • Widely distributed among the population	• Permanent elimination of special advantages for specific groups
Main government challenge	• Macroeconomic management by insulated technocratic elites	• Institutional development highly dependent on midlevel public-sector management

Source: Naím (1994).

Table 10.2 The Washington Consensus is dead; long live the new Washington Consensus

Original Washington Consensus	Augmented Washington Consensus
	The original list plus
• Fiscal discipline	• Legal and political reform
• Reorientation of public expenditures	• Regulatory institutions
• Tax reform	• Anticorruption
• Financial liberalization	• Labor market flexibility
• Unified and competitive exchange rates	• World Trade Organization agreements
• Trade liberalization	• Financial codes and standards
• Openness to foreign direct investment	• "Prudent" capital account opening
• Privatization	• Nonintermediate exchange rate regimes
• Deregulation	• Social safety nets
• Secure property rights	• Poverty reduction

Source: Reprinted from Rodrik (2002) with permission.

lower tariffs and unions in parastatals facing privatization, the "victims" of the first-stage reforms were often atomistic or too poor to matter politically. By contrast, the set of interests potentially affected in the next stage reads like a *Who's Who* of highly organized and vocal groups: teachers' and judicial unions, the upper echelons of the public bureaucracy, state and local governments, owners and managers of private monopolies, and the medical establishment.

The complications of second-generation reforms have been evident in countries attempting to move forward. Public school teachers and public health-sector employees have been in a state of semipermanent warfare against governments that have attempted to meddle in their affairs. Chile under Patricio Aylwin and Eduardo Frei and Bolivia under the first administration of Gonzalo Sánchez de Losada are examples. Similarly, cleaning up the finances of free-spending provincial governments proved a politically formidable task for Carlos Menem, Fernando de la Rúa, and Eduardo Duhalde in Argentina and for Fernando Henrique Cardoso and his team in Brazil.

The political process required by second-generation reforms is turning out to be very different from that for first-generation reforms. The first wave of changes was often carried out in unique emergency situations. Many of the measures (e.g., monetary and exchange rate stabilization) did not require parliamentary approval; in areas that normally should (e.g., deregulation or fiscal reform), even democratic governments were able to resort to "emergency rule by decree." By contrast, deep changes in such priority areas as judicial and regulatory systems can hardly be carried out without lengthy discussion and the participation and technical expertise of the affected parties. Rule by committee and consensus has to be the norm from now on. But as governments everywhere are finding out, that is more easily said than done.

All of this necessarily requires that the institutions of democracy be strengthened. There is much talk in the revamped Washington Consensus about the importance of institutions. But as Rodrik (2002, 3) puts it, "The question before policy-makers therefore is no longer 'do institutions matter' but which institutions matter and how does one acquire them?" In his words, such institutions must facilitate the development and consolidation of a "clearly designated system of property rights, a regulatory apparatus curbing the worst forms of fraud, anti-competitive behavior and moral hazard, a moderately cohesive society exhibiting trust and social cooperation, social and political institutions that mitigate risks and manage social conflicts, the rule of law and clean government."

The study of institutions and their relation to economic performance is just beginning in the region. Questions on how institutional features shape and influence public policy and social interactions in Latin American countries have only recently captured the attention of scholars who possess the methodological training to produce research designs that can be replicated and lend themselves to comparative studies. Simple cross-country regressions that introduce institutional or political variables have not yet shown much explanatory power.[1] But we have learned a few lessons, which we review below.

Some Necessary Disclaimers

Two disclaimers are necessary when writing about second-generation reforms. The first is that one may view them as desirable goals in themselves (who could be against less corrupt courts or better hospitals?) without having many illusions about their broader economic impact. In some particularly exalted moments, the authors of the several Washington Consensuses promised that the sum of first- and second-generation reforms would provide the answer to the question of development in general and of economic growth in particular. But cooler heads and some research have revealed that these reforms are no panacea, particularly when it comes to generating long-term growth. More schooling may be a great thing, but its empirical link to increases in per capita income is tenuous indeed, as Pritchett (2001) and Easterly (2001) have found. Not even the relationship between trade and growth is clear. Sachs and Warner (1995) and Frankel and Romer (1999) were early optimists, claiming that greater openness means faster growth; Rodríguez and Rodrik (2000) are skeptical.

1. In his study of the determinants of first-generation reforms, Lora (2000, 13) introduces several political variables, acknowledging that "we are aware that none of the variables considered is a satisfactory indicator of the concepts used in the theoretical literature." Unsurprisingly, he concludes that "the timing and composition of reforms do not appear to be strongly influenced by the political variables highlighted in the theoretical literature. Neither the number of effective parties, nor governing party representation, which are proxies of political fragmentation, has explanatory power in the regressions."

The second disclaimer has to do with the political labels of reform. Policies associated with the Washington Consensus are often thought to strengthen the market and weaken the state. Yet in many areas, second-generation reforms involve "bringing the state back in." Regulation, judicial adjudication, and (to a lesser extent) the provision of social services are government activities almost by definition. The question, then, is how to strengthen the state without allowing it to again become bloated. Or in the words of former Spanish prime minister Felipe González, how to acquire a "small but muscular state."

The fact that second-generation reforms may imply strengthening the state is important for identifying the opponents of reform. Public-sector employees and their privileges are the plausible villains in some stories—health care and education, most prominently. But in other areas, the villains come well dressed and directly from the private sector. The strengthening of regulation is vehemently opposed by the powerful owners—both domestic and foreign—of privatized electricity, telecommunications, and water companies; greater disclosure in financial markets is sure to upset bankers and their friends; and enhanced competition will find enemies both in protected farmers and among shipping and airline owners granted monopolies over domestic transport. This means, in plain but old-fashioned language, that second-generation reform mongering need not be a right-wing affair; it can be a progressive or left-wing affair just as well.

How Much Reform?

Lora (2001) has developed the most comprehensive measure of Latin American first-generation reforms (what he calls "structural" policies). He computes regionwide indices in five areas—trade, finance, taxation, privatization, and labor—normalized so that zero is the lowest rating in any country at any time in the sample, and one the highest. Therefore, the levels of the index are rather hard to interpret, but the changes in the index over time offer a good measure of progress in these areas.[2]

Figure 10.1 shows such changes between 1985 and 1999. The results are consistent with conventional wisdom. Two sets of first-generation reforms—trade and finance legislation—have gone farthest, with the relevant index rising by more than 75 percent during the period. Two other sets of reforms—privatization and tax changes—are in an intermediate category, with the index rising by about 25 percent in both cases. Finally, in labor market regulations—hiring and firing costs, nonwage costs, rules on overtime, and part-time work—there has been hardly any change at all since the mid-1980s. Some countries, such as Argentina, have attempted

2. Notice that Lora classifies changes in labor laws as a first-generation reform, whereas Naím and Rodrik relegate them to the second stage.

Figure 10.1 The advance of first-generation reforms in Latin America, 1985-99

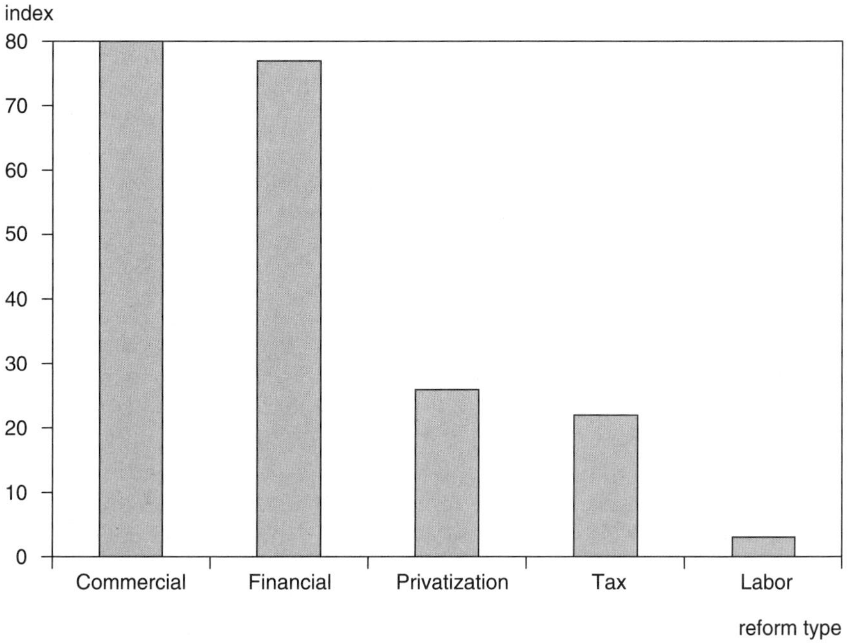

Note: The advance is calculated as the change in the respective index between 1985 and 1999, divided by 1 minus the value of the index in 1985.

Source: Lora (2001).

labor reform again and again, only to have bills defeated or passed in highly watered-down form. In others, such as Chile, firing costs have actually risen in the past decade.

We know of no similar attempt to assess the progress of second-generation reforms across countries and across time. It is revealing that a special International Monetary Fund conference on second-generation reforms held in October 1999 had papers on every topic imaginable, but nothing on the extent of such reforms in the real world. The evidence, therefore, is mostly informal. But the general picture that emerges is quite clear: in Latin America, second-generation reforms are in their infancy at best. There is one area—social security and pensions—where change has been widespread (though one might argue that this was really a first-generation tax reform).[3]

On other fiscal issues, such as relations between national and subnational governments, much has been tried in such countries as Brazil and

3. See Lora and Pages-Serra (2000).

Argentina, with mixed results. (There is also the case of Colombia, where fiscal decentralization has made great strides since 1990, though not necessarily for the better.) Regulatory and prudential systems in finance have improved vastly, if for no other reason than that recurrent financial crises made change inevitable; Chile, Colombia, and Mexico (and in some domains Argentina) stand out in this regard. Modern regulation for some privatized utilities has also sprung up here and there, again with Argentina and Chile taking the lead (though the regulation of telecommunications in Argentina has been far from successful).[4]

But the farther one goes from macroeconomics or big-ticket items such as electricity, and the closer one gets to institutional and microeconomic reform, the less hopeful the panorama becomes. State reform is much talked about but seldom clearly defined and even more rarely implemented. When it comes to poverty alleviation, the tendency has been not to reform existing policies and institutions but to bypass them. First came the fashion for social-emergency funds, invented in Bolivia in 1985 and widely copied elsewhere; then the fashion shifted to contingent cash-transfer programs, paid to female heads of households: Mexico's Progresa is the best-known such scheme, but Ecuador under Jamil Mahuad tried something similar (Skoufias and Parker 2001). Judicial reform is also just starting; perhaps Chile's wide-ranging changes to its penal system are the most striking example.[5] And finally there is the most important of second-generation reforms: education. Progress here is also spotty, as chapter 8 of this book reports.

In one sense, it is not surprising that Latin America has not gone very far in implementing second-generation reforms. We saw above that they are typically defined in terms of outputs (eliminate poverty) instead of inputs (change this or that regulation). But those are the outputs that make advanced nations advanced. If Latin America had alleviated poverty, guaranteed good education and decent health care, acquired upstanding police officers and judges, and learned to regulate highly sophisticated private banks and companies, it would have advanced—and all in a mere decade and a half.

Just as George Orwell's animals are all equal, but some are more equal than others, Latin America's countries are all underdeveloped, but some a great deal more so than others. This difference can be attributed to varying endowments and initial conditions but also to widely varying policy regimes. The political determinants of such policy options, and the polit-

---

4. On regulating the electric sector, see Serra and Fischer (2000); on telecommunications, see Estache, Manacorda, and Valletti (2002).

5. In this case, what such a reform ought to entail is particularly contentious and unclear. There is a vast literature on the efficiency of legal systems in industrial countries, but applications to developing nations are few and far between. See López-de-Silanes (2002) for a review of the issues.

ical circumstances that make policy reform more or less likely, are the very big topics to which we now turn.

The Timing and Sequencing of Reforms

In this section, we revisit two questions that received much attention in the early literature on the political economy of reform. First, do economic crises, either domestic or international, cause reform? Second, what determines the sequence and bundling of different reform initiatives? Our aim is to ascertain what importance, if any, these two issues have for the prospects of second-generation reforms in Latin America.

Are Crises Necessary for Reform?

In the frenzy of reform activity of the early to mid-1990s, it became a truism that economic crises facilitate or outright cause reform. Aside from Colombia, which at that time undertook deep policy changes without a crisis (and, outside Latin America, Australia), in almost every other country reform seemed to be triggered by default, hyperinflation, or worse. The consensus among prominent analysts was almost unanimous. According to Bates and Krueger (1993a, 454), "In all cases, of course, reforms have been undertaken in circumstances in which economic conditions were deteriorating. There is no recorded instance of the beginning of a reform program at a time when economic growth was satisfactory and when the price level and balance of payments situations were stable." In short, things had to get very bad before they could get better.

This idea was appealing and intuitive, but not without problems. Rodrik (1996) provided the most cogent criticisms, pointing out that there is an element of tautology in the explanation: "Reform naturally becomes an issue only when policies are perceived to be not working. A crisis is just an extreme case of policy failure. That reform should follow crisis, then, is no more surprising than smoke following fire."

There were plenty of models around built to formalize how the politico-economic equilibrium changes to permit reform, and of what role crises can play in this context. In all these models, agents (groups) decide what to do by comparing expected streams of payoffs. Typically, the (flow) payoff associated with "nonreform" is expected to deteriorate.[6] A reform occurs in this context when the payoff associated with the policy change first exceeds that associated with the status quo. What role do crises play in all of this?

6. This deterioration can come about because of exogenous (terms of trade and other) shocks, as in Velasco (1994) and Tomell (1995), or because of the endogenous evolution of state variables—financial adaptation in Labán (1994) and Mondino, Sturzenegger, and Tommasi (1996), or government debt in Alesina and Drazen (1991) and Velasco (1999).

Two papers dealt with this question of crises explicitly. Drazen and Grilli (1993), using the model in Alesina and Drazen (1991), looked at a case in which the cost of inflation increases exogenously, and showed that by making delay more costly this shock can accelerate the arrival of stabilization. Velasco (1999) showed that an adverse shock to government revenue could cause debt to accumulate more quickly and thereby bring forward in time the occurrence of fiscal reform. More strikingly, both papers showed that crises can be "good" for welfare; if the indirect (beneficial) effect of reducing delay outweighs the direct (adverse) effect of the crisis, then a bad shock can make everyone better off.

When applied to first-generation reforms, the crises-cause-reform hypothesis found some empirical confirmation. Lora (2000), using data from 1985 to 1995, regressed his policy reform index (both the average and its components) on a crisis proxy, defined as the gap in a year's income per capita relative to its previous peak. The corresponding coefficient, which he found to be robust to the inclusion of all other explanatory variables, indicated that a gap of 10 percent in income per capita leads to an annual increase in the total index of between 0.005 and 0.008. The result was strikingly significant in statistical terms. The coefficient, however, was also strikingly small; the average increase in the total reform index between 1985 and 1995 was 0.25, so the measured contribution of crises to this change turned out to be tiny.

All this intellectual activity (to which one of us contributed) was exciting. But from the vantage point of the time of this writing, 2001 and 2002, and especially when thinking about second-generation reforms, it all seems like *much ado about little*. A decade has passed since the peak of the reforming frenzy. During that period, the economic performance of the countries of the region has varied widely, from outright success stories (Chile and the Dominican Republic), to volatile but positive growth (Mexico), to outright crisis (Argentina and Ecuador since 1998). Yet the process of reform has slowed down almost everywhere, regardless of economic circumstances.[7]

One possible retort is that the most recent crises have not been deep enough. But a moment's thought robs this alternative of much plausibility. The 1995 tequila crisis in Mexico, with its repercussions in South America, and the 1999 blowups in Brazil and Ecuador were very costly, as was the recent meltdown in Argentina. In all of these countries, macroeconomic stabilization policies of varied effectiveness were implemented. Brazil reduced its social security deficit, and Argentina tinkered with its

7. The index of first-generation reforms computed by Lora (2001) shows an average annual rate of increase of 4.5 percent between 1986 and 1994. For 1995-99, the equivalent figure is 3.1. If second-generation reforms were to be included, the region's performance in 1995-99 would be weaker. Note, however, that with much already done in some areas—e.g., trade liberalization—some slowing down of reform was inevitable.

labor code. But in none of these nations did the crises prompt deep structural changes.

A more important objection is that the crises-cause-reform literature failed to distinguish between macroeconomic blowups and those of other types. Most actual crises were macroeconomic: hyperinflation, debt default, and the like. Hence, they prompted a temporary political consensus (or "special politics," or honeymoon) to do something about *that*. If budget cuts and wage freezes were what it took, so be it. But once the macroeconomic emergency evaporated, so did the political consensus. What is so surprising about that?

Just as important, the consensus often extended to policies that had a plausible link with the collapsing macroeconomic variables, but no further. A few governments tried to sneak in other policy changes. Others were forced by the international financial institutions to bundle macroeconomic and microeconomic structural reforms. Tariff cuts (which also had an immediate anti-inflation impact) and privatization (which often reduced the fiscal deficit) were the most conspicuous example of such bundling (more on this below). But in retrospect, it seems clear that the political system's newfound tolerance for reform did not amount to carte blanche for reforming technocrats to do as they pleased—certainly not to change the way teachers are paid or the system by which electricity rates are set.

The point is important, for macroeconomic changes have a very different structure of costs and benefits than do other kinds of policy changes. A reform's political viability depends crucially on its political cost-benefit ratio. Macroeconomic stabilization provides huge efficiency gains (and hence has large political benefits) that are widely spread across the population while redistributing relatively little income across groups (hence, its immediate political costs are limited).[8] A crisis, in this context, is nothing but a deepening of the distortions associated with inflation and the like, and hence a sharp rise in the potential efficiency and political gains associated with stabilization. It is not surprising, therefore, that macroeconomic crises seem to lead to macroeconomic reforms.

The situation is much different for other kinds of reforms. Take public education or garbage collection, two public services that ought to improve under second-generation reforms. Deterioration in these services typically occurs gradually rather than over a few months, as can happen with inflation. (True, there are cases when garbage simply goes uncollected, but these are the exception rather than the rule.) Moreover, in cases such as education or judicial proceedings, monitoring the quality of the service can be hard (is that math teacher really no good?), and a population used to dismal standards of service can take a while to notice a decline.

8. To be sure, macroeconomic stabilization has a distributional impact, because the costs are not born homogeneously by everyone. It is precisely the struggle over who will bear certain costs of adjustment that drives the delayed stabilization models of Alesina and Drazen (1991) and Drazen and Grilli (1993).

However much politicians may like to talk about a "crisis in education," no such thing exists from the perspective of the immediate political costs of *not* reforming. And reforming these sectors, as we saw above, involves large redistributions of income, with the losses being concentrated among relatively few people and sectors. This is true with or without a crisis. In short, it is hard to envision a situation in which the political cost-benefit ratio of educational or public service reform is altered drastically, all of a sudden making change more likely.

Reform and the International Economic Cycle

A closely related question is how domestic reform correlates with the international economic cycle. It is painfully well known that economic activity in Latin America tends to move hand in hand with activity in the countries belonging to the Organization for Economic Cooperation and Development, with prices of primary commodities, and especially with the size of capital flows to the region. But is an upturn or a downturn in the world economy more likely to provoke reform at home? The crisis hypothesis would readily suggest that downturns are the necessary catalyst. But as we have seen, this theory provides little help when it comes to second-generation reforms. More important, a period of capital inflows and affluence may provide fiscal resources with which to compensate the losers, making reform more likely.

Start with the connection between first-generation reforms and capital movements. It is suggestive that the largest increases in the index occurred in the first half of the 1990s (4.5 percent a year between 1986 and 1994, against 3.1 percent for 1995-99), at a time when foreign capital was plentiful (especially after 1992). This just amounts to eyeballing the data, but more formal work suggests the same conclusion. Lora (2000) incorporated the capital-flows variable into a regression using data only to 1995. He found that, except for labor, all other areas of reform were facilitated by capital flows to the region. The coefficients were large and robust to the inclusion of other regressors. In particular, an increase in capital flows of 1 percent of Latin American GDP was associated with "an improvement of between 1 and 2 percent in the total index of structural policies" (p. 17). These results have to be taken with more grains of salt than usual, for causality very much remains to be sorted out.[9] However, they do lend

9. In a very influential paper, Calvo, Leiderman, and Reinhart (1993) argued that, in contrast to received wisdom, capital flows to Latin America had been until then largely exogenous—i.e., not influenced statistically by the region's domestic developments. This would allow one to think that it is capital flows that prompt reform, and not vice versa. Lora (2000) tests this hypothesis by carrying out causality tests. He finds that, when using an appropriate number of lags, the reforms appear to have caused capital flows to the region as a whole, though not to individual countries. So causality does seem to be an issue.

some credence to the intuitive notion that international capital flows have helped push reform forward.

These are mostly private capital flows, which do not come with overt conditionality attached. Hence, it is unlikely that the enlightened advice of the IMF or the World Bank is what stands behind the increase in first-generation reforms reported by Lora (2001). What accounts then for this correlation? One possibility is the already mentioned availability of funds to compensate losers. But this hypothesis also has problems. One is that it is hard to identify real-life compensation schemes. "Virtue is its own reward," the then-US trade representative used to tell Latin American ministers in the early 1990s, and many seemed to take it to heart. Note also that statistically it is not clear that compensation mechanisms mattered that much. Lora (2000) considered real depreciations (which compensate producers of import-competing goods) and trade pacts (which presumably help potential exporters). Neither seemed to be associated with movements in the index of trade reforms.

Probably more important is that the capital abundance of the early 1990s came at a time when several countries were already experimenting with trade liberalization and, more important, with exchange-rate-based stabilizations. We know from the work of Calvo and his fellow researchers (e.g., see Calvo and Vegh 1994) that such stabilization packages more often than not are associated with a temporary consumption boom and a sharp appreciation of the real exchange rate.

Given that governments in the region rely mostly on value-added taxes, the rise in consumption typically also meant an increase in tax revenues. The combination of plentiful capital and (at least temporarily) sound public finances made it easier to undertake fiscal reform and to reduce remaining controls on capital outflows. If the current account deficit was not too large, the situation was ripe to cut tariffs further. Governments also tended to loosen bank regulation, allowing cash-rich banks to relend more freely.[10] Put it all together, and it is not surprising that the period of capital inflows coincided with an increase in measured first-generation reforms.[11]

This suggests that the connection between capital inflows and fiscal, financial, and trade reforms may have been fairly specific and is unlikely to be replicated automatically when capital returns to the region. This is es-

10. Of course, this procyclical movement in prudential requirements turned out to be a fatal mistake. Pre-1994 Mexico is the perfect example of the problem.

11. In Chile and Colombia in the early 1990s, concerns over an excessively appreciated exchange rate were the main reason to reduce controls on outflows and cut tariffs. Both policies were intended to cause dollars to leave the country, helping weaken the exchange rate—something that did not happen in earnest until overall capital flows turned around as a result of the Asian crisis. Note that this happened in both countries during a boom and not a crisis, explaining why both countries—and especially Colombia—appeared to defy the crises-cause-reform hypothesis.

pecially true where second-generation reforms are concerned. Enlightened policymaking may ensure that next time dollars are plentiful, they will get spent improving education, health care, and the judiciary, but we would not bet on it.

In any case, the question may be mostly academic. Flows to Latin America have never recovered from the Asian and Russian crises. Today, with Argentina and Uruguay near bankruptcy, asset prices down almost everywhere, international financial markets in disarray, and investors' appetite for risk diminished even further by the terrorist attacks on the United States of September 11, 2001, the scarcity of foreign funds may be with us for a long time. Indeed, for many countries in the region, the next few years may be ones of muddling through—not so crisis ridden that some reform becomes inevitable, but not so flush with dollars that anyone's political support can be bought off.

Big Bangs, Sequencing, Bundling, and All That

Once, for one reason or another, a government is willing and reasonably able to pursue market-oriented reform, a whole set of issues arises on how to proceed. One question that was at the forefront of the academic and policy discussion in the early to mid-1990s involved the appropriate sequencing of reforms. Should political leaders endeavor to push for as many reforms as possible at once, or should they introduce them one after the other?

The optimal sequence of reforms depends on both economic and political criteria. The neoclassical economics benchmark is simple: If you can, do all reforms simultaneously. Radical or big-bang reform is the best reform strategy, Mussa (1982) argued early during the debate. As long as the perceived private costs and benefits correspond to the true social costs and benefits, private economic agents will choose the socially correct pace of adjustment following a full-scale liberalization.[12] Things looked different on the ground, however. In Latin America, the literature on the sequencing of economic reforms was spurred by the failed Southern Cone stabilizations of the late 1970s and early 1980s. One influential view attributed these unfortunate outcomes to mistakes in the order of liberalization.[13]

12. The only caveat applies when one can clearly identify a distortion that places the economy in a second-best world; if that is the case, one might be able to design a particular sequencing strategy that can take care of the second-best problem. Put differently, arguments for unbundling must be based on the existence of an unremovable distortion or market failure—or perhaps concerns over income distribution—and of a sequencing second-best solution.

13. That view was due to Díaz Alejandro. Debate centered on the order of liberalization of the trade and capital accounts, with most researchers in favor of opening the former before the latter to avoid destabilizing capital flows; see Edwards (1984) and McKinnon (1991).

Subsequent research was more precise in identifying potential welfare gains or losses associated with different sequences. One possible argument for gradualism rested on the need to minimize short-term changes in income distribution (Gavin 1996). Another relied on the presence of preexisting distortions (policy-induced or otherwise) in one or several markets that cannot be removed at the time the reform plan is announced. Potential candidates were labor market interventions, domestic capital market imperfections, and limits to foreign indebtedness that are not perceived as binding by individual agents (Edwards and Van Wijnbergen 1986 and Edwards 1992). In all of these cases, one could imagine circumstances in which the second-best reform strategy should involve some degree of gradualism—for instance, in the sequencing of trade and capital account liberalization.[14]

In that early literature, the arguments for one type of sequence or another were mostly economic. Where did politics come in? The simplest political case was implied in Jeffrey Sachs's 1994 "emergency room" metaphor: While the patients are in there, treat them not just for the symptoms but also for the underlying disease as well. This view was predicated on the huge uncertainty the patient was likely to face once out of the hospital. Reforming administrations often face a nontrivial likelihood of being ejected from office. In that situation, the only strategy is "do as much as you can."

Other arguments for bundling suggested that political constraints could be loosened if different reform policies were bundled together. Rodrik (1994, 1996) emphasized the agenda-setting role of reformist governments. He asked: How could wide-ranging trade and industrial policy reforms be rendered palatable to the interest groups that had been their beneficiaries for so long? His answer was that macroeconomic crises enabled reformist governments to package fiscal reforms—which were absolutely crucial for the return to price stability—with trade and industrial-policy reforms—which may have been desirable in the long run but were incidental to the immediate crisis.[15]

Dewatripont and Roland (1994) argued for unbundling, because it has lower experimentation costs than does a big bang. At each stage of the transition, the choice is between accepting the next set of reforms and re-

14. A related argument by Calvo (1989) emphasized that imperfect credibility is equivalent to an intertemporal distortion. If the public wrongly believes that trade liberalization will be reversed in the future, some control of the capital account may be called for.

15. Martinelli and Tommasi (1997) also argued that political-economy considerations tended to cause several possible reforms to be carried out simultaneously. Their point was that in societies with powerful interest groups and characterized by a cobweb of redistributive and distortionary policies, "optimal" unbundled plans will be time inconsistent: winners of early reforms who are hurt by later reforms have an incentive to stop the gradual path in its later stages. Knowing that, losers from reform will oppose the earlier measures.

versing the previous one. If the initial reforms have been a success, people are more willing to accept less popular reforms so as not to lose the gains of the first reforms and to save on reversal costs.[16] In some situations, the degree of complementarity could be such that the logic is reversed. Shleifer, Murphy, and Vishny (1992) argued that in former socialist countries, where the basis of a market economy was completely absent, partial reform would be infeasible in the long run. Political sustainability would then argue for bundling.

This was a hopeful view. It emphasized that one could not have inflation stabilization without fiscal reform, but that in turn required better tax enforcement, which in turn necessitated both civil service reform and a revamping of the judiciary. But of course none of it made sense without capable administrators and an educated population, so educational reform was also a must. The reform plan started with the lowly goal of limiting price increases, and soon this logic had the government trying to reinvent practices and institutions that had been in place for decades if not centuries. The perspective was hopeful indeed—too much so. Panglossian is a better label.

We know today that a market economy can survive in Latin America for a long time (it has been almost 200 years since independence, and 10 since most big reforms kicked in) with an inefficient state, imperfect contract enforcement, and dismal public schools. By the same token, capitalism is alive (if not well) in Russia, but so are rampant insider trading, huge private monopolies, an increasingly corrupt state, and a system of property rights that gives mafiosi, former apparatchiks, and new oligarchs a big upper fist.

Bundling and big bangs were indeed prevalent in the early efforts of reform. A key reason must have been the "emergency room" or "window of opportunity" logic. A good politician does not waste an opportunity to do as he or she pleases, and the initial crises afforded precisely such an opportunity, however transitory. Just as important, there was strong complementarity among many of the early first-generation reforms. One cannot lower inflation if the budget deficit is 10 percent of GDP and there is no market for government bonds. Some monetary, fiscal, and financial reforms had to go hand in hand.

But complementarity between first- and second-generation reforms seems to be much weaker, both economically and politically. We also know that we do not even know enough to make statements about that with any degree of confidence. Labor market flexibility may have much to recommend itself, but Europe lived without it for decades, even if it meant high unemployment.

Even more troubling is our ignorance about such matters as education. The notion that human capital investment is key to long-term growth

16. Another argument in favor of unbundling was advanced by Wei (1998). He argued that gradual sequencing might allow the building of constituencies for reform, in the presence of individual specific uncertainty, as in the framework of Fernández and Rodrik (1991).

seems unexceptionable. But as Pritchett (2001) has forcefully argued, that link is awfully hard to find in the data.[17] If policymakers are unsure about the outcome of economic reforms and worry about the costs of experimentation, as Dewatripont and Roland (1995) argued, all this conflicting advice is likely to make them even more risk averse and to strengthen the case for a very careful and gradual phasing in of the reforms—perhaps so gradual that second-generation reforms only get implemented in the indefinite future.[18]

All the resulting unbundling may be prudent, but it also has political costs of its own. Rodrik's point (1994, 1996) remains valid: crafty packaging of reform initiatives can offer *something for everyone* and therefore weaken opposition. By letting a decade or more elapse between first- and second-generation reforms, many possibilities for creative dealmaking have been wasted; the history of health care reform in Chile provides an example.

The democratic administration of President Aylwin came to power in 1990 mindful of polls that showed that public dissatisfaction with health care services was a main force behind the vote against Augusto Pinochet and his handpicked candidate. The finance minister, Alejandro Foxley, raised value-added taxes in 1990 and used the additional revenue to finance greater social expenditures, of which health care was a big beneficiary. A revamping of the public health system was postponed as too politically troublesome; the governing team was also unsure what kind of health care model it wanted to adopt—European or US style?

A decade and several strikes by health care workers later, Chile's real public spending on health care has doubled, but total output in the state-run health care system has barely increased. Technocrats today are aware that the system is a black hole and that a thoroughgoing reform of its management and incentives is essential. But they have no more money with which to placate the vehement opposition of doctors and hospital workers. Prospects for health care reform look very dim indeed.

Does It Matter Who the Reformers Are?

The political affiliations of those who undertake reforms also matter. Even when reforms are identical, they will most likely be perceived differently by the electorate when they are promoted by leftist governments than

17. Hanushek and Kimko (2000) do find an effect of labor force quality (as opposed to years of schooling) on growth.

18. This of course does not mean that second-generation reforms are unimportant. It just means that policymakers have received much contradictory advice. Naím (2000) stresses the extent to which supposed wisdom emanating from Washington has been subject to fads and fashions, starting in the 1950s but especially in the past decade.

when rightist leaders push for them. There is no agreement, however, as to whether right-handed or left-handed leaders will fare better when driving their countries through the next level of reforms. Although some argue that it takes a Richard Nixon to go to China, others correctly point to how difficult it is to get a government to adopt policies that adversely affect its constituencies. With the advent of a number of social democratic governments in the larger countries of Latin America, this question seems more pressing than ever.

Neoliberalism by Surprise

One striking feature of first-generation reforms in many countries is the degree to which they were done by stealth. Presidents Carlos Menem in Argentina (1989-99), Alberto Fujimori in Peru (1990-2000), and to a much lesser extent Patricio Aylwin in Chile (1990-94) were elected on antistructural-reform platforms. The most radical conversion from antireformist to militant reformist was that of Fujimori. As a candidate, he denounced the structural reforms proposed by conservative leader Mario Vargas Llosa as destructive and damaging to the interests of the Peruvian poor. Despite the skyrocketing inflation, economic stagnation, and widespread poverty, Fujimori managed to build political support without a clear plan for how he intended to address these pressing issues. As a political unknown, Fujimori was elected primarily because he was perceived as the only way to prevent the reformist Vargas Llosa from winning office.

Yet once elected, Fujimori experienced a radical change of mind and turned himself into a champion of reform. The economy was stabilized after the populism of the Alan García years and began a period of tentative growth. For a few years, Peru was the darling of international investors. And Fujimori was also popular at home. Public opinion in Peru even approved of his 1992 decision to dissolve Congress and the judiciary, and—with the support of the military—to take on dictatorial power (Stokes 2001). International actors—not yet converted to the gospel of good governance—seemed more concerned with the adoption of Washington Consensus policies than with the destruction of these institutions.

In the end, of course, the Fujimori experience was a disaster. In addition to adopting structural reforms, his government committed widespread human rights violations and had little respect for constitutional provisions—even after his custom-made Constitution was adopted in 1993. After 10 years of Fujimori, Peru's economic policies reflected the Washington Consensus, but no groundwork had been done to build second-generation reforms. Institutions were weak, and the rapid and dramatic fall of Fujimori from power further weakened the only two institutions that had apparently worked reasonably well: the military and the secret police. The Fujimori experience underscores an important point: Even if it takes a Nixon to go to China, it might very well be that some Nixons turn out to be crooks.

Menem and Aylwin (less drastically) also carried out a "policy switch." Democracy was consolidated in Argentina and Chile during their terms in power, and economic performance was quite good (in Argentina, better in Menem's first term than in his second). In Chile, where the reversal was less dramatic, the economy began a boom that lasted until the Asian crisis.

How should we understand the apparent success of these policy reversals? Przeworski, Stokes, and Manin (1999) have posed an interesting question: Do voters care about policies or about results? If they care about policies, the policy switches experienced in Argentina, Chile, Peru, and Venezuela should worry those who believe in institutions, accountability, and responsiveness. Conversely, if voters care about results more than policies, changing one's avowed policy might be in the best interest of one's constituency. It is true that voters often use policies as proxies for results. Yet if a politician elected on a certain policy platform learns once in office that those policies led to positive results in the past but will no longer work, should that politician stay with the policies she campaigned on? Or should she adopt policies that will maximize the possibilities of achieving the results voters expect?

The Nixons of the world might go to China because they realize that it is no longer convenient or that it has become much more costly not to be on talking terms with China. They can command the support of public opinion in their countries because they can credibly claim that they have changed their policy preferences upon learning new information. They can also credibly present themselves as economic reformers committed to helping ease the costs for their constituencies—a "social-oriented market economy" was the phrase that Aylwin used to portray his adoption of the economic policy framework inherited from Pinochet, mitigated by a tax reform that allowed for more social spending. Aylwin's and the Concertación alliance's economic policy conversion paved the way for the acceptance of the market-based model by a large majority of Chileans.

To continue with the analogy, when Nixons go to China, they also help reduce national animosity against China. It is true that the positive economic results of the model in Chile helped convince the population that the model worked, but these results, which were visible before 1988, were not sufficient to allow Pinochet to win that year's plebiscite.

Although policy reversals were very common in the early 1990s, they have vanished in recent years. After more than a decade—almost 20 years in the case of Argentina—of regular elections, parties and leaders have built track records on their positions on structural reforms. There are two other reasons why "neoliberalism by surprise"[19] seems to be on the de-

19. The phrase is due to Stokes (2001).

cline. One is that presidential candidates are less and less inclined to commit themselves to strict policy initiatives. This reflects politicians' greater concern with winning and holding onto office than with policies themselves. Moreover, "mandates are not instructions." As Przeworski, Stokes, and Manin (1999, 13) put it: "At the beginning of the term voters need not even have a clear view of what to expect and to demand. It is up to the incumbent to guess what voters will reward and what they will punish." What politicians are increasingly doing is filling out the agenda after being elected, rather than throwing out the old agenda and adopting a new one.

This is especially so for second-generation reforms, which are much less clear-cut than first-generation ones. It is one thing to promise to end inflation or to stick to a given parity between the peso and the dollar. All voters can understand the promise and monitor whether it is fulfilled. It is a very different thing to promise "health care reform" or "educational reform." Because the candidate's advisers themselves are unlikely to know exactly what this means, they will inevitably be vague about it. Monitoring is also trickier; people may perceive easily whether waiting time at public hospitals goes down, but how many can evaluate the quality of teaching their children are receiving? With vague promises and fuzzy results, surprises are less likely.

Betraying Your Constituents?

But the Nixon-in-China hypothesis is not just about policy surprises. It is also about constituent accountability, about politicians doing things on behalf of "their" people. It may be, as we argued above, that in a competitive democracy politicians are concerned with results. But not all results affect people equally. Nixon's achievement was to persuade the American right wing and the business community that a rapprochement with China was in their interest. But what if a reform is in the national interest but not in the specific interest of the group that voted for this or that politician? What is a budding Nixon to do then?

The question is relevant for today's Latin America for two reasons. Second-generation reforms have many winners but some highly visible losers, concentrated in a few sectors. From labor unions to the owners of monopoly utilities, from public health employees to judges, from protected farmers to agricultural workers, those affected by second-generation reforms are ready to use the tools available to them in democracies to retain their acquired rights. Social democratic leaders elected in Argentina (1999), Brazil (1998), Chile (2000), Peru (2001), and, arguably, Mexico (2000) were faced with the choice of adopting reforms that may have general benefits but, that, in the short run, would adversely affect some of their basic constituencies. Are radicals in Argentina or Socialists in Chile likely to cut the privileges enjoyed by large numbers of state workers? Are social democratic (or more left-wing) governments bad news for second-generation reforms? Or on the contrary, can Nixon's logic prevail once again?

Social democrats have generally refrained from adopting reforms that could damage their electoral support among their core constituencies, even when by not acting they risk losing support elsewhere. Public employee unions strongly supported the candidacy of Ricardo Lagos in Chile, despite Lagos's promises to undertake radical health care and education reforms. Health care reform would most likely result in policies that are detrimental to the public health workers' union. Rather than abandoning one of his constituencies and cultivating a different electoral base elsewhere, the president has mostly chosen to avoid a confrontation with the union, watering down a much-needed health care reform. The decision may be wise for short-term electoral reasons; it is easier to stay with a winning coalition than to try to build a new one.

In Brazil, Fernando Henrique Cardoso was somewhat bolder in adopting reforms that are opposed by some of his constituencies. But he was perceived within Brazil more as a right-wing president than as a socialist. His heart might have been with the international left, but the left in Brazil votes for the Workers' Party and against him. Mexican president Vicente Fox gathered his support from a combination of traditional conservatives and those whose main interest was to see the Institutional Revolutionary Party (PRI) defeated. In his first months in office, Fox's two main campaign pledges were derailed or blocked by his own constituency.

Paradoxically, taking on vested interests should be less of a problem for social democratic leaders today than two decades ago. With less influential unions than decades ago and a growing number of voters who are not members of organized groups and show less partisan identification, all candidates are adopting catchall electoral platforms.

The experience of the early 1990s showed that politicians do adopt policies that adversely affect their constituencies when they know that new constituencies can be fostered, so that, measured in electoral support and public opinion approval, the benefits of reform become greater than the costs of alienating some of their constituencies. An example is the rise of export-oriented sectors in almost every country, which bitterly oppose the currency overvaluation common in previous decades.

The strength of the opposition might also help left-of-center leaders to rally their constituencies behind certain reforms. Public employees' unions might prefer to negotiate a reform with a friendly government than risk having to face a hostile right-wing government in the future. High levels of political competition might facilitate reform; uncertainty about what party will be in power in the future can lead key constituencies to agree to limited reforms today as a way of preempting more drastic reforms tomorrow.

Electoral Uncertainty Can Be the Ally of Reform

Social democrats and right-wingers alike face similar incentives in competitive electoral democracies: they need to foster electoral majorities to stay in power. Although they are naturally more inclined to appease their constituencies and adopt policies that will have distributional consequences in favor of their constituencies, they are also inclined to adopt policies that will strengthen and protect their constituencies in the future. Uncertainty about future electoral outcomes will make it easier for politicians to actively build new bases of support.

This growing uncertainty comes from two sources. The first is long-term cultural and social change. With voters behaving much less ideologically and declining traditional clientelistic practices, attachments to political parties are weakening. As reported by IDB (2000b, 174-82), the percentage of people in Latin America that "feel very close or fairly close to a political party" is low by international standards and tending to fall over time.[20] Changing social structure also matters. The traditional middle class linked to the state (teachers, some professionals, and public-sector employees) owed its very existence to its ability to extract redistribution through the political system. Hence, its political preferences were strong and sharply defined. The newer middle classes (e.g., owners of small and medium-sized firms and the self-employed) that arguably provide the pivotal voter in many countries today have much less clear political attachments. Their preferences can be volatile, as recent presidential elections in Brazil, Chile, Mexico, and Peru suggest.

The other source of growing electoral uncertainty is the transformation of the rules of the political game (IDB 2000b). Government financing for presidential campaigns—so that all candidates who qualified can have enough resources to get their message across—facilitates competition and makes outcomes less predictable.[21] The adoption of runoff provisions for presidential elections—rather than plurality rule or throwing the election to the parliament—helps make elections more competitive and reduces the influence of loyal voting blocks. Independent electoral oversight agencies and simplified electoral registration and voting procedures also help foster turnout and weaken the power of organized voting blocks.

In short, uncertainty about future electoral results leads politicians to adopt policies that will maximize their chances of winning future elec-

20. An exception is Uruguay, where more than 40 percent of people claim to feel very close or fairly close to a political party.

21. This does not require limits to campaign spending, but only enough government support so that all qualifying candidates can have their message heard. The Chilean and Brazilian system of free television time during peak hours—with the obvious inconveniences—provides such access even better than televised presidential debates.

tions. This can weaken the attachment to traditional constituencies (holding on to your "core" or "traditional" vote may not be enough to get you elected) and make leaders of all political stripes bolder in pushing reform. That provides one reason for optimism about the future of second-generation reforms in the region.

Improving the Institutions of Democracy

During the 1990s, democratic institutions became, as US president Bill Clinton told the Santiago Summit of the Americas, the only game in town. But the rules under which this game is played vary substantially across the Western Hemisphere's countries. Moreover, some of the rules have changed within individual countries, and many more institutions will change as democracy consolidates in some countries and dissatisfaction with democracy grows in others (IDB 2000b).

When asking whether political institutions work well in Latin America, four issues call for attention: (1) executive-legislative relations, (2) federal versus provincial and local governments, (3) majoritarian versus proportional representation electoral systems, and (4) the timing of elections. Here we review each, trying to draw some preliminary inferences about what institutional features constitute obstacles to good governance and to adopting second-generation reforms.

Executive-Legislative Relations

Who controls the legislative agenda? Does the president have the ability to govern by decree? What prerogatives does the legislative power have in shaping the budget and government expenditures in general? How does the parliament actually produce legislation? These questions matter a great deal for the quality of governance and the ability to carry out policy reforms.

From the 1960s to the 1980s, when scholars of the developing world were concerned with authoritarian regimes and transitions to democracy, useful models to understand executive-legislative relations were being produced in well-established democracies. Using these theoretical models, recently published studies of legislative-executive relations in Brazil (Figueiredo and Limongi 2000; Mainwaring 1999), Chile (Siavelis 2000; Londregan 2000; Baldez and Carey 1999), Mexico (Negretto 2001), Argentina (Jones et al. 2001, 2002; Tommasi, Saiegh, and Sanguinetti 2001), and Uruguay (Altman 2001), among others, have mapped out how parliaments actually work and how executive-legislative relations lead to the adoption of laws and regulations, beyond the constitutional framework in specific countries. These contributions have made it clear that small variations in institutional design or different informal social and political norms may lead to drastically different outcomes.

Latin American countries are for the most part presidentialist. The president holds overwhelming power compared with that of Congress. In countries with term limits for members of parliament, the executive tends to exert even more power and influence. When the president has influence in determining the government party's electoral lists of candidates, party discipline in Congress is easier to achieve. Government by decree also facilitates party discipline, but it weakens the power of the legislature (Negretto 2001).

The works of Jones et al. (2001, 2002) and Jones, Sanguinetti, and Tommasi (2000) on the Argentine Congress and the comparative project on legislative politics in Latin America by Morgenstern and Nacif (2001) have helped clarify how executive-legislative relations play themselves out in the region. These studies not only have utilized the rigorous models developed in the field of executive-legislative relations in the United States and Europe but have gone a step further by adapting them to the particular characteristics of most Latin American governments (i.e., strong presidentialism, multiparty systems, and short-lived parties). They have sought to answer basic questions: Can an effective and independent legislature exist in a country marked by strong presidentialism? For the legislature to be strong—and for checks and balances to exist—does the president need to lose power and the legislature acquire more constitutional prerogatives? Is a strong legislature a recipe for inaction and red tape? And, ultimately, does a strong legislature foster or hinder the adoption of second-generation reforms?

The answers found by researchers of course depend on the country. Figueiredo and Limongi (2000) identify more features associated with strong and efficient legislatures in the Brazilian Congress than previously believed. The Chilean Congress has asserted itself as a player, despite Chile's strong presidential system. The Mexican Congress has played an important role and challenged the overwhelming power of the president since 1997. Conversely, the Argentine and Ecuadorian Congresses have acted irresponsibly and have jeopardized economic and political stability in recent years.

Institutional features that promote the formation of stable, disciplined majorities in parliament, and that do not give overwhelming power to the executive, facilitate the consolidation of democratic institutions and may reduce political obstacles for the implementation of second-generation reforms. It is true that the implementation of first-generation reforms in Latin America has been championed by presidents, not legislatures. Legislators have historically been reluctant to undertake reform. But this has been the case in no small part because when reforms are successful the president, not the legislature, takes the credit.

This situation has led to the common but misguided view that the weaker the legislature, the better for reform. This may have been true for some first-generation reforms, but is unlikely to be the case from now on. If second-generation reforms are all about strengthening institutions, a balance of power is a necessary condition to reduce corruption levels and increase accountability. As the experience of Peru taught us recently, an overwhelmingly powerful president can help facilitate the adoption of some changes, but excessive concentration of power ends up jeopardizing the whole reform effort.

However, simply transferring constitutional powers to a weak and corruption-prone legislature will not eliminate the negative by-products of presidentialism. When presidents are accountable to the national electorate and legislators are accountable to their local constituents—rather than to the executive, their party bosses, or local caudillos—the balance of power between both branches of government is grounded on their distinct representation. A bottom-up enforcement mechanism is more efficient than a top-to-bottom approach that relies on constitutional provisions that challenge the existing balance of power and are impossible to enforce.

A priority is to design institutional reforms that can help create professional legislatures that are made up of career legislators who are independent of the executive or local party bosses. This helps avoid what Jones et al. (2002) have termed the syndrome of "professional politicians and amateur legislators." For legislatures to work effectively, the structure of incentives for legislators must be different from that of the executive, party bosses, or local leaders. If an individual legislator owes his career to the state governor, he cannot be expected to act independently in Congress.

In some circumstances, a stronger legislature might ultimately represent an obstacle for a reform-oriented president. But a legislature made up of career professional legislators accountable to their local constituencies will also counterbalance an ineffectual president. In other presidential systems with strong legislators—for example, the United States—the president and members of Congress are accountable to different constituencies and yet both benefit from good economic performance. In the United States, parties are strong—not as strong as in Chile or Uruguay, but certainly much stronger than in Peru or Venezuela—but not enough to hinder the strong constituent-based political careers of professional legislators.

To strengthen the legislature and make it more professional, the system must differentiate the sources of political power (electorate, financing, etc.) that the president, parties, and individual legislators have access to. If they all derive their political strength from the same source, little can be gained by reducing the existing strong presidential tendencies in those countries.

Federal versus Provincial and Local Governments

In recent conventional wisdom, decentralization and the strengthening of local and provincial governments are positive steps toward making governments more efficient, responsive, and accountable. Targeted social spending also heavily relies on local and provincial governments to reduce waste and minimize deadweight losses. Health and educational reforms often call for greater local government involvement and give local governments more autonomy. Local governments are often seen as potential allies of national governments in the effort to reduce the strong bargaining power of influential teachers' and health workers' labor unions.

However, decentralization might also lead to unforeseen difficulties. When local governments realize that they can avoid paying the full costs of some of their actions, a problem of the commons arises (Velasco 1999). Argentina and Brazil in the 1980s and 1990s were prime examples. In those countries, provincial or state governments, through a variety of mechanisms, could get the federal government to finance their deficits. This created a situation in which the benefits of spending were local but the costs were born nationally. Understanding that at least part of the cost would be borne by others, subfederal governments were tempted to overspend and overborrow. The result was big deficits at both the local and national levels.

That is not the only problem of decentralization. The sharing of responsibilities between local and national officials, and the lack of clear demarcation between the two, can cause agency problems. Voters and public opinion need to have the ability to punish unresponsive and corrupt politicians. When voters have difficulties identifying those responsible for mismanagement, government performance will suffer. Corruption can flourish when politicians pilfer public funds and freely engage in the business of auctioning regulations and laws (IDB 2000b, 170).

Contributions to the study of federalism in Argentina (Jones et al. 2001; Jones, Sanguinetti, and Tommasi 2000) have highlighted the way in which the federal government and the provinces trade political support for financial assistance. Regional redistribution of wealth and taxes also takes places in more complex ways than a simplistic top-down, two-party analysis would lead one to believe. The work by Jones et al. (2001, 2002) points to the dependency that many national legislators have on provincial governments.

Rather than representing the interest of the federal government, legislators in Argentina often serve the interests of the provincial governors who sent them to Congress in the first place and will give them provincial government positions when their short careers in Buenos Aires are over. Legislators seek to protect the interests of their constituencies, but in Argentina the constituencies are often local party leaders and not voters.

Though Brazil and Argentina are the paradigmatic cases of irresponsible state, provincial, and local governments, decentralization efforts going on in Chile, Colombia, Mexico, and much of the region also suggest that poorly designed reforms can turn ineffectual subnational governments into players that obstruct rather than facilitate structural reform. Local accountability generated by the election of local officials might lead to an outburst of pork barrel politics, much as in the United States.

Yet federalism and strong local governments need not be enemies of second-generation reforms. In theory, certain institutional design features can make local and provincial governments more accountable for the decisions they make. For instance, though central governments are unlikely to give up their monopolies on tax collection, they might find it in their best interest to link financing for provincial governments to provinces' success in improving tax collection. Local government officials must be given a share of the political costs of adopting policies that will hurt particular constituencies. The paradigm of the bad central government and the good and understanding local government results from bad political institutional design.

Concurrent elections of provincial or state governors with the presidential election may facilitate political alliances between the president and provincial governors and could make it more difficult for provincial governments to blame the central government for their own mistakes and reckless budget behavior. Although some have advocated separating local and national elections (IDB 2000b), there are good reasons why voters are better served when they force candidates for national and local office to define in advance their future interactions if elected. Holding concurrent elections might in fact facilitate ticket splitting, reduce the influence of party bosses, and foster constituent accountability for all candidates for all offices.

Electoral Rules: Majoritarian versus Proportional Representation

Although the interaction of electoral rules and the party system is one of the best-studied fields in political science, the relationship between electoral rules and political stability and governability is far from settled. In Latin America, most countries are strongly presidentialist, but the electoral rules used to elect the members of the mostly—but not exclusively—bicameral parliaments vary widely (Jones 1995, 1997).

Most countries have parliaments chosen through proportional representation, but some countries use closed lists (party-vote) and others open lists (candidate-vote). There are also wide regional differences on malapportionment, redistricting provisions, and the timing of elections, and periodic electoral reforms have been common in many countries. From Mexico to

Brazil, from Bolivia to Guatemala, agricultural regions are overrepresented. Urbanized regions (especially recently urbanized ones) are severely underrepresented.

After the restoration of democracy in most Latin American countries, the overwhelming sense of relief led many to overlook the problem of malapportionment resulting from political negotiations with the outgoing military regimes or inherited from the old democratic regimes. Recent reports point to a growing sense of discontent and disillusionment with democracy in the region (IDB 2000b). One cause is the failure of most countries to guarantee the principle that all votes have the same weight.

Rules for presidential elections vary widely throughout the region. Whereas Mexico has a simple first-past-the-post system, Brazil and Chile have a runoff if no candidate obtains more than 50 percent of the votes. In Bolivia, the election of the president falls to the parliament if no candidate wins more than 50 percent in the first round. Uruguay recently adopted runoff provisions between the two presidential candidates with the most votes. This is one area where a great deal of change has occurred, much of it for the better. It is far easier to govern if rules for presidential elections require that the winner obtain a clear majority of votes. This is usually defined as more than 50 percent, but Argentina devised an interesting formula to avoid a runoff when the first-round winner obtains more than 40 percent of the vote and is well ahead of the runner-up.[22]

Electoral rules also influence the president's ability to build parliamentary majorities. The size of electoral districts (district magnitude) varies dramatically across countries. In Brazil, each state is guaranteed a minimum of 8 seats in the Chamber of Deputies, but the most populous states elect 70 (São Paulo) and 46 (Rio de Janeiro) deputies each. The larger the district's delegation to the chamber, the more party fragmentation is likely to occur. The rule of thumb among students of electoral rules is that proportional representation works best when districts have a magnitude close to five seats per district.

Malapportionment should be fiercely combated. If a country, for political or historical reasons, allows certain regions to be overrepresented in one chamber (as the United States does with less populous states in the Senate), the other chamber should be organized to promote equal representation for all regions.

Permissive proportional representation systems also make it difficult for a president to achieve commanding majorities, although when presidential and parliamentary elections are held concurrently, the winning presidential candidate is more likely to command an electoral majority—or plurality—in congress. Proportional representation has worked in Europe

22. Since the most recent "update" on the electoral systems of the Americas was published in 1997, Brazil, Ecuador, Peru, Uruguay, and Venezuela have made nontrivial changes to their electoral rules.

because political parties are strong and stable. In the absence of strong and stable parties in Latin America, proportional representation—especially under closed-list systems—has facilitated the formation of temporary factions and loose electoral coalitions and the rise of populist leaders.

Although proportional representation systems foster pluralism and representation for minorities, their drawbacks include hurdles to majority formation and clientelism, especially when associated with closed lists and large districts. If proportional representation is to be the formula of choice, legislators should strive to provide mechanisms for open lists (which allow voters to select individual candidates and make it easier to throw the rascals out), and for seat-allocation rules that foster the formation of majorities.[23]

The system of first-past-the-post (single-member district) is used very little in the region, and then only in former British colonies. Mexico used single-member districts until the mid-1970s, when it adopted a mixed system for the Chamber of Deputies (300 deputies elected in single-member districts and 200 elected in proportional-representation districts). The adoption of first-past-the-post systems might facilitate the formation of commanding majorities in Latin American parliaments if congressional elections were held concurrently with presidential elections, but it might also help increase reelection rates for incumbents.

One alternative is for countries to adopt single-member districts that allow for regular malapportionment corrections (e.g., after each census). These smaller districts, where legislators can relate to and understand the needs of their constituencies, provide an effective mechanism of political accountability. If anything, with single-member districts, electors have an easier time of throwing the rascals out. When voters are forced to select from a closed party list that includes individual politicians that they dislike or do not know, accountability is not well served. Similarly, when voters have to select candidates from an open list in very large districts, they often end up sending their favorite candidate along with that candidates' court of political protégés, who get elected with the trickle-down votes of the popular candidate.

Although most countries have no restriction on immediate parliamentary reelection—with the notable exceptions of Costa Rica and Mexico—the reelection rates of members of parliament is strikingly low when compared with those of industrial nations. That creates incentives for the development of "professional politicians and amateur legislators," as has been the case in Argentina. The persistence of amateur legislators whose political careers depend on their strength within their political party, their

23. The d'Hondt allocation formula, rather than Saint-Laguë or Largest Remainder, favors the formation of majorities because it overrepresents the party with the largest number of votes. For an explanation of different seat-allocation formulas, see the Administration and Cost of Elections Projects, www.aceproject.org.

influence with the local political bosses, or their proximity to the president hinders the quality and effectiveness of Congress. Chile and after that Colombia are the countries with the highest rates of incumbency reelection. The parliaments of these two countries also rank among the most influential in the region.

The Timing of Elections

Perhaps the clearest enemy of first- and second-generation reforms alike is the excessive number of elections in many Latin American countries. Elections are central to democracy. But holding many and frequent consecutive elections hinders the good functioning of government. Because governments need to win elections to stay in power, the nature of incentives is such that incumbents will act differently when elections are around the corner than if the next election is scheduled for 3 years down the road. It is well documented that government spending increases in election years. There are also other negative effects associated with frequent elections. When elected politicians are candidates, their productivity falls in parliament. Fewer laws are passed in the months preceding parliamentary elections. And the legislation that is passed is often a response to short-term electoral concerns.

Even in countries where fiscal responsibility has been the rule in recent years, the incentive to increase government spending during election years is almost irresistible. Chile held presidential elections in 1999, municipal elections in 2000, and parliamentary elections in 2001. The fiscal year beginning in 2002 was the first time in 3 years that no electoral considerations were in play when choices were made as to how to allocate the government's budget. With an ongoing electoral calendar, Mexican governments often switched their policy priorities and spending priorities to accommodate immediate electoral concerns. The logic was flawless. A victory by an opposition candidate would be interpreted as a rejection of government policies. So even if the government was committed to maintaining fiscal austerity, increasing government expenditure in particular states or provinces would actually facilitate achieving the goal of fiscal discipline at the national level.

Holding presidential and parliamentary elections concurrently provides a number of positive incentives to candidates and parties. The winning presidential candidate is more likely to command majority support in parliament, the new president will not need to negotiate with a congress already in session, and the same issues that define the presidential election will be present in the voters' choice for the senate and chamber. Although a majority of Latin American democracies now hold presidential and parliamentary elections concurrently, Chile is an exception.

In addition to holding concurrent presidential and parliamentary elections, there are strong arguments for reducing the number of elections. Argentina is an emblematic case. Although all deputies serve 4-year terms, half of the Chamber of Deputies is elected concurrently with the presidential elections and the other half is elected in the midterm elections 2 years after the presidential election. Although Argentina has carried out some important electoral reforms in recent years—which include the direct election of senators and the concurrent election of the president and Parliament—it has failed to modify this unusual way of electing its lower chamber. The timing of elections in Argentina always fuels political calculations of actors in the opposition who, rather than working together with the government to build consensus, choose to wait until the next election in the hope of improving their bargaining position.

In countries with a federal system of government, state elections are often held independently of national elections. Mexico is the emblematic case. Every year, there are gubernatorial elections in some of Mexico's 31 states. Although many of those elections fail to capture the attention of the Mexican national press, some of Mexico's larger state elections are seen as tests of the government's popularity, and the results of these elections are often used to mount opposition to government reform programs. Having too many elections—whether they are national or local elections—is not conducive to the successful implementation of the next generation of reforms.

Several Latin American countries have straightened and simplified their electoral calendars. For example, Chile is close to approving a constitutional reform that will make presidential and parliamentary elections concurrent after 2005. But few countries have reduced or simplified their calendar for local elections. Combining the election of regional or provincial governors with that of the president and standardizing the legislative districts to equate the constituencies for local officials and national legislators will simplify the decision of the voter and will make the election more important. When people perceive an election to be important, we know well, they turn out to vote in high numbers. More electoral legitimacy should strengthen the position of reform-minded elected officials, and fewer elections will reduce the incentives proreform politicians have to deviate from the path of second-generation reforms.

Reform-Mongering Strategies

The question of how to make economic reforms politically palatable is certainly not a new one. The modern classic on this subject (as on many others) was written by Albert O. Hirschmann, who proposed "reform-mongering" strategies that might render land reform feasible in the face of opposition by politically powerful landowners. As summarized by Haggard and Kaufman (1995), Hirschmann called for "the use of ambiguity and obfuscation, less visible extractive instruments, and timing of initiatives to exploit moments of high popular support." The recipe is still valid for contemporary politicians pushing second-generation reforms.

Honeymoons

The natural moment of "high popular support" is those weeks and months after a new government has been inaugurated. The case studies in Williamson (1994) found little evidence to link these "honeymoons" with first-generation reforms. Perhaps that was because such reforms were often triggered by crises or other exogenous events. But that is unlikely to happen again, and especially not with regard to second-generation reforms. In the second stage, the politically savvy use of a government's early time in office is turning out to be of the utmost importance.

Honeymoons are key because they give governments political capital—be it the result of a landslide victory in an election or because the new president symbolizes some type of profound change in the country (e.g., the first opposition leader in 70 years, the first woman to be elected, the first indigenous leader, or a beloved national figure). The literature on the US presidency tells us that presidents are more productive, and successful, during their first 100 days in office than during any other 100-day period during their terms. Although there is no technical reason for this honeymoon, the usual explanation has to do with the legitimacy earned in the election and the perception that elections also carry mandates to which all elected officials—not just the president—should pay attention.[24]

Although we are not aware of any comprehensive study on the success of honeymoon initiatives for Latin American democracies, the concept of the honeymoon has penetrated the region and has shaped the policy calendar of new presidents. Some have chosen to solve existing territorial disputes with neighboring countries; for example, Jamil Mahuad used most of his political capital as newly elected president of Ecuador in 1998 to settle the long-standing border dispute with Peru. Others have sought to solve internal political conflicts—Colombian president Andrés Pastrana held his first round of talks with the guerrilla leaders even before taking office in 1998—or to settle scores with a troubled national past, as

24. Note that the concept of honeymoon in the United States also relates to the new composition of Congress resulting from the last concurrent presidential and congressional election. When legislative elections are not held concurrently with presidential elections or when proportional representation, rather than single-member districts, is the electoral formula of choice, a new president may not enjoy a legislative majority, and a honeymoon may be impossible.

Argentine president Raúl Alfonsín did in 1983. All have attempted to turn initial successes in these endeavors into lasting political strength, but few have succeeded. The political capital embedded in the honeymoon is like venture capital. It helps some leaders consolidate their public stature; it leads others to embarrassing political setbacks.

How can "honeymoon venture capital" be converted into lasting political capital? The example of Chile in 1990 and Mexico in 2000 helps clarify what to do and what not to do. In Chile in 1990, the incoming Concertación government—an alliance of Christian Democrats and Socialists—took office amid growing demands for democratic consolidation, a complex human rights dilemma (human rights violators were protected by the powerful military, but human rights victims were demanding justice), and pressing social needs (half of Chileans lived in poverty).

Contrary to widespread expectations, the new Chilean government chose to postpone tackling human rights conflicts and instead used its first 100 days in office to negotiate a tax increase with the conservative opposition. After the passage of the tax reform, the government concentrated on building support for a change in labor laws, which was also approved. Patricio Aylwin's gamble paid off, and his honeymoon period extended well beyond his first 100 days.

In Mexico, incoming president Vicente Fox chose to give priority to the initiative for an indigenous-rights law agreed upon by the government of former president Ernesto Zedillo and the Zapatista rebels. A key tax increase was saved for later. The strategy backfired. The indigenous-rights law was opposed by Fox's own National Action Party. A watered-down version was eventually passed, but the president lost precious honeymoon time in pushing for a proposal that ended up not leaving anyone happy. Fox completed his first year in office without securing passage of his tax increase, a cornerstone of his ambitious program of social spending and human capital formation. His honeymoon period ended without any major legislative initiatives having passed the opposition-controlled Congress.

The need for newly elected officials to be strategic in choosing their first legislative initiatives cannot be overemphasized. Much of the future success of a president's legislative package will depend on how effectual he was when first in office in securing congressional approval for his first initiative and in sustaining little damage from his opponents in congress. Latin American presidential systems give little actual decision-making power to the legislative branch. Legislators can gain influence only by obstructing the president's initiatives. If the president's first legislative initiative is significantly damaged by the legislature, the executive will be weakened and the legislature strengthened. However, because of institutional design, the legislature will never be strong enough to control the entire lawmaking process. A weak executive irremediably leads to stalemate in government.

All Politics Is Local

Former US House of Representatives speaker Tip O'Neill's famous dictum that "all politics is local" also applies to structural reforms in the region. A judicial reform or a reduction in the defense budget is more likely in Peru after Fujimori's scandalous exodus than in Chile after Pinochet's departure from the presidency but not the army in 1990. A tax increase made more sense in poverty-stricken but fast-growing Chile in 1990 than in Nicaragua that same year. A successful reforming politician needs to be able to identify these opportunities and act upon them swiftly. For that she must be endowed with a strong sense of national history and a good nose for changing opportunities.

Thus the starting point for a successful reformer is the role of history. Countries have memories, and these shape what is politically possible and what is not. The recent history of judicial reform in Chile illustrates the point. The changes put in motion by the Frei administration entail a complete revamping of the judicial system. They are still moving forward, in spite of the initial opposition of judges and portions of the legal establishment. The political success of the reforms can be traced to 1990, and to the difficulties found by the entering Aylwin government as it struggled to prosecute the most notorious cases of human rights violations.

Before leaving office, Pinochet packed the Supreme Court with justices who were strongly committed to upholding the Amnesty Law passed in 1978. Seeking to shift the balance within the 17 life-term members of the Supreme Court, the Concertación governments (Aylwin and Frei) sought to draw justices into voluntary retirement with attractive retirement packages. Limited success and the fact that most Courts of Appeal—from which all nominees for the Supreme Court were drawn—were also packed with Pinochet loyalists led the Concertación government to seek a reform that made retirement mandatory at 75 years of age for all judges and increased the number of justices in the Supreme Court from 17 to 21, providing for the appointment of lawyers and legal scholars from outside the judicial branch. The government's interest in reforming the entire judicial system would have been much weaker if the Supreme Court had not been so strongly identified with the protection of those who committed human rights violations during the dictatorship.

Efforts to push judicial reform through Parliament were thus made simpler by the judiciary's diminished prestige, for it was widely perceived as ineffectual in defending victims of human rights abuses and in upholding the law during the dictatorship. The active opposition of the judiciary to the entire reform initiative during the Frei government had little influence because the judiciary could draw little support from public opinion. In contrast to the teachers' union or the public health workers, judges and judicial bureaucrats failed to make their case in the court of public opinion, and the government thus was able to force a radical reform upon them.

It Is OK to Be Opportunistic

Politicians live not only in a hostile environment, but in an ever-changing one as well. When Mexican president Vicente Fox visited Washington in early September of 2001, relations among the North American Free Trade Agreement partners were the best ever. Fox's initiatives to regularize the legal status of 3.5 million Mexicans in the United States seemed to be gaining momentum in the White House and the Capitol.

Then the terrorist attacks of September 11 dramatically shifted the US international agenda. When hosting Fox in Washington a few days before the attacks, President George W. Bush had declared that the United States has "no more important relationship in the world than the one we have with Mexico." But when Bush spoke to Congress two days after the attacks, the message was clear: "America has no truer friend than Great Britain." Although Fox vowed to keep on pushing for a speedy regularization of the 3.5 million undocumented workers, his chances for success had undoubtedly dimmed.

Policymakers always deal with the not-so-trivial question of how best to take advantage of unpredictable national or international developments. Having a battery of reform initiatives ready to send to congress and sell to public opinion, whenever a domestic or international shock creates a favorable environment for those reforms, should be a priority of all reform-oriented governments. Just as players on the bench must be ready to come into the field when called upon, reform-oriented governments need to have teams of experts preparing reforms even if they are uncertain about the immediate political feasibility of those reforms.

Corruption scandals often provide a formidable opportunity to reform bureaucracies or sectors with strong labor unions or other interest groups. They also constitute prime opportunities for privatization efforts. The Chilean severance pay scandal in 2000 is a good example. Several top executives in state-owned companies, all of whom were politically appointed during the Frei administration, wrote themselves substantial severance pay agreements in case the next government asked for their resignation.

The Chilean national oil company (Empresa Nacional del Petróleo, or ENAP), long seen as a candidate for privatization, was the most deeply touched by the scandal. Voices quickly rose calling for privatization. This idea had many advocates within the governing coalition. But they were mostly reluctant to go public; even worse, they did not have a concrete plan to sell ENAP. Opponents soon decried the calls for privatization as an exaggerated and reckless reaction to the scandal. Top ministers balked, and the idea was soon discarded. But one is tempted to ask what if. Had privatization advocates in the government had a plan ready for ENAP, perhaps they could have successfully convinced the administration that a swift sale would reduce the political costs of the scandal, at a time when vested interests were severely weakened.

Groom Your Potential Allies

It is a truism of political economy that a reform effort will succeed only if the groups supporting it are more numerous and politically more influential than the groups opposing it. The obvious but sensible conclusion is that a reform-mongering politician should spend time grooming potential allies among those who would benefit from reform. The problem arises when these potential allies do not exist politically—that is, when they are unorganized and have little or no political weight. This is especially likely to be the case with second-generation reforms, which, as we and many others have noted before, tend to generate diffuse benefits for many and losses highly concentrated among a few.

Yet the situation need not be hopeless. Successful reformers have found two ways for giving allies the necessary tender loving care. The first can be labeled *whetting the appetite of consumers*. Gradual trade reform is one example. Consumers who have never tried the pleasures of higher-quality imported goods are unlikely to be strong advocates of tariff reform but perceptions change once the forbidden fruit has been tasted. Pollsters from several countries that have carried out an initial round of tariff cuts report similar results. When citizens are asked if the government should help domestic producers against imported competition, a majority says yes; but when asked if imported goods should be made more expensive or less readily available, an overwhelming majority says no.

Another example comes from the delivery of public services. Political perceptions change once at least a portion of the public has been treated to timely garbage collection or decent health clinics. One way to accomplish this, in the words of Graham and Naím (1998), is to create "pockets of good performance within the public sector, even among very inefficient institutions, which can then serve as examples or provide impetus for further reform."

Consumers' appetites can be whetted even more drastically if they are provided with the *exit* option of purchasing the same services from the private sector, with the bill still being footed by the state. School vouchers, subsidies to buy privately built housing, and portable, government-financed health insurance all operate with the same logic. These schemes can facilitate further reform through two mechanisms: users become more demanding, and public providers feel the pressure of a withering clientele.

This last point is not without dangers. Competition from the private sector will help further public-sector reform *only* if fewer users mean fewer resources for inefficient providers. But this need not be so if funds for public hospitals or schools are allocated in the budget and are not contingent on the services provided. Political pressures may also militate against budget cuts and layoffs in the inefficient state providers. Then one can end up in the worst of all possible worlds: with a public sector that refuses to shrink while continuing to suck in large quantities of resources, and with a private sector that provides high-quality but also high-cost services at the state's expense. This is a nightmare scenario for finance ministers everywhere.

Whetting the appetite of consumers can be useful, but the political leverage of unorganized consumers has its limits. That is why it is also important to vest the interests of producers. Early reforms can give rise to a whole class of new producers; they, in turn, can become powerful advocates for further change. Trade reform again provides an example. Tariff cuts on imported inputs have led to a new range of exports in many developing countries. The new exporters, in turn, have become effective watchdogs against the dangers of overvalued exchange rates, inefficient customs services, and the like.

Pension reform provides another example. Making possible individual retirement accounts, as in Argentina, Chile, Colombia, and Peru, created a new class of savers who are advocates of macroeconomic prudence and low inflation. But perhaps more important is the lobby of pension fund administrators, who are now likely to be agitating for greater transparency in financial markets, laws against insider trading, and the like. The logic extends even to the realm of social policy. The school voucher system adopted in Chile created the *sostenedores*, who run private schools with public monies. On some issues, they have been a political force for improved education.

Of course, just as Plato had to worry about who would guard the guardians, reforming governments ought to fret over who will control the new vested interests. After all, the desires of these newfangled producers may, but need not, coincide with the general good. New exporters can already be seen lobbying for subsidies, and pension fund managers have opposed conflict-of-interest laws that could restrict board members in corporations of which they hold stock. There is no easy cure for this problem, just a need for eternal vigilance.

Politicians versus Technopols

The last item on our list of helpful reform-mongering strategies has to do with the credentials of the reformers. In their summary of the political conditions for economic reform, Williamson and Haggard (1994, 594) underlined the role of economists and economic teams in facilitating the adoption of first-generation reforms. In their words, "The only other feature that we have suggested to be a virtual prerequisite for successful reforms was a coherent economic team enjoying strong executive support . . . and there need to be some economists available who are sufficiently responsible to accept, and even sufficiently ambitious to seek, high political office, rather than limit their sights to academic debate or lucrative consulting." But their call for "technopols *al poder*" should be qualified when it comes to second-generation reforms.[25]

In consolidated democracies with regular elections and higher degrees of accountability, economists have long assumed an advisory rather than an executive advisory role. An elementary rule in parliamentary democracies—and even in presidential democracies such as the United States—is that the prime minister or president should reap the benefits of successful policies but should be shielded from paying the costs of failing initiatives. In strong presidential systems such as those in Latin America, presidents often concentrate both the benefits and costs of different policy initiatives.

When a president champions second-generation reforms—or for that matter, any policy initiative—the failure of one reform can take a heavy toll on the president's popularity and political capital. The short-term electoral success might ultimately do more harm than good to the long-term health of second-generation reforms. The overall prospects for reform are better served by technocrats who can successfully implement particular reforms and allow the president to reap the electoral benefits of success but themselves pay the political costs of failure.[26] If the president appoints a reform-minded technocrat to implement certain reforms, the president can successfully shield herself from failure. But if the technopol is the same person as the president, the failure of one second-generation reform may derail all future reform initiatives.

Conclusion

The success of second-generation reforms will be measured in long-term improvements in social welfare. In contrast to first-generation reforms, the effect of the new wave of reforms will not be felt immediately. Some of these reforms might, paraphrasing George W. Bush's description of the

25. The term *technopol* was originally coined by Domínguez and Feinberg (see Domínguez 1997).

26. This has been the case with influential finance ministers who were eventually thrown to the lions when the economy turned sour. The case of Domingo Cavallo in Argentina in 1996 comes to mind. The problem is that Cavallo and others like him (Pedro Aspe in Mexico, Alejandro Foxley in Chile, and Pedro Malan in Brazil) also illustrate the opposite phenomenon: that of a finance minister who becomes so influential and respected by financial markets that his success and that of the reform program become indistinguishable.

war on terrorism, be secret even in success. But in spite of that (perhaps *because* of that), they are important. It is hard to imagine a fairer and more prosperous Latin America without better public services and modernized government agencies.

If politics was important in achieving the first round of reforms, it is even more important in this next wave. At the beginning of the chapter, we discussed who is likely to provide the necessary political leadership, and under what circumstances. And just above, we outlined strategies that have worked to push second-generation reforms forward.

But there is more to the reform process than skillful politicking. The drive toward reform needs fewer generals and more foot soldiers. The leaders who individually championed reform, who were crucial for the success of first-generation reforms, must give way to strong and independent institutions that can foster, strengthen, and consolidate a reform-friendly environment. The success of second-generation reforms will only be assured when institutions replace visionary leaders as the foundation upon which reform rests. Above, we reviewed some changes in the rules of the political game—in electoral systems, for instance—that may render that goal somewhat less forbidding.

With the growth slowdown in Latin America becoming more pronounced, the prospects for swift second-generation reforms look dim. Analysts used to fret about reform fatigue; today, the talk is of impending populism and backsliding. But the only surprising thing about this is that it should come as a surprise. Any economy, rich or poor, advanced or underdeveloped, can achieve low inflation or tariffs. Building better schools and hospitals and more effective legal and regulatory systems is what advancing is mostly about. Who ever said that could be done easily?

11

Summing Up

JOHN WILLIAMSON

The preceding chapters have reviewed the economic situation of Latin America and developed a set of policy proposals intended to address the major problems facing the countries of the region, so as to put them back on the road of catch-up growth that most people thought they had achieved before the debt crisis. The aim of this chapter is to summarize these proposals and place them in the context of past and competing ideas, as well as relating them to other major areas of social concern.

The book started by examining where Latin America has come during the past decade, since market-oriented reforms became widespread. The record is a mixed one. The per capita growth that was so conspicuously absent in the 1980s did return in the 1990s, but at less than half the rate recorded during Latin America's golden age, between 1950 and 1980,[1] and it was much lower in the second half of the decade than the first.

The obvious explanation for this deterioration in performance is the series of crises that erupted in emerging markets, starting with Mexico in 1994. Even at the rates achieved in the first half of the decade, however, it would have taken many more decades for incomes in Latin America to reach the levels that already prevail in industrial countries, let alone to catch up with where those countries can expect to be by then. Income

1. Per capita growth per year was 2.9 percent between 1950 and 1980, –0.1 percent in the 1980s, and 1.3 percent from 1990 to 2000 (data from *ECLAC Notes* and World Bank, *World Development Indicators*).

distribution just about stopped getting worse, at least in the region as a whole, but there was no widespread improvement, despite the fact that distribution is more inegalitarian than almost anywhere else in the world.[2] Social indicators have continued to improve, but that was true even during the debt crisis. The region has witnessed major crises in its three largest economies and in Ecuador, Venezuela, and Uruguay. This was far from the dramatic improvement in the region's performance that reformers had expected to result from widespread adoption of the liberalizing reforms that they advocated. What went wrong?

One hypothesis is that the whole strategy of what critics label "neoliberal reform" was mistaken. If that hypothesis were correct, then presumably one would expect to see the countries that had most resolutely resisted "neoliberalism," which means Cuba and Venezuela, enjoying the biggest advance in living standards, whereas those that had embraced it first and most decisively, like Chile, would be lagging behind. Statistics do not confirm this hypothesis; setting per capita income as 100 in 1990, in Cuba it had fallen to 79 and in Venezuela to 97 in 2000, whereas in Chile it had risen to 147.[3] It is true that the price of copper (still Chile's staple export) did better than that of either sugar (Cuba's staple) or petroleum (Venezuela's staple) in the 1990s, but the price of commodity exports is not a good predictor of economic performance over a period as long as a decade.

A second hypothesis is the exact opposite of this: that the reforms were not pushed far enough. Fernandez-Arias and Montiel (1997) estimated econometrically (on the basis of data from all developing countries) that the reforms had accelerated growth by about 2 percent a year, which was partly offset by a deterioration in the international environment. They estimated that more vigorous reform along the same lines, to match the performance of the East Asian countries, could have produced a further acceleration of about 2.5 percent a year. A later paper by Lora and Panizza (2002, 13) estimates that, despite a somewhat smaller payoff from reform than had been estimated earlier, per capita income in 2000 was on average 11 percent higher than it would have been without reform. Even smaller, though still positive, effects are found by Stallings and Peres (2000). In short, the verdict of serious work is that the impact of the reforms was indeed positive, although disappointingly small.

---

2. The unweighted average of the Gini coefficient for the 26 countries reported in the United Nations Development Program's 2001 *Human Development Report* is 50.4 percent, as against an average for the rest of the world of 36.9 percent. Only in southern Africa is income distribution comparably skewed. The poorest 10 percent of the population gets an unweighted average of 1.5 percent of total income (varying from a maximum of 2.9 percent in Jamaica to a minimum of 0.4 percent in Honduras), whereas the richest 10 percent gets an unweighted average of 40.2 percent (varying from a minimum of 28.9 percent in Jamaica to a maximum of 48.8 percent in Nicaragua).

3. This is according to *ECLAC Notes*.

A third hypothesis is that it takes time to benefit from market-oriented reforms. Thus it took well over a decade from the time in 1974 when Chile first started implementing such reforms until many people were prepared to call it an economic success story, and only after this did it become a model that other countries might find attractive to emulate. But then of course one is led to ask why it took so long. China did not have to wait for 15 years after it initiated market reforms in 1978 to benefit, nor did India have to wait 15 years after 1991; both started to benefit within a couple of years. What did they do right that Latin America did wrong?

The obvious answer is that they avoided macroeconomic crises of the sort that devastated Chile in 1982, Mexico in 1994, Argentina in 2001, and so on. Remember that there was a false dawn in Chile in the late 1970s when it looked as though Chile might be a success story in the making. But then mistaken macroeconomic policies—a fixed exchange rate to reduce inflation regardless of the loss of competitiveness this entailed, combined with relative freedom for capital inflows and financial deregulation without effective supervision—led to the disaster of the 1982 collapse.[4] In the following years, Chilean policy became far more pragmatic. The authorities aimed to achieve and maintain a competitive real exchange rate, and they were content with a very gradual approach to disinflation. Supervision of the financial system became a priority. After the restoration of democracy in 1990, they adopted the *encaje* to limit capital inflows and pursued an anticyclical fiscal policy (Ffrench-Davis 2000). In conjunction with the market-oriented microeconomic policies that were then securely in place, the result was the impressive Chilean progress of the 1990s.

A fourth hypothesis is that the region was hit by a series of exogenous shocks that repeatedly disrupted the progress that was beginning to be achieved. The tequila crisis in Mexico in 1994-95, the falloff in capital inflows and the decline in commodity prices after the East Asian crisis in 1997 and the Russian crisis in 1998, and the Brazilian crisis in 1999 all reverberated around the region, as did the Argentine crisis and the new Brazilian panic as this was being written. But then one has to ask whether these shocks were truly exogenous to the policies being pursued in the region; surely the East Asian and Russian crises were, but the other crises originated within the region. The crisis vulnerability of the region was one of the major reasons for its disappointing performance.

In sum, the second and fourth hypotheses help to explain why the growth performance of Latin America was so disappointing. Although the reforms of the 1990s were in the right direction, they could usefully have been pushed a lot further. And crises, sometimes exogenous but too often due to short-sighted policy choices within the region, played an overwhelmingly important role in interrupting progress. Crises have some-

4. People tend to forget it now, but the 14 percent collapse in GDP was even larger than that experienced by Argentina in 2002.

times been caused by bad—that is, dogmatic—macroeconomic policies, as argued in the discussion of why it took so long to benefit from the new policy regime in Chile.

To elaborate on the last point, it is clear that at times the reform process was less than ideal. Although the evidence (some of which is cited in chapter 2) shows conclusively that privatization has in most cases brought important benefits, the fact is that on occasion privatizations were carried out without the necessary care to ensure that the privatized firm was selling in a competitive market or, where that was impractical, was properly regulated. Trade was liberalized without the necessary complementary concern to make sure that the exchange rate was sufficiently competitive to induce vigorous export growth. Perhaps because they are largely in the public sector, education and training did not receive the priority necessary to nurture the growth of a modern knowledge-based economy.

A deeper problem was that the institutional basis for an ambitious program of policy reform was weak: civil services, judiciaries, and the teaching profession were ill adapted for the modern world. And the reform programs themselves were too narrowly focused on restoring growth, and never really faced up to the need to expand employment in particular and opportunities in general so as to give poor people a chance to contribute their talents and begin to correct the highly unequal income distributions that history has bequeathed to the region. It is true that those who have worried about income distribution in the past have tended to be populists whose programs ended up impoverishing those they were supposed to help along with the rest of society, but that just says that one needs to be more intelligent in tackling the problem, not that it should be brushed under the rug.

Given this diagnosis of the reasons for Latin America's disappointing performance in the past decade, this book's next nine chapters sought to develop an agenda for the future. The following section of this chapter summarizes what they say.

The New Agenda

The first topic addressed is how to modernize the state (chapter 2, by Pedro-Pablo Kuczynski). Much of the focus in around 1990 was on cutting back the bloated role that the state had assumed in most Latin American countries during the decades that culminated in the debt crisis. Fiscal deficits got far too large; the government set itself up as producer of many goods and services that can be provided more efficiently by the private sector; government regulation of economic activity was oppressive; and government was far too centralized. But a desire to prune back government in those areas is not the same as a desire for minimalist government:

"A strong and capable state is necessary to support markets, and an arbitrary and corrupt state can impede their development."[5]

The most important reason for wanting to prune the state of those activities it does not do well is to allow it to concentrate on the key functions that it alone can fulfill: providing security, the institutional infrastructure of a market economy, and public goods; internalizing externalities; and looking after those members of society least able to care for themselves. The agenda of "second-stage reforms" (Naím 1994; Burki and Perry 1998) is devoted to building the institutions—a modern, efficient, noncorrupt civil service and judiciary being perhaps the most central of them—that will permit those core functions to be fulfilled efficiently.

The duty of looking after those members of society least able to care for themselves is one that the historical legacy of Iberian colonialism has led Latin American states to perform particularly poorly. The result is that the region features the most inegalitarian income distributions in the world. In seeking to remedy this, one must recognize that most of the first-generation reforms do not have much traction (as Nancy Birdsall and Miguel Székely show in chapter 3), although except for financial reforms they appear to be marginally helpful rather than massively unhelpful, as the antiglobalization ideologues (e.g., Houtart and Polet 2001) maintain.[6] The legitimate criticism of the reforms is not that they have contributed to poverty, but that they have so far failed to address the structural causes of poverty. The next generation of policy reform clearly needs to pursue that challenge.

Birdsall and Székely look less to the traditional antidote to unequal income distribution, a massive redistribution of income through the tax system ("Band-Aids"), than to measures to empower poor people to exploit the potentialities of a market economy ("bootstraps"). Of course, one should still strive to make both the system of taxation and the pattern of public expenditures progressive, but one of the things that money is good at buying is the ability to minimize tax obligations. Even with careful attention to tax design and enforcement, one may not be able to do much better than achieve a roughly proportionate tax system, at least without serious damage to incentives. The fiscal system as a whole can still have a progressive impact if the pattern of public expenditure is biased toward poor people, by focusing heavily on the universal provision of such basic, opportunity-enhancing public services as education and health. These are

---

5. World Bank, *World Development Report 2001/2: Building Institutions for Markets*, 26.

6. However, both Berry (1997) and Morley (2001) concluded that reforms have generally tended to increase inequality. Morley estimates that trade reforms were regressive, whereas opening the capital account had a progressive impact, the exact opposite of Birdsall and Székely's results. What everyone agrees on is that the impact of the reforms was small "compared to other factors like growth, inflation, and changes in education structure" (Morley 2001, 20).

perhaps the most potent instruments available to empower poor people, although they can usefully be supplemented by land reform, access to microcredit, and legal recognition of de facto property rights in the informal sector (de Soto 2000).[7] These are the major instruments that have been identified as ways of empowering poor people to take advantage of a market economy, and their deployment should be high on the policy agenda.

Revamping the fiscal system so as to reverse its traditional tendency in Latin America to aggravate income inequalities is one of several challenges to fiscal policy discussed by Daniel Artana, Ricardo López Murphy, and Fernando Navajas in chapter 4. Now that the region has made progress in overcoming the problem of secular fiscal deficits that was so troubling in the 1980s, attention needs to turn to another of the traditional roles of public finance that was ill served in Latin America in the past: that of stabilizing the macroeconomy over the business cycle. López Murphy and his colleagues explain the procyclicality of fiscal policy in political-economy terms as an equilibrium between political pressures to increase spending during booms and the response of an executive branch concerned with deficits and distortions that gets leverage only in bad times.

Their prescription includes more transparency regarding hidden debts and tax expenditures and rules analogous to the European Union's Maastricht criteria—though both more stringent and more sophisticated—to govern the reaction of expenditure and debt policies to exogenous shocks. The greater sophistication is required because the Maastricht criteria actually curb the ability to pursue anticyclical fiscal policies, whereas a major objective of fiscal rules in Latin America should be to promote anticyclical policies. These will have to start by restraining the temptation to splurge in the good times[8] (it is no good criticizing the IMF for pressing fiscal austerity on Argentina in 2002; the only way of financing fiscal relaxation would be by inflating, and that would certainly not benefit poor people).

Another area needing attention in a number of countries is reconciling the new and welcome measures of fiscal decentralization with the maintenance of overall national fiscal discipline. This again needs the design and acceptance of rules, in this case rules designed to confront subnational governments with hard budget constraints without depriving them

7. This is not to suggest that any property grab should be subsequently ratified by the state; that would make a mockery of the very concept of property rights. Nonetheless, there are large extralegal settlements in most Latin American countries where the former owners have long ago abandoned any attempt to exercise property rights but the current de facto owners are denied the advantages that come with legalization.

8. Note that this is what Chile did in the early 1990s (in part by imposing the *encaje*). Its reward was to be the fastest-growing Latin American country, and one of the few to avoid a major macroeconomic crisis, during the decade that followed. Similarly, Colombia stood out as the country that followed anticyclical policies in the 1970s, and it too was rewarded with the region's best growth performance in the 1980s.

of the autonomy that will allow them to act on the basis of regional or local preferences. That means that they need a substantial tax base of their own on which they can levy regional or local taxes to reflect regional or local priorities. The obvious tax to employ is a property tax, which is fairly progressive and systematically underutilized in the region. The chapter also argues that transfers from central to regional or local governments should be based on a formula related to the *expenditures* (rather than the *revenue*) of the central government, so as to avoid a national anticyclical policy being undermined by variations in regional or local spending.

Although fiscal deficits are not the drag on national savings that they used to be, the change has not been sufficiently pronounced to make the budget a big contributor to savings. In addition to pushing fiscal reform further, there is a need for a financial system that is capable of mobilizing private savings and intermediating them to where they will be invested productively. That is not the case at present, as Pedro-Pablo Kuczynski explains in chapter 5, as a result of which the region is excessively dependent on capital inflows, which helps explain its vulnerability to financial crises.

Firms declare that by far the most important obstacle to their development is a lack of finance, which is manifest in both the difficulty in raising equity finance and the very low gearing ratio of Latin American firms (35 percent on average, less than half the average in South East Asia and a third that in the average industrial country; IDB 2001c). Banking systems continue to have a high proportion of nonperforming loans, limited coverage, too many inefficient state banks, and little medium-term lending. Bond markets have improved but remain weak, whereas mortgage markets are virtually nonexistent outside Chile. After briefly flourishing in the first half of the 1990s, equity markets have once again gone to ground. The most hopeful financial development of the past decade is the growth of private pension funds, which were pioneered by Chile and have since been copied in a number of countries.

The challenge now is to implement a range of "second-generation reforms" needed to enable the capital markets and the banks to fill the void that will be left if capital inflows never revive—as they may not, given that the international banks are still feeling burned, the surge in foreign direct investment associated with privatization has largely run its course, and the shine has gone off emerging markets among international investors. The rather unglamorous but very necessary reforms needed to build domestic bond markets include improving the legal protection of creditors by facilitating prompt recovery of assets pledged as collateral in the event of default; developing credit registries; privatizing state banks; upgrading accounting standards; providing a level playing field on regulatory and tax issues; and creating a benchmark government bond. Kuczynski argues that reviving equity markets will mainly depend upon a change in the present unfavorable market perceptions of growth prospects in Latin America but could usefully be aided by greater transparency and a strengthening of the rights of minority investors.

Even if large-scale capital inflows do not revive, it would be a mistake to suppose that Latin America will in the future regain the insulation from the international capital market of the earlier postwar period. Barring strong and costly, perhaps prohibitively costly, policy actions to close the capital account, exchange rate policy will in the future have to be conducted on the assumption of capital mobility. In fact, the speculative crises spawned by capital mobility have already led to a big change in the exchange rate policies employed in the region, away from temporarily fixed rates and the varieties of crawling band that were widely employed in the past toward the "two-corner solution." One of the corners is a fixed exchange rate backed up by institutional measures to create confidence that its fixity will be sustained, which advocates used to assume could be provided by a currency board (as in Argentina), but now look to dollarization to provide (as in Ecuador and El Salvador). The other corner is a floating exchange rate, with the nominal anchor being provided by inflation targeting (as in Brazil, Chile, and Mexico).

But questions still abound about whether this two-corner solution is going to provide a lasting resolution to the crises that have dogged the region in the past. Does Argentina's experience not demonstrate that a hard peg may impose costs even greater than those of classic currency crises? Are the countries that claim to be floating allowing their exchange rates to move freely, or do their actions demonstrate a "fear of floating"? Is it true that no principles of exchange rate management can be devised that will improve on the behavior of a floating rate?

Liliana Rojas-Suarez argues in chapter 6 that the best answer for the larger countries (though not necessarily for the small countries of Central America and the Caribbean, where dollarization may be appropriate if it is politically acceptable) is likely to involve inflation targeting with a floating exchange rate qualified by clear and limited rules for foreign exchange intervention.[9] But even this regime cannot be expected to work satisfactorily unless it is accompanied by complementary institutional innovations. Banks must be required to internalize the risks that they take in accepting foreign exchange exposure or lending in dollars to the nontradable sector, perhaps by requiring them to insure such risks. Shocks need to be countered, both by an ability to adjust the exchange rate and by building up and running down reserves and stabilization funds. The operation of such stabilization funds should be guided by public and transparent information on what is considered "normal."

9. There is a difference of view between Liliana Rojas-Suarez and the author of this chapter about the form that such rules should take. She favors intervention directed toward liquidity management, and with no concern for the level of the rate, whereas I favor an attempt to guide markets by indicating what rate is believed consistent with the fundamentals, with intervention directed to the objective of limiting deviations from that rate ("misalignments").

Chapter 7, on trade, by Roberto Bouzas and Saúl Keifman, describes both the process of trade liberalization in the region during the past decade and its consequences. One consequence they note is that import growth has vastly outpaced export growth, which on average accelerated very little in volume terms from the previous two decades. There were two major reasons for this. One was the limited gains in market access to countries belonging to the Organization for Economic Cooperation and Development (OECD) achieved by most Latin American countries, except for Mexico and those of Central America, as a result of which there was a minimal shift in the composition of trade from primary commodities to manufactures. The other was the widespread real appreciation of Latin American currencies in the 1990s.

Although some recovery from the depreciated rates of the crisis years was to be expected, in many cases real appreciation went much further than was desirable, particularly in countries that used the exchange rate as a nominal anchor to reduce inflation, but even in those such as Chile and Colombia that tried to resist appreciation by imposing an *encaje* on capital inflows. More competitive exchange rates are going to be imperative in the future if the region is to reap less unbalanced, and therefore greater, benefits from liberal trade. Given what was just said about the limited possibility of administrative management of the exchange rate in the brave new world of capital mobility, this implies that the fiscal-monetary mix will need to be chosen with a view to keeping the exchange rate competitive, which reinforces the earlier call for budget surpluses on average over the cycle and a better framework for mobilizing private savings. The dramatic turnaround in the Brazilian trade balance, including a year-on-year increase in exports of more than 20 percent as this is written in late 2002, shows how crucial it is to have a competitive exchange rate in order to expand exports.

Another consequence of trade liberalization noted by Bouzas and Keifman is that it did not have the effects on employment and real wages that had been predicted. These expectations were based on a simple two-factor model in which developing countries are all assumed to be labor-abundant so that free trade will raise the demand for labor and therefore employment and the wage rate. It transpires that the abundant factor in most Latin American countries is natural resources rather than labor, so that the impact on wages and income distribution is ambiguous.

This is something that should have been appreciated sooner. It implies that it would be a mistake to treat further trade liberalization as a reliable weapon for overcoming the region's inherited inequality.[10] It is perfectly

10. It still seems even more implausible to imagine that trade restrictions can be used as a weapon for systematically improving income distribution. Table 3.3 in this volume suggests that the impact of trade liberalization on income distribution was minor (not significant), though the point estimate is that it was helpful rather than harmful. However, Stallings and Peres (2000, chap. 6) and Morley (2001) both find a small negative effect.

reasonable to seek further trade liberalization on efficiency grounds; the point is that this one stone cannot be relied on to kill two birds. The big issue is what strategy should be adopted to liberalize trade: unilateral, multilateral through the World Trade Organization (WTO), minilateral (through a Free Trade Area of the Americas, or FTAA), regional, multiple bilateral (i.e., by signing as many bilateral free trade agreements as possible), or all of the foregoing?

Because unilateral liberalization has now largely run its course in the region, there is certainly a need to exploit multilateral, minilateral, and regional possibilities, and doubtless the bilateral route will continue further for some time yet. The minilateral—FTAA—route seems particularly promising in the Latin American context.[11] Allied with competitive exchange rates and the sort of measures to improve competitiveness that Bouzas and Keifman advocate, the result should be much greater export increases and substantially lower trade deficits than the region experienced in the 1990s, thus enabling it to grow without the need for large capital inflows.

A country that is lucky enough to have natural resources would be foolish not to take advantage of them. Nonetheless, if Latin Americans are to be more than hewers of wood and drawers of water, they will need to be able to command the tools of the knowledge economy. This means that they will need to overcome the longstanding weakness of the region in providing education to its children,[12] and to move progressively toward the lifetime learning that is fast becoming the norm for a large proportion of the labor force in the more technologically advanced societies. Chapter 8, by Laurence Wolff and Claudio de Moura Castro, surveys the present weaknesses in the region, but notes also the signs of recent progress. A variety of approaches will be necessary to extend these further. More money is an essential condition for further advances; good education does not come cheap. But simply throwing more money at education is not enough. The money needs to be spent by what the chapter's authors call a smart state: one that will promote decentralization, exploit testing, foster parental involvement, use technology in teaching, and constantly experiment.

Public funding needs to be redeployed down from the universities toward the primary and increasingly the secondary level, which is as far as the bulk of the population gets. That is not to call for curtailing university spending, which is going to be key to the technological upgrading that

11. Unfortunately, the US insistence on including a clause emasculating their right to use well-designed measures to influence capital flows in the bilateral free trade agreements it negotiated with Chile and Singapore suggests that it may try to include something similar in an FTAA. That could go a long way to negating the trade benefits that Latin America can expect from an FTAA.

12. Fernandez-Arias and Montiel (1997, table 3) attribute about 0.5 percent of the lag of Latin America's growth rate behind East Asia's to the education lag.

will allow the region to retain its place as the most advanced of the developing regions of the world. Rather, it calls for cost recovery, by expecting students to pay a substantial part of the cost of their university education. By all means provide student loans practically on demand and scholarships to the truly needy, but middle-class students who riot against being charged for access to a lifetime of privilege are the true enemies of an assault on inequality, and they need to be told so.

The field in which there has been the least progress in implementing liberalizing reforms is without much question the labor market. Roughly half of the labor force in most countries had the good fortune to get jobs in the formal labor market while economies were rapidly expanding. They tried to give themselves a high degree of protection through labor market legislation, although this has come under pressure as a result of the liberalizing reforms of the past decade. But the principal problem is that their benefits come at the cost of closing the door to others. This presents a major challenge in designing a reform program that will not unduly encroach on the acquired rights of the incumbents but will nevertheless break down the barriers that prevent so many of those in the informal economy from aspiring to anything better.

The challenge of designing such a program is taken up by Jaime Saavedra in chapter 9. He points to the need to reduce severance payments, because they constitute contingent claims on companies that tend to be exercised at the time a company can least afford to pay them, and thus constitute an important disincentive to hiring in the formal sector. He suggests replacing them by a system of individual accounts (as in Colombia) so as to make the burden of providing a measure of income security to workers more predictable and to spread the cost out over time. And he notes the benefit of tying pension benefits to contributions, so that workers are less likely to regard that part of their social security payment as a tax.

Saavedra urges unions to recognize that their interests are not always antagonistic to those of the employers, but that both share important common interests in raising productivity so as to permit companies to pay high real wages and provide generous nonwage benefits. He points to the benefits of improved labor market information, skill certification, and occupational training systems, so as to improve the ability of the labor market to match demand and supply.

Chapter 10, by Patricio Navia and Andrés Velasco, deals with the political economy of reform, and specifically the political problems of achieving implementation of second-generation reforms. The political problem of achieving economic reform was characterized by Haggard and Williamson (in Williamson 1994, 531) as gaining acceptance of changes that promise benefits that may be large but are long term, diffuse, and with unknown beneficiaries while the costs are immediate, concentrated, and readily evident to those who will lose. Navia and Velasco argue that this tends to be far more true of second-generation reforms than of most first-generation reforms: "the set of interests potentially affected in the [second] stage reads like a *Who's Who* of highly organized and vocal groups: teachers' and judicial unions, the upper echelons of the public bureaucracy, state and local governments, owners and managers of private monopolies, and the medical establishment." Many of the reforms recommended in this volume fall into the category they are describing, so their light on how to win political acceptance for this agenda is much needed.

They do not give much credence to some of the standard prescriptions for reform. Crises may help induce reform, but the empirical evidence does not assign them a major role, and in any event going out to stir up crises so as to nurture support for reform hardly sounds like a promising strategy. Bundling reforms into big bangs may be sensible where the political conditions to permit bundling are present, but we need to learn how to make reforms where they are not. Reform by stealth—policy reversals—has become far less common in recent years than it was a decade ago.

They regard a more promising avenue as exploiting the political uncertainty that forces politicians to look beyond their traditional constituencies to a more fluid electorate that votes on the basis of perceived results. A legislature composed of career professionals who are dependent on their constituents rather than their party improves the chance that legislators will perceive political benefits in strong economic performance. If election is by proportional representation, the electoral district should be of modest size (something like five representatives), to limit party fragmentation. Election dates should be consolidated, to avoid the phenomenon of the permanent election campaign. A reform-minded government should exploit its honeymoon—and it should keep a drawer of reform plans ready to launch whenever political circumstances appear favorable.

Finally, Navia and Velasco argue that presidents should not invest their own political capital too heavily in pushing reform, which should instead be led by those who can be politically sacrificed without fatally damaging the administration for which they work should a particular reform fail to win acceptance. Obviously there is no panacea on offer here, just some guidance on how to begin to think about exploiting the opportunities offered by the democratic environment that the region now boasts.

Supplementing the Agenda

No book of reasonable length can expect to contain a full treatment of every topic that is important to the future development of Latin America. Let me therefore try to compensate somewhat by a brief consideration of five crucial issues that were not treated in individual chapters: democracy, social progress, illegal drugs, the environment, and the policies of the rest of the world.

Latin America, like Europe, is now almost universally democratic. Both regions now have only one regime that cannot claim democratic legitimacy with reasonable plausibility. It is true that much of the fervor that accompanied the revival or initiation of democracy has ebbed as democratic regimes have shown themselves just as vulnerable to corruption and just as capable of economic failure as those they replaced. Nevertheless, the whole mindset of what is a normal and acceptable form of government in Latin America, and what sort of actions would trigger hostile reactions by neighboring countries, has been transformed since the authoritarian epoch of the 1960s and 1970s. Democracy has ridden out the debt crisis and the adoption of market economics, despite the warnings of the Jeremiahs that it would perish if subjected to such stresses. Today no one believes that only authoritarian regimes are capable of introducing market-oriented economic reforms or stabilizing inflation. If there were a decade of decent economic progress comparable to that which Chile achieved in the 1990s, Latin America could be expected to emerge with democracy as securely entrenched as it is in North America or in Western Europe.

Perhaps surprisingly, given the facts about income distribution that have already been alluded to, Latin America on average seems to have somewhat better social indicators than would be expected given its level of per capita income. At least, more countries rank higher on the human development index than in terms of per capita income (21 countries higher and 10 lower, according to table 1 of the appendix to the 2002 UN *Human Development Report*). Comparing the figures for 2000 in the 2002 *Human Development Report* with those for 1990 in the 1991 report, one finds that life expectancy increased by just over 2 years to 70 years (as against 78.2 years in the high-income OECD countries), adult literacy increased from 84.0 to 88.3 percent, and, rather impressively, mortality for children under 5 years of age almost halved, from 65 to 37 per thousand (though that is still a lot higher than the 6 per thousand in the OECD countries).[13]

Latin America is still ahead of East Asia in both longevity and literacy, although the gap is much smaller than that in per capita income, but at least the region's poor income distribution does not completely nullify the advantage that one would expect it to gain from its higher income level. Faster economic growth concentrated disproportionately on those lower down the income distribution, the objective of the policy agenda developed in this book, can be expected to improve the social indicators further. Progress could be accelerated even more by an increased focus of public expenditures on the social sectors, although this should of course be accompanied by concern for the quality of expenditures (which may again need a second-generation reform program).

13. These figures are all unweighted country averages.

One of the great unmentionable topics in discussions of economic policy in Latin America is the illegal drug problem. It is time to recognize that this is in fact a critically important issue for a number of Latin American countries, namely those whose climate and geography give them the ability to produce marijuana and cocaine, meaning Bolivia, Ecuador, Peru, and above all Colombia. If these products were traded legally, their production would provide a modest income for a significant number of peasants and their commercialization would also generate a number of jobs, but there would be no large profits in the business because competition would keep prices close to the cost of production. But countries outside the producing region have decided to combat consumption through prohibition and have enlisted the producing countries in an effort to suppress production and trade. Because demand is highly inelastic, this attempted suppression results in high prices, and therefore tempts producers and traders into taking risks, for which they as individuals, but not the societies of which they are a part, get handsomely rewarded.

The war between those involved in the drug trade and the governments that try to suppress it results not just in the brutalization of society, but also in economic costs that surely outweigh the economic benefits of drug production. It is difficult to see how this will ever change except by some form of legalization in the drug-consuming countries, which is a topic well beyond the scope of this study.[14] That leaves a large cloud hanging indefinitely over a significant part of Latin America.

The source of the rich natural resource endowment of the region noted above is its unique natural environment, involving inter alia one of the two great mountain chains of the world, the world's largest tropical rain forest, its deepest topsoil, and its tallest and most beautiful waterfalls. Biologists and all those with any aesthetic sense worry about the possible loss of this inheritance. The person in the street is perhaps even more concerned about local environmental ills, such as the air and water pollution that are prevalent particularly in low-income urban areas. (And the region is now overwhelmingly urban; 74 percent of its people lived in urban areas in 1997, as against 78 percent in high-income countries, far higher than in other regions of the developing world.)

These local environmental problems have begun to receive attention, and some places—like Cubatão in Brazil, which was in the 1970s reputed to be the most polluted place on earth—have already been transformed for the better. The slowdown in population growth, which is now down to 1.6 percent a year as a result of declining fertility (which is forecast to reach replacement level within about 20 years), also gives hope that local environmental problems may be on the road to solution.

---

14. But let us just note that, if demand really is highly inelastic, then the price fall resultant from legalization would not stimulate a large increase in demand. Or are we supposed to believe in a kinked demand curve?

The big outstanding questions concern *global* environmental issues. The region is a small player in carbon emissions, but a major one in biodiversity. Many of the logging companies continue to despoil the continent's forests, an action that in the future will surely win them the same revulsion that in our generation we feel toward the slave ship captains of old. If this were a case of making environmental issues take a back seat until living standards had risen, because of an environment-growth trade-off, tolerating the destruction of the forests would be sad but perhaps understandable. However, the evidence suggests that allowing uncontrolled logging is a lose-lose policy from a social standpoint, with the logging companies and those they may need to bribe to get access to the forests as the only gainers.

This study has focused on what Latin America can do for itself. That does not mean that we believe that its future is independent of what happens in the rest of the world. Although in the long run a country's fate is primarily dependent on its own choices, in the short run the progress of any region is closely bound up with what happens in the outside world. Latin America clearly has an interest in the industrial countries' avoiding recessions, and in their allowing access to their markets for the goods in which the region has a comparative advantage, especially agricultural products. Latin America would surely benefit if the industrial countries were to agree to a renegotiation of the intellectual property rights provisions in the WTO, to give more weight to the aim of achieving rapid and cheap diffusion of inventions and less to maximizing the rewards for inventing.

The region would certainly benefit if the recent phobia against emerging markets in industrial-country capital markets were to be replaced by a more balanced view. Latin America would stand to gain if international measures were taken to improve protection against such exogenous shocks as sudden falls in commodity prices (e.g., by strengthening the IMF's Compensatory Financing Facility). It will need help, in terms of a willingness in the industrial countries to sign tax information-sharing agreements, if it is ever to collect income tax on the bulk of the income earned on flight capital.

Latin America could also hope to benefit if the international community were to decide that it was prepared to pay for global public goods like the preservation of biodiversity, and it decided to raise real money to pay countries for safeguarding such global treasures as tropical forests. And a few countries (mainly the poor ones, notably Bolivia, Haiti, Honduras, and Nicaragua) will benefit if foreign aid programs are rebuilt in pursuit of the UN Millennium Development Goals. So there is much that the international community could do to help the region, only a small part of which could be described as charity. But regardless of the extent to which the rest of the world helps, Latin America will help itself by implementing the agenda laid out above.

Concluding Comments

Thirteen years ago, I summarized the "first-generation" policy reforms that were then being implemented in many Latin American countries in 10 pithy points, which I termed the Washington Consensus (see the discussion in the appendix). There is significant overlap between that list and the agenda laid out above. Fiscal discipline is still not completely secure. Many countries still need tax reforms to broaden the revenue base and cut marginal tax rates, and better tax administration to make tax yields more progressive without reverting to prohibitive marginal rates. Public expenditures still need to be redirected, away from indiscriminate subsidies and toward productive social spending like health and education. There is still useful scope for further liberalizing trade. It is as important now as it was then that exchange rates should be competitive. Privatization still needs to be pushed further, especially regarding state banks. Creating new enterprises, or at least incorporating them into the formal sector, is still impeded by a raft of pointless regulations. There is still much to be done to register the property rights of those in the informal sector.

At the same time, the overlap is far from complete. Some of the reforms that then seemed important—such as allowing foreign direct investment to enter or liberalizing interest rates—have been accomplished. Other things have come onto the agenda, such as empowering the poor to contribute to (and thus benefit from) economic growth, or the focus on crisis proofing the economy. There are two quite distinct reasons for those changes that have occurred. One is that time has progressed, and what was relevant then may not be so now, while both research and the march of events have resulted in new reforms being perceived as urgent. The other reason is that the original list represented an attempt to distill a consensus among third parties, whereas the agenda presented above consists of the reforms that the authors of this book believe are needed. Our agenda can be summarized under four headings:

- *Crisis proofing*. This can be furthered by anticyclical fiscal policies, hard budget constraints on subnational governments, stabilization funds, flexible exchange rates,[15] inflation targeting, further strengthening of fiscal positions and completion of pension reform so as to reduce dependence on foreign savings, and regional peer monitoring of Maastricht-like commitments to fiscal responsibility.

- *Completion of first-generation reforms*. It is important to liberalize the labor market so as to give those currently in the informal sector the opportunities that come only with formality; we believe this should be sought by cooperation rather than confrontation. The labor market

15. Except where the economy is so dominated by the United States as to make dollarization an economically viable option.

could also be made more flexible through a comprehensive program of labor retraining. Trade reforms need to focus primarily on improving market access to industrial countries, via the FTAA and WTO. There are still many enterprises, including state-owned banks, to be privatized.

- ***Aggressive second-generation (institutional) reforms***. Needs differ by country, and we have not developed this agendum with the same detail as elsewhere, but leading candidates include the political system, the civil service, the judiciary, and the financial sector.
- ***Income distribution and the social agenda***. Efforts should be made to make the fiscal system more progressive, not by reverting to penal marginal tax rates but by such actions as imposing property taxes and by focusing expenditures on the universal provision of high-quality basic education and health care. Poor people need to be empowered by giving them access to the assets that will enable them to earn a decent living in a market economy: education, land, credit, and titling.

It perhaps needs saying explicitly that we commend this agenda given what we know in 2002, but it is not presented as ultimate truth.

Finally, the agenda is for the medium term, rather than one addressed to resolving the short-term crises that seem likely to be again preoccupying the region when this book is published. This is deliberate. Latin America will never break out of the crisis syndrome unless it pays more attention to long-term issues, particularly but not exclusively if the good times eventually return.

Appendix

Our Agenda and the Washington Consensus

JOHN WILLIAMSON

The editors of this volume were both deeply involved in the development of what became known as the "Washington Consensus," a phrase that we have endeavored to avoid repeating ad nauseam in the main text of this book. But in view of our past, as well as the title of the volume, there are bound to be some readers who will be curious about how we conceive the relationship between the proposals that have been developed in this volume and the Washington Consensus. The purposes of this appendix are to spell out this relationship, and to explain why we have chosen to title the volume *After the Washington Consensus*.

Origin of the Term

The story starts with a reform agenda first developed in the depths of the debt crisis in a publication of the Institute for International Economics, in which Pedro-Pablo Kuczynski, my coeditor of this volume, was one of the authors (as he recounts in chapter 1). It was entitled *Toward Renewed Economic Growth in Latin America* (Balassa et al. 1986). The agenda advocated competitive exchange rates to provide an incentive for export growth, import liberalization, the generation of adequate domestic savings to finance investment (primarily by tightening fiscal policy), and cutting back the bloated role of government to allow it to concentrate on the provision of core public services and a framework for economic activity. In the light of subsequent events, it is worth noting that the call for import liberalization was coupled with a call for competitive exchange rates; the authors were not naive enough to imagine that import liberalization alone would guarantee export growth.

This document initially had a very frosty reception in Latin America, for it did indeed call for upheaval in the region's traditional approach to economic policy. But opinion started to change quite quickly, and by the time of the Brady Plan in 1989 a number of countries were implementing the sort of reforms that *Toward Renewed Economic Growth in Latin America* had advocated. This was not widely appreciated in Washington, so to enlighten local opinion, the Institute for International Economics decided to convene a conference devoted to exploring the extent to which these reforms were being pursued in the region (Williamson 1990). To give some coherence to this conference, I made a list of ten reforms that I judged Washington could agree were widely needed in Latin America as of 1989 (see chapter 2 in Williamson 1990, now accessible at www.iie.com/jwilliamson.htm). I dubbed this agenda the "Washington Consensus." It embraced the following ten points:

1. Budget deficits . . . small enough to be financed without recourse to the inflation tax.
2. Public expenditures redirected from politically sensitive areas that receive more resources than their economic return can justify . . . toward neglected fields with high economic returns and the potential to improve income distribution, such as primary education and health, and infrastructure.
3. Tax reform . . . so as to broaden the tax base and cut marginal tax rates.
4. Financial liberalization, involving an ultimate objective of market-determined interest rates.
5. A unified exchange rate at a level sufficiently competitive to induce a rapid growth in nontraditional exports.
6. Quantitative trade restrictions to be rapidly replaced by tariffs, which would be progressively reduced until a uniform low rate in the range of 10 to 20 percent was achieved.
7. Abolition of barriers impeding the entry of foreign direct investment.
8. Privatization of state-owned enterprises.
9. Abolition of regulations that impede the entry of new firms or restrict competition.[1]
10. The provision of secure property rights, especially to the informal sector.

1. Although not explicitly stated, this applied to the labor market as well as product markets, which is why in this volume labor market liberalization is treated as an unfulfilled first-generation reform.

Ten country authors were then asked to analyze the extent to which this agenda was being implemented in their country (or countries, in the case of the smaller ones). The conference concluded that acceptance of this agenda was intellectually incomplete and that action lagged even more, but that there had nonetheless been a sea change in attitudes to economic policy within the region in the late 1980s.

Like most of the rest of the world, the countries of Latin America were aiming at macroeconomic stabilization, developing a market economy, and integrating into the global economy. They had freed themselves of the intellectual apartheid that earlier in the postwar period had divided the world into industrial countries (those belonging to the Organization for Economic Cooperation and Development), where price stability, the market economy, and open trade were good things; and developing countries, where inflation was due to structural causes, the state had to play a leading role, and import-substituting industrialization provided a royal road to growth. And there was in the following years a wave of optimism that the new agenda would succeed in putting the region firmly back on the road to modernization and catch-up growth from which it had been deflected by the debt crisis of the 1980s.

Criticisms of the Term

Right from the start, the term "Washington Consensus" evoked controversy. One of the discussants of my paper, Richard Feinberg, argued that I should have called it the "universal convergence," because (1) the change in economic thought that I was summarizing was worldwide rather than confined to Washington, and (2) the extent of agreement fell far short of consensus. Feinberg was of course correct in both these points, but it was too late to change the brand name.

The criticism that hurt me the most came from within Latin America. Many reformers felt that I had slighted them by implying that this was a reform agenda made in Washington rather than designed by them. That is certainly not what I intended or believed;[2] "Washington" reflected the fact that, insofar as the original intention was to make propaganda, the target of the propaganda was envisaged as being those Washingtonians who were skeptical of whether there was a reform process under way in Latin America. Had my intention been to make propaganda for reform in Latin America, the last city in the world that I would have associated with the cause of reform is Washington.

The reason is obvious: This was a godsend to all those unreconstructed opponents of reform who yearned for socialism or import-substituting industrialization or a state in which they could play a leading role. The term

2. See Williamson (1990, 354-58) for an account of my experiences in Bolivia in 1985 for an authentication of this denial.

fed the desire to believe that reforms were designed by the United States in its own interests and imposed by the Washington-based international financial institutions under its thumb, notably the International Monetary Fund and World Bank, and perhaps also the Inter-American Development Bank. Anyone with a smidgen of anti-Americanism could be persuaded to foam at the mouth with indignation at the idea that Washington was seeking to impose its interests, and then they would, it was hoped, be easy to recruit to the antireform cause. Before long, the term had escaped from its original meaning of a list of 10 specific reforms that most influential people in a certain city agreed would be good for a specific region of the world at a certain date in history, to mean an ideological agenda valid for all time that was supposedly being imposed on all countries.

The ideological agenda was asserted to be that of neoliberalism, meaning the set of ideas emanating from the Mont Pellerin Society and developed primarily by Milton Friedman and Friedrich von Hayek, and then to some extent implemented by Ronald Reagan and Margaret Thatcher when they were in power. There were of course important areas of overlap between my original meaning and the neoliberal interpretation of the term, for most neoliberals believe in macroeconomic discipline, privatization, a market economy, and free trade. (So do lots of non-neoliberals; that is to say that there was a consensus that these ideas make sense. Indeed, non-neoliberals seem to be much better at implementing some of them, notably fiscal discipline, at least to judge by what happens in Washington.)

But there were also fundamental differences, in that I never claimed to detect a consensus in favor of free capital movements, monetarism, minimal tax rates (whether or not rationalized by "supply-side economics"), or the minimal state that accepts no responsibility for correcting income distribution or internalizing externalities. Curiously, no one who used the term in this sense ever seems to have thought it necessary to ask whether such policies commanded a consensus in Washington before treating them as a part of the Washington Consensus. They simply used the term to mean the full conservative agenda of the Reagan and Thatcher administrations, rather than distinguishing between those things that outlasted Reagan and Thatcher (like globalization and privatization) and those that were unceremoniously ditched when their rule ended (like monetarism and supply-side economics and belief in minimalist government), as I had intended.

This neoliberal meaning appears to me to be the way most self-styled opponents of the Washington Consensus have used the term in recent years. This is the sense in which, for example, Stiglitz (2002) uses it. This allows him to inveigh against the Washington Consensus without actually disagreeing with anything much that I wrote in 1990.[3] And perhaps this usage was to some extent legitimized by the fact that at least for a period

3. I once attempted to engage Stiglitz in a debate about the Washington Consensus. He declined to participate on the ground that he and I disagree little about substance as opposed to semantics and he did not consider semantics to be worth debating.

in the 1990s some of the Washington institutions—the IMF and key agencies of the US government like the Treasury Department—did indeed urge parts of this extended agenda, most damagingly a pace of capital account liberalization that most people agree in retrospect to have been precipitate.

Did the Washington Consensus Fail?

As Naím (2002) has said, it is certainly true that the phrase "Washington Consensus" has become something of a damaged brand name. But before one can decide whether something that has been used to mean such different things to different people worked or failed, one obviously needs to be clear about the sense in which one is using the term.

If one uses the term in its neoliberal sense, then it is easy to be among the critics. One of the reasons that Chile did well in the 1990s and avoided a major crisis was precisely because it used the *encaje* to limit the entry of short-term funds as occurred in other Latin American countries when the markets were enthusiastic about emerging markets. Excessive capital inflows both discouraged investment in tradable-goods industries as currencies became overvalued, thus reducing the ability to service debt, and built up a debt overhang whose subsequent exit at the first whiff of trouble turned problems into crises.

Similarly, one of the reasons that so many people were disappointed by the outcomes of the 1990s is that the rewards from such growth as was achieved, in dimensions like expanding employment and reducing poverty, were disappointing. That is to be expected when growth is slow and the benefits to those lower down the income scale are exclusively those that result from trickle-down; better outcomes for poor people demand either faster growth or a better distribution of the fruits of growth, or preferably both. A neoliberal agenda, by precluding any concern for the distribution issue, makes it that much more likely that outcomes will disappoint.

But it would be too easy to dismiss the criticisms of the Washington Consensus as exclusively attributable to the fact that many people have used the term in a different sense than I did. The fact is that the results of the past decade have been disappointing, as already acknowledged. We need to ask why.

In acknowledging disappointment in the outcomes, let me emphasize that I am not agreeing that the Washington Consensus was responsible for the tragedy in Argentina. Argentina undertook many good reforms, but it also made two fatal errors: it nailed its mast to a currency board that resulted in its exchange rate becoming grossly uncompetitive, and it failed to follow the strict fiscal policies that would have been needed to give the currency board a chance to work. Both run directly counter to the policies recommended in what I meant by the Washington Consensus, so it is unambiguously wrong to blame the latter for Argentina's tragedy.

The present volume makes a more general attempt to diagnose the reasons for the disappointing performance of Latin America. We identify three (or four, depending on how you classify them) reasons.

The first, and surely the one that has been most damaging to economic growth, is the series of crises that emerging markets have suffered, starting with that in Mexico at the end of 1994. The second is that reform was incomplete. Some first-generation reforms were never tackled, and few countries launched much of an agenda of second-generation reforms. Third, the objectives of reform were too narrowly drawn, being restricted essentially to restoring growth without any specific concern for employment, poverty, income distribution, mobilizing the poor to contribute to growth, or the social agenda. The question is whether these failings can legitimately be attributed to the Washington Consensus.

As far as crises are concerned, it is true that my version of the Washington Consensus did not emphasize crisis avoidance. No country that took as a textbook the Consensus as I wrote it would have been *obliged* to do the sort of things that led countries into crisis—by opening up the capital account prematurely and letting money flood in and overvalue the currency, or using the exchange rate as a nominal anchor, or pursuing a procyclical fiscal policy. But neither were they warned against such foolish acts. Those were not the urgent issues in the late 1980s, so a warning against them did not get included in what I wrote at the time. Moreover, it has to be said that what became widely known as the Washington Consensus—the version preached at the time by some of the international financial institutions and US government agencies and enthusiastically endorsed by much of the Latin American elite—was indeed guilty of a reckless enthusiasm for capital account liberalization.

The second reason argues that the problem was not too much reform, but too little. We consider that the most conspicuous act of neglect regarding first-generation reforms concerns the labor market, which has remained strongly dualistic everywhere, resulting in ever-growing informality. In other key areas, reform was incomplete (e.g., with regard to fiscal reform, where the massive budget deficits were eliminated but opportunity was not taken during the good times in the first half of the decade to run budget surpluses that would provide a buffer to allow a move to deficit spending when times turned difficult). Presumably, even the most ardent critics of the Washington Consensus will not blame it for the failure to push reform far enough.

In addition, there is a whole agenda of so-called second-generation reforms, involving the strengthening of the institutions that provide the foundations for market-oriented growth. Although some countries have indeed reformed some of their institutions, most notably by the wave of decentralization in the region, institutional reforms were not in general given high priority, and even the decentralization is in many cases seriously incomplete. In this respect, it has to be conceded that the Washington Consensus was not ahead of its time; it focused on policies, not institutions. Recognition of the key role of institutions in nurturing development was the big change in development economics in the 1990s.

The third reason for disappointing performance listed above is that the objective that underlay policy was excessively narrow: it consisted in accelerating growth without worsening income distribution. This was as much as I judged official Washington would subscribe to in 1989,[4] so that is what I incorporated into the Washington Consensus. I regard the narrow focus of the Consensus as a legitimate target for criticism, if one interprets it as offering a policy manifesto. Birdsall and de la Torre (2001) wrote a tract that aims to complement the Consensus by listing a set of 10 reforms intended to improve income distribution without reducing growth (chapter 3 takes up some of those themes). That provides an admirable complement to the Consensus.

So even my version of the Washington Consensus fell short as a manifesto for guiding economic policy in the 1990s. It failed to warn countries about some of the risks that they encountered. It neglected institutional reforms. And it was too narrowly focused on growth. The successor agenda that we have developed in this volume has sought to remedy those weaknesses.

Of course, none of this argues for abandoning what I meant by the Washington Consensus. It certainly does not argue for returning to the high inflation of yesteryear. Nor does it argue for giving socialism another chance. Some want to revive industrial policy, which may not be a promising idea, or to build a national innovation system, which looks more hopeful (see chapters 7, 8, and 11), but both are a long way from ubiquitous state intervention. Nor does it argue for closing economies again. Perhaps it would be nice to go back to closed capital accounts, if we could make exchange controls work, but it would be silly to abandon export promotion in favor of a new wave of import substitution. Critics criticize, quite understandably, the hypocrisy of Western governments that urge liberalization on developing countries while maintaining trade restrictions on the specific commodities that developing countries are in a position to export to them, or that have pushed intellectual property protection into the World Trade Organization. But endorsing those criticisms does not mean returning to the intellectual apartheid of the days before the Washington Consensus.

4. Remember that the origin of the Washington Consensus was a list of policy prescriptions that would command general assent in the Washington of George H.W. Bush shortly after Ronald Reagan had left office.

The Relationship to our Agenda

Our agenda builds directly on the diagnosis that was offered in the preceding section of why outcomes in the past decade have been disappointing. We offer an extensive set of proposals designed to avoid a succession of future crises similar to those that have had such a devastating effect on growth since 1994. We discuss how to liberalize the labor market in a civilized way, not by riding roughshod over the interests of those who already have formal-sector jobs. We outline some of the institutional reforms that countries need, though our discussion in this area is admittedly not as complete as elsewhere.

We also discuss how to broaden the agenda so as to improve income distribution and increase the antipoverty impact of growth, which means mainly by focusing more on aspects of the social agenda. We argue that this is essential if the region is ever to offer living standards to its average citizens comparable to those available in advanced countries; it is simply not possible to imagine that the average person will ever catch up if the elite continues to receive the lion's share of the income. Of course, it will be far easier for the elite to acquiesce in a reduction in their *share* in the context of vigorous growth that avoids asking them also to accept losses in their *absolute* level of income.

From the standpoint of the task attempted in this book, it does not really matter whether one chooses to use the term "Washington Consensus" in my original sense or in the neoliberal sense used by Stiglitz and many others. Someone who uses the term as an economic cuss word will surely want to identify a policy agenda to succeed the Consensus. And anyone who thought that my summary of the reform agenda for Latin America in about 1989 was a reasonably accurate and enlightened description of what was then thought to be needed should also be interested in considering how the agenda needs to be updated. The main difference between the two groups is that the former will wish to present a new agenda as a repudiation of the Consensus whereas the latter group will regard it as going beyond the Consensus. Both groups can welcome an analysis of what the policy agenda should consist of after the Consensus.

The search for a new agenda did not lead us to denounce the first-generation reforms that were adumbrated in *Toward Renewed Economic Growth in Latin America* and summarized in my version of the Washington Consensus. On the contrary, we argue that an important part of the new policy agenda needs to be a completion of those reforms. But it is only a part of the new agenda: we also argue that first-generation reforms need to be complemented by second-generation reforms, that crisis proofing the economies of the region needs to become a new priority, and that growth needs to be complemented by a new concern with poverty and the distribution of income.

A new reform agenda needs to contain a third element as well as completing and complementing the reforms of the early 1990s: it needs where necessary to correct them. Several candidates appear prominently in the book. On the macroeconomic level, the major errors were failing to seek cyclical stabilization and premature liberalization of the capital account. It is much easier to avoid liberalizing than it is to close up again once liberalization has happened, and indeed it can be argued that a reimposition of administrative controls on capital outflows would amount to breach of an implicit contract by the government (chapter 6).

Nevertheless, limited and strategic departures from an open capital account may be possible and worthwhile, such as an *encaje* if the problem of excessive capital inflows ever recurs, or a requirement that foreign financial institutions must seek authorization to borrow in local currency (as was required in Singapore during the Asian crisis, which impeded foreign speculators selling the currency short). On the microeconomic level, the major errors concerned the way in which some privatizations were carried out. Every privatization must offer net advantages to the public, which implies that it must be accompanied by creation of an efficient regulatory system if the privatized enterprise is not selling into a competitive market. In some cases, it may be possible to use the act of privatization to further the strategic objective of fostering competition.[5]

Finally, with regard to trade policy, it is important to undertake import liberalization in the context of a competitive exchange rate and adequate foreign market access, and with supporting policies geared to helping any company that wishes to improve its competitiveness to do so (see chapter 7). This will allow export industries to grow and create new jobs in parallel to the expected contraction of import-competing industries, thus reaping the efficiency benefits of more trade without imposing net contractionary pressures on the economy. There is much here that parallels Ffrench-Davis's call to "reform the reforms" (2000).

In short, we do not see our agenda as a rejection of the Washington Consensus. If one wishes, one can regard it as completing, complementing, and where necessary correcting the policy program summarized in my use of the term. But if some people are fed up with the whole debate, they are welcome to treat our title as an invitation to discuss policy reform free of any ideological albatrosses from the past.

5. A less important point looking forward than it was in the past, because most of the large privatizations have already happened: privatization must also avoid any appearance of impropriety in the way the sale is conducted, especially because Latin American opinion has now become sensitized to corruption.

References

Aghion, Philippe, Eve Caroli, and Cecilia Garcia-Penalosa. 1999. Inequality and Economic Growth: The Perspective of the New Growth Theories. *Journal of Economic Literature* 37, no. 4: 1615-60.

Agosin, M. 1999. Trade and Growth in Chile. *CEPAL Review* 68 (Santiago): 79-100.

Agosin, M., and R. Ffrench Davis. 1993. La Liberalización Comercial en América Latina. *Revista de la CEPAL* 50 (Santiago): 41-62.

Agosin, Manuel R., and Ricardo Ffrench-Davis. 2001. Managing Capital Flows in Chile. In *Short-term Capital Flows and Economic Crises*, ed. Stephany Griffith-Jones, Manuel F. Montes, and Anwar Nasution. World Institute for Development Economics Research (WIDER) Studies in Development Economics. New York: Oxford University Press.

Alesina, A., and A. Drazen. 1991. Why Are Stabilizations Delayed? *American Economic Review* 81, no. 5: 1170-88.

Alesina A., R. Hausmann, R. Hommes, and E. Stein. 1996. *Budget Institutions and Fiscal Performance in Latin America.* NBER Working Paper 5586. Cambridge, MA: National Bureau of Economic Research.

Alesina, Alberto, and Dani Rodrik. 1994. Distributive Politics and Economic Growth. *Quarterly Journal of Economics* 109: 465-89.

Altman, D. 2001. The Politics of Coalition Formation and Survival in Multiparty Presidential Democracies: The Case of Uruguay (1989-1999). *Party Politics* 6, no. 3: 259-83.

Amadeo, Edward, Indermit Gill, and Marcelo Neri. 2000. *Brazil: The Pressure Points in Labor Legislation.* Ensaios Econômicos da EPGE 395. Rio de Janeiro: Fundação Getúlio Vargas.

Arancibia, V., and R. Rosas. 1994. *Medicion de la Calidad de la Educación en América Latina*, volume III. Santiago: UNESCO/Orealc.

Arango, Carlos, and William Maloney. 2000. Unemployment Dynamics in Latin America: Estimates of Continuous Time Markov Models for Mexico and Argentina. Washington: The World Bank. Photocopy (June).

Artana, Daniel. 1996. Políticas Públicas y Crecimiento: El Caso de Tucumán. In *La Economía de Tucumán*, ed. V. Elías. San Miguel de Tucumán, Argentina: Fundación del Tucumán.

Artana, Daniel, M. Cristini, and S. Urbiztondo. 1995. Un Análisis Económico del Poder Judicial en la Argentina. In *Anales de la XXX Reunión Anual de la Asociación Argentina de Economía Política.* Córdoba: Universidad Nacional de Rio Cuarto.

Artana, Daniel, and Ricardo López Murphy. 1995. Descentralización Fiscal: Algunas Lecciones para Latinoamérica. In *Finanzas Públicas y Economía Espacial: En Honor de H. Nuñez Miñana*, ed. A. Porto. Buenos Aires: Universidad Nacional de La Plata.

Artana, Daniel, and Ricardo López Murphy. 1996. *Descentralización Fiscal y Aspectos Macroeconómicos: Una Perspectiva Latinoaméricana*. Santiago: Comisión Económica para América Latina y el Caribe.

Atkinson, Anthony. 1997. Bringing Income Distribution in from the Cold. *The Economic Journal* 107, no. 441: 297-321.

Attanasio, Orazio, and Miguel Székely. 2001. Going Beyond Income: Redefining Poverty in Latin America. In *A Portrait of the Poor: An Asset Based Approach*, ed. Orazio Attanasio and Miguel Székely. Baltimore: Johns Hopkins University Press.

Balassa, Bela. 1982. The Process of Industrial Development and Alternative Development Strategies. In *The Newly Industrializing Countries in the World Economy*, ed. B. Balassa. Oxford: Pergamon Press.

Balassa, Bela, Gerardo Bueno, Pedro-Pablo Kuczynski, and Mario Henrique Simonsen. 1986. *Toward Renewed Economic Growth in Latin America*. Mexico City: El Colegio de Mexico; Washington: Institute for International Economics.

Baldez, L., and J.M. Carey. 1999. Presidential Agenda Control and Spending Policy: Lessons from General Pinochet's Constitution. *American Journal of Political Science* 43, no. 1: 29-55.

Barro, Robert J. 2000. Inequality and Growth in a Panel of Countries. *Journal of Economic Growth* 5, no. 1: 87-120.

Barro, Robert J., and Jong-Wha Lee. 2000a. *International Comparisons of Educational Attainment*. NBER Working Paper 4349. Cambridge, MA: National Bureau of Economic Research.

Barro, Robert J., and Jong-Wha Lee. 2000b. *International Data on Educational Attainment: Updates and Implications*. NBER Working Paper 7911. Cambridge, MA: National Bureau of Economic Research.

Bates, R., and A. Krueger. 1993a. Generalizations Arising from the Country Studies. In *Political and Economic Interactions in Economic Policy Reform: Evidence from Eight Countries*, ed. R. Bates and A. Krueger. Oxford: Basil Blackwell.

Bates, R., and A. Krueger, eds. 1993b. *Political and Economic Interactions in Economic Policy Reform: Evidence from Eight Countries*. Oxford: Basil Blackwell.

Behrman, Jere, Nancy Birdsall, and Miguel Székely. 2000a. *Economic Reform and Wage Differentials in Latin America*. Working Paper 435. Washington: Inter-American Development Bank.

Behrman, Jere, Nancy Birdsall, and Miguel Székely. 2000b. Intergenerational Mobility in Latin America: Deeper Markets and Better Schools Make a Difference. In *New Markets, New Opportunities? Economic and Social Mobility in a Changing World*, ed. Nancy Birdsall and Carol Graham. Washington: Brookings Institution Press and Carnegie Endowment for International Peace.

Behrman, Jere, Nancy Birdsall, and Miguel Székely. 2001a. *Economic Policy and Wage Differentials in Latin America*. Working Paper 01-048. Philadelphia: Penn Institute for Economic Research, University of Pennsylvania.

Behrman, Jere, Nancy Birdsall, and Miguel Székely. 2001b. Pobreza, Desigualdad, y Liberalización Comercial y Financiera en América Latina. In *Liberalización, Desigualdad y Pobreza: América Latina y el Caribe en los 90s*, ed. Eduardo Ganuza, Ricardo Paes de Barros, Lance Taylor, and Rob Vos. Buenos Aires: United Nations Development Program and Editorial Universitaria de Buenos Aires.

Bell, Linda. 1997. The Impact of Minimum Wages in Mexico and Colombia. *Journal of Labor Economics* 15, no. 3: 103-35.

Benabou, Roland. 1996. Inequality and Growth. In *NBER Macroeconomics Annual*, ed. Ben Bernanke and Julio Rotenberg. Cambridge, MA: National Bureau of Economic Research.

Bergoeing, Raphael, and Felipe Morande. 2002. Labor Taxes, Employment and Growth: Chile 1998-2001. Working Paper No. 131. Stanford, CA: Center for Research on Economic Development and Policy Reform, Stanford University.

Bernanke, Ben, Thomas Laubach, Frederic Mishkin, and Adam Posen. 1999. *Inflation Targeting: Lessons from the International Experience.* Princeton, NJ: Princeton University Press.

Berry, Albert. 1997. The Income Distribution Threat in Latin America. *Latin American Research Review* 32, no. 2: 3-40.

Berry, Albert, and María Teresa Mendez. 1999. Policies to Promote Adequate Employment in Latin America. Employment and Training Papers No. 46. Geneva: International Labor Office.

Bhagwati, Jagdish. 1987. Outward Orientation: Trade Issues. In *Growth-Oriented Adjustment Programs*, ed. V. Corbo, M. Goldstein, and M. Khan. Washington: International Monetary Fund and World Bank.

Birdsall, Nancy. 1999. *Education: The People's Asset.* Center on Social and Economic Dynamics Working Paper 5. Washington: Brookings Institution Press.

Birdsall, Nancy. 2002. Da Política Social para um Contrato Social de Económia Aberta na América Latina. In *Desenvolvimento em Debate: Novos Rumos de Desenvolvimento no Mundo*, ed. Ana Celia Castro. Rio de Janeiro: Banco Nacional de Desenvolvimento Económico e Social. Available in English at www.cgdev.org/pubs/workingpapers.

Birdsall, Nancy, and Augusto de la Torre. 2001. *Washington Contentious.* Washington: Carnegie Endowment for International Peace.

Birdsall, Nancy, and Frederick Jasperson. 1997. *Pathways to Growth: Comparing East Asia and Latin America.* Washington: Inter-American Development Bank.

Birdsall, Nancy, and Juan Luis Londoño. 1997. Asset Inequality Does Matter: Lessons from Latin America. *American Economic Review* 87, no. 2: 32-37.

Birdsall, Nancy, and John Nellis. 2002. *Winners and Losers: Assessing the Distributional Impacts of Privatization.* CGD Working Paper 6. Washington: Center for Global Development.

Birdsall, Nancy, Thomas Pinckney, and Richard Sabot. 1999. Why Low Inequality Spurs Growth: Savings and Investment by the Poor. In *Social Inequality: Values, Growth and the State*, ed. Andrés Solimano. Ann Arbor, MI: University of Michigan Press.

Birdsall, Nancy, David Ross, and Richard Sabot. 1995. Inequality and Growth Reconsidered: Lessons from East Asia. *World Bank Economic Review* 9, no. 3: 477-508.

Blom, Andreas, Lauritz Holm-Nielsen, and Dorte Verner. 2001. Education, Earnings, and Inequality in Brazil 1982-1998: Implications for Education Policy. Policy Research Working Paper No. 2686. Washington: World Bank.

Bouzas, Roberto. 1999. Regional Trade Arrangements: Lessons from Past Experience. In *Trade Rules in the Making: Challenges in Regional and Multilateral Negotiations*, ed. M. Rodríguez Mendoza, P. Low, and B. Kotschwar. Washington: Organization of American States and Brookings Institution Press.

Bowen, H., E. Leamer, and L. Sveikauskas. 1987. Multicountry, Multifactor Tests of the Factor Abundance Theory. *American Economic Review* 77, no. 5: 791-809.

Braun, M., and R. Hausmann. 2002. Financial Development and Credit Crunches: Latin America and the World. In *The Latin American Competitiveness Report 2001-2002*, ed. K. Schwab, J. Sachs, P. Cornelius, and J. Vial. New York: Oxford University Press.

Braun, M., and M. Tommasi. 2002. Fiscal Rules for Subnational Governments: Some Organizing Principles and Latin American Experiences. Paper presented for the IMF/World Bank conference "Rules-based Fiscal Policy in Emerging-Market Economies," Oaxaca, Mexico, February 14-16.

Bravo, J., and A. Uthoff. 1999. *Transitional Fiscal Costs and Demographic Factors in Shifting from Unfunded to Funded Pensions in Latin America.* Serie Financiamiento del Desarrollo 88. Santiago: Economic Commission for Latin America and the Caribbean.

Brunner, José Joaquín. 2001. Chile: Informe e Indice sobre Capacidad Tecnologica. Universidad Adolfo Ibanez, Instituto de Economia Politica, Santiago. Photocopy.

Brunner, José Joaquín. 2002. Colombian Higher Education in the Context of Reform in Latin America. World Bank, Washington. Photocopy (July).
Burki, Javed, and Guillermo Perry. 1998. *Beyond the Washington Consensus: Institutions Matter.* Washington: World Bank.
Buitelaar, R. 2000. Policies to Build Competitive Advantages Around Natural Resources. Paper presented at the Conference on Export Development in the Millennium: Challenges and Opportunities for Latin America and the Caribbean, September 18-19.
Calderon, Angel. 2000. *Job Stability and Labor Mobility in Urban Mexico: A Study Based on Duration Models and Transition Analysis.* Working Paper R-419. Washington: Inter-American Development Bank.
Calvo, Guillermo. 1989. Incredible Reforms. In *Debt, Stabilization, and Development,* ed. J. Braga de Macedo, G. Calvo, P. Kouri, and R. Findlay. Oxford: Basil Blackwell.
Calvo, Guillermo, Leonardo Leiderman, and Carmen Reinhart. 1993. Capital Inflows and Real Exchange Rate Appreciation in Latin America: The Role of External Factors. *IMF Staff Papers* (March).
Calvo, Guillermo, and Carmen Reinhart. 2002. Fear of Floating. *Quarterly Journal of Economics* 117, no. 2: 379-408.
Calvo, Guillermo, and Carlos Vegh. 1994. Inflation Stabilization and Nominal Anchors. *Contemporary Economic Policy* (July).
Calvo, Guillermo, and Carlos Vegh. 1999. Inflation Stabilization and Balance of Payments Crises in Developing Countries. In *Handbook of Macroeconomics,* vol. 1C, ed. J. Taylor and M. Woodford. Amsterdam: Elsevier Science.
Camargo, José Márcio, Marcelo Nerí, and Maurício Cortez Reis. 2000. Emprego e Produtividade no Brasil na Década de 1990. In *Brasil: Uma década em transição,* ed. Renato Baumann. Rio de Janeiro: Campus.
Cárdenas, Mauricio, and Raquel Bernal. 1999. *Changes in the Distribution of Income and the New Economic Model in Colombia.* Reformas Económicas No. 36. Santiago: Economic Commission for Latin America and the Caribbean.
Carkovic, M., and R. Levine. 2002. Does Foreign Direct Investment Accelerate Economic Growth? University of Minnesota, Minneapolis. Photocopy (May).
Carstens, Agustin, and Alejandro Werner. 1999. *Mexico's Monetary Policy Framework under a Floating Exchange Rate Regime.* Serie Documentos de Investigacion Documento 9905. Mexico City: Banco de México.
Cartaya, Vanessa. 2000. Empleo, Productividad e Ingresos en Venezuela, 1990-98. In *Apertura Económica y Empleo,* ed. Phillipe Egger and Norberto García. Lima: International Labor Organization.
Cassoni, Adriana, Steven G. Allen, and Gaston J. Labadie. 2000. *Unions and Employment in Uruguay.* Research Network Working Paper R-392. Washington: Inter-American Development Bank.
CEPAL (UN Comisión Económica para América Latina y el Caribe). 2002. *Globalización y Desarrollo.* Santiago: CEPAL.
Chisari, Omar, A. Estache, and C. Romero. 1999. Winners and Losers from the Privatization and Regulation of Utilities: Lessons from a General Equilibrium Model of Argentina. *World Bank Economic Review* 13, no. 2: 357-78.
Chong, Alberto, and Florencio López-de-Silanes. 2003. Benefits of Privatization in Latin America: What Do We Know? In *Costs and Benefits of Privatization in Latin America,* ed. by Alberto Chong and Florencio López-de-Silanes. Stanford University Press (forthcoming).
Chong, Alberto, and Alejandro Micco. 2001. On Information Technology and Competitiveness in Latin America. Inter-American Development Bank, Santiago. Photocopy.
Clark, Gregory, and Robert Feenstra. 2001. Technology in the Great Divergence. University of California, Davis. Photocopy (October).
Clavijo, F., and S. Valdivieso. 2000. *Reformas Estructurales y Política Macroeconómica: El Caso de México 1982-1999.* CEPAL Serie Reformas Económicas 67. Santiago: UN Comisión Económica para América Latina y el Caribe.

Contreras, Dante, David Bravo, and P. Medrano. 1999. Measurement Error, Unobservables, and Skill Bias in Estimating the Return to Education in Chile. University of Chile, Santiago. Photocopy (January).

Cook, Maria Lorena. 1998. Toward Flexible Industrial Relations? Neo-Liberalism, Democracy and Labor Reform in Latin America. *Industrial Relations* 37, no. 3: 311-36.

Cornia, Giovanni, Richard Jolly, and Frances Stewart. 1987. *Adjustment with a Human Face: Protecting the Vulnerable and Promoting Growth.* New York: UNICEF and Oxford University Press.

Cottarelli, Carlo, and Curzio Giannini. 1997. *Credibility without Rules? Monetary Frameworks in the Post-Bretton Woods Era.* Occasional Paper 154. Washington: International Monetary Fund.

Cunningham, Wendy, and W. Maloney. 2001. Heterogeneity among Mexico's Micro-enterprises: An Application of Factor and Cluster Analysis. *Economic Development and Cultural Change* 50: 131-56.

Datt, Gaurav, and Martin Ravallion. 1992. Growth and Redistribution Components of Changes in Poverty: A Decomposition with Application to Brazil and India. *Journal of Development Economics* 38: 275-95.

Dayal-Gulati, A., and C. Thimann. 1997. *Saving in Southeast Asia and Latin America Compared: Searching for Policy Lessons.* Working Paper WP/97/110. Washington: International Monetary Fund.

De Ferranti, David, Guillermo Perry, Indermit S. Gill, and Luis Servén. 2000. *Securing Our Future in a Global Economy.* Latin America and Caribbean Studies. Washington: World Bank.

De Ferranti, David, G. Perry, D. Lederman, and W. Maloney. 2002. *From Natural Resources to the Knowledge Economy: Trade and Job Quality.* Washington: World Bank.

De Gregorio, José, Sebastian Edwards, and Rodrigo Valdés. 1998. Capital Controls in Chile: An Assessment. Paper presented at the 11th Inter-American Seminar on Economics, Rio de Janeiro, December 3-5.

De Janvry, Alain, and Elisabeth Sadoulet. 2000. Growth, Poverty, and Inequality in Latin America: A Causal Analysis, 1970-94. *Review of Income and Wealth* 46, no. 3: 267-88.

De Soto, Hernando. 2000. *The Mystery of Capital: Why Capitalism Triumphs in the West and Fails Everywhere Else.* London: Black Swan.

Deininger, Klaus, and Pedro Olinto. 2000. *Asset Distribution, Inequality, and Growth.* Policy Research Working Paper 2375. Washington: World Bank.

Deininger, Klaus, and Lyn Squire. 1996. Measuring Income Inequality: A New Data Base. *World Bank Economic Review* 10, no. 3: 565-91.

Devlin, R., and A. Estevadeordal. 2000. *What's New in the New Regionalism in the Americas?* INTAL-ITD-STA Working Paper 6. Buenos Aires: Inter-American Development Bank (May).

Dewatripont, M., and G. Roland. 1995. The Design of Reform Packages Under Uncertainty. *American Economic Review* 85, no. 5: 1207-23.

Diamond, P., and S. Valdés-Prieto. 1994. Social Security Reform. In *The Chilean Economy: Policy Lessons and Challenges*, ed. B. Bosworth, R. Dornbusch, and R. Labán. Washington: Brookings Institution Press.

Díaz, A. 1995. *La industria Chilena entre 1970-1994: De la Sustitución de Importaciones a la Segunda Fase Exportadora.* CEPAL LC/R 1535. Santiago: UN Comisión Económica para América Latina y el Caribe.

Dollar, David, and Aart Kraay. 2000. Growth Is Good for the Poor. *Journal of Economic Growth* 7, no. 3: 195-225.

Domínguez, J.I., ed. 1997. *Technopols: Freeing Politics and Markets in Latin America in the 1990s.* University Park, PA: Pennsylvania State University Press.

Drazen, A., and V. Grilli. 1993. The Benefits of Crises for Economic Reforms. *American Economic Review* 83, no. 3: 598-607.

Duryea, Suzanne, Alejandra Cox-Edwards, and Manuelita Ureta. 2001. Women in the Latin American Labor Market: The Remarkable 1990s. Paper prepared for the Annual Meeting of the Latin American and the Caribbean Economic Association, Montevideo (October).

Duryea, Suzanne, and Miguel Székely. 1998. Labor Markets in Latin America: A Supply Side Story. Paper prepared for the Inter-American Development Bank and Inter-American Investment Corporation Annual Meeting, Cartagena (March).

Easterly, William. 2001. *The Elusive Quest for Growth: Economists' Adventures and Misadventures in the Tropics.* Cambridge, MA: MIT Press.

Easterly, William, and R. Levine. 2001. What Have We Learned from a Decade of Empirical Research on Growth? It's Not Factor Accumulation: Stylized Facts and Growth Models. *World Bank Economic Review.* No 15: 177-219.

ECLAC (UN Economic Commission for Latin America and the Caribbean). 1995. *Latin America and the Caribbean: Policies to Improve Linkages with the Global Economy.* Santiago: ECLAC.

Edwards, Sebastian. 1984. *The Order of Liberalization in Developing Countries.* Princeton, NJ: Princeton Essays in International Finance.

Edwards, Sebastian. 1986. Are Devaluations Contractionary? *Review of Economics and Statistics* (August): 500-08.

Edwards, Sebastian. 1992. *The Sequencing of Structural Adjustment and Stabilization.* ICEG Occasional Paper 34. San Francisco: International Center for Economic Growth.

Edwards, Sebastian. 1993a. *Latin America and the Caribbean: A Decade After the Debt Crisis.* Washington: Latin American and Caribbean Regional Office, World Bank.

Edwards, Sebastian. 1993b. Openness, Trade Liberalization and Growth in Developing Countries. *Journal of Economic Literature* 31, no. 3: 1358-393.

Edwards, Sebastian, and Alejandra Cox-Edwards. 2000. *Economic Reforms and Labor Markets: Policy Issues and Lessons from Chile.* NBER Working Paper 7646. Cambridge, MA: National Bureau of Economic Research.

Edwards, Sebastian, and Miguel Savastano. 1999. *Exchange Rates in Emerging Economies: What Do We Know and What Do We Need to Know?* NBER Working Paper 7228. Cambridge, MA: National Bureau of Economic Research.

Edwards, Sebastian, and Sweder van Wijnbergen. 1986. The Welfare Effects of Trade and Capital Market Liberalization. *International Economic Review* 27, no. 1: 141-48.

Egger, Phillipe, and Norberto García. 2001. *Apertura y Empleo: Los Países Andinos en los Noventa.* In *Apertura Económica y Empleo,* ed. Phillipe Egger and Norberto García. Lima: International Labor Organization.

Ehrenberg, R., D. Brewer, A. Gamoran, and J.D. Willms. 2001. Does Class Size Matter? *Scientific American* (November).

Eichengreen, Barry. 1999. *Toward a New International Financial Architecture.* Washington: Institute for International Economics.

Eichengreen, Barry. 2002. Can Emerging Markets Float? Should They Inflation Target? University of California, Berkeley. Photocopy (February).

Elley, W.B. 1992. *How in the World Do Students Read?* Newark, DE: The International Reading Association.

Espinola, Viola. 2001. School Decentralization in Latin America. Inter-American Development Bank, Washington. Photocopy.

Estache, Antonio, Marco Manacorda, and Tommaso M. Valletti. 2002. Telecommunications Reforms, Access Regulation and Internet Adoption in Latin America. *Economía* 2, no. 2 (Spring).

Ethier, W. 1998. Regionalism in a Multilateral World. *Journal of Political Economy* 106, no. 6: 1214-45.

Fanelli, J., M. González Rosada, and S. Keifman. 2001. Comercio, Régimen Cambiario y Volatilidad: Una Visión desde la Argentina de la Coordinación Macroeconómica en el Mercosur. In *Coordinación de Políticas Macroeconómicas en el Mercosur,* ed. J. Fanelli. Buenos Aires: Siglo XXI Editores.

Favero, Carlo, and Francesco Giavazzi. 2002. Why Are Brazil's Interest Rates So High? Universite Bocconi, Milano. Photocopy (July 14).

Fernández, R., and Dani Rodrik. 1991. Resistance to Reform: Status Quo Bias in the Presence of Individual-Specific Uncertainty. *American Economic Review* 81, no. 5: 1146-55.

Fernandez-Arias, Eduardo, and Peter Montiel. 1997. *Reform and Growth in Latin America: All Pain, No Gain?* Working Paper 351. Washington: Inter-American Development Bank.

Ffrench-Davis, Ricardo. 2000. *Reforming the Reforms in Latin America*. London: Macmillan.

Ffrench-Davis, Ricardo, P. Leiva, and R. Madrid. 1993. Trade Liberalization and Growth: The Chilean Experience, 1973-1989. In *Trade and Growth: New Dilemmas in Trade Policy*, ed. M. Agosin and D. Tussie. London: Macmillan.

FIEL (Fundación de Investigaciones Económicas Latinoaméricanas). 1988. *Regulaciones y Estancamiento: El Caso Argentino*. Buenos Aires: Ediciones Manantial.

FIEL (Fundación de Investigaciones Económicas Latinoaméricanas). 1993. *Hacia una Nueva Organización del Federalismo Fiscal en la Argentina*. Buenos Aires: FIEL.

FIEL (Fundación de Investigaciones Económicas Latinoaméricanas). 1998a. *La Reforma Previsional en la Argentina*. Buenos Aires: FIEL.

FIEL (Fundación de Investigaciones Económicas Latinoaméricanas). 1998b. *La Reforma Tributaria en la Argentina*. Buenos Aires: FIEL.

Figueiredo, A.C., and F. Limongi. 2000. Presidential Power, Legislative Organization, and Party Behavior in Brazil. *Comparative Politics* 32, no. 2: 151.

Filmer, Deon, and Lant Pritchett. 1999. The Effect of Household Wealth on Educational Attainment: Evidence from 35 Countries. *Population and Development Review* 25, no. 1: 85-120.

Forbes, Kristin. 2000. A Reassessment of the Relationship Between Inequality and Growth. *American Economic Review* 90, no. 4: 869-87.

Foster, James, J.E. Greer, and Eric Thorbecke. 1984. A Class of Decomposable Poverty Indices. *Econometrica* 52: 761-66.

Foster, James, and Miguel Székely. 2001. *Is Economic Growth Good for the Poor? Tracking Low Incomes Using General Means*. Research Department Working Paper 453. Washington: Inter-American Development Bank.

Frankel, Jeffrey. 1999. *No Single Currency Regime Is Right for All Countries or At All Times*. Princeton Essays in International Finance 215. Princeton, NJ: Princeton University Press.

Frankel, Jeffrey, and David Romer. 1999. Does Trade Cause Growth? *American Economic Review* 89, no. 3 (June).

Frankel, Jeffrey, Sergio Schmukler, and Luis Servén. 2000. Global Transmission of Interest Rates: Monetary Independence and Currency Regime. World Bank, Washington. Photocopy (August 14).

Frankel, Jeffrey, E. Stein, and S. Wei. 1997. *Regional Trading Blocs in the World Economic System*. Washington: Institute for International Economics.

Frenkel, Roberto, and Martin González Rosada. 2000. Balance of Payments Liberalization: Effects on Growth, Employment, and Income in Argentina. *CEPA Working Paper Series I, Working Paper No. 13*. Center for Economic Policy Analysis. New York: New York University (February).

Frenkel, Roberto, and Martin González-Rosada. 2001. Comportamiento Macroeconómico, Empleo y Distribución de Ingresos: Argentina en los Noventa. In *Liberalización, Desigualdad y Pobreza*, ed. Enrique Ganuza, Ricardo Paes de Barros, Lance Taylor, and Rob Vos. Buenos Aires: United Nations Development Program and Editorial Universitaria de Buenos Aires.

Frieden, Jeffry, and Ernesto Stein, eds. 2001. *The Currency Game: Exchange Rate Politics in Latin America*. Washington: Inter-American Development Bank.

Fukasaku, K., and R. Hausmann, eds. 1998. *Democracy, Decentralisation, and Deficits in Latin America*. Paris: Inter-American Development Bank and Organization for Economic Cooperation and Development.

Galiani, Sebastian. 2001. Labor Market Reform in Argentina: Where Do We Stand? Universidad de San Andres, Buenos Aires. Photocopy (November).

Galindo, A., and A. Micco. 2001. *Creditor Protection and Financial Cycles.* Working Paper 443. Washington: Inter-American Development Bank.

Gasparini, Leonardo, Mariana Marchionni, and Walter Sosa-Escudero. 2000. *A Characterization of Changes in Argentina Through Microeconomic Decompositions.* Buenos Aires: University of la Plata.

Gavin, M. 1996. Unemployment and the Economics of Gradualist Reform. *Journal of Policy Reform* 1, no. 3: 239-58.

Gavin, M., R. Hausmann, R. Perotti, and E. Talvi. 1996. *Managing Fiscal Policy in Latin America and the Caribbean: Volatility, Procyclicality, and Limited Creditworthiness.* Washington: Inter-American Development Bank.

Gavin, M., R. Hausmann, and E. Talvi. 1997. *Saving Behavior in Latin America: Overview and Policy Issues.* Washington: Inter-American Development Bank.

Gibson, Hill, José Molinas, and Margarita Moli. 2001. Liberalización del Sector Externo en Paraguay: Efectos sobre el Crecimiento, la Distribución del Ingreso y la Pobreza. In *Liberalización, Desigualdad y Pobreza,* ed. Enrique Ganuza, Ricardo Paes de Barros, Lance Taylor, and Rob Vos. Buenos Aires: United Nations Development Program and Editorial Universitaria de Buenos Aires.

Gindling, Thomas, and Donald Robbins. 1999. Trade liberalization and the relative wages for more-skilled workers in Costa Rica. *Review of Development Economics* 3, no. 2: 140-54.

Giugale, M., and S. Webb, eds. 2000. *Achievements and Challenges of Fiscal Decentralization: Lessons from Mexico.* Washington: World Bank.

Goldberg, Pinelopi, and Nina Pavcnik. 2001. Trade Protection and Wages: Evidence from the Colombian Trade Reforms. Yale University and Dartmouth College. Photocopy (September).

Goldfajn, Ian. 2002. *Are There Reasons to Doubt Fiscal Sustainability in Brazil?* Technical Note 25. Brasília: Banco Central do Brasil.

Goldfajn, Ilan, and Sergio Werlang. 2000. The Pass-Through from Depreciation to Inflation: A Panel Study. Departamento de Economia, PUC-RIO. Photocopy (April).

Goldstein, Morris. 2002. *Managed Floating Plus.* POLICY ANALYSES IN INTERNATIONAL ECONOMICS 66. Washington: Institute for International Economics.

Gonzaga, Gustavo, Naércio Menezes Filho, and Cristina Terra. 2002. *Trade Liberalization and the Evolution of Skill Earnings Differentials in Brazil.* Ensaios Econômicos da EPGE 457. Rio de Janeiro: Fundação Getúlio Vargas.

Gonzalez Anaya, José Antonio. 2000. Exchange Rate Pass-Through and Partial Dollarization: Is There a Link? Paper presented at the World Bank Conference on Dollarization in Latin America, Buenos Aires (June 5-7).

Gonzalez, José A. 1999. *Labor Market Flexibility in Thirteen Latin American Countries and the U.S.* Washington: World Bank.

Graham, Carol, and Moisés Naím. 1998. The Political Economy of Institutional Reform in Latin America. In *Beyond Tradeoffs: Market Reform and Equitable Growth in Latin America,* eds. N. Birdsall, C. Graham, and R. Sabot. Washington: Brookings Institution Press.

Graham, Carol, and Stefano Pettinato. 2002. *Happiness and Hardship: Opportunity and Insecurity in New Market Economies.* Washington: Brookings Institution.

Grandolini, G., and L. Cerda. 1998. *The 1997 Mexican Pension Reform: Genesis and Design Features.* Financial Markets and Pension Reform Project, Policy Research Working Paper WPS 1733. Washington, DC: World Bank.

Grosse, R. 1996. A Privatization Nightmare: Aerolíneas Argentinas. In *Privatizing Monopolies: Lessons from the Telecommunications and Transport Sectors in Latin America,* ed. R. Ramamurti. Baltimore: Johns Hopkins University Press.

Haggard, Stephan, and Robert R. Kaufman. 1995. *The Political Economy of Democratic Transitions.* Princeton, NJ: Princeton University Press.

Hamermesh, Daniel. 2002. International Labor Economics. Presidential Address to the Society of Labor Economists. *Journal of Labor Economics* 20, no. 4: 709-32.

Hanushek, E.A., and D.D. Kimko. 2000. Schooling, Labor Force Quality, and the Growth of Nations. *American Economic Review* 90, no. 5: 1184-208.

Hausmann, Ricardo. 1999. Should There Be Five Currencies or One Hundred and Five? *Foreign Policy*, no. 116: 65-79.

Hausmann, Ricardo, and Liliana Rojas-Suarez. 1996. *Banking Crises in Latin America*. Washington: Inter-American Development Bank.

Heckman, James. 2001. *Policies to Foster Human Capital*. Working Paper 2, no. 1. Joint Center for Poverty Research, Northwestern University/University of Chicago.

Heckman, James, and Carmen Pages, eds. 2003. *Law and Employment: Lessons from Latin America and the Caribbean*. Chicago: National Bureau of Economic Research and University of Chicago Press.

Herran, Carlos. 2001. *Why Do Youngsters Drop Out of School in Argentina and What Can Be Done Against It?* Washington: Inter-American Development Bank.

Heymann, D., and F. Navajas. 1989. Fiscal Policies in High Inflation Economies: A Macro Perspective. In *Public Finance and Steady Economic Growth, Proceedings of the 45th Congress of the International Institute of Public Finance*, ed. G. Krause Junk. Buenos Aires.

Hoffman, A. 1999. *Crecimiento y Productividad en América Latina: Una Visión Comparativa de Largo Plazo*. CEPAL LC/R 1947. Santiago: Comisión Económica para América Latina y el Caribe.

Hopenhayn, Hugo. 2000. *Labor Market Policies and Employment Duration: The Effects of Labor Market Reform in Argentina*. Research Network Working Paper R-407. Washington: Inter-American Development Bank.

Houtart, François, and François Polet. 2001. *The Other Davos: The Globalization of Resistance to the World Economic System*. New York: Zed Books.

IDB (Inter-American Development Bank). 1997. *Latin America After a Decade of Reforms: Economic and Social Progress Report*. Baltimore: Johns Hopkins University Press.

IDB (Inter-American Development Bank). 1999. *Facing Up to Inequality in Latin America: Economic and Social Progress Report 1998-1999*. Baltimore: Johns Hopkins University Press.

IDB (Inter-American Development Bank). 2000a. *Reforming Primary and Secondary Education in Latin America and the Caribbean*. IDB Strategy Paper. Washington: IDB.

IDB (Inter-American Development Bank). 2000b. *Economic and Social Progress in Latin America: Development Beyond Economics*. Washington: IDB.

IDB (Inter-American Development Bank). 2001a. *Competitiveness: the Business of Growth*. Washington: IDB.

IDB (Inter-American Development Bank). 2001b. *Science and Technology for Development*. IDB Strategy Paper. Washington: IDB.

IDB (Inter-American Development Bank). 2001c. *Latin American Economic Policies*, vol. 13, first quarter. Washington: Research Department, IDB.

IEA (International Association for the Evaluation of Educational Achievement). 2000. Third International Mathematics and Science Study. *International Mathematics Report*. Boston: Boston College.

IFPRI (International Food Policy Research Institute). 2000. Evaluating a Mexican Strategy for Reducing Poverty. Washington: IFPRI.

ILO (International Labor Organization). 2001. *Panorama Laboral*. Lima: ILO.

Instituto Apoyo. 2000. *Reforma del Poder Judicial*. Lima: Instituto Apoyo.

INTAL (Instituto para la Integración de América Latina y el Caribe). 2001. *Informe MERCOSUR 2000-2001*. Buenos Aires: INTAL.

Jones, M.P. 1995. A Guide to the Electoral Systems of the Americas. *Electoral Studies* 14, no. 1: 5-21.

Jones, M.P. 1997. A Guide to the Electoral Systems of the Americas: An Update (vol. 14: 5). *Electoral Studies* 16, no. 1: 13-15.

Jones, M.P., S. Saiegh, P. Spiller, and M. Tommasi. 2001. Keeping a Seat in Congress: Provincial Party Bosses and the Survival of Argentine Legislators. Paper presented at the Annual Conference of the American Political Science Association, San Francisco (August 30-September 2).

Jones, M.P., S. Saiegh, P. Spiller, and M. Tommasi. 2002. Professional Politicians: Amateur Legislators: The Argentine Congress in the 20th Century. *American Journal of Political Science* 46, no. 3: 656-69.

Jones, M.P., P. Sanguinetti, and M. Tommasi. 2000. Politics, Institutions, and Fiscal Performance in a Federal System: An Analysis of the Argentine Provinces. *Journal of Development Economics* 61, no. 2: 305-33.

Kane, C., and R. Palacios. 1996. The Implicit Pension Debt. *Finance and Development* (June): 36-38.

Karl, Terry. 2001. The Vicious Cycle of Inequality in Latin America. In *The Politics of Injustice in Latin America*, ed. S.E. Eckstein and T. Wickhman-Crowley. Berkeley: University of California Press.

Kennedy, S., and J. Robbins. 2001. *The Role of Fiscal Rules in Determining Fiscal Performance.* Working Paper 2001-16. Ottawa: Department of Finance, Canada.

Kritz, Ernesto. 2002. La Crisis Argentina: Una Mirada desde el Mercado de Trabajo. Buenos Aires: Sociedad de Estudios Laborales. Photocopy (June).

Kuczynski, Pedro-Pablo. 2002. A Year as Finance Minister of Peru. In *Exeter College Association Register 2002*. Oxford: Exeter College.

Kugler, Adriana. 2002. *From Severance Pay to Self Insurance: Effects of Severance Payment Savings Accounts in Colombia.* Discussion Paper 434. Bonn: Institute for the Study of Labor (IZA).

Kugler, Adriana, and Mauricio Cardenas. 2003. The Incidence of Job Security Regulations on Labor Market Flexibility and Compliance in Colombia: Evidence from the 1990 Reform. In *Law and Employment: Lessons from Latin America and the Caribbean*, ed. James Heckman and Carmen Pages. Chicago: National Bureau of Economic Research and University of Chicago Press (forthcoming).

Kugler, Adriana, and Maurice Kugler. 2001. The Effects of Payroll Taxes on Employment and Wages: Evidence from the Colombian Social Security Reform. Paper prepared for the Latin America Conference of the Center for Research on Economic Development and Policy Reform, Stanford (November). Photocopy.

La Porta, R., F. López-de-Silanes, and A. Shleifer. 2000. *Government Ownership of Banks.* NBER Working Paper 7620. Cambridge, MA: National Bureau of Economic Research.

Labán, R., and F. Sturzenegger. 1994a. Fiscal Conservatism as a Response to the Debt Crisis. *Journal of Development Economics* 45, no. 2: 305-24.

Labán, R., and F. Sturzenegger. 1994b. Distributional Conflict, Financial Adaptation and Delayed Stabilization. *Economics & Politics* 6, no. 3: 257-78.

Laird, S., and P. Messerlin. 2001. Trade Policy Regimes and Development Strategies: A Comparative Study. In *Regional Integration and Trade in the Development Agenda*, ed. R. Devlin and A. Estevadeordal. Washington: Inter-American Development Bank.

Larraín, F., and M. Selowsky. 1991. *The Public Sector and the Latin American Crisis.* San Francisco: ICS Press.

Leamer, E. 1984. *Sources of International Comparative Advantage.* Cambridge, MA: MIT Press.

Levine, Ross, and William Easterly. 2002. *Tropics, Germs, and Crops: How Endowments Influence Economic Development.* Working Paper 15. Washington: Center for Global Development. www.cgdev.org/wp.cgd_wp015.doc.

Li, Hongyi, Lyn Squire, and Hengfu Zhu. 1998. Explaining International and Intertemporal Variations in Income Inequality. *Economic Journal* 108: 26-43.

Lindauer, David. 1999. Labor Market Reforms and the Poor. Background Paper for the 2000/2001 World Development Report on Poverty. Washington: The World Bank. Photocopy (October).

Londoño, Juan Luis, and Miguel Székely. 2000. Persistent Poverty and Excess Inequality. *Journal of Applied Economics* 3, no. 1: 93-134.

Londregan, J. 2000. *Legislative Institutions and Ideology in Chile: The Political Economy of Institutions and Decisions.* New York: Cambridge University Press.
López-Córdova, J.E. 2001. *NAFTA and the Mexican Economy: Analytical Issues and Lessons for the FTAA.* INTAL-ITD-STA Occasional Paper 9. Washington: Instituto para la Integración de América Latina y el Caribe and Inter-American Development Bank's Integration, Trade, and Hemispheric Issues Division and Statistics and Quantitative Analysis Unit.
López-de-Silanes, F. 2002. The Politics of Legal Reforms. *Economía* 2, no. 2 (Spring).
López Murphy, Ricardo. 1988. La Política Fiscal Compensatoria. *Económica* (La Plata), 33, no. 1: 85-112.
López Murphy, Ricardo. 1994. *Los Programas de Estabilización: Algunas Experiencias Recientes en Latinoamérica.* Serie Seminarios 19/1994. Buenos Aires: Instituto Torcuato di Tella.
López Murphy, Ricardo, and Fernando Navajas. 1998. Domestic Savings, Public Savings and Expenditures on Consumer Durable Goods in Argentina. *Journal of Development Economics* 57: 97-116.
Lora, Eduardo. 1997. *Una Década de Reformas Estructurales en América Latina: Qué se ha Reformado y Cómo Medirlo.* Research Department Working Paper 348. Washington: Inter-American Development Bank.
Lora, Eduardo. 2000. *What Makes Reforms Likely? Timing and Sequencing of Structural Reforms in Latin America.* Working Paper 424. Washington: Inter-American Development Bank.
Lora, Eduardo. 2001. *Structural Reforms in Latin America: What Has Been Reformed and How to Measure It.* Research Department Working Paper 466. Washington: Inter-American Development Bank.
Lora, Eduardo, and Carmen Pagés-Serra. 2000. *Hacia un envejecimiento responsable: Las reformas de los sistemas pensionales en América Latina.* Inter-American Development Bank Working Paper 433 (October).
Lora, Eduardo, and Ugo Panizza. 2002. *Structural Reforms in Latin America under Scrutiny.* Washington: Inter-American Development Bank.
Lora, Gustavo. 1998. *The Employment Problem in Latin America: Perceptions and Stylized Facts.* Research Network Working Paper No. 371. Washington: Inter-American Development Bank.
Lustig, Nora, ed. 1995. *Coping with Austerity: Poverty and Inequality in Latin America.* Washington: Brookings Institution Press.
Lustig, Nora. 2000a. Crises and the Poor: Socially Responsible Macroeconomics. *Economia* 1, no. 1: 1-30.
Lustig, Nora. 2000b. *Shielding the Poor.* Washington: Brookings Institution.
Lustig, Nora. 2001. Life Is Not Easy: Mexico's Quest for Stability and Growth. *Journal of Economic Perspectives* 15, no. 1: 85-106.
Macario, C. 2000. *Export Growth in Latin America: Policies and Performance.* Boulder, Co: Lynne Rienner.
Mainwaring, S.P. 1999. *Rethinking Party Systems in the Third Wave of Democratization. The Case of Brazil.* Stanford, CA: Stanford University Press.
Maloney, William. 1999. Does Informality Imply Segmentation in Urban Labor Markets? Evidence from Sectoral Transitions in Mexico. *World Bank Economic Review* 13, no. 2: 275-302.
Maloney, William. 2001. Distortion and Protection in the Mexican Labor Market. World Bank, Washington. Photocopy (November).
Maloney, William, and Jairo Nuñez. 2001. *Measuring the Impact of Minimum Wages: Evidence from Latin America.* Policy Research Working Paper 2597. Washington: World Bank.
Manin, Bernard, Adam Przeworski, and Susan C. Stokes. 1999. Elections and Representation. In *Democracy, Accountability and Representation*, ed. Adam Przeworski, Susan C. Stokes, and Bernard Manin. New York: Cambridge University Press.
Márquez, Gustavo. 2002. Capacitación de la Fuerza Laboral en América Latina. ¿Qué Debe Hacerse? Seminar "Desarrollando Consensos en torno al Mercado de Trabajo y las

Políticas de Empleo en el Área Andina", Inter-American Development Bank and Grupo de Analisis para el Desarrollo, Lima (July).
Marrufo, Grecia. 2001. Financing Social Security Programs in Mexico: Who Bears the Cost? Paper prepared for the Conference on Labor Market Reform in Latin America, Stanford (November). Photocopy.
Martinelli, C., and M. Tommasi. 1995. *Economic Reforms and Political Constraints: On the Time Inconsistency of Gradual Sequencing*. UCLA Department of Economics Working Paper 736. Los Angeles: University of California.
Martinelli, C., and M. Tommasi. 1997. Sequencing of Economic Reforms in the Presence of Political Constraints. *Economics & Politics* 9: 115-31.
Mathieson, Donald J., and Liliana Rojas-Suarez. 1993. *Liberalization of the Capital Account: Experiences and Issues*. IMF Occasional Paper 103. Washington: International Monetary Fund.
Mazza, Jacqueline. 2001. Labor Intermediation Services: A Review for Latin America and Caribbean Countries. Seminar "Desarrollando Consensos en torno al Mercado de Trabajo y las Políticas de Empleo en el Área Andina," Inter-American Development Bank and Grupo de Analisis para el Desarrollo, Lima (July).
McKinnon, R. 1991. *The Order of Economic Liberalization*. Baltimore: Johns Hopkins University Press.
Melo, Alberto. 2001. The Innovation Systems of Latin America and the Caribbean. Inter-American Development Bank, Washington. Photocopy.
Menezes Filno, Naércio, Helio Zylberstain, José Paulo Chahad, and Elaine Pazello. 2002. *Unions and Economic Performance of Brazilian Establishments*. Research Network Working Paper R-464. Washington: Inter-American Development Bank.
Michalopoulos, C. 1987. World Bank Programs for Adjustment and Growth. In *Growth-Oriented Adjustment Programs*, ed. V. Corbo, M. Goldstein, and M. Khan. Washington: International Monetary Fund and World Bank.
Michalopoulos, C. 1999. Trade Policy and Market Access Issues for Developing Countries: Implications for the Millennium Round. Washington: World Bank. Photocopy (September 2).
Mihaljek, Dubravko, and Marc Klau. 2001. A Note on the Pass-through from Exchange Rate and Foreign Price Changes to Inflation in Selected Emerging Market Economies. In *Modeling Aspects of the Inflation Process and the Monetary Transmission Mechanism in Emerging Market Countries*. BIS Paper 8. Basel: Bank for International Settlements.
Mishkin, Frederic, and Klaus Schmidt-Hebbel. 2001. *One Decade of Inflation Targeting in the World: What Do We Know and What Do We Need to Know?* NBER Working Paper 8397. Cambridge, MA: National Bureau of Economic Research.
Mondino, Guillermo, and Silvia Montoya. 2002. *The Effect of Labor Market Regulations on Employment Decisions by Firms: Empirical Evidence for Argentina*. Research Network Working Paper R-391. Inter-American Development Bank, Washington.
Mondino, G., F. Sturzenegger, and M. Tommasi. 1996. Recurrent High Inflation and Stabilization: A Dynamic Game. *International Economic Review* 37, no. 4: 981-96.
Montenegro, Armando, and Carmen Pages. 2002. Who Benefits from Labor Market Regulations? Chile 1960-1998. Inter-American Development Bank, Washington. Photocopy (May).
Morawetz, David. 1977. *Twenty-Five Years of Economic Development, 1950 to 1975*. Washington: World Bank.
Moreira, M., and S. Najberg. 1999. O Impacto da Abertura Comercial sobre o Emprego, 1990-97. In *A Economía Brasileira nos Anos 90*, ed. F. Giambiaggi and M. Moreira. Rio de Janeiro: Banco Nacional de Desenvolvimento Económico e Social.
Morgenstern, S., and B. Nacif, eds. 2001. *Legislative Politics in Latin America*. New York: Cambridge University Press.
Morley, Samuel. 1994. *Poverty and Inequality in Latin America: Past Evidence, Future Prospects*. Policy Essay 13. Washington: Overseas Development Council.

Morley, Samuel. 1995. *Poverty and Inequality in Latin America: The Impact of Adjustment and Recovery in the 1980s*. Baltimore: Johns Hopkins University Press.
Morley, Samuel. 2000. *La Distribución del Ingreso en América Latina y el Caribe*. Santiago: Comisión Económica para América Latina y el Caribe.
Morley, Samuel. 2001. *Distribution and Growth in Latin America in an Era of Structural Reform*. TMD Discussion Paper 66. Washington: International Food Policy Research Institute.
Morley, Samuel, and David Coady. 2003. *Targeted Education Subsidies in Developing Countries: A Review of Recent Experiences*. Washington: Center for Global Development. Forthcoming.
Morley, Samuel, Ricardo Machado, and Stefano Pettinato. 1999. *Indexes of Structural Reform in Latin America*. ECLAC Serie de Reformas Economicas 12. Santiago: Economic Commission for Latin America and the Caribbean.
Mussa, Michael. 1982. Government Policy and the Adjustment Process. In *Import Competition and Response*, ed. J. Bhagwati. Chicago: University of Chicago Press.
Mussa, Michael. 2002. *Argentina and the Fund: From Triumph to Tragedy*. Washington: Institute for International Economics.
Naím, Moisés. 1994. Latin America: The Second Stage of Reform. *Journal of Democracy* 5, no. 4 (October): 32-48.
Naím, Moisés. 2000. Fads and Fashion in Economic Reforms: Washington Consensus or Washington Confusion? *Foreign Policy* 118, no. 86 (Spring).
Naím, Moisés. 2002. Washington Consensus: A Damaged Brand. *Financial Times*, October 28.
Navarro, Juan Carlo. 1999. Postponing Reform: Achievements and Shortcomings of Higher Education in Venezuela. *International Higher Education*, no. 15. Boston, MA: Boston College.
Negretto, G.L. 2001. Government Capacities and Policy Making by Decree in Latin America: The Cases of Brazil and Argentina. Paper prepared for the Annual Meeting of the American Political Science Association, San Francisco (August 30-September 2).
Nickson, R.A. 1995. *Local Government in Latin America*. Boulder, CO: Lynne Rienner.
Noland, Marcus, and Howard Pack. 2003. *Industrial Policy in an Era of Globalization: Lessons from Asia*. Washington: Institute for International Economics.
Ocampo, José Antonio. Forthcoming. Capital Account and Counter-Cyclical Prudential Regulations in Developing Counties. In *From Capital Surges to Drought: Stabilizing Emerging Economies*, ed. Ricardo Ffrench-Davis and Stephany Griffith-Jones. Basingstoke: Palgrave/Macmillan.
Ocampo, José Antonio, Fabio Sánchez, and Camilo Ernesto Tovar. 2001. Cambio Estructural, Mercado Laboral y Distribución del Ingreso: Colombia en la década de los noventa. In *Liberalización, Desigualdad y Pobreza*, ed. Enrique Ganuza, Ricardo Paes de Barros, Lance Taylor, and Rob Vos. Buenos Aires: United Nations Development Program and Editorial Universitaria de Buenos Aires.
O'Connell, Lesley. 1999. *Collective Bargaining in Six Latin American countries: Degrees of Autonomy and Decentralization*. Research Network Working Paper No. R-399. Washington: Inter-American Development Bank.
OECD (Organization for Economic Cooperation and Development). 1999. *Managing National Innovation Systems*. Paris: OECD.
OECD (Organization for Economic Cooperation and Development). 2001a. *Knowledge and Skills for Life*. Paris: OECD.
OECD (Organization for Economic Cooperation and Development). 2001b. *Science, Technology, and Industry Outlook: Drivers of Growth*. Paris: OECD.
Okun, Arthur. 1975. *Equality and Efficiency: The Big Trade-Off*. Washington: Brookings Institution Press.
OLADE (Organización Latinoamericana de Energía). 1993. *El Déficit de Financiamiento de la Inversión Eléctrica*. Quito: OLADE.
Oliveira, João Batista Araújo. 1998. *A Pedagogia do Suceso*. Sao Paulo: Instituto Ayrton Senna.
Ortíz de Zevallos, G., and P. Pollarolo, eds. 2000. *Seguridad Ciudadana*. Lima: Instituto Apoyo.

Packard, Truman. 2001. *Is There a Positive Effect from Privatizing Social Security? A Panel Analysis of Pension Reforms in Latin America.* Working Paper No. 2719. Washington: The World Bank.

Paes de Barros, Ricardo and Carlos Enrique Corseuil. 2001. *The Impact of Regulations on Brazilian Labor Market Performance.* Research Network Working Paper R-427. Washington: Inter-American Development Bank.

Pagés, Carmen, Suzanne Duryea, and Olga Jaramillo. 2001. Mercados de Trabajo en América Latina: Descifrando la Década de los Noventa. Paper prepared for "Seminario técnico de consulta regional sobre temas laborales," Panama (November). Photocopy.

Pagés, Carmen, and Jaime Saavedra. 2002. Legislación Laboral: Algunos Principios Fundamentales, Evidencia Empírica y Opciones de Política en América Latina. Nota de Política, Seminar "Desarrollando Consensos en Torno al Mercado de Trabajo," Inter-American Development Bank and Grupo de Analisis para el Desarrollo, Lima (July).

Pascó-Font, Alberto, and Jaime Saavedra. 2001. Reformas Estructurales y Bienestar: Una Mirada al Perú de los Noventa. Grupo de Analisis para el Desarrollo, Lima.

Pascó-Font, Alberto, and Máximo Torero. 2001. *El Impacto Social de la Privatización y de la Regulación de los Servicios Públicos en el Perú.* Documento de Trabajo 35. Lima: Grupo de Analisis para el Desarrollo.

Perry, Guillermo, and Luis Servén. 2002. The Anatomy of a Multiple Crisis: Why Was Argentina Special and What Can We Learn from It? World Bank, Washington. Photocopy (May 19).

Persson, Torsten, and Guido Tabellini. 1994. Is Inequality Harmful for Growth? Theory and Evidence. *American Economic Review* 84, no. 3: 600-21.

Pessino, Carola. 2001. Convertibility and the Labor Market. Paper prepared for the conference "The Currency Board's First Decade: Argentina and the Convertibility Law". Buenos Aires (April). Photocopy.

Poterba, J., and J. von Haguen, eds. 1999. *Fiscal Institutions and Fiscal Performance.* Chicago: University of Chicago Press.

PREAL (Partnership for Educational Revitalization in the Americas). 2001. *Lagging Behind: A Report Card on Education in Latin America.* Washington: PREAL.

Pritchett, Lant. 2001. Where Has All the Education Gone? *World Bank Economic Review* 15, no. 3: 367-91.

Przeworski, Adam, Susan C. Stokes, and Bernard Manin, eds. 1999. *Democracy, Accountability, and Representation.* New York: Cambridge University Press.

Rama, Martin. 1997. Organized Labor and the Political Economy of Product Market Distortions. *World Bank Economic Review* 11, no. 2: 357-95.

Rama, Martin. 1998. *Wage Misalignment in CFA Countries: Are Labor Market Policies to Blame?* Policy Research Working Paper 1873. Washington: World Bank.

Ramamurti, R., ed. 1996. *Privatizing Monopolies: Lessons from the Telecommunications and Transport Sectors in Latin America.* Baltimore: Johns Hopkins University Press.

Ramos, Lauro. 2002. *A Evolução da Informalidade no Brasil Metropolitano 1991-2001.* Texto para discussão No. 914. Rio de Janeiro: Instituto de Pesquisa Econômica Aplicada.

Reinhart, Carmen, and Kenneth Rogoff. 2002. *The Modern Theory of Exchange Rate Arrangements: A Reinterpretation.* NBER Working Paper 8963. Cambridge, MA: National Bureau of Economic Research.

Reinhart, Carmen, and R. Todd Smith. 1998. Too Much of a Good Thing: The Macroeconomic Effects of Taxing Capital Inflows. In *Managing Capital Flows and Exchange Rates: Lessons from the Pacific Basin,* ed. R. Glick. Cambridge: Cambridge University Press.

Reyes, Alvaro. 2000. *Tendencias Recientes en el Empleo en Colombia.* In *Apertura Económica y Empleo,* ed. Phillipe Egger and Norberto García. Lima: International Labor Organization.

Robles, Miguel, Jaime Saavedra, Máximo Torero, Néstor Valdivia, and Juan Chacaltana. 2001. *Estrategias y Racionalidad de la Pequeña Empresa.* Lima: International Labor Organization.

Rodríguez, Francisco, and Dani Rodrik. 2001. Trade Policy and Economic Growth: A Skeptic's Guide to the Cross-National Evidence. *Macroeconomics Annual 2000,* ed. Ben Bernanke and Kenneth S. Rogoff. Cambridge, MA: MIT Press for NBER.

Rodrik, Dani. 1994. The Rush to Free Trade: Why So Late? Why Now? Will It Last? In *Voting for Reform: Democracy, Political Liberalization, and Economic Adjustment*, ed. S. Haggard and S.B. Webb. New York: Oxford University Press.

Rodrik, Dani. 1996. Understanding Economic Policy Reform. *Journal of Economic Literature* 34, no. 1: 9-41.

Rodrik, Dani. 1999. Why Is There So Much Economic Insecurity in Latin America? Cambridge: John F. Kennedy School of Government, Harvard University (October). Photocopy.

Rodrik, Dani. 2002. After Neoliberalism, What? Remarks at the BNDES seminar on "New Paths of Development," Rio de Janeiro, September 12-13.

Rojas-Suarez, Liliana. 2003. What Exchange Rate Arrangements Work Best for Latin America. In *The Dollarization Debate*, ed. James Dean, Dominick Salvatore, and Thomas Willet. Oxford University Press (forthcoming).

Rojas-Suarez, Liliana, and Steven Weisbrod. 1995. *Financial Fragilities in Latin America: The 1980s and the 1990s*. IMF Occasional Paper 132. Washington: International Monetary Fund.

Ros, J. 2001. Política Industrial, Ventajas Comparativas y Crecimiento. *CEPAL Review* 73 (Santiago): 129-48.

Saavedra, Jaime. 1998. *¿Crisis Real o Crisis de Expectativas? El empleo en Perú antes y después de las reformas estructurales*. Research Network Working Paper No. 388. Washington: Inter-American Development Bank.

Saavedra, Jaime. 2003. The Economics of Social Exclusion in Peru: An Invisible Wall? 4th Annual Global Development Conference. Cairo (January).

Saavedra, Jaime, and Alberto Chong. 1999. Structural Reforms, Institutions, and the Informal Sector in Peru. *Journal of Development Studies* 35, no. 4: 95-116.

Saavedra, Jaime, and Eduardo Maruyama. 1999. Los Retornos a la Educación y a la Experiencia en el Perú, 1985-1997. In *Pobreza Economía Social: Análisis de la Encuesta ENNIV-1997*, ed. Richard Webb and Moisés Ventocilla. Lima: Instituto Cuánto.

Saavedra, Jaime, and Máximo Torero. 2003. *Labor Market Reforms and Their Impact on Formal Labor Demand and Job Market Turnover: The Case of Peru*. In *Law and Employment: Lessons from Latin America and the Caribbean*, ed. James Heckman and Carmen Pagés. Chicago: NBER and University of Chicago Press (forthcoming).

Saavedra, Jaime, and Máximo Torero. 2002. *Union Density Changes and Union Effects On Firm Performance in Peru*. Research Network Working Paper R-465. Washington: Inter-American Development Bank.

Sachs, Jeffrey, and Felipe Larraín. 1999. Why Dollarization Is More Straitjacket than Salvation. *Foreign Policy*, no. 116: 80-92.

Sachs, Jeffrey, and Andrew Warner. 1995. Economic Reform and the Process of Global Integration. *Brookings Papers on Economic Activity* 1995:1. Washington: Brookings Institution.

Sachs, Jeffrey, and Andrew Warner. 1997. Natural Resource Abundance and Economic Growth. Center for International Development and Harvard Institute for International Development, Cambridge, MA. Photocopy (November).

Sala-i-Martin, Xavier. 1997. I Just Ran Two Million Regressions. *American Economic Review* 87, no. 2: 178-83.

Salinas, C. 2000. *México: Un Paso Difícil a la Modernidad*. Barcelona: Plaza y Janés.

Schaechter, Andrea, Mark Stone, and Mark Zelmer. 2000. *Adopting Inflation Targeting: Practical Issues for Emerging Market Countries*. IMF Occasional Paper 202. Washington: International Monetary Fund.

Schmidt-Hebbel, K. 1996. La Reforma Pensional Colombiana: Efectos Fiscales y Macroeconómicos. Bolsa de Bogotá y ASOFONDOS, Bogotá. Photocopy.

Serra, P., and R. Fischer. 2000. Regulating the Electricity Sector in Latin America. *Economía* 1, no. 1: 155-98 (Fall).

Shleifer, A., K. Murphy, and R. Vishny. 1992. Transitions to a Market Economy: Pitfalls of Partial Reform. *Quarterly Journal of Economics* (August).

Shome, P., ed. 1995. *Tax Policy Handbook*. Washington: International Monetary Fund.
Siavelis, P. 2000. *The President and Congress in Post-Authoritarian Chile: Institutional Constraints to Democratic Consolidation*. University Park, PA: Pennsylvania State University Press.
Silva, V. 2001. *Estrategia y Agenda Comercial Chilena en los Años Noventa*. CEPAL Serie Comercio Internacional 11. Santiago: Comisión Económica para América Latina y el Caribe.
Silvani, C., and J. Brondolo. 1993. Medición del Cumplimiento Tributario en el IVA y Análisis de sus Determinantes. International Monetary Fund and Centro Internacional de Agricultura Tropical, Cali, Colombia. Photocopy (November).
Skoufias, Emmanuel, and Susan W. Parker. 2001. Demand-Side Interventions and their Impact on Child Labor and School Enrollment: Evidence from the PROGRESA Program in Mexico. *Economía* 2, no. 1 (Fall).
Spilimbergo, Antonio, Juan Luis Londoño, and Miguel Székely. 1999. Income Distribution, Factor Endowments, and Trade Openness. *Journal of Development Economics* 59: 77-101.
Stallings, Barbara, and Wilson Peres. 2000. *Growth, Employment, and Equity: The Impact of the Economic Reforms in Latin America and the Caribbean*. Washington: Brookings Institution Press.
Stein, E., E. Talvi, and A. Grisanti. 1998. *Institutional Arrangements and Fiscal Performance: The Latin American Perspective*. Working Paper Series 367. Washington: Inter-American Development Bank.
Stiglitz, Joseph E. 1996. Some Lessons from the East Asian Miracle. *World Bank Research Observer* 11, no. 2: 151-77.
Stiglitz, Joseph E. 2002. *Globalization and Its Discontents*. New York: Norton.
Stokes, S.C. 2001. *Markets, Mandates, and Democracy: Neoliberalism by Surprise in Latin America*. New York: Cambridge University Press.
Superintendencia de Administradoras de Fondos de Pensiones. 1998. *Boletín Estadístico 145*. Santiago: Superintendencia de Administradoras de Fondos de Pensiones.
Svensson, Lars. 1999. Price Level Targeting vs. Inflation Targeting: A Free Lunch? *Journal of Money, Credit and Banking* 31: 277-95.
Székely, Miguel. 1998. *The Economics of Poverty, Inequality, and Wealth Accumulation in Mexico*. London: Macmillan.
Székely, Miguel. 2001a. Introduction. In *A Portrait of the Poor: An Asset Based Approach*, ed. Orazio Attanasio and Miguel Székely. Baltimore: Johns Hopkins University Press.
Székely, Miguel. 2001b. *The 1990s in Latin America: Another Decade of Persistent Inequality, but with Somewhat Lower Poverty*. Research Department Working Paper 454, Washington: Inter-American Development Bank.
Székely, Miguel, and Marianne Hilgert. 1999. *What's Behind the Inequality We Measure? An Investigation Using Latin American Data*. Research Department Working Paper 409. Washington: Inter-American Development Bank.
Talvi, E., and C. Vegh. 2000. *Tax Base Variability and Procyclical Fiscal Policy*. NBER Working Paper 7499. Cambridge, MA: National Bureau of Economic Research.
Tanzi, V., and H. Zee. 1998. *Taxation and the Household Saving Rate: Evidence from OECD Countries*. IMF Working Paper WP/98/36. Washington: International Monetary Fund.
Ten Kate, Adrian, Carla Macario, and Gunnar Niels. 2000. Mexico: Export Promotion Policies on the Cutting Edge. In *Export Growth in Latin America. Policies and Performance*, ed. Carla Macario. Boulder, CO: Lynne Rienner.
Thorp, Rosemary. 1998. *Progress, Poverty and Exclusion: An Economic History of Latin America in the 20th Century* Baltimore: Johns Hopkins University Press for the Inter-American Development Bank and the European Union.
Tomell, A. 1995. Are Economic Crises Necessary for Trade Liberalization and Fiscal Reform? The Mexican Experience. In *Reform, Recovery and Growth: Latin America and the Middle East*, ed. R. Dornbusch and S. Edwards. Chicago: University of Chicago Press for National Bureau of Economic Research.
Tommasi, M., S. Saiegh, and P. Sanguinetti. 2001. Fiscal Federalism in Argentina: Policies, Politics, and Institutional Reform. *Economía* 1, no. 2: 147-201.

Torre, Juan Carlos, and Pablo Gerchunoff. 1999. *La Economía Política de las Reformas Institucionales en Argentina. Los casos de la Política de Privatización de ENTEL, la Reforma de la Seguridad Social y la Reforma Laboral*. Research Network Working Paper R-349. Washington: Inter-American Development Bank.

Trefler, D. 1993. International Factor Price Differences: Leontief Was Right! *Journal of Political Economy* 101, no. 6: 961-87.

Trefler, D. 1995. The Case of the Missing Trade and Other Mysteries. *American Economic Review* 85, no. 5: 1028-46.

Truman, Edwin. 2002. Inflation Targeting Around the World. Paper presented at the Central Bank of Brazil Conference on Three Years of Inflation Targeting, Rio de Janeiro (May 17).

UNESCO (United Nations Educational, Scientific, and Cultural Organization) and Oficina Regional de Educación de la UNESCO para América Latina y el Caribe (Orealc). 1998. *First International Comparative Study of Learning in Third and Fourth Grades*. Santiago: UNESCO/Orealc.

UNESCO (United Nations Educational, Scientific, and Cultural Organization) and Oficina Regional de Educación de la UNESCO para América Latina y el Caribe (Orealc). 2000. *Informe Sub-regional de América Latina de EFA*. Santiago: UNESCO.

UNESCO (United Nations Educational, Scientific, and Cultural Organization). 2001a. *Latin America and the Caribbean: Regional Report*. Paris: UNESCO Institute of Statistics.

UNESCO (United Nations Educational, Scientific, and Cultural Organization) and Oficina Regional de Educación de la UNESCO para América Latina y el Caribe (Orealc). 2001b. *Balance de los 20 anos del Proyecto Principal de Educacion en América Latina y el Caribe*. Santiago: UNESCO.

Vega, María Luz. 2001. *La Reforma Laboral en América Latina: Un Analisis Comparado*. Lima: Oficina Internacional del Trabajo, Oficina Regional para América Latina y el Caribe.

Velasco, A. 1994. The State and Economic Policy: Chile 1952-1992. In *The Chilean Economy: Policy Lessons and Challenges*, ed. B. Bosworth, R. Dornbusch, and R. Labán. Washington: Brookings Institution Press.

Velasco, A. 1999. A Model of Endogenous Fiscal Deficits, and Delayed Fiscal Reforms. In *Fiscal Institutions and Fiscal Performance*, ed. J. Poterba and J. von Hagen. Chicago: University of Chicago Press for the NBER.

Von Gersdorff, H. 1997. *The Bolivian Pension Reform*. Financial Markets and Pension Reform Project. Washington: World Bank.

Wei, Shang-Jin. 1998. Gradualism versus Big Bang: Speed and Sustainability of Reforms. In *The Political Economy of Reform*, ed. F. Sturzenegger and M. Tommasi. Cambridge, MA and London: MIT Press.

Weller, Jurgen. 2000. *Reformas Económicas, Crecimiento y Empleo: Los Mercados de Trabajo en América Latina y el Caribe durante los años Noventa*. Comisión Económica para América Latina y el Caribe and Facultad de Ciencias de la Educación, Santiago.

Williamson, John, ed. 1990. *Latin American Adjustment: How Much Has Happened?* Washington: Institute for International Economics.

Williamson, John, ed. 1994. *The Political Economy of Policy Reform*. Washington: Institute for International Economics.

Williamson, John. 2000. *Exchange Rate Regimes for Emerging Markets: Reviving the Intermediate Option*. POLICY ANALYSES IN INTERNATIONAL ECONOMICS 60. Washington: Institute for International Economics.

Williamson, John, and Stephan Haggard. 1994. The Political Conditions for Economic Reform. In *The Political Economy of Policy Reform*, ed. J. Williamson. Washington: Institute for International Economics.

Wolff, Laurence, and Douglass Albrecht. 1992. *Higher Education Reform in Chile, Brazil and Venezuela: Toward a Redefinition of the Role of the State*. World Bank Working Paper. Washington: World Bank.

Wolff, Laurence, and Claudio de Moura Castro. 2000. *Secondary Education in Latin America and the Caribbean: The Challenge of Growth and Reform*. Washington: Inter-American Development Bank.

Wolff, Laurence, Pablo Gonzalez, and Juan Carlos Navarro. 2002. *Educación Privada y Politica Publica en América Latina*. Santiago: PREAL.
Wolff, Laurence, Ernesto Schiefelbein, and Paulina Schiefelbein. 2002. *Primary Education in Latin America: The Unfinished Agenda*. Washington: Inter-American Development Bank.
Wolff, Laurence, Ernesto Schiefelbein, and Jorge Valenzuela, 1992. *Improving the Quality of Primary Education in Latin America and the Caribbean: Towards the 21st Century*. Washington: World Bank.
World Bank. 1993. *Argentina: From Insolvency to Growth*. Washington: World Bank.
World Bank. 2001. *Attacking Poverty: World Development Report 2000/2001*. Baltimore: Johns Hopkins University Press.

About the Contributors

Daniel Artana, Argentina's former secretary of the treasury, is a chief economist at Fundación de Investigaciones Económicas Latinoamericanas (FIEL) in Buenos Aires and professor of economics at the National University of La Plata and the Universities of Torcuato di Tella and San Andrés. He was a consultant at the World Bank, the Inter-American Development Bank, and private foundations in and governments of several Latin American countries. He has contributed to journals and books on public economics, applied macroeconomics, and industrial organization.

Nancy Birdsall is president of the Center for Global Development. She was formerly with the Carnegie Endowment for International Peace and director of the Economic Reform Project there. She was the executive vice president of the Inter-American Development Bank (1993-98) and before that director of the Policy Research Department at the World Bank. She is the author of numerous publications on labor markets, human resources, economic inequality, the relationship between income distribution and growth, and other development issues. She is coauthor of *Delivering on Debt Relief: From IMF Gold to a New Aid Architecture* (2002) with John Williamson. She serves on various boards, including the Population Council, and is a special adviser to the administrator of the United Nations Development Program (UNDP).

Roberto Bouzas is a professor at the University of San Andrés and a senior research fellow at the National Science Research Council. He is also the academic director of the master of philosophy program in international relations and negotiations cosponsored by the University of San

Andrés, Facultad Latinoamericana de Ciencias Sociales (FLACSO), and the University of Barcelona. He was a visiting professor at Stanford, Duke, and Notre Dame universities and adviser to the Argentine government and international institutions such as the Inter-American Development Bank and the UN Economic Commission for Latin America and the Caribbean (ECLAC). He is the author of *Realidades Nacionales Comparadas* (Grupo Editor Altamira, Buenos Aires, 2002).

Saúl Keifman is a professor of economics at the University of Buenos Aires and chair of the master in economics program at the same university. He is also a researcher at the National Council for Scientific and Technical Research (CONICET). He has been a researcher at Facultad Latinoamericana de Ciencias Sociales (FLACSO) and Centro de Estudios de Estado y Sociedad (CEDES) and has taught at FLACSO, Instituto de Desarrollo Económico y Social (IDES), Instituto Superior de los Economistas de Gobierno (ISEG), the National University of La Plata, and the University of Palermo. He has published extensively on international economic policy issues.

Pedro-Pablo Kuczynski was minister of economy and finance of Peru in 2001-02 and minister of energy and mines in 1980-82. He has been president and chief executive officer of the Latin America Enterprise Fund LP since its inception in 1994. From 1992 to 1994, he was vice chairman of CAP SA, a steel and forest products company in Chile. From 1982 to 1992, he was chairman of First Boston International and managing director of First Boston Corporation. He was also a partner at Kuhn, Loeb & Company International (1973-75), deputy director of the Peruvian Central Bank (1967-69), and president and chief executive officer of Halco Mining (1977-80). He began his career at the World Bank in 1961 and held senior positions there and at the International Finance Corporation. He is the author of several books on the economics of Latin America.

Ricardo López Murphy, Argentina's former minister of economy and former minister of defense, founded the *Movimiento Recrear Argentina* political party in 2002 and is standing as its candidate for president of Argentina in the 2003 election. He is a chief economist at Fundación de Investigaciones Economicas Latinoamericanas (FIEL) in Buenos Aires and professor of economics at the National University of La Plata and the University of San Andrés. He has contributed to numerous journals and has written and edited books on macroeconomics, fiscal and monetary policies, and public policy. He has also been an adviser to governments in Latin America and consultant to multilateral agencies.

Claudio de Moura Castro is president of the advisory council of Faculdade Pitágoras in Brazil. He taught at the Catholic University of Rio de

Janeiro, Vargas Foundation, University of Chicago, University of Brasília, University of Geneva, and University of Burgundy (Dijon). He was technical coordinator of the ECIEL research project on education (comprising 10 Latin American countries), director of CAPES (Brazil's agency for postgraduate education), executive secretary of CNRH (social policy institute of the planning secretariat in Brazil), chief of the training policies branch of the International Labor Organization (Geneva) between 1986 and 1992, and senior human resource economist in the technical division of the World Bank. He was chief of the social programs division of the Inter-American Development Bank and also chief educational adviser there. He has published over 30 books and 300 scholarly articles.

Fernando Navajas is a chief economist at Fundación de Investigaciones Económicas Latinoamericanas (FIEL) in Buenos Aires and professor of economics at the National University of La Plata and the University of San Andrés. He was previously with the UN Economic Commission for Latin America and the Caribbean (ECLAC). He was also a council member of the Argentine Association for Political Economy and chief of the Cabinet of Advisers of the Ministry of Economy in Argentina.

Patricio Navia is the outreach coordinator for the Center for Latin American and Caribbean Studies at New York University where he also teaches Latin American politics and Latin American and Caribbean culture. He has published articles in the *Journal of Democracy*, *Democratization*, and *Social Science Quarterly*. He is a regular columnist in *La Tercera* newspaper (Chile), *Capital* magazine (Chile), and *Revista Época* magazine (Spain). He has done consulting work for the Chilean ministries of interior (on electoral reform) and economics (on foreign investment), the Ford Foundation, and the Americas Society in New York.

Liliana Rojas-Suarez is a senior adviser at the Inter-American Development Bank and a nonresident fellow at the Center for Global Development. She is also the chair of the Latin American Shadow Financial Regulatory Committee and a member of the Advisory Committee of the North American Economics and Finance Association. From March 1998 to October 2000, she was managing director and chief economist for Latin America at Deutsche Bank. Before joining Deutsche Bank, she was the principal adviser in the Office of the Chief Economist at the Inter-American Development Bank. Between 1984 and 1994, she held various positions at the International Monetary Fund, including deputy chief of the capital markets and financial studies division of the research department. She was a visiting fellow at the Institute for International Economics, professor at Anahuac University in Mexico, and an adviser for PEMEX, Mexico's national petroleum company. She has published widely on macroeconomic policy, international economics, and financial markets. Her most recent publications include *Why So High? Understanding Interest Rate Spreads in Latin America* (with P. Brock, IDB, 2000) and *Financial Regulation: Why, How and Where Now?* (with C. Goodhart et al., Routledge, 1998).

Jaime Saavedra is principal researcher and executive director of Grupo de Análisis para el Desarrollo (GRADE), a think tank based in Lima, Peru. He teaches economics at the Pontificia Universidad Católica del Peru. He is also a member of the National Council of Labor and the Consultative Commission of the Ministry of Labor. He chaired the Executive Committee of the LACEA/IDB/WB Network on Inequality and Poverty and was a researcher and consultant with the World Bank, Inter-American Development Bank, the United Nations Development Program (UNDP), the UN Economic Commission for Latin America and the Caribbean (ECLAC), the International Labor Organization, and the Ministries of Education, Finance, and Labor in Peru. He was a visiting researcher at the Center for International Studies at the University of Toronto.

Miguel Székely is the undersecretary for planning at Mexico's Ministry for Social Development. He was with the Office of the President of Mexico in 2001 and a researcher in the Inter-American Development Bank between 1996 and 2001. He has published four books and 34 articles on poverty, inequality, and social development in Mexico and Latin America.

Andrés Velasco is Sumitomo-FASID Professor of International Finance and Development at Harvard University's Kennedy School of Government. He joined Harvard in 2000, after a decade on the faculty at New York University where he taught economics and directed the Center for Latin American and Caribbean Studies. He has published widely in the areas of international economics, economic development, and political economy. He is affiliated with the National Bureau of Economic Research in Cambridge, Massachusetts, and the Center for Applied Economics at the University of Chile. In 1990-92, he served as chief of staff to Chile's finance minister and later as director of international finance at that ministry. In 1995, he served as chief economist and deputy lead negotiator in Chile's NAFTA accession team. Since then, he has been an adviser to the governments of Ecuador and El Salvador and to the Central Bank of Chile and a consultant to the World Bank, International Monetary Fund, Inter-American Development Bank, UN Economic Commission for Latin America and the Caribbean, and Federal Reserve Bank of Atlanta.

John Williamson, senior fellow at the Institute for International Economics since 1981, was project director for the UN High-Level Panel on Financing for Development (the Zedillo Report) in 2001; on leave as chief economist for South Asia at the World Bank during 1996-99; economics professor at Pontifícia Universidade Católica do Rio de Janeiro (1978-81), University of Warwick (1970-77), Massachusetts Institute of Technology (1967, 1980), University of York (1963-68), and Princeton University (1962-63); adviser to the International Monetary Fund (1972-74); and economic consultant to the UK Treasury (1968-70). He is author, coauthor, editor, or coeditor of numerous studies on international monetary and developing-world debt issues, including *Dollar Overvaluation and the World Economy* (2003), *Delivering on Debt Relief: From IMF Gold to a New Aid Architecture* (2002), and *Exchange Rate Regimes for Emerging Markets: Reviving the Intermediate Option* (2000).

Laurence Wolff has been a consultant at the Inter-American Development Bank since 1998. Previously he worked for 22 years at the World Bank where he was responsible for education projects in Latin America, Africa, and the Middle East. He has written on a variety of subjects related to education in developing countries including cost effectiveness; the role of the private sector in providing educational services; the relationships of science, technology, and education; and the uses of educational assessments.

Index

Other Publications from the **Institute for International Economics**

* = out of print

POLICY ANALYSES IN INTERNATIONAL ECONOMICS Series

1 **The Lending Policies of the International Monetary Fund*** John Williamson
August 1982 ISBN 0-88132-000-5
2 **"Reciprocity": A New Approach to World Trade Policy?*** William R. Cline
September 1982 ISBN 0-88132-001-3
3 **Trade Policy in the 1980s***
C. Fred Bergsten and William R. Cline
November 1982 ISBN 0-88132-002-1
4 **International Debt and the Stability of the World Economy*** William R. Cline
September 1983 ISBN 0-88132-010-2
5 **The Exchange Rate System,*** Second Edition
John Williamson
Sept. 1983, rev. June 1985 ISBN 0-88132-034-X
6 **Economic Sanctions in Support of Foreign Policy Goals***
Gary Clyde Hutbauer and Jeffrey J. Schott
October 1983 ISBN 0-88132-014-5
7 **A New SDR Allocation?*** John Williamson
March 1984 ISBN 0-88132-028-5
8 **An International Standard for Monetary Stabilization*** Ronald L. McKinnon
March 1984 ISBN 0-88132-018-8
9 **The Yen/Dollar Agreement: Liberalizing Japanese Capital Markets*** Jeffrey A. Frankel
December 1984 ISBN 0-88132-035-8
10 **Bank Lending to Developing Countries: The Policy Alternatives*** C. Fred Bergsten, William R. Cline, and John Williamson
April 1985 ISBN 0-88132-032-3
11 **Trading for Growth: The Next Round of Trade Negotiations***
Gary Clyde Hufbauer and Jeffrey R. Schott
September 1985 ISBN 0-88132-033-1
12 **Financial Intermediation Beyond the Debt Crisis*** Donald R. Lessard, John Williamson
September 1985 ISBN 0-88132-021-8
13 **The United States-Japan Economic Problem***
C. Fred Bergsten and William R. Cline
October 1985, 2d ed. January 1987
ISBN 0-88132-060-9
14 **Deficits and the Dollar: The World Economy at Risk*** Stephen Marris
December 1985, 2d ed. November 1987
ISBN 0-88132-067-6
15 **Trade Policy for Troubled Industries***
Gary Clyde Hufbauer and Howard R. Rosen
March 1986 ISBN 0-88132-020-X
16 **The United States and Canada: The Quest for Free Trade*** Paul Wonnacott, with an Appendix by John Williamson
March 1987 ISBN 0-88132-056-0
17 **Adjusting to Success: Balance of Payments Policy in the East Asian NICs***
Bela Balassa and John Williamson
June 1987, rev. April 1990 ISBN 0-88132-101-X
18 **Mobilizing Bank Lending to Debtor Countries*** William R. Cline
June 1987 ISBN 0-88132-062-5
19 **Auction Quotas and United States Trade Policy*** C. Fred Bergsten, Kimberly Ann Elliott, Jeffrey J. Schott, and Wendy E. Takacs
September 1987 ISBN 0-88132-050-1
20 **Agriculture and the GATT: Rewriting the Rules*** Dale E. Hathaway
September 1987 ISBN 0-88132-052-8
21 **Anti-Protection: Changing Forces in United States Trade Politics***
I. M. Destler and John S. Odell
September 1987 ISBN 0-88132-043-9
22 **Targets and Indicators: A Blueprint for the International Coordination of Economic Policy**
John Williamson and Marcus H. Miller
September 1987 ISBN 0-88132-051-X
23 **Capital Flight: The Problem and Policy Responses*** Donald R. Lessard and John Williamson
December 1987 ISBN 0-88132-059-5
24 **United States-Canada Free Trade: An Evaluation of the Agreement***
Jeffrey J. Schott
April 1988 ISBN 0-88132-072-2
25 **Voluntary Approaches to Debt Relief***
John Williamson
Sept.1988, rev. May 1989 ISBN 0-88132-098-6
26 **American Trade Adjustment: The Global Impact*** William R. Cline
March 1989 ISBN 0-88132-095-1
27 **More Free Trade Areas?***
Jeffrey J. Schott
May 1989 ISBN 0-88132-085-4
28 **The Progress of Policy Reform in Latin America*** John Williamson
January 1990 ISBN 0-88132-100-1
29 **The Global Trade Negotiations: What Can Be Achieved?*** Jeffrey J. Schott
September 1990 ISBN 0-88132-137-0
30 **Economic Policy Coordination: Requiem or Prologue?*** Wendy Dobson
April 1991 ISBN 0-88132-102-8

31 **The Economic Opening of Eastern Europe***
John Williamson
May 1991 ISBN 0-88132-186-9

32 **Eastern Europe and the Soviet Union in the World Economy***
Susan M. Coffins and Dani Rodrik
May 1991 ISBN 0-88132-157-5

33 **African Economic Reform: The External Dimension*** Carol Lancaster
June 1991 ISBN 0-88132-096-X

34 **Has the Adjustment Process Worked?***
Paul R. Krugman
October 1991 ISBN 0-88132-116-8

35 **From Soviet disUnion to Eastern Economic Community?***
Oleh Havrylyshyn and John Williamson
October 1991 ISBN 0-88132-192-3

36 **Global Warming The Economic Stakes***
William R. Cline
May 1992 ISBN 0-88132-172-9

37 **Trade and Payments After Soviet Disintegration*** John Williamson
June 1992 ISBN 0-88132-173-7

38 **Trade and Migration: NAFTA and Agriculture*** Philip L. Martin
October 1993 ISBN 0-88132-201-6

39 **The Exchange Rate System and the IMF: A Modest Agenda** Morris Goldstein
June 1995 ISBN 0-88132-219-9

40 **What Role for Currency Boards?**
John Williamson
September 1995 ISBN 0-88132-222-9

41 **Predicting External Imbalances for the United States and Japan***William R. Cline
September 1995 ISBN 0-88132-220-2

42 **Standards and APEC: An Action Agenda***
John S. Wilson
October 1995 ISBN 0-88132-223-7

43 **Fundamental Tax Reform and Border Tax Adjustments*** Gary Clyde Hufbauer
January 1996 ISBN 0-88132-225-3

44 **Global Telecom Talks: A Trillion Dollar Deal***
Ben A. Petrazzini
June 1996 ISBN 0-88132-230-X

45 **WTO 2000: Setting the Course for World Trade** Jeffrey J. Schott
September 1996 ISBN 0-88132-234-2

46 **The National Economic Council: A Work in Progress *** I. M. Destler
November 1996 ISBN 0-88132-239-3

47 **The Case for an International Banking Standard** Morris Goldstein
April 1997 ISBN 0-88132-244-X

48 **Transatlantic Trade: A Strategic Agenda***
Ellen L. Frost
May 1997 ISBN 0-88132-228-8

49 **Cooperating with Europe's Monetary Union**
C. Randall Henning
May 1997 ISBN 0-88132-245-8

50 **Renewing Fast Track Legislation*** I. M.Destler
September 1997 ISBN 0-88132-252-0

51 **Competition Policies for the Global Economy**
Edward M. Graham and J. David Richardson
November 1997 ISBN 0-88132 -249-0

52 **Improving Trade Policy Reviews in the World Trade Organization** Donald Keesing
April 1998 ISBN 0-88132-251-2

53 **Agricultural Trade Policy: Completing the Reform** Timothy Josling
April 1998 ISBN 0-88132-256-3

54 **Real Exchange Rates for the Year 2000**
Simon Wren Lewis and Rebecca Driver
April 1998 ISBN 0-88132-253-9

55 **The Asian Financial Crisis: Causes, Cures, and Systemic Implications** Morris Goldstein
June 1998 ISBN 0-88132-261-X

56 **Global Economic Effects of the Asian Currency Devaluations**
Marcus Noland, LiGang Liu, Sherman Robinson, and Zhi Wang
July 1998 ISBN 0-88132-260-1

57 **The Exchange Stabilization Fund: Slush Money or War Chest?** C. Randall Henning
May 1999 ISBN 0-88132-271-7

58 **The New Politics of American Trade: Trade, Labor, and the Environment**
I. M. Destler and Peter J. Balint
October 1999 ISBN 0-88132-269-5

59 **Congressional Trade Votes: From NAFTA Approval to Fast Track Defeat**
Robert E. Baldwin and Christopher S. Magee
February 2000 ISBN 0-88132-267-9

60 **Exchange Rate Regimes for Emerging Markets: Reviving the Intermediate Option**
John Williamson
September 2000 ISBN 0-88132-293-8

61 **NAFTA and the Environment: Seven Years Later** Gary Clyde Hufbauer, Daniel Esty, Diana Orejas, Luis Rubio, and Jeffrey J. Schott
October 2000 ISBN 0-88132-299-7

62 **Free Trade between Korea and the United States?** Inbom Choi and Jeffrey J. Schott
April 2001 ISBN 0-88132-311-X

63 **New Regional Trading Arrangements in the Asia Pacific?**
Robert Scollay and John P. Gilbert
May 2001 ISBN 0-88132-302-0

64 **Parental Supervision: The New Paradigm for Foreign Direct Investment and Development**
Theodore H. Moran
August 2001 ISBN 0-88132-313-6

65 **The Benefits of Price Convergence: Speculative Calculations**
Gary Clyde Hufbauer, Erika Wada, and Tony Warren
December 2001 ISBN 0-88132-333-0

66 **Managed Floating Plus**
Morris Goldstein
March 2002 ISBN 0-88132-336-5

67 **Argentina and the Fund: From Triumph to Tragedy**
Michael Mussa
July 2002 ISBN 0-88132-339-X

68 **East Asian Financial Cooperation**
C. Randall Henning
September 2002 ISBN 0-88132-338-1

BOOKS

IMF Conditionality* John Williamson, editor
1983 ISBN 0-88132-006-4

Trade Policy in the 1980s* William R. Cline, editor
1983 ISBN 0-88132-031-5

Subsidies in International Trade*
Gary Clyde Hufbauer and Joanna Shelton Erb
1984 ISBN 0-88132-004-8

International Debt: Systemic Risk and Policy Response* William R. Cline
1984 ISBN 0-88132-015-3

Trade Protection in the United States: 31 Case Studies* Gary Clyde Hutbauer, Diane E. Berliner, and Kimberly Ann Elliott
1986 ISBN 0-88132-040-4

Toward Renewed Economic Growth in Latin America* Bela Balassa, Gerardo M. Bueno, Pedro-Pablo Kuczynski, and Mario Henrique Simonsen
1986 ISBN 0-88132-045-5

Capital Flight and Third World Debt*
Donald R. Lessard and John Williamson, editors
1987 ISBN 0-88132-053-6

The Canada-United States Free Trade Agreement: The Global Impact*
Jeffrey J. Schott and Murray G. Smith, editors
1988 ISBN 0-88132-073-0

World Agricultural Trade: Building a Consensus*
William M. Miner and Dale E. Hathaway, editors
1988 ISBN 0-88132-071-3

Japan in the World Economy*
Bela Balassa and Marcus Noland
1988 ISBN 0-88132-041-2

America in the World Economy: A Strategy for the 1990s* C. Fred Bergsten
1988 ISBN 0-88132-089-7

Managing the Dollar: From the Plaza to the Louvre* Yoichi Funabashi
1988, 2nd ed. 1989 ISBN 0-88132-097-8

United States External Adjustment and the World Economy* William R. Cline
May 1989 ISBN 0-88132-048-X

Free Trade Areas and U.S. Trade Policy*
Jeffrey J. Schott, editor
May *1989* ISBN 0-88132-094-3

Dollar Politics: Exchange Rate Policymaking in the United States*
I.M. Destler and C. Randall Henning
September 1989 ISBN 0-88132-079-X

Latin American Adjustment: How Much Has Happened?* John Williamson, editor
April 1990 ISBN 0-88132-125-7

The Future of World Trade in Textiles and Apparel* William R. Cline
1987, 2d ed. June *199* ISBN 0-88132-110-9

Completing the Uruguay Round: A Results-Oriented Approach to the GATT Trade Negotiations* Jeffrey J. Schott, editor
September 1990 ISBN 0-88132-130-3

Economic Sanctions Reconsidered (2 volumes)
Economic Sanctions Reconsidered: Supplemental Case Histories
Gary Clyde Hufbauer, Jeffrey J. Schott, and Kimberly Ann Elliott
1985, 2d ed. Dec. 1990 ISBN cloth 0-88132-115-X
ISBN paper 0-88132-105-2

Economic Sanctions Reconsidered: History and Current Policy
Gary Clyde Hufbauer, Jeffrey J. Schott, and Kimberly Ann Elliott
December 1990 ISBN cloth 0-88132-140-0
ISBN paper 0-88132-136-2

Pacific Basin Developing Countries: Prospects for the Future* Marcus Noland
January 1991 ISBN cloth 0-88132-141-9
ISBN paper 0-88132-081-1

Currency Convertibility in Eastern Europe*
John Williamson, editor
October 1991 ISBN 0-88132-128-1

International Adjustment and Financing: The Lessons of 1985-1991* C. Fred Bergsten, editor
January 1992 ISBN 0-88132-112-5

North American Free Trade: Issues and Recommendations*
Gary Clyde Hufbauer and Jeffrey J. Schott
April 1992 ISBN 0-88132-120-6

Narrowing the U.S. Current Account Deficit*
Allen J. Lenz
June 1992 ISBN 0-88132-103-6

The Economics of Global Warming
William R. Cline/*June 1992* ISBN 0-88132-132-X

U.S. Taxation of International Income: Blueprint for Reform* Gary Clyde Hutbauer, assisted by Joanna M. van Rooij
October 1992 ISBN 0-88132-134-6

Who's Bashing Whom? Trade Conflict in High-Technology Industries Laura D'Andrea Tyson
November 1992 ISBN 0-88132-106-0

Korea in the World Economy* Il SaKong
January 1993 ISBN 0-88132-183-4

Pacific Dynamism and the International Economic System*
C. Fred Bergsten and Marcus Noland, editors
May 1993 ISBN 0-88132-196-6

Economic Consequences of Soviet Disintegration*
John Williamson, editor
May 1993 ISBN 0-88132-190-7

Reconcilable Differences? United States-Japan Economic Conflict*
C. Fred Bergsten and Marcus Noland
June 1993 ISBN 0-88132-129-X

Does Foreign Exchange Intervention Work?
Kathryn M. Dominguez and Jeffrey A. Frankel
September 1993 ISBN 0-88132-104-4

Sizing Up U.S. Export Disincentives*
J. David Richardson
September 1993 ISBN 0-88132-107-9

NAFTA: An Assessment
Gary Clyde Hufbauer and Jeffrey J. Schott/ *rev. ed.*
October 1993 ISBN 0-88132-199-0

Adjusting to Volatile Energy Prices
Philip K. Verleger, Jr.
November 1993 ISBN 0-88132-069-2

The Political Economy of Policy Reform
John Williamson, editor
January 1994 ISBN 0-88132-195-8

Measuring the Costs of Protection in the United States
Gary Clyde Hufbauer and Kimberly Ann Elliott
January 1994 ISBN 0-88132-108-7

The Dynamics of Korean Economic Development* Cho Soon
March 1994 ISBN 0-88132-162-1

Reviving the European Union*
C. Randall Henning, Eduard Hochreiter, and Gary Clyde Hufbauer, editors
April 1994 ISBN 0-88132-208-3

China in the World Economy Nicholas R. Lardy
April 1994 ISBN 0-88132-200-8

Greening the GATT: Trade, Environment, and the Future Daniel C. Esty
July 1994 ISBN 0-88132-205-9

Western Hemisphere Economic Integration*
Gary Clyde Hufbauer and Jeffrey J. Schott
July 1994 ISBN 0-88132-159-1

Currencies and Politics in the United States, Germany, and Japan
C. Randall Henning
September 1994 ISBN 0-88132-127-3

Estimating Equilibrium Exchange Rates
John Williamson, editor
September 1994 ISBN 0-88132-076-5

Managing the World Economy: Fifty Years After Bretton Woods Peter B. Kenen, editor
September 1994 ISBN 0-88132-212-1

Reciprocity and Retaliation in U.S. Trade Policy
Thomas O. Bayard and Kimberly Ann Elliott
September 1994 ISBN 0-88132-084-6

The Uruguay Round: An Assessment*
Jeffrey J. Schott, assisted by Johanna W. Buurman
November 1994 ISBN 0-88132-206-7

Measuring the Costs of Protection in Japan*
Yoko Sazanami, Shujiro Urata, and Hiroki Kawai
January 1995 ISBN 0-88132-211-3

Foreign Direct Investment in the United States, 3rd Ed. Edward M. Graham and Paul R. Krugman
January 1995 ISBN 0-88132-204-0

The Political Economy of Korea-United States Cooperation*
C. Fred Bergsten and Il SaKong, editors
February 1995 ISBN 0-88132-213-X

International Debt Reexamined* William R. Cline
February 1995 ISBN 0-88132-083-8

American Trade Politics, 3rd Ed. I.M. Destler
April 1995 ISBN 0-88132-215-6

Managing Official Export Credits: The Quest for a Global Regime* John E. Ray
July 1995 ISBN 0-88132207-5

Asia Pacific Fusion: Japan's Role in APEC*
Yoichi Funabashi
October 1995 ISBN 0-88132-224-5

Korea-United States Cooperation in the New World Order*
C. Fred Bergsten and Il SaKong, editors
February 1996 ISBN 0-88132-226-1

Why Exports Really Matter!* ISBN 0-88132-221-0
Why Exports Matter More!* ISBN 0-88132-229-6
J. David Richardson and Karin Rindal
July 1995; February 1996

Global Corporations and National Governments
Edward M. Graham
May 1996 ISBN 0-88132-111-7

Global Economic Leadership and the Group of Seven C. Fred Bergsten and C. Randall Henning
May 1996 ISBN 0-88132-218-0

The Trading System After the Uruguay Round*
John Whalley and Colleen Hamilton
July 1996 ISBN 0-88132-131-1

Private Capital Flows to Emerging Markets After the Mexican Crisis* Guillermo A. Calvo, Morris Goldstein, and Eduard Hochreiter
September 1996 ISBN 0-88132-232-6

The Crawling Band as an Exchange Rate Regime: Lessons from Chile, Colombia, and Israel
John Williamson
September 1996 ISBN 0-88132-231-8

Flying High: Liberalizing Civil Aviation in the Asia Pacific*
Gary Clyde Hufbauer and Christopher Findlay
November 1996 ISBN 0-88132-227-X

Measuring the Costs of Visible Protection in Korea* Namdoo Kim
November 1996 ISBN 0-88132-236-9
The World Trading System: Challenges Ahead
Jeffrey J. Schott
December 1996 ISBN 0-88132-235-0
Has Globalization Gone Too Far? Dani Rodrik
March 1997 ISBN cloth 0-88132-243-1
Korea-United States Economic Relationship*
C. Fred Bergsten and Il SaKong, editors
March 1997 ISBN 0-88132-240-7
Summitry in the Americas: A Progress Report
Richard E. Feinberg
April 1997 ISBN 0-88132-242-3
Corruption and the Global Economy
Kimberly Ann Elliott
June 1997 ISBN 0-88132-233-4
Regional Trading Blocs in the World Economic System Jeffrey A. Frankel
October 1997 ISBN 0-88132-202-4
Sustaining the Asia Pacific Miracle: Environmental Protection and Economic Integration Andre Dua and Daniel C. Esty
October 1997 ISBN 0-88132-250-4
Trade and Income Distribution William R. Cline
November 1997 ISBN 0-88132-216-4
Global Competition Policy
Edward M. Graham and J. David Richardson
December 1997 ISBN 0-88132-166-4
Unfinished Business: Telecommunications after the Uruguay Round
Gary Clyde Hufbauer and Erika Wada
December 1997 ISBN 0-88132-257-1
Financial Services Liberalization in the WTO
Wendy Dobson and Pierre Jacquet
June 1998 ISBN 0-88132-254-7
Restoring Japan's Economic Growth
Adam S. Posen
September 1998 ISBN 0-88132-262-8
Measuring the Costs of Protection in China
Zhang Shuguang, Zhang Yansheng, and Wan Zhongxin
November 1998 ISBN 0-88132-247-4
Foreign Direct Investment and Development: The New Policy Agenda for Developing Countries and Economies in Transition
Theodore H. Moran
December 1998 ISBN 0-88132-258-X
Behind the Open Door: Foreign Enterprises in the Chinese Marketplace
Daniel H. Rosen
January 1999 ISBN 0-88132-263-6
Toward A New International Financial Architecture: A Practical Post-Asia Agenda
Barry Eichengreen
February 1999 ISBN 0-88132-270-9
Is the U.S. Trade Deficit Sustainable?
Catherine L. Mann
September 1999 ISBN 0-88132-265-2
Safeguarding Prosperity in a Global Financial System: The Future International Financial Architecture, Independent Task Force Report Sponsored by the Council on Foreign Relations
Morris Goldstein, Project Director
October 1999 ISBN 0-88132-287-3
Avoiding the Apocalypse: The Future of the Two Koreas Marcus Noland
June 2000 ISBN 0-88132-278-4
Assessing Financial Vulnerability: An Early Warning System for Emerging Markets
Morris Goldstein, Graciela Kaminsky, and Carmen Reinhart
June 2000 ISBN 0-88132-237-7
Global Electronic Commerce: A Policy Primer
Catherine L. Mann, Sue E. Eckert, and Sarah Cleeland Knight
July 2000 ISBN 0-88132-274-1
The WTO after Seattle Jeffrey J. Schott, editor
July 2000 ISBN 0-88132-290-3
Intellectual Property Rights in the Global Economy Keith E. Maskus
August 2000 ISBN 0-88132-282-2
The Political Economy of the Asian Financial Crisis Stephan Haggard
August 2000 ISBN 0-88132-283-0
Transforming Foreign Aid: United States Assistance in the 21st Century Carol Lancaster
August 2000 ISBN 0-88132-291-1
Fighting the Wrong Enemy: Antiglobal Activists and Multinational Enterprises Edward M.Graham
September 2000 ISBN 0-88132-272-5
Globalization and the Perceptions of American Workers
Kenneth F. Scheve and Matthew J. Slaughter
March 2001 ISBN 0-88132-295-4
World Capital Markets: Challenge to the G-10
Wendy Dobson and Gary C. Hufbauer, assisted by Hyun Koo Cho
May 2001 ISBN 0-88132-301-2
Prospects for Free Trade in the Americas
Jeffrey J. Schott
August 2001 ISBN 0-88132-275-X
Lessons from the Old World for the New: Constructing a North American Community
Robert A. Pastor
August 2000 ISBN 0-88132-328-4
Measuring the Costs of Protection in Europe: European Commercial Policy in the 2000s
Patrick A. Messerlin
September 2001 ISBN 0-88132-273-3
Job Loss from Imports: Measuring the Costs
Lori G. Kletzer
September 2001 ISBN 0-88132-296-2

No More Bashing: Building a New Japan-United States Economic Relationship
C. Fred Bergsten, Takatoshi Ito, and Marc Noland
October 2001 ISBN 0-88132-286-5
Why Global Commitment Really Matters!
Howard Lewis III and J. David Richardson
October 2001 ISBN 0-88132-298-9
Leadership Selection in the Major Multilaterals
Miles Kahler
November 2001 ISBN 0-88132-335-7
The International Financial Architecture: What's New? What's Missing? Peter Kenen
November 2001 ISBN 0-88132-297-0
Delivering on Debt Relief: From IMF Gold to a New Aid Architecture
John Williamson and Nancy Birdsall, with Brian Deese
April 2002 ISBN 0-88132-331-4
Imagine There's No Country: Poverty, Inequality, and Growth in the Era of Globalization
Surjit S. Bhalla
September 2002 ISBN 0-88132-348-9
Reforming Korea's Industrial Conglomerates
Edward M. Graham
January 2003 ISBN 0-88132-337-3
Industrial Policy in an Era of Globalization: Lessons from Asia
Marcus Noland and Howard Pack
March 2003 ISBN 0-88132-350-0
Reintegrating India with the World Economy
T.N. Srinivasan and Suresh D. Tendulkar
March 2003 ISBN 0-88132-280-6
After the Washington Consensus: Restarting Growth and Reform in Latin America John Williamson and Pedro-Pablo Kuczynski, editors
March 2003 ISBN 0-88132-347-0

SPECIAL REPORTS

1 **Promoting World Recovery: A Statement on Global Economic Strategy***
by Twenty-six Economists from Fourteen Countries
December 1982 ISBN 0-88132-013-7
2 **Prospects for Adjustment in Argentina, Brazil, and Mexico: Responding to the Debt Crisis*** John Williamson, editor
June 1983 ISBN 0-88132-016-1
3 **Inflation and Indexation: Argentina, Brazil, and Israel*** John Williamson, editor
March 1985 ISBN 0-88132-037-4
4 **Global Economic Imbalances***
C. Fred Bergsten, editor
March 1986 ISBN 0-88132-042-0
5 **African Debt and Financing***
Carol Lancaster and John Williamson, editors
May 1986 ISBN 0-88132-044-7
6 **Resolving the Global Economic Crisis: After Wall Street***
by Thirty-three Economists from Thirteen Countries
December 1987 ISBN 0-88132-070-6
7 **World Economic Problems***
Kimberly Ann Elliott and John Williamson, editors
April 1988 ISBN 0-88132-055-2
Reforming World Agricultural Trade*
by Twenty-nine Professionals from Seventeen Countries
1988 ISBN 0-88132-088-9
8 **Economic Relations Between the United States and Korea: Conflict or Cooperation?***
Thomas O. Bayard and Soogil Young, editors
January 1989 ISBN 0-88132-068-4
9 **Whither APEC? The Progress to Date and Agenda for the Future***
C. Fred Bergsten, editor
October 1997 ISBN 0-88132-248-2
10 **Economic Integration of the Korean Peninsula**
Marcus Noland, editor
January 1998 ISBN 0-88132-255-5
11 **Restarting Fast Track***
Jeffrey J. Schott, editor
April 1998 ISBN 0-88132-259-8
12 **Launching New Global Trade Talks: An Action Agenda** Jeffrey J. Schott, editor
September 1998 ISBN 0-88132-266-0
13 **Japan's Financial Crisis and Its Parallels to U.S. Experience**
Ryoichi Mikitani and Adam S. Posen, eds.
September 2000 ISBN 0-88132-289-X
14 **The Ex-Im Bank in the 21st Century: A New Approach?** Gary Clyde Hufbauer and Rita M. Rodriguez, eds.
January 2001 ISBN 0-88132-300-4
15 **The Korean Diaspora in the World Economy**
C. Fred Bergsten and Inbom Choi, eds.
January 2003 ISBN 0-88132-358-6
16 **Dollar Overvaluation and the World Economy**
C. Fred Bergsten and John Williamson, eds.
February 2003 ISBN 0-88132-351-9

WORKS IN PROGRESS

The Decline of US Labor Unions and the Role of Trade
Robert E. Baldwin
Changing Direction: The New Economy in the United States, Europe, and Japan
Martin Baily

New Regional Arrangements and the World Economy
C. Fred Bergsten
The Globalization Backlash in Europe and the United States
C. Fred Bergsten, Pierre Jacquet, and Karl Kaiser
China's Entry to the World Economy
Richard N. Cooper
The ILO in the World Economy
Kimberly Ann Elliott
Can Labor Standards Improve under Globalization?
Kimberly Ann Elliott and Richard B. Freeman
Reforming Economic Sanctions
Kimberly Ann Elliott, Gary C. Hufbauer, and Jeffrey J. Schott
Free Trade in Labor Agency Services
Kimberly Ann Elliott and J. David Richardson
IMF and the World Bank
Michael Fabricius
NAFTA: An Eight-Year Appraisal
Gary C. Hufbauer and Jeffrey J. Schott
New Agricultural Negotiations in the WTO
Timothy Josling and Dale Hathaway
Food Regulation and Trade: Toward a Safe and Open Global Food System
Timothy Josling, David Orden, and Donna Roberts
Imports, Exports, and American Industrial Workers since 1979
Lori G. Kletzer and Robert Lawrence
Crimes and Punishments? An Analysis of Retaliation under the WTO
Robert Lawrence
Paying the Price: The Costs of Fragmented International Markets
Robert Lawrence and Scott Bradford
Globalization and Creative Destruction in the US Textile and Apparel Industry
James Levinsohn
Reforming OPIC for the Twenty-first Century
Theodore Moran
International Financial Architecture
Michael Mussa
Foreign Direct Investment, Taxes, and Tax Competition
John Mutti
Dollarization, Currency Blocs, and US Policy
Adam S. Posen
Germany and the World Economy
Adam S. Posen
Sizing Up Globalization: The Globalization Balance Sheet Capstone Volume
J. David Richardson
Private Sector Investment and Debt Workouts
Nouriel Roubini and Brad Setser
Inflation Targeting
Edwin Truman
Curbing the Boom-Bust Cycle
John Williamson

Australia, New Zealand, and Papua New Guinea
D.A. Information Services
648 Whitehorse Road
Mitcham, Victoria 3132, Australia
tel: 61-3-9210-7777
fax: 61-3-9210-7788
email: service@adadirect.com.au
http://www.dadirect.com.au

United Kingdom and Europe
(including Russia and Turkey)
The Eurospan Group
3 Henrietta Street, Covent Garden
London WC2E 8LU England
tel: 44-20-7240-0856
fax: 44-20-7379-0609
http://www.eurospan.co.uk

Japan and the Republic of Korea
United Publishers Services, Ltd.
KenkyuSha Bldg.
9, Kanda Surugadai 2-Chome
Chiyoda-Ku, Tokyo 101 Japan
tel: 81-3-3291-4541
fax: 81-3-3292-8610
email: saito@ups.co.jp
For trade accounts only. Individuals will find IIE books in leading Tokyo bookstores.

Thailand
Asia Books
5 Sukhumvit Rd. Soi 61
Bangkok 10110 Thailand
tel: 662-714-07402 Ext: 221, 222, 223
fax: 662-391-2277
email: purchase@asiabooks.co.th
http://www.asiabooksonline.com

Canada
Renouf Bookstore
5369 Canotek Road, Unit 1
Ottawa, Ontario KIJ 9J3, Canada
tel: 613-745-2665
fax: 613-745-7660
http://www.renoufbooks.com

India, Bangladesh, Nepal, and Sri Lanka
Viva Books Pvt.
Mr. Vinod Vasishtha
4325/3, Ansari Rd.
Daryaganj, New Delhi-110002
India
tel: 91-11-327-9280
fax: 91-11-326-7224
email: vinod.viva@gndel.globalnet.ems.vsnl.net.in

Southeast Asia (Brunei, Cambodia, China, Malaysia, Hong Kong, Indonesia, Laos, Myanmar, the Philippines, Singapore, Taiwan, and Vietnam)
Hemisphere Publication Services
1 Kallang Pudding Rd. #0403
Golden Wheel Building
Singapore 349316
tel: 65-741-5166
fax: 65-742-9356

Visit our Web site at:
http://www.iie.com
E-mail orders to:
orders@iie.com